The Italian Lakes

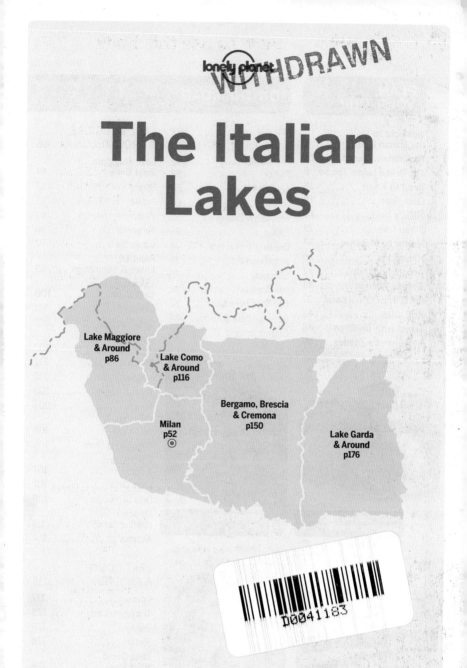

Lake Maggiore & Around p86

Lake Como & Around p116

Milan p52

Bergamo, Brescia & Cremona p150

Lake Garda & Around p176

D0041183

Paula Hardy, Marc Di Duca, Regis St Louis

PLAN YOUR TRIP

ON THE ROAD

PANETTONE, PASTICCERIA
MARCHESI, MILAN P71

VARENNA P139

PALAZZO BORROMEO,
ISOLA BELLA P93

CAPPELLA COLLEONI,
BERGAMO P155

SUSAN WRIGHT / LONELY PLANET ©

JUSTIN FOULKES / LONELY PLANET ©

MARINADA / SHUTTERSTOCK ©

ARGALIS / GETTY IMAGES ©

Contents

On the Wine Trail

Welcome to the Italian Lakes

Formed at the end of the last ice age, and a popular holiday spot since Roman times, the Italian Lakes have an enduring, beguiling beauty.

Artful Landscapes

Travellers traversing the Alps wind down from snowcapped mountains to be greeted by a Mediterranean burst of colour: gardens filled with rose-red camellias, hot-pink oleanders, lemon trees and palms surrounding cerulean blue lakes. It's impossible not to be seduced. Fishing boats bob in tiny harbours, palaces float in the Borromean Gulf and grand belle époque hotels line the waterfronts in towns such as Stresa, Como, Bellagio and Salò. No wonder European aristocrats, Arab princes and Hollywood celebrities choose to call this home.

A Modern Legacy

Since Leonardo da Vinci broke all the rules in his stunning *Last Supper,* the indefatigably inventive Lombards seem to have skipped straight from the Renaissance to the 21st century. Not only is Milan a treasure trove of modern and contemporary art, but art deco and rationalist architecture abound. Around the lakes, Michelin-starred restaurants push the boundaries of traditionalism, and vintners, oil producers and textile houses experiment with sustainable technologies and techniques. Even now, jackhammers are hard at work on Milan's futuristic new skyline modelled by star architects Zaha Hadid, Daniel Libeskind, Arata Isozaki and César Pelli.

Living by Design

Though Italian design is distributed globally, seeing it in its home context offers a fresh appreciation. From Como's silk weavers to Brianza's furniture makers and the violin artisans of Cremona, this region has an outstanding craft heritage. Today Milan is home to all the major design showrooms and an endless round of trade fairs. But it's not just insiders who have all the fun. Northern Italian design houses have branched out into spas, bars, galleries and restaurants. So why not join them for a touch of *la vita moda* (the stylish life).

The Lake Lifestyle

Home to many of Italy's foremost musical talents, writers and artists, Milan and Verona are on the tour circuit of the best international music acts, dance troupes, opera and theatre. In summer, film, music and art festivals abound in city theatres, lakeside gardens and historic villas, while at weekends, urbanites escape to the mountains and lakes for morning markets, sailing, hiking and long afternoon lunches. The key to it all is an unswerving dedication to life's fine print.

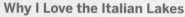

Why I Love the Italian Lakes

By Paula Hardy, Writer

From cutting-edge textiles to high-tech olive presses and a sidewalk scene that makes Fashion Week seem entirely redundant, Milan and the lakes are both thrilling and fun. Everyone here is fizzing with ideas, ambition and energy, and it's catching. Unlike nonna's Italy further south, Lombards, like New Yorkers, are refreshing modernists and natural entrepreneurs. A surprising number of people here care deeply about marrying the region's craft heritage with modern, sustainable technology. As such, they're pioneering an exciting and beautiful vision of the future that inspires me.

For more about our writers, see p280

Above: Terrace dining in Varenna (p139), overlooking Lake Como

Italian Lakes

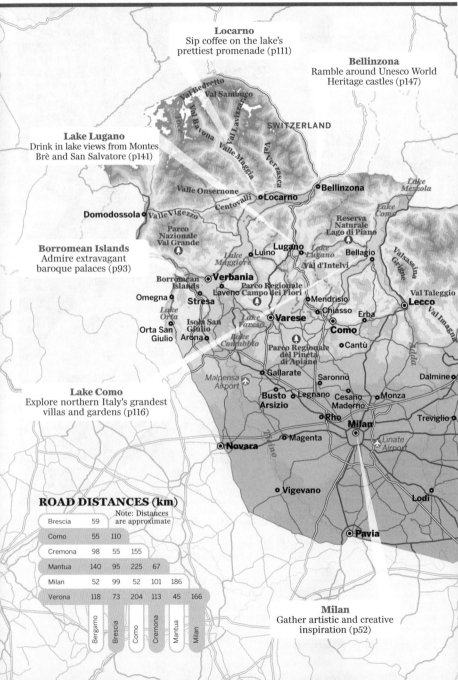

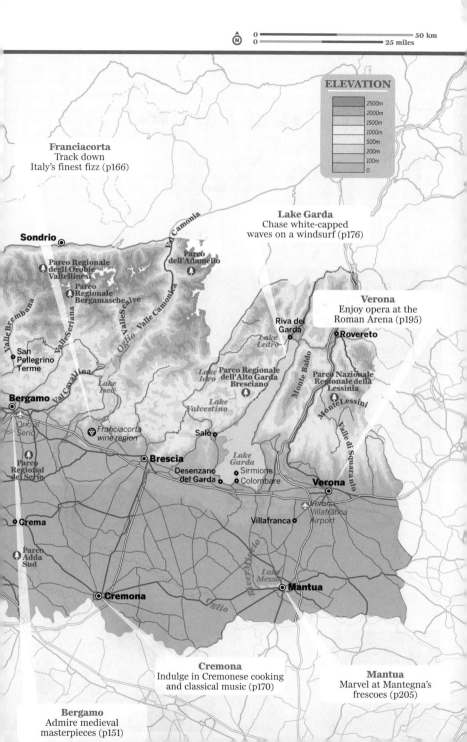

N

| 0 | | 50 km |
| 0 | | 25 miles |

ELEVATION

2500m
2000m
1500m
1000m
500m
200m
100m
0

Franciacorta
Track down
Italy's finest fizz (p166)

Lake Garda
Chase white-capped
waves on a windsurf (p176)

Val Camonia

Sondrio

Parco Regionale
degli Orobie
Valtellinesi

Parco
Regionale
Bergamasche alve

Valle Camonica

Parco
dell'Adamello

Riva del
Garda

Lake
Ledro

Verona
Enjoy opera at the
Roman Arena (p195)

Rovereto

Valle Brembana

Valle Seriana

Oglio

San
Pellegrino
Terme

Lake
Iseo

Val Cavallina

Lake
Idro

Parco Regionale
dell'Alto Garda
Bresciano

Monte Baldo

Parco Nazionale
Regionale della
Lessinia

Monte Lessini

Bergamo

Orio al
Serio

Lake
Valvestino

Franciacorta
wine region

Salò

Lake
Garda

Valle di Squaranto

Parco
Regional
del Serio

Brescia

Desenzano
del Garda

Sirmione
Colombare

Verona

Crema

Verona
Villafranca
Airport

Parco
Adda
Sud

Villafranca

River Mincio

Lake
Messo

Oglio

Cremona

Mantua

Cremona
Indulge in Cremonese cooking
and classical music (p170)

Mantua
Marvel at Mantegna's
frescoes (p205)

Bergamo
Admire medieval
masterpieces (p151)

The Italian Lakes'
Top 14

The Last Supper

1 When Leonardo da Vinci was at work on *The Last Supper* (p59), a star-struck monk noted that he would sometimes arrive in the morning, stare at yesterday's effort then promptly call it quits for the day. Your visit may be similarly brief (and it's no mean feat nabbing a ticket in the first place), but the baggage of a thousand dodgy reproductions and one very dubious best-selling novel is quickly shed once actually face to face with the astonishing beauty and enthralling psychological drama as Christ reveals one of the apostles will betray him.

Milan's Duomo

2 Whether it's your virgin visit to Milan or your 50th, your first glimpse of the city's cathedral (p56) with its organic ferment of petrified sky-piercing pinnacles and buttresses will never fail to elicit a gasp of awe. Under the ever-watchful gaze of the golden Madonnina, you can also wander the rooftop, feeling just a little closer to heaven. It's said that you can see the Matterhorn on a clear day, but given Milan's notorious haze, you'll probably have to call in favours from Our Lady to guarantee that.

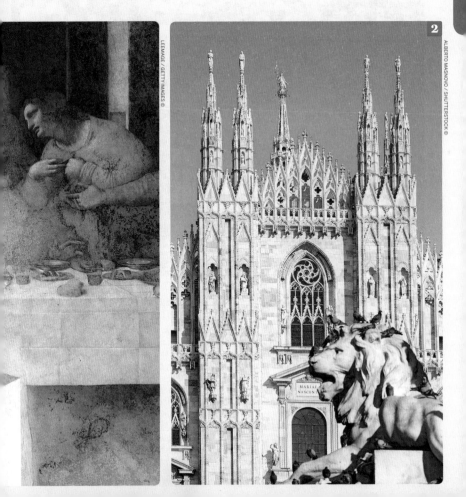

LEEMAGE / GETTY IMAGES ©

ALBERTO MASNOVO / SHUTTERSTOCK ©

TRAVELVIEW / SHUTTERSTOCK ©

MORES, MAURO PICCARDI / SHUTTERSTOCK ©

Verona's Roman Arena

3 Even those normally immune to arias will be swept up in the occasion. On summer nights, when 14,000 music lovers fill Verona's Roman Arena (p195) and light their candles at sunset, expect goosebumps even before the performance starts. The festival, which runs from mid-June to the end of August, was started in 1913 and is now the biggest open-air lyrical music event in the world. It draws performers such as Placido Domingo and the staging is legendary – highlights have included Franco Zeffirelli's productions of *Carmen* and *Aida*.

Mantegna in Mantua

4 Maverick Mantegna was a carpenter's son who married into the Bellini clan in Venice, painted a golden altar in Verona, frescoed the Belvedere chapel in Rome and finally became court painter in Mantua in 1460. His landscapes and scenes of arrested energy demonstrate a sculptural approach to painting reminiscent of classical antiquity. *Cristo Morto*, his most famous work, in Milan's Brera gallery and the *Camera degli Sposi* (Bridal Chamber) in Palazzo Ducale (pictured above; p205) in Mantua still have the power to shock and amaze.

Bellagio

5 Beautiful Bellagio (p125) has been a favoured summer resort since Roman times. Its position on a promontory jutting out into the centre of Lake Como made it the object of much envy, hence its tumble-down fortifications and Como-esque church of San Giovanni. While the Romans planted olive and laurel trees, their descendants surrounded their villas with camellias and rhododendrons. In summer, lovers come to promenade among them while modern hedonists launch into the blue lake from the Lido deck.

Wineries in Valpolicella

6 From Oltrepò Pavese in the east to Leonardo da Vinci's favourite Valtellina vintages in the foothills of the Alps and Italy's finest fizz in Franciacorta, Lombardy offers up kilometres of vineyards perfect for touring and tastings. Most famous of all is the blockbuster red Amarone produced in the region of Valpolicella using a 6th-century process developed by the Greeks. Sample some of the best at Villa della Torre (p201), designed by Giulio Romana and now part of the august Allegrini winery. Villa della Torre

Shopping in Milan's 'Quad'

7 For anyone interested in the fall of a frock or the cut of a jacket, a stroll around Quadrilatero D'Oro (p79), the world-famous shopping district, should be on your lifetime to-do list. And even if you don't have the urge to carry a swag of glossy bags, the people-watching is priceless. Bespoke-suited silver foxes prowl, gazelle-limbed models lope up and down, and aggressively accessorised matrons crowd the bar at Pasticceria Marchesi and Pasticceria Cova for short blacks and some obligatory flirting with the baristas.

Borromean Palaces

8 The Borromean Gulf forms Lake Maggiore's most beautiful corner, and the Borromean Islands (p93) harbour its most spectacular sights: the privately owned palaces of the Borromei family. On Isola Bella, the grandiose Palazzo Borromeo (pictured right) presides over 10 tiers of gardens and a gilt-encrusted Throne Room, while on Isola Madre white peacocks stalk gardens around an older family residence complete with a puppet theatre designed by La Scala's set designer. In summer, the Borromei family reside in the palace.

7

Italian Masters

9 Founded in the late 18th century, Milan's Pinacoteca di Brera and Bergamo's Accademia Carrara (p151) housed many Italian masters including Titian, Tintoretto, Botticelli, Raphael, Caravaggio and the Bellini brothers. The masterpieces number in their hundreds and represent the arc of Italian artistic development between the 15th and 18th centuries. In 2015, after seven years of renovation and a €10 million investment, the Accademia Carrara reopened and is once again a world-class museum. Santacroce's *John the Merciful in Alexandria,* Accademia Carrara, Bergamo

Mountain Hikes

10 Ringed with a range of spectacular Alpine peaks reflected gloriously in dozens of glassy glacial lakes, northern Italy is a paradise for hikers and strollers alike. The more populous southern towns of Stresa, Como and Salò sport flower-fringed promenades from where pilgrim paths and mule tracks disappear into the hills. One of the best is La Dorsale del Triangolo Lariano (p44), which snakes along a high ridge above Lake Como (take the funicular up to Brunate to reach the trailhead) and connects the glamorous town of Como to bijou Bellagio. Lake Como

PETER STEIN / SHUTTERSTOCK ©

IRYNAI / SHUTTERSTOCK ©

Locarno (Switzerland)

11 Once part of the Lombard duchy of Anghera, Locarno (p111) made its name in 1925 with the Treaty of Locarno, a noble attempt at fixing Europe's borders. Since then the town has taken a less serious bent, devoting itself to pleasure: cultivating a beautiful waterfront, running cable cars up the mountain to frescoed chapels and stunning viewpoints, and hosting summer festivals, including the International Film Festival with shows screened nightly in Piazza Grande. Santuario della Madonna del Sasso (p111)

Villa Carlotta

12 Imagine a landscape caught between fantasy and reality, a green theatre where statues might move, fountains and sculpture embody encoded messages, and the air is full of strange noises as water trickles down walls and gurgles in grottos. No, this isn't Shakespeare's magical isle in *The Tempest,* but the gardens of Villa Carlotta (p136) on Lake Como. Given to a Prussian princess on her wedding, the villa is stuffed with Canova statues, while the gardens bloom with Europe's finest collection of rhododendrons, azaleas and camellias.

Water Sports on Lake Garda

13 Sailors, windsurfers, kitesurfers and paragliders come to test their mettle at Riva del Garda's Punta Lido (p187), on winds first mentioned by Virgil. The Pelèr swoops south from the mountains in the morning, catching the sails of speedmeisters until noon, when the gentler Ora puffs north from the southern valleys in the afternoon and early evening. Experts fine-tune their experiences on some of the 20 other winds that skim across the lake, like the Ander and Fasanella as well as the violent Vinesa from Verona. Sailing, Lake Garda

ULLI SEER / LOOK-FOTO / GETTY IMAGES ©

Medieval Bergamo

14 There's no shortage of fresh air, breath-taking views and urban appeal in this medieval Lombard town (p151), perched atop a hill at the foot of the Orobie Alps. The city's defining feature is its double identity. The ancient hilltop Città Alta (Upper Town) is a tangle of tiny medieval streets and Lombard Romanesque architecture. Le Corbusier considered Piazza Vecchia (pictured right) the most beautiful square in Europe, lined as it is with fine Renaissance palaces, such as the pearly-white Palazzo Nuovo, which houses one of Italy's most prestigious libraries.

ALEXANDER SPATARI / GETTY IMAGES ©

Need to Know

For more information, see Survival Guide (p253)

Currency
Euro (€),
Swiss franc (Sfr)

Language
Italian, Swiss, German

Visas
Not required for EU citizens. Nationals of Australia, Brazil, Canada, Japan, New Zealand and the US do not need visas for visits of up to 90 days.

Money
ATMs are widely available and credit cards accepted at most hotels, restaurants and shops. To change money, you'll need to present your ID.

Mobile Phones
GSM and tri-band phones can be used in Italy with a local SIM card.

Time
Central European Time (GMT/UTC plus one hour)

When to Go

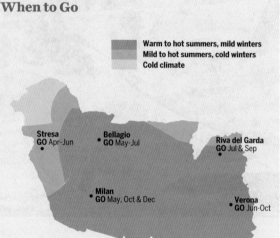

Warm to hot summers, mild winters
Mild to hot summers, cold winters
Cold climate

Stresa
GO Apr-Jun

Bellagio
GO May-Jul

Riva del Garda
GO Jul & Sep

Milan
GO May, Oct & Dec

Verona
GO Jun-Oct

High Season
(Mar & Apr, Jul & Aug, Oct)

➡ Accommodation prices rise at least 50%.

➡ Cities and lake resorts are hot and crowded in July and August.

➡ Trade fairs are held in Milan and Verona in March, April and October.

Shoulder (May & Jun, Sep)

➡ Perfect weather and gardens are in bloom.

➡ By June, lake resorts are buzzing and the water is warming up.

➡ September is harvest time and perfect for touring wine roads.

Low Season
(Nov–Feb)

➡ Accommodation bargains abound, but many lake and mountain hotels close.

➡ Some tourist info offices close and many restaurants operate with reduced hours.

➡ Christmas fairs are held in Milan and Verona.

Useful Websites

inLombardia (www.in
-lombardia.it) Lombardy's
official tourism website.

Provincia di Verona (www.
tourism.verona.it) Covers
Verona, Lake Garda and
Valpolicella.

Turismo Milano (www.turismo.
milano.it) Milan's excellent
official city guide.

Lake Maggiore (www.illago
maggiore.com) Covers the
southern (Italian) half of the
lake, as well as Lake Orta, Varese
and the Ossola valleys.

Lake Como (www.lakecomo.org)
Covers the whole Como area.

Lonely Planet (www.lonely
planet.com/italy/lombardy
-and-the-lakes) Destination
information, hotel bookings and
traveller forum.

Important Numbers

Italy country code	☏39
International access code	☏00
Ambulance (Italy)	☏118
Ambulance (Switzerland)	☏144
Local police	☏113
All emergency services from a mobile phone	☏112

Exchange Rates

Australia	A$1	€0.68
Canada	C$1	€0.68
Japan	¥100	€0.80
New Zealand	NZ$1	€0.63
UK	UK£1	€1.18
USA	US$1	€0.91

For current exchange rates see
www.xe.com.

Daily Costs

**Budget:
Less than €110**

➡ Dorm bed: €20–30

➡ Sandwich: €2.50–4

➡ Pizza or pasta: €8–12

➡ Coffee drunk at bar: €1

**Midrange:
€110–€200**

➡ Midrange double room:
€110–200

➡ Two-course lunch and wine
in a trattoria: €25–45

➡ *Aperitivo* cocktail and all-
you-can-eat buffet: €8–15

➡ Average museum entry:
€5–10

**Top end:
More than €200**

➡ Top-end hotel double: €200
and over

➡ Fine-dining restaurant meal:
€50–150

➡ Top-end *aperitivo:* €15–20

➡ Hotel parking: €10–20 per
day

Opening Hours

Opening hours in Italy tend to be
longer in summer. In August in
Milan, many shops and restaurants close for several weeks, or
have reduced hours, and clubs
move their activities out of town.
Conversely, in winter around the
lakes, many places are shut.

Banks 8.30am–1.30pm and
3.30–4.30pm Monday–Friday

Cafes & bars 7.30am–8pm;
most serve alcoholic drinks in
the evening

Restaurants noon–2.30pm and
7.30–11pm (kitchens close at
10pm); most close at least once
a week

Shops 9am–1pm and 3.30–
7.30pm (or 4–8pm) Monday–
Saturday; some shops only open
for half the day on Monday

Arriving in the Italian Lakes

**Aeroporto Malpensa Malpensa
Express** (p85) trains run to
the city centre (one-way €13,
50 minutes) every 30 minutes
from 5.40am to 10.40pm; the
Malpensa Shuttle (p85) (€10
one-way) continues a limited
service between 10.45pm and
5.30am. Taxis to Milan are a €90
set fare (50 minutes).

Aeroporto Orio al Serio The
Orio al Serio Bus Express runs
to Milan's Central Station
(adult/child €5/4, one hour)
every 30 minutes from 4.25am
to 10.20pm; Autostradale (p261)
also runs a half-hourly service
to Milan (adult/child €5/3.50)
between 7.45am and 12.15am.
ATV buses depart every 20
minutes to Bergamo (€2.30, 15
minutes).

Aeroporto Verona-Villafranca
An ATV Aerobus (p262) runs
to/from the train station (€6,
15 minutes) every 20 minutes
from 6.30am to 11.30pm. A taxi
into Verona costs between €25
and €30.

Medical Services

**American International Medi-
cal Centre** (p255) Private, international health clinic in Milan
with English-speaking staff.

ASST Papa Giovanni XXIII
(p255) Located 4km west of
Bergamo, this modern, state-
of-the-art hospital has excellent
facilities.

Ospedale Borgo Trento (p255)
Verona's health centre is of
national importance and offers
top-quality diagnostics, surgery
and outpatient care.

Ospedale Maggiore Policlinico
(p255) Milan's main hospital;
offers an outpatient service.

For much more on
getting around,
see p262

First Time in the Italian Lakes

For more information, see Survival Guide (p253)

Checklist

➡ Ensure your passport is valid for at least six months.

➡ Check visa requirements at www.esteri.it.

➡ Check airline baggage restrictions.

➡ Inform your debit-/credit-card company that you'll be visiting Italy.

➡ Organise appropriate travel insurance, especially for activity holidays.

➡ Book popular sights, exhibitions and high-end restaurants.

➡ Download the Milan transport app at www. atm-mi.it.

What to Pack

➡ Good walking shoes

➡ A corkscrew for picnicking

➡ Mosquito repellent – a must in summer

➡ Warm clothes and a jacket for cool evenings, and an umbrella in winter and spring

➡ Swimming costume, hat, sunglasses and sunscreen

➡ Smart threads and shoes for dining

➡ Electrical adapter

Top Tips for Your Trip

➡ The best time to be out and about is between 5pm and 9pm, when northern Italians take to the piazzas for *passeggiata* (a stroll), *spritz* (a *prosecco*-based cocktail) and *aperitivo* (complimentary snacks). Join the throng and save some money on dining out.

➡ Northern Italians are fairly formal. Make eye contact and say *buongiorno/buonasera* (good morning/evening) and *piacere* (pleased to meet you) when greeting people.

➡ Get off the main roads – not only will you avoid paying tolls, but you'll enjoy the region's best scenery, photo ops and villages.

➡ When planning itineraries, bear in mind the mountainous terrain surrounding the lakes. Fast motorways link the lakes at the northern and southern ends; otherwise, you're in for a lot of zigzagging north and south.

What to Wear

In northern Italy, especially fashion-conscious Milan, maintaining *la bella figura* (ie making a good impression) is extremely important. It's all very well being a nice soul, but northern Italians expect a well-cut suit, shiny shoes and neatly coiffed hair to boot. In general, T-shirts, shorts and flip-flops don't cut the mustard unless you're on the beach, and topless sunbathing is a no-no around the family-friendly lakes. A smart-casual dress code should cover most situations, though trainers, short-sleeved shirts and light-blue jeans are frowned upon for evening wear.

Money

Credit and debit cards are widely accepted. Visa, MasterCard and Cirrus are the preferred options; American Express is only accepted by international hotel chains, luxury boutiques and major department stores. Always check if restaurants take cards before you order; most bars and cafes do not. Chip-and-pin is the norm for card transactions – few places accept signatures as an alternative.

Bancomats (ATMS) are everywhere; most offer withdrawal from overseas savings accounts and cash advances on credit cards. Both transactions will incur international transaction fees. You can change cash and travellers cheques at a bank, post office or *cambio* (exchange office). Bring ID.

Bargaining

Gentle haggling is common in flea markets and antiques markets; in all other instances you're expected to pay the stated price.

Tipping

Cafes & bars Most Italians just leave small change (€0.10 to €0.20 is fine).

Hotels At least €2 per bag or night, for porter, maid or room service.

Restaurants Tips of 10% are standard – though check to see that a tip hasn't already been added to your bill, or included in the flat *coperto* (cover) charge.

Transport Round up taxi fares to the nearest euro.

Language

With its business focus, industrial hinterland and extensive program of international trade fairs, English is widely spoken in Lombardy and around the lakes, as is German and, to some degree, French. That said, locals are always pleased when visitors deploy some Italian, and a few choice phrases will enhance your travel experience no end.

Phrases to Learn Before You Go

 What's the local speciality?
Qual'è la specialità di questa regione?
kwa·le la spe·cha·lee·ta dee kwes·ta re·jo·ne

A bit like the rivalry between medieval Italian city-states, these days the country's regions compete in speciality foods and wines.

 Which combined tickets do you have?
Quali biglietti cumulativi avete?
kwa·lee bee·lye·tee koo·moo·la·tee·vee a·ve·te

Make the most of your euro by getting combined tickets to various sights; they are available in all major Italian cities.

 Where can I buy discount designer items?
C'è un outlet in zona? che oon owt·let in zo·na

Discount fashion outlets are big business in major cities – get bargain-priced seconds, samples and cast-offs for *la bella figura*.

 I'm here with my husband/boyfriend.
Sono qui con il mio marito/ragazzo.
so·no kwee kon eel mee·o ma·ree·to/ra·ga·tso

Solo women travellers may receive unwanted attention in some parts of Italy; if ignoring fails have a polite rejection ready.

 Let's meet at 6pm for pre-dinner drinks.
Ci vediamo alle sei per un aperitivo.
chee ve·dya·mo a·le say per oon a·pe·ree·tee·vo

At dusk, watch the main piazza get crowded with people sipping colourful cocktails and snacking the evening away: join your new friends for this authentic Italian ritual!

Etiquette

Greetings The standard form of greeting is a handshake. If you know someone well, air-kissing on both cheeks (starting on the left) is the norm.

Be polite Say *mi scusi* to attract attention or say 'I'm sorry'; *grazie* (*mille*) to say 'thank you (very much)'; *prego* to say 'you're welcome' or 'please, after you' and *permesso* if you need to get past.

Cafe culture Don't linger at an espresso bar; drink your coffee and go. It's called espresso for a reason.

Paying the bill Whoever invites usually pays. Splitting the bill between friends is OK, but itemising it is *molto vulgare* (very vulgar).

Boating Allow passengers to disembark before boarding boats. For those in need of assistance, the crew are happy to lend a hand.

What's New

Accademia Carrara

Bergamo's blockbuster fine art gallery is open once again after a seven-year restoration program. The wait has been worth it, and it now ranks among Italy's finest galleries. (p151)

Fondazione Feltrinelli

One of the most extraordinary new structures to arise in Milan is Herzog & de Meuron's grand glass conservatory. It's home to the Milanese publisher Feltrinelli and hosts a great bookstore, bar and cultural events. (p61)

VOLT

Milan has a long history as a music town, and new club VOLT has its sights set on European Top Club's chart with its state-of-the-art sound system and top-notch DJs. (p77)

Jungle Raider Park Xtreme

The first extreme adventure park in Italy has opened on the forested slopes of Lake Como, where you can climb spider nets, zipline through the treetops and cross ravines on wire bridges. (p125)

Noi

Internationally trained chef Tommaso Spagnolo learned his craft in New York and London. Now he presides over his own creative osteria in Bergamo. (p157)

Casinò di San Pellegrino Terme

This art nouveau gambling house is now fully restored and open to the public. Tour the lavish interiors and then bathe in mineral-rich waters next door at QC Terme. (p162)

Budget Digs on Lake Como

The latest trend on northern Italy's most exclusive lake is top-notch budget accommodation at places like Ostello Bello. (p32)

Orta Jazz Festival

Between June and September, this new jazz festival takes place in Piazza Motta against the lovely backdrop of Lake Orta. (p109)

Museo di Castelvecchio

Seventeen old master paintings stolen from Verona's Castelvecchio in 2015 have now been returned to the museum. They include works by Rubens, Tintoretto and Mantegna. (p195)

Il Sereno Lago di Como

The hottest new hotel on Lake Como is this striking contemporary beauty, replete with a pool that overhangs the lake, a restaurant by Andrea Berton and a stunning vertical garden. (p33)

La Rucola 2.0

This revamped, Michelin-starred eatery in Sirmione is even better following a refit, with more up-to-date decor lending it a refined, contemporary ambience. (p180)

For more recommendations and reviews, see lonelyplanet.com/italy/lombardy-and-the-lakes

If You Like...

The Great Outdoors

Greenway del Lago di Como An easygoing, 10km walk on the sunny western side of Lake Como. (p133)

Surfsegnana Make the best of the Pelèr and Ora winds to windsurf, kitesurf and sail around Lake Garda. (p189)

Santuario della Madonna del Ghisallo Head to this 17th-century church above Bellagio and leave your memento to the patron saint of cyclists. (p126)

Monte Mottarone Attracts families for mountain biking, bobsledding and lake views. (p87)

Guti Bike Rent Get off the beaten track and cycle scenic trails beside Lake Como. (p132)

Parco Sempione Join the joggers, rollerbladers and picnickers in Milan's grand public park. (p59)

Rockmaster Festival Made famous by the likes of Maurizio Zanolla, Arco hosts this festival and is a must-visit list for climbers. (p188)

Fabulous Food

Sauce Milan Tours by professional food writers reveal that Milan is a serious food town. (p73)

Eataly Along with a bevy of Michelin stars, a huge Eataly emporium puts Milan at the forefront of Lombard food. (p81)

Locanda 4 Cuochi Meet the young chefs at the vanguard of Veronese cooking. (p199)

Mantua Sample heritage dishes spiced with pumpkin and cinnamon that can trace their origins back to the Renaissance. (p205)

Bellagio Cooking Classes A great introduction to lakeside cuisine, including a trip to market. (p127)

Peck Italy's biggest cheese-producer, its Lombard cheeses have conquered the world. This deli has an exhaustive selection. (p69)

Comincioli Producers of award-winning olive oil from the shores of Lake Garda. (p182)

Art

The Last Supper Milan is home to the world's most famous painting by Leonardo da Vinci. (p59)

Monastero di Santa Giulia Hidden in Brescia's urban sprawl, this museum encloses two frescoed Roman villas. (p167)

Museo del Novecento The home of Milan's best modern art. (p58)

Museo Poldi Pezzoli Milan's private house museums are as impressive as any museum. (p59)

Pinacoteca di Brera Come to see the Italian masters at Milan's fine art gallery. (p58)

Palazzo Ducale Mantegna executed his biggest commission in this Mantua palace. (p205)

Villa Olmo Como's art nouveau landmark now hosts blockbuster exhibits in its ornate interiors. (p117)

Accademia Carrara Bergamo's top-notch gallery full of Renaissance masterpieces. (p151)

Architecture

Duomo Milan's great Gothic cathedral is architecturally unique. (p56)

Certosa di Pavia One of the most notable buildings of the Renaissance is this lavish monastery. (p82)

Piazza Vecchia Le Corbusier considered this square in Bergamo's medieval hilltop town to be the finest in Europe. (p151)

Fondazione Prada Rem Koolhaas' converted brandy factory is contemporary architecture at its best. (p61)

Basilica di San Zeno Maggiore A masterpiece of Romanesque architecture with a frescoed interior in Verona. (p197)

Casinò di San Pellegrino Terme
This stylish gaming house is the epitome of art nouveau style. (p162)

Il Vittoriale degli Italiani Poet Gabriele d'Annunzio's lakeside villa showcases every architectural excess. (p184)

Villa Gardens

Villa Taranto One of Europe's finest botanic gardens, planted with over 20,000 different species. (p95)

Palazzo Borromeo The Borromeo's outdoor baroque fantasy is adorned with classical statuary and white peacocks. (p93)

Villa Carlotta A 17th-century villa stuffed with sculpture by Antonio Canova and gardens filled with azaleas, rhododendrons and camellias. (p136)

Villa Balbianello Located at Lenno on Lake Como, these terraced gardens drip down the promontory like ice cream on a cone. (p133)

Villa Melzi d'Eril Neat neoclassical elegance combines with the studied informality in Lake Como's first English-style garden in Bellagio. (p126)

Parco Scherrer Exotic gardens devised by textile merchant Hermann Arthur Scherrer, bristling with tropical foliage and architectural follies. (p146)

Grotte di Catullo The lakes' largest Roman ruin sits amid olive trees at the tip of Sirmione's promontory. (p177)

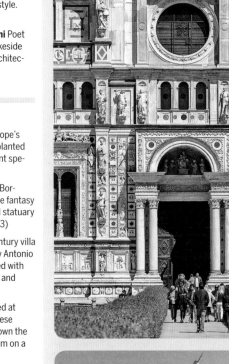

Top: Certosa di Pavia (p82)

Bottom: Palazzo Borromeo (p93)

Month by Month

February

Cold mountain winds and shuttered doors signal the quietest month of the year. Cities in the Po valley shrug off the winter blues with Carnival celebrations.

✨ Carnevale

In the period leading up to Ash Wednesday, many Italian towns stage pre-Lenten carnivals; the best are in Milan, Lecco, Bellinzona and Verona, the latter led by King Gnoco.

March

The weather in March is capricious. If you get lucky, you could bag some sunshine at great prices. Towards the end of the month, early-blooming camellias herald spring.

◉ Mostra Nazionale della Camelia

Verbania gets a splash of extra floral colour in late March from a display of more than 200 varieties of camellia. (p96)

April

Lakeside gardens burst into bloom, although temperatures still retain their chilly edge. Easter sees the tourist season kick off in earnest, and global fairs pack hotels in Milan and Verona.

◉ Salone Internazionale del Mobile

Milan's Furniture Fair is the design industry's premier global event, even bigger than the fashion shows. The main event takes place at the Fiera Milano, but satellite events, showcasing the work of emerging talents, are held all over town in the Fuorisalone. (p68)

◉ Settimana del Tulipano

Forty thousand tulips erupt in bloom on the grounds of Villa Taranto; the dahlia path is also in bloom, as is the dogwood. (p96)

May

The month of roses, May is a perfect time to travel, especially for walkers and cyclists. Hotel prices are also good value, and river cruises launch for the season.

MILAN'S FASHION WEEK(S)

Glimpse the future of wardrobes worldwide four times a year, when leading designers parade next season's collections at Milan's Fashion Weeks. The men's shows head the A/W (autumn/winter) schedule in January, with the women's following in February. Men's S/S (spring/summer) takes place in June and the women's in September. For event listings and a full timetable of designer showcases, check with the Camera Nazionale della Moda Italiana (National Chamber of Italian Fashion; www.cameramoda.it). Access to most shows is by invitation only.

☆ Festival di Cremona Claudio Monteverdi

This month-long festival celebrating composer Claudio Monteverdi, among others, draws the big performers of ancient music. (p173)

July

Temperatures crank up. Walkers and cyclists head for the mountains, but everyone else heads for the beach, meaning prices at lakeside accommodation soar. Summer music festivals kick off.

☆ Arena di Verona Opera Festival

Verona's open-air Roman Arena is a spectacular location for opera; the season kicks off in mid-June and runs to the end of August. Book tickets online.

☆ Orta Jazz Festival

Against the backdrop of lovely Lake Orta, Piazza Motta becomes an open-air stage for free jazz concerts during the summer. One jam a month is held from June to September. (p109)

☆ Bellagio Festival

From June to early September, catch weekly classical music concerts in Bellagio (www.bellagiofestival.com) and some of Lake Como's most spectacular villas.

August

Locals take their annual holidays and life in the cities slows to a snail's pace. Be warned: the weather can be stifling on the plains and lakeside beaches are crowded.

☆ Stresa Festival

Classical concerts and midsummer jazz in lakeside gardens are held from mid-July to early September. (p91)

☆ Festival Internazionale di Film

This two-week film festival (www.pardolive.ch) in Locarno, one of Europe's most important, has been going since 1948. An open-air screen is pitched in Piazza Grande so the public can attend for free.

☆ Blues to Bop

Lugano's picturesque piazzas become an outdoor stage for 50 musicians who perform over 40 blues and jazz concerts (www.bluestobop.ch) over three days at the end of August.

September

Autumn is when the grape harvest is celebrated alongside the rice harvest. Mountain forests proffer scented porcini mushrooms and creamy chestnuts.

🏎 Italian F1 Grand Prix

Hosted at the autodrome (www.monzanet.it) in the royal park of Monza, this is one of the longest-running races in Formula One and is a must-see for enthusiasts.

☆ Stradivari Festival

Between mid-September and mid-October, Cremona's Museo del Violino hosts this month-long festival that focuses on music for string instruments. (p173)

🍷 Bardolino Grape Festival

Sit down at outdoor tables and drink and dine with local families at the Bardolino wine festival (Festa dell'Uva e del Vino), held on the last weekend in September. (p193)

November

Summer resorts have shut for the season and there's a chill in the northern air, but late-season produce and truffles from Piedmont fill menus with tasty treats.

🍴 Festa del Torrone

A weekend celebration packed with over 250 events celebrating Cremona's Christmas sweet *torrone* (nougat). Aside from tastings, there's opera and medieval pageantry. (p173)

December

December is rainy, but cities stave off the grey with Christmas markets, roasted chestnuts and festive illuminations. Alpine resorts open for the ski season.

☆ Festa di Sant'Ambrogio & Fiera degli Obej Obej

The feast day of Milan's patron saint is celebrated on 7 December with a large Christmas fair at Castello Sforzesco. La Scala's opera season kicks off the same day.

Itineraries

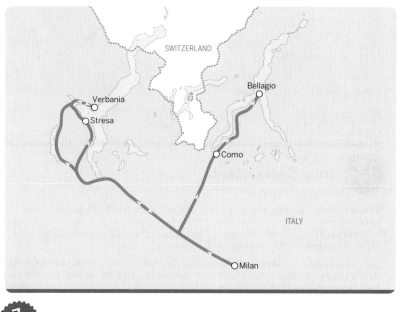

7 DAYS Greatest Hits

Squeeze the most out of a seven-day itinerary with this city-and-lake combo, which combines Milan's best highlights with some chic lakeside living in Stresa, Como and Bellagio.

Modernist **Milan** gets this whirlwind tour off to a spectacular start with big-city treats like Leonardo da Vinci's *The Last Supper,* Michelin-starred dining at Seta and world-class art in the Pinacoteca di Brera. Give yourself at least two days to eat, shop and sight-see, and take in an opera at La Scala. Then head for belle époque **Stresa** and ferry-hop to the Borromean palaces on Isola Bella and Isola Madre. On your second day, swing up Monte Mottarone or launch off on a ferry to **Verbania** to visit the voluptuous gardens at Villa Taranto. From Stresa, continue to **Como** by car or train (via Milan). Here you can amble the flower-laden promenade to Villa Olmo, visit the frescoed Basilica di San Fedele and zip up to Brunate for pretty walks and panoramic views. Then press on to **Bellagio**, which sits in the centre of the lake, allowing you to ferry-hop to Tremezzo and Varenna. Back in Bellagio, round off the tour with a romantic sunset boat cruise.

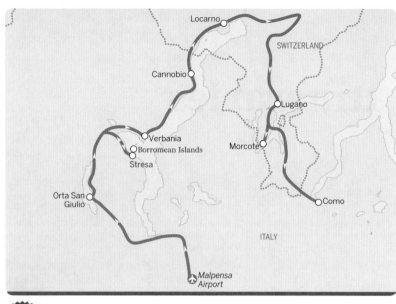

Into Switzerland

This two-week tour takes you from tiny Lake Orta to the bustling southern shores of Lake Maggiore and up to the lake's wilder northern reaches before crossing the border to Locarno in Switzerland. From here, the drive south to Lake Lugano and Como cuts through the most spectacular mountain scenery.

Head straight from **Malpensa Airport** to the medieval town of **Orta San Giulio** on the thickly wooded shores of Lake Orta. Spend the following day meandering the medieval streets, visiting the 12th-century basilica on Isola di San Giulio and romancing over dinner. In the morning, depart for **Stresa** on the southern shore of Lake Maggiore. From here you can take the ferry to the **Borromean Islands** for a day trip to explore their extravagant palaces and gardens. After a day or two, move north up the eastern shore of the lake to **Verbania**, where you can dip into the interesting Troubetzkoy sculpture collection at Museo del Paesaggio and wander through the vast gardens of Villa Taranto. Dine at charming Osteria Castello or romantic Ristorante Milano before moving on in the morning to **Cannobio**. This dreamy little cobbled town is one of the quietest on the lake and is a lovely place to spend a day or two lounging on the beach, sailing or exploring the Cannobino River valley. Start the second week by crossing the border to **Locarno**, where you can pack two days exploring the quaint old town, swimming at the lakeside *lido,* and visiting the Castello Visconteo, Isole di Brissago gardens and hilltop Santuario della Madonna del Sasso. In July and August, Locarno also hosts a fantastic film and music festival. The drive south from Locarno to bewitching **Lago di Lugano** offers spectacular mountain scenery. You'll need two or three days here to explore the lakeside towns of Gandria, Meride and Morcote. At Meride you'll find Mario Botta's fascinating Museo dei Fossili, while at Gandria you can wander the 5km Sentiero di Gandria with its outstanding views over the lake. Base yourself in photogenic **Morcote**, which has been voted Switzerland's most beautiful village. Finally, tear yourself away and head south to the silk town of **Como**, for a final taste of glamour and, perhaps, a swoop over the lakes with the Aero Club.

Top: Orta San Giulio
(p108)
Bottom: Morcote
(p146)

7 DAYS · A Wine Meander

Lombardy produces some of Italy's finest wines and the area around Verona and Lake Garda are prime grape-growing territory. This tour combines the cultural highlights of Verona with the heady flavours of Soave, Valpolicella, Franciacorta and the Valtenesi.

Fly into **Verona** and enjoy two days of sightseeing in the city's frescoed churches and grand castle museum. On the third day, day trip to **Soave**, where you can sample the lemony Soave Classico at the Azienda Agricola Coffele in the old town. The following day, set off for **Valpolicella** to sample the full bodied Amarone and Recioto reds. Prebook for tastings at wineries. A leisurely lunch at Enoteca della Valpolicella is also a must. Then continue on through the vine-covered hills to **Bardolino** on the shores of Lake Garda. This tiny town is surrounded by 70 wineries, one of which, Zeni, houses a wine museum. You can also sample wines here. The next day loop round the bottom of the lake into the **Valtenesi**. Base yourself in **Salò** and strike out for innovative wineries like Comincioli. Round up this wine-fuelled feast with lunch at Michelin-starred Due Colombe in **Franciacorta**, where you'll get to sample some of Italy's finest fizz.

10 DAYS · Art Cities

For an architectural and artistic tour of northern Italy's glittering medieval and Renaissance heydays, look no further than the elegant cities of the Po valley.

Start this tour in **Milan**, one of medieval Italy's most important city-states. Spend four days here exploring the Castello Sforzesco, the collection of old masters in the Pinacoteca di Brera and Leonardo da Vinci's *The Last Supper*. Make day trips to **Monza** and **Pavia** to see the Villa Reale and the Certosa di Pavia. Journey to **Bergamo** on your fifth day to find some of Lombardy's finest Renaissance architecture in the Upper Town. Dedicate a morning to the collection in the Accademia Carrara, one of the most impressive galleries in Italy. From Bergamo it's a short hop to **Brescia**, a city which hides a fascinating historic core in its ugly suburban sprawl, including two preserved Roman houses with floor mosaics. The Roman theme continues in **Verona**, your next stop. Verona's Roman Arena hosts the world's largest open-air opera festival. With three final days here, you'll have time to wander, drink some of the region's fine wines and maybe even day trip to **Mantua** to see Mantegna's frescoes in the Palazzo Ducale.

7 DAYS Action-Packed Adventure

The northern reaches of Lake Garda are hemmed in by high mountains, making this perfect hiking, biking and climbing territory. Regular winds also draw water-sports enthusiasts to this outdoor paradise.

Hire a car in **Verona** and head straight for the lakeside town of **Garda**, where you can overnight and take your first dip in the lake at the beautiful Parco Baia delle Sirene beach. The next day, drive to **Malcesine** and ascend massive Monte Baldo in the cable car. Cyclists can hire bikes at Xtreme Malcesine and take them on board, walkers can access panoramic mountaintop trails and paragliders can launch off the mountain and soar over the lake. On day three, arrive at **Riva del Garda** at the northern tip of the lake. Base yourself here for the next three or four days in order to pack in the wind- and kitesurfing, sailing, swimming, hiking, canyoning and rock climbing. Finish with a spot of R&R at B&B Peter Pan above the village of **Gargnano**, from where you can enjoy off-the-beaten-track walking trails in the Parco dell'Alto Garda Bresciano or flop on the beach at Parco la Fontanella.

7 DAYS Lake Garda's Southern Shore

The southern shore of Lake Garda with its mild Mediterranean climate has been attracting travellers since Roman times. Hence the tumbledown Roman ruins, patrician villas, elegant lakeside towns and vine- and olive-covered hinterland. This itinerary encompasses them all.

From **Verona** drive straight to **Sirmione**, the southernmost town on Lake Garda. It sits on a peninsula that juts out into the lake and is surrounded on all sides by water. Spend the night wandering the cobbled lanes, soaking in the thermal springs and, in the morning, explore the Grotte di Catullo, a ruined Roman villa set in two pretty hectares. Then drive to Salò, via **Desenzano del Garda**, where you can visit another Roman villa. Base yourself in **Salò** for four days. It was once Garda's capital and is full of lovely Liberty-style buildings. From here, you can visit the aristocratic residence on the Isola del Garda, as well as Valtenesi wineries, olive farms and the archaeological park of Rocca di Manerba. Finally, head on to **Gardone Riviera** for the last two nights to take in André Heller's beautiful botanical garden and the extraordinary Il Vittoriale degli Italiani, the estate of poet and Fascist Gabriele d'Annunzio.

Off the Beaten Track: The Italian Lakes

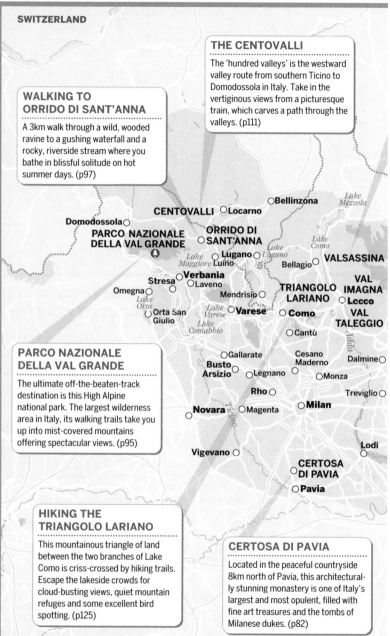

SWITZERLAND

THE CENTOVALLI

The 'hundred valleys' is the westward valley route from southern Ticino to Domodossola in Italy. Take in the vertiginous views from a picturesque train, which carves a path through the valleys. (p111)

WALKING TO ORRIDO DI SANT'ANNA

A 3km walk through a wild, wooded ravine to a gushing waterfall and a rocky, riverside stream where you bathe in blissful solitude on hot summer days. (p97)

CENTOVALLI ○Locarno ○Bellinzona Lake Mezzola

Domodossola○

PARCO NAZIONALE DELLA VAL GRANDE ○**ORRIDO DI SANT'ANNA** Lake Como

Lake Maggiore Luino ○Lugano○ Lake Lugano Bellagio○ **VALSASSINA**

Stresa○ **Verbania** ○Laveno **VAL**

Omegna○ Mendrisio○ **TRIANGOLO LARIANO** **IMAGNA** ○**Lecco**

Lake Orta ○Orta San Giulio Lake Varese ○**Varese** ○**Como** **VAL TALEGGIO**

Lake Comabbio ○Cantù

PARCO NAZIONALE DELLA VAL GRANDE

The ultimate off-the-beaten-track destination is this High Alpine national park. The largest wilderness area in Italy, its walking trails take you up into mist-covered mountains offering spectacular views. (p95)

○Gallarate Cesano Maderno Dalmine○

Busto Arsizio○ ○Legnano ○Monza

Rho○ Treviglio○

○**Novara** ○Magenta ○**Milan**

Vigevano ○ Lodi ○

CERTOSA DI PAVIA

○**Pavia**

HIKING THE TRIANGOLO LARIANO

This mountainous triangle of land between the two branches of Lake Como is criss-crossed by hiking trails. Escape the lakeside crowds for cloud-busting views, quiet mountain refuges and some excellent bird spotting. (p125)

CERTOSA DI PAVIA

Located in the peaceful countryside 8km north of Pavia, this architecturally stunning monastery is one of Italy's largest and most opulent, filled with fine art treasures and the tombs of Milanese dukes. (p82)

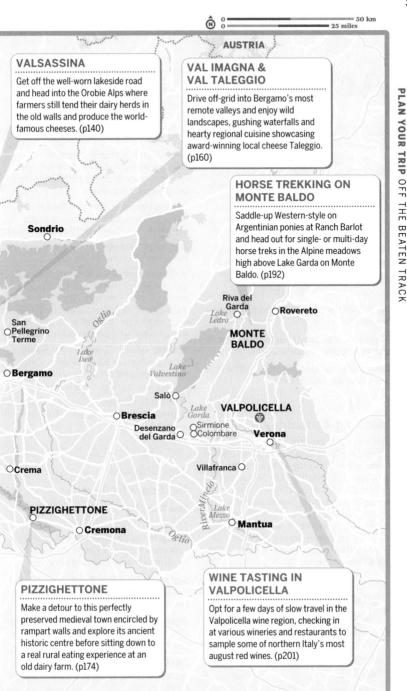

0 ——————————— 50 km
0 ——————————— 25 miles

AUSTRIA

VALSASSINA

Get off the well-worn lakeside road and head into the Orobie Alps where farmers still tend their dairy herds in the old walls and produce the world-famous cheeses. (p140)

VAL IMAGNA & VAL TALEGGIO

Drive off-grid into Bergamo's most remote valleys and enjoy wild landscapes, gushing waterfalls and hearty regional cuisine showcasing award-winning local cheese Taleggio. (p160)

HORSE TREKKING ON MONTE BALDO

Saddle-up Western-style on Argentinian ponies at Ranch Barlot and head out for single- or multi-day horse treks in the Alpine meadows high above Lake Garda on Monte Baldo. (p192)

Sondrio

Oglio

San Pellegrino Terme

Riva del Garda
Lake Ledro
Rovereto

MONTE BALDO

Lake Iseo

Bergamo

Lake Valvestino

Salò

VALPOLICELLA

Brescia
Lake Garda
Sirmione
Desenzano del Garda
Colombare
Verona

Crema

Villafranca

River Mincio

PIZZIGHETTONE
Lake Mezzo
Mantua
Cremona
Oglio

PIZZIGHETTONE

Make a detour to this perfectly preserved medieval town encircled by rampart walls and explore its ancient historic centre before sitting down to a real rural eating experience at an old dairy farm. (p174)

WINE TASTING IN VALPOLICELLA

Opt for a few days of slow travel in the Valpolicella wine region, checking in at various wineries and restaurants to sample some of northern Italy's most august red wines. (p201)

Accommodation

Accommodation Types

Northern Italy has a good range of accommodation. In summer, you should book at least a month in advance, and in popular places such as Como and Bellagio a minimum two-night stay may be required. Availability in Milan and Verona is affected by trade fairs and popular festivals.

Hotels Range from one- to three-star *pensione* (guesthouses) through to exclusive lakeside villas.

B&Bs The best-value accommodation. More luxurious versions border on boutique hotels.

Agriturismi (farm stays) Working farms offering accommodation.

Rifugi (mountain huts) Mountain huts in the Alps offering basic accommodation.

Camping Campgrounds cluster around the lakes and include spots for caravans.

Booking Accommodation

The most popular type of accommodation around the lakes is in hotels, B&Bs and *agriturismi* (farm stays). Villa rentals are available, but usually at the higher end of the market. Home Away (www.homeaway.com), Olivers Travels (www.oliverstravels.com), Lake Como Homes (www.lakecomo homes.com) and Hidden Italy (www.hidden italy.com) are good resources. Airbnb (www.airbnb.com) is useful mainly in Milan and Verona.

➡ Many lakeside hotels only open from Easter to October.

➡ Around the lakes, prices fluctuate considerably depending on the season, with Easter, summer and the Christmas/New Year being the most expensive.

➡ In popular places like Como, Bellagio and Stresa bookings should be made at least a month (and sometimes even further) in advance.

➡ During peak season some places demand a two- or three-night minimum stay.

➡ Milan is a case of its own, with price variations and availability linked to the trade fair and events calendar – the bigger the fair, the higher the price and the greater the degree of difficulty in locating a room. If travelling during these times, book at least a month or two in advance.

➡ During Milan's Salone del Mobile in April, prices can increase 200%. Likewise, Verona's summer opera festival and large-scale concerts put pressure on prices and availability.

➡ All hotels in the region now apply a tourist tax to overnight stays (€0.60 to €3.50 per person per night).

Top Choices
Best on a Budget

Casa Base, Milan (http://base.milano.it; €) An on-trend co-living artists' residence.

Central Hostel Bergamo, Bergamo (www.centralhostelbg.com; €) Bergamo's hostel has an excellent location and plenty of extras.

Campeggio Fornella, Valtenesi (www.fornella.it; €) A luxury, four-star campground with a private beach, lagoon pool and children's club.

Ostello Bello, Como (www.ostellobello.com; €) Milan's popular hostel brand reimagined on the shores of Lake Como.

Villa Giuliana, Menaggio (€) An early-20th-century villa with a lovely garden and thoughtful extras.

Traditional *agriturismo* with vineyard and olive grove

AGRITURISMI (FARM STAYS)

Live out your bucolic fantasies at one of northern Italy's growing number of *agriturismi* (farm stays). A long-booming industry in Tuscany and Umbria, farm stays are spreading across the country like freshly churned butter. While all agriturismi are required to grow at least one of their own products, the farm stays themselves range from rustic country houses with chickens and horses where guests can pitch in with farm work to elegant country estates with sweeping olive groves and sparkling pools.

To find lists of *agriturismi*, ask at any tourist office or check online at www.agriturismo.it, www.agriturismo.net and www.agriturismo.com.

Best Agriturismi

Agriturismo Casa Clelia, Bergamo (www.casa clelia.com; €) Ten beautiful rooms in a restored 16th-century farmhouse.

Agriturismo Le Radici, Lake Como (www.le radiciagriturismo.it; €) Relax amid open fields and sweeping views of Monte Generoso.

Agriturismo San Mattia, Verona (www. agriturismosanmattia.it; €) A 14-room farm with a Slow Food–focused restaurant serving Valpolicella vintages.

Agriturismo Scuderia Castello, Toscolano-Maderno (www.scuderiacastello.it; €) A lofty farm overlooking Lake Garda in the idyllic village of Gaino.

Best for Romance

Palazzo Parigi, Milan (www.palazzoparigi.com; €€€) A historic palazzo decked out in an opulent turn-of-the-century style.

Villa Arcadio, Salò (www.hotelvillaarcadio.it; €€€) Perched above Salò, this converted convent is the essence of lakeside glamour.

Locanda San Vigilio, San Vigilio (www.punta -sanvigilio.it; €€€) An enchanting 16th-century inn in the mould of an English manor house.

Il Sereno Lago di Como, Lake Como (www.il sereno.com; €€€) Elegant lines and a bold modern design beside Lake Como.

Hotel Pironi, Cannobio (www.pironihotel.it; €€) A 15th-century mini-monastery up high in Cannobio.

Best for Families

Residence Filanda, Riva del Garda (www. residencefilanda.com; €€) An apart-hotel with a heated pool and close to 1 hectare of child-friendly gardens.

La Garzonera, Lake Maggiore (www.garzonera.it; €) A rural inn offering horse riding, bike riding and long lakeside walks.

Agriturismo San Mattia, Verona (www.agriturismo sanmattia.it; €) Kids can make friends with the chickens at this Veronese farm stay.

Camping Conca d'Oro, Lake Maggiore (www. concadoro.it; €) Family-friendly camping and caravan park with sites overlooking Lake Maggiore.

Getting Around

For more information, see Transport (p260)

Travelling by Car

Driving in northern Italy is easy and, if you want to explore the hinterland around the lakes, a car is essential.

Car Hire

Multinational car-rental agencies can be found at regional airports and in larger towns. Most firms accept a standard licence or International Driving Permit (IDP) as identification. Consider hiring a small car, which you'll appreciate when negotiating narrow city or village lanes.

Driving Conditions

Roads in northern Italy are well-maintained, particularly privatised motorways, where tolls are payable. Usually this involves taking a ticket when you join the network and paying with cash or credit card at an automated ticket booth as you exit the network.

The main A4 motorway, which runs east–west across Lombardy, connects Milan with Eastern Europe. As a result, it is heavily trafficked by heavy goods vehicles (HGVs), which can make for a tiring and stressful drive. When possible, avoid it.

Away from the motorways connecting major towns, you'll be doing most of your travelling on the spiderweb network of *strade statali* (state highways; coded SS), *strade regionali* (regional highways; SR) and *strade provinciali* (provincial routes; SP).

Around the lakes and in mountain areas, driving on spring and summer weekends can be a real test of patience as half of Milan's population heads northward.

➡ Fuel prices are among the highest in Europe. Lead free (*senza piombo*; 95 octane) costs up to €1.55/L.

➡ Motorway tolls are around €1 for every 7km travelled.

➡ All vehicles must use headlights by day on the autostradas.

➡ Speed cameras operate in Italy and Switzerland.

➡ Seatbelts are compulsory for all passengers.

➡ Roadside parking costs between €2 and €3 per hour. Guarded parking costs from €15 per day.

No Car?

Bus

Services are mainly organised around provincial capitals (such as Bergamo, Brescia, Como, Cremona, Mantua and Verona), which act as hubs for the towns nearby. You will rarely be able to scoot from one lake directly to another by bus. Generally, it is easiest to get to your chosen lake by rail and use buses locally.

Switzerland's network of postal buses comes into its own for reaching into the fascinating back valleys that wind off north of Locarno and Bellinzona. Timetables are posted at stops.

Boat

There's an extensive network of ferries and faster hydrofoils (which are more expensive) on all of the lakes. In summer, this means you can reach almost anywhere around the lakes by boat, so if you are without a car, base yourself in a well-connected hub like Como, Bellagio, Stresa or Riva del Garda.

➡ If you plan on exploring the lakes by boat, enquire about multiday and multidestination tickets, which are good value.

➡ Off-season (November to Easter) services are cut back drastically.

Train

From Milan, all the main cities are easily reached by train. Brescia, the south-shore towns on Lake Garda and Verona are on the main line connecting Milan with Venice. Other lines link Milan with Bergamo, Cremona, Mantua and Pavia. Bergamo and Cremona are also linked directly to Brescia, as is Mantua to Verona.

➡ You can buy tickets at the station counter or machines.

➡ Tickets must be validated (time stamped) before boarding, or you risk a fine.

➡ Only on some services (such as Eurostar City and Cisalpino) will you need a seat reservation, but this can be made when you buy the ticket.

➡ Most major train stations have a left-luggage service or lockers.

PLAN YOUR TRIP GETTING AROUND

DRIVING FAST FACTS

Right or left: Right

Legal driving age: 25

Top speed limit: 130km/h (80mph)

Signature car: Alfa Romeo Giulietta

Daily cost to enter Milan's congestion zone: €5

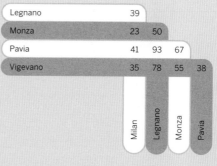

	Milan	Legnano	Monza	Pavia
Legnano	39			
Monza	23	50		
Pavia	41	93	67	
Vigevano	35	78	55	38

Don't Miss Drives

Lakes & Mountains This picturesque drive starting in the hamlet of Cannobio takes you high into the mountains around the Parco Nazionale della Val Grande. (p98)

High Into the Hills Escape to a quieter rural world high above Lake Como and enjoy sensational views from Cima Sighignola, the 'Balcony of Italy'. (p130)

Castle Circuit A circular tour around the castles and strongholds of Bergamo's southern plains where Visconti and Venetian dukes held sway, and Caravaggio was born. (p158)

Valpolicella Wine Tour Weave your way among Valpolicella's world-famous wineries and discover mannerist villas and big, bold wines made using a technique developed by the Greeks. (p202)

Casoncelli (ravioli stuffed with sausage meat)

Plan Your Trip

Eat & Drink Like a Local

Let's be honest: you came for the food. Just don't go expecting the stock-standards served at your local Italian. Northern Italian food features a broad spectrum of flavours from freshwater fish to exotic saffron risotto and hearty helpings of goose and spiced pheasant. Fizzy and aromatic white wines and light reds from Alpine valleys make for a perfect match.

The Year in Food

Spring (March–May)

Early spring cheeses are curdled and markets burst with artichokes, green and pink Mezzago asparagus from Monza, *radicchio* (chicory) and, towards the season's end, cherries and courgette flowers.

Summer (June–August)

Summer treats include strawberries, peppers, figs and citrus fruit as well as an abundance of freshwater fish. Chickpeas and beans are harvested.

Autumn (September–November)

Food festivals galore, the olive and grape harvests, and forest gems such as chestnuts, porcini mushrooms and game birds. Oenophiles head to Bardolino in September for the wine fair. By mid-October truffle season starts in nearby Piedmont.

Winter (December–February)

The rice and corn harvest commences. Winter greens such as cabbage and kale feature heavily, but pumpkins add a warm glow to Mantuan specialities. The year ends with Milan's speciality Christmas cake, *panettone*.

Food Experiences

Meals of a Lifetime

Dal Pescatore (p208) The first female Italian chef to hold three Michelin stars, Nadia Santini is a self-taught culinary virtuoso.

Seta (p70) The most talked about dining destination in Milan, headed up by acclaimed chef Antonio Guida.

Da Vittorio (p157) This triple-Michelin-starred restaurant delivers exquisite seafood plates, courtesy of famed Bergamo-born chef Enrico Chicco Cerea.

Il Sole (p102) Creative, nouvelle cuisine in a near-perfect setting in Ranco on the banks of Lake Maggiore.

Locanda 4 Cuochi (p199) The definition of a modern trattoria, run by four exceptional chefs

with a zealous attention to fresh, seasonal ingredients. Fine dining at democratic prices.

Cheap Treats

Panzerotti Milan's signature pizza-dough parcels stuffed with mozzarella, tomato, ham or spicy salami, and then fried or baked in a wood-fired oven.

Arancini Sicilian rice balls are now gaining in popularity as *aperitivi* (pre-dinner snacks) in Milan.

Mortadella di Ossola A Slow Food Movement–protected sausage from Lake Maggiore made with pork and liver flavoured with salt, wine and spices.

Polentone (p157) Italy's first takeaway polenta place in Bergamo's old town.

Sciatt Deep-fried buckwheat balls filled with cheese, a speciality of the Valtellina.

Sbrisolona A cornmeal cake flavoured with almonds, lemon rind and vanilla found in Mantua and Verona.

Local Specialities

The stretch of northern Italy marked by its glittering glacial lakes covers four distinct culinary zones, from the western Piedmontese shores of Lake Maggiore and the upper Alpine reaches of Lombardy and the Valtellina valley to the soupy rice paddies of the Po valley and the spice-laden flavours of the Veneto, bounding Lake Garda's eastern shore.

Milan

Milan is Italy's wealthiest city and its cuisine is similarly golden-hued. *Cotoletta,* sliced buttery veal, mellow yellow risotto and Yuletide *panettone* are cases in point. Since the Renaissance, the Milanese have been great meat eaters – pork, veal, beef, offal and game are all popular, as are hefty casseroles and *minestre* (soups) bulked up with rice or pasta. Surrounded by freshwater rivers and home to the largest wholesale fish market in Europe, fish is another staple of the diet.

➡ **Coffee & cake** Meeting at Milan's historic *pasticcerie* (pastry shops) for a *brioche* (sweet bread) or slice of strudel.

➡ **Aperitivo** Milanese often forgo dinner and feast for free on copious buffets fashioned by trendy *aperitivo* bars from 7pm onwards.

→ **Risotto alla Milanese** Milan's signature dish is a risotto simmered in marrow stock, wine, butter and saffron. Ratanà (p73) is the place to try it.

→ **Panettone** The eggy, brioche-like Yuletide bread is now a national Easter and Christmas tradition. Pasticceria Marchesi (p71) is a proud keeper of heritage recipes.

→ **Cotoletta alla Milanese** Thick cutlets from the loin of a milk-fed calf, dipped in breadcrumbs and fried. Try the real deal at Peck Italian Bar (p69).

Brescia Province

The cuisine of Brescia and Bergamo is Alpine-Venetian, combining strong flavours in simple dishes. In Bergamo, polenta is served 'wet' with almost everything, including sweets. Alpine herds provide an ample supply of meat for braised stews *(brasato),* oven baking *(al forno)* and spit roasts, while their milk is transformed for famous Lombard cheeses such as Grana Padano, Bagoss and Rosa Camuna.

→ **Bergamo** Famous for *schisöl* (polenta cooked with cheese and mushrooms) and the *polenta e osei* (sweet polenta cake), garnished with *osei* (chocolate birds).

→ **Brescia** A porcine paradise, the window of Brescia's Salumeria Fratelli Castiglioni overflows with sausages, *cotechino* (boiled pork sausage), *lardo* (lard), *guanciale* (pig cheek) and *pestöm* (a minced pork salami).

→ **Casoncelli** (or *casoncèi*) Bergamo's distinctive ravioli stuffed with sausage meat.

Lake Como

Isolated within a steep mountain valley, the cuisine of Lake Como is fish focused. Perch, pike, tench, shad, sardines, local *lavarello* (white fish) and eels are all plentiful. Often fish is served lightly fried *(fritto),* grilled or poached. More elaborate treatments include fish soups, marinades and risottos. The surrounding mountain valleys yield up Taleggio, Bitto and Formagella cheeses along with cured meats.

→ **Bellagio** Renowned for its super-rich Toc polenta, blended with butter and cheese. Sample it straight from the fire at Ristorante Silvio (p127).

→ **Lavarello in salsa verde** A local white fish marinated in a green parsley and garlic sauce.

Bergamo bakery display

Lake Garda

Influenced by the regions of Lombardy, Trentino and the Veneto, which border its expansive shoreline, Garda's cuisine combines fish and meat with the more Mediterranean flavours of citrus and olives. Mountain meat dishes and Austro-Hungarian influences linger on in the north, while the southern shores of the lake are characterised by fish flavoured with fruity olive oils and citrus, and accompanied by zesty local wines from the vineyards of Bardolino and Lugana.

→ **Riva del Garda** This is the place to sample Austrian-style *carne salata* (thinly sliced salted beef).

→ **Valpolicella** Young vintners at Massimago (p201) and Fratelli Vogadori (p203) are reviving the region's reputation as a producer of some of Italy's finest red wines.

→ **Valtenesi** This corner of Lake Garda is famous for its superior olive oils. Comincioli (p182) is an award-winning producer.

Lake Maggiore

Combining the blockbuster cuisines of Piedmont and Lombardy, the area surrounding Lake Maggiore boasts many celebrated products, including Bettelmatt and gorgonzola cheeses, chestnuts and rhododendron-flavoured honeys from Verbano and Varese, herb-flavoured lard from Macugnaga and cured goat's leg from the Vigezzo Valley. To the south, around Novara, farms cultivate innumerable rice varieties, including the rare Black Venus rice.

➡ **Ticino** The Swiss tradition of grotto restaurants is the ideal setting for a platter of Ticino mountain cheeses.

➡ **Stresa** In 1857 Princess Margherita of Savoy graced Stresa with a visit. In commemoration they created the lemon, butter biscuit *Margheritine di Stresa*.

➡ **Varese** Exquisite soft-centred, almond-based biscuits, *amaretti di Gallarate*, have impressed internationally recognised chef Giorgio Locatelli.

➡ **Val d'Ossola** Venture north to Domodossola or into the Val Grande and look out for *Mortadella di Ossola* (pork salami with liver, wine and spices).

Po Valley

Vegetable gardens, orchards, rice and maize fields stretch between the prosperous patrician towns of Pavia, Lodi, Cremona and Mantua. Traditionally a land of peasant farmers, fruits, vegetables and polenta loom large on the menu as do river fish, frogs, poultry, wild boar, horse, salami and game birds.

➡ **Cremona** Sample typical dishes of *bollito* (boiled meats), *marubini* (meat and cheese stuffed pasta boiled in broth) and *cotechino* (boiled pork sausage). Or attend the nougat festival in November.

➡ **Mantua** Renaissance Mantua remains addicted to spiced pumpkin *tortelli alla zucca*.

➡ **Pavia** Pavia's most traditional dish is a soupy *risotto alla certosina* (risotto with frog's legs). Eat it riverside at **Antica Osteria del Previ** (☑0382 2 62 03; www.anticaosteriadelprevi. com; Via Milazzo 65; meals €15-30; ☺12.30-2.30pm & 7.30-10pm Mon-Sat, 12.30-2.30pm Sun).

➡ **Salami d'oca di Mortara** Originally a Jewish speciality, goose sausage is now a favourite throughout the Po valley.

Valtellina

Stretching across the northern reaches of Lombardy, this Alpine valley is famous for its rich, red wines, Bitto cheese, *bresaola* (air-cured beef) and buckwheat pasta. Otherwise, expect to see a menu generously supplied with goat, lamb, beef and plenty of dairy products.

➡ **Sondrio** Sample Austrian-influenced *chisciöl* (buckwheat pancake topped with Casera cheese), *pizzocheri alla Valtellinese* (buckwheat pasta with cabbage and Grana Padano cheese) and *sciatt* (deep-fried buckwheat balls).

➡ **Violino di capra della Valchiavenna** A slow-cured goat shank, traditionally served by slicing the meat as a violin player moves their bow.

Verona

Combining both simple rural fare with sophisticated sweets, Veronese cuisine is much influenced by its proximity to Venice. Risotto, polenta and potato gnocchi provide the staples, accompanied by braised horse, pork, beef, donkey, duck and freshwater fish from the Tincio river. Cabbages from Castagnaro, bitter red *radicchio*, apples and Soave cherries are seasonal treats. Those with a sweet tooth will enjoy *pandoro* (the Veronese yeast bread equivalent of *panettone*).

DARE TO TRY

Anguilla alla gardesana Eels marinated with Garda lemons, oil, salt and pepper and cooked on an open grill.

Missoltini A boldly flavoured Como speciality of sun-dried shad cured in salt and bay leaves.

Pastissada de caval Verona's wine-drenched horse-meat stew is served with lashings of polenta.

Rane in umido alla Pavese Frogs sautéed with leeks in a tomato sauce typical of Pavia.

Zampone Pork sausage stuffed in a pig's trotter, typical of Cremona.

Where to Eat

➡ **Ristorante (restaurant)** Crisp linen, formal service and refined dishes make restaurants the obvious choice for special occasions.

➡ **Trattoria** A family-owned version of a restaurant, with cheaper prices, more relaxed service and classic regional specialities. Avoid places offering tourist menus.

➡ **Osteria** Intimate and relaxed, the *osteria* has its roots in a traditional tavern serving wine with a little food on the side; these days, they are hard to distinguish from trattorias, although the menu is usually more limited and, sometimes, verbal.

➡ **Enoteca (wine bar)** A real trend in cities, wine bars are affordable and atmospheric places to dine and sample regional wines by the glass.

➡ **Agriturismo (farm stay)** A working farmhouse offering accommodation as well as food made with farm-grown produce.

➡ **Braceria (grill)** A meat-focused menu often with a meat counter displaying different cuts of meat. The selected portion is then cut and cooked to order on an open grill.

Menu Decoder

➡ **Menu a la carte** Choose whatever you like from the menu.

➡ **Menu di degustazione** Degustation menu; usually consisting of six to eight 'tasting size' courses.

➡ **Menu turistico** Good value as it might appear, tourist menus usually feature non-regional standards and can be mediocre quality.

➡ **Pane e coperto** 'Bread and cover' charges range from €1 to €6 at most restaurants.

➡ **Piatto del giorno** Dish of the day.

➡ **Antipasto** A hot or cold appetiser. For a tasting plate of different appetisers, request an *antipasto misto* (mixed antipasto).

➡ **Primo** First course; usually a substantial rice, pasta or *zuppa* (soup) dish.

➡ **Secondo** Second course; either *carne* (meat) or *pesce* (fish).

➡ **Contorno** Side dish; typically *verdure* (vegetables).

➡ **Dolce e frutta** 'Sweet and fruit', consisting of either *torta* (cake), pudding or fresh fruit.

➡ **Nostra produzione (or fatti in casa)** Made in-house; used to describe anything from bread and pasta to *liquori* (liqueurs).

➡ **Surgelato** Frozen; usually used to indicate fish or seafood that has not been freshly caught.

Cotechino (boiled pork sausage)

How to Eat & Drink Like a Local

When to Eat

➡ **Colazione (breakfast)** Lombards rarely eat a sit-down breakfast, but instead bolt down a cappuccino with a brioche or other type of pastry (generically known as *pastine*) at a coffee bar before heading to work.

➡ **Pranzo (lunch)** Served from noon to 2.30pm; few restaurants take orders for lunch after 2.30pm. Traditionally, lunch is the main meal of the day, though many Lombards now share the main family meal in the evening. Smaller shops and businesses close to accommodate a proper sit-down meal between 1pm and 4pm.

➡ **Aperitivo (aperitif)** At the strike of 6pm local bars swell with crowds of workers indulging in that all-essential post-work, pre-dinner ritual of *aperitivo,* when the price of your cocktail (€8 to €20 in Milan) includes an eat-yourself-silly buffet of finger food, salads, pasta and even sushi.

➡ **Cena (dinner)** Served between 7pm and 10pm. Opening hours vary, but many places begin filling up by 7.30pm. In summer, and in larger cities like Milan, hours may extend to midnight.

Cycling along the shores of Lake Garda in Malcesine (p190)

Plan Your Trip
Activities

Northern Italy's Alpine landscape offers outdoor enthusiasts a plethora of activities. Blessed with rolling hills, riverine deltas, glacial lakes and soaring mountains, you can take your pick of hiking, biking, climbing, skiing, horse riding, sailing and surfing, or you can simply sit back and enjoy the view.

Best Outdoors

Best Short Walks

Up the wooded Valle delle Cartiere, around Lake Ledro, along Como's Passeggiata Lino Gelpi and down from the funicular stations of Monte Brè or Monte San Salvatore and Cimetta.

Best Easy Bike Rides

Around the vineyards of Franciacorta and the Valtenesi, as well as around Lake Orta and beside the lakes in Verbania Pallanza and Mantua.

Best for Water Sports

Make the best of the Pelèr and Ora winds to windsurf, kitesurf and sail on Lake Garda, or in Cannobio at the northern end of Lake Maggiore.

Best Scenic Drives

Through the Brasa Gorge and up the Val Cannobino; from Como to the peak of Cima Sighignola; from Cernobbio to Monte Bisbino; and from Salò to Riva del Garda.

When to Go

Spring and autumn, with their abundance of wildflowers and forest fruits, are the prettiest times to be outdoors.

➡ **April–June** Warm days, wildflowers in valleys – perfect for cyclists, walkers and climbers.

➡ **July** Great for watersports in Lake Garda and the northern end of Lake Maggiore. Hiking in the mountains is best this month.

➡ **September & October** Still warm enough for water sports, but cooler days mean mellow hikes and cycle rides through vineyards.

➡ **December–February** The best skiing months for atmosphere (particularly at Christmas).

Where to Go

➡ **Orobie Alps** Rising to the northeast of Lake Como with valleys funnelling down to Bergamo, the Orobie Alps peak at 3000m and are covered in forests and pastures.

➡ **Lake Como** Hit Gravedona for water sports, the western mountains for scenic drives, and the rugged Triangolo Lariano for scenic hikes between Como, Bellagio and Lecco.

➡ **Lake Garda** A veritable outdoor playground with world-class windsurfing and sailing at Riva del Garda, Torbole and Gargnano; championship rock climbing in Arco; paragliding, biking, hiking and skiing on Monte Baldo; horse riding on the Tremonsine plateau and through Bardolino vineyards; and cycling through the olive groves of the Valtenesi.

➡ **Lake Iseo** Bordering the region of Franciacorta, Lake Iseo is a perfect spot for easy cycling, either around Monte Isola or through Franciacorta's vineyards.

➡ **Lake Maggiore** Set sail from Cannobio; ascend Monte Mottarone for biking, hiking and skiing; or escape northwest from Locarno to explore the Ticino valleys on foot.

➡ **Mantua** Family-friendly walking, cycling and river cruising around Mantua's three lakes and beside the Mincio and Po rivers.

➡ **Parco Nazionale della Val Grande** Get back to nature in one of Italy's wildest national parks with guided walks amid majestic chestnut forests.

Cycling

Northern Italians are cycling fanatics. On weekends you can see whole gangs of cyclists scooting up hill and down dale with frightening alacrity.

More relaxed cycling is possible on the Lombard plains, in Mantua, along the Mincio river and through the Franciacorta and Valtenesi wine territory. Tourist offices in Como, Lecco and Varese can supply maps with suggested cycle routes between Lake Maggiore and the east bank of Lake Como.

For more challenging trails, head to the eastern shore of Lake Como, Monte Mottarone on Lake Maggiore and Monte Baldo on Lake Garda, where numerous off-road trails snake down the mountainsides. Most famous of all, though, is the challenging climb from Bellagio to the Santuario della

Madonna del Ghisallo (p126). Apart from being a classic Giro d'Italia stage, the chapel is an extraordinary shrine to cycling.

If you're bringing your own bike, check with your airline if there's a fee and how much, if any, disassembling is required. Bikes can be transported by train in Italy, either with you or to arrive within a couple of days. Bike hire or city cycle schemes are available in most towns and resorts.

Top Trails

➡ **Dorsale** Ideal for a day of mountain biking.

➡ **Monte Mottarone** (p87) Rent a mountain bike for the 20km to 30km descent to Stresa.

➡ **Madonna del Ghisallo** (p126) Feel like a champion on this classic climb from Bellagio.

➡ **Monte Isola** Cycle round Lake Iseo's island.

➡ **Rocca di Garda** An 11km trail from Garda to Costermano and Albarè.

➡ **The Valtenesi** (p181) A 38km circular route travels from the Castle of Padenghe through Rocca di Manerba and Puegnago del Garda.

Windsurfing in Torbole, Lake Garda (p189)

THOMAS QUACK / SHUTTERSTOCK ©

Walking

In many towns on the lakes, you can simply head for a stroll along the shoreline. Some of the best include the waterfront promenades in Lugano, Verbania on Lake Maggiore, Sarnico on Lake Iseo, Salò and Riva del Garda on Lake Garda, and Como on Lake Como.

On Lake Como, the Greenway del Lago di Como links Cadenabbia and Colonna, while on Lake Orta it is possible to walk right around the lake in three relaxed days, and west of Garda and Bardolino easy, scenic trails snake through the hills.

In some cases, no more than a couple of hours of walking can bring you to lovely sights and viewpoints. A 3km walk north out of Riva del Garda, for example, leads to the Varone waterfall (p187), or take the old Ponale Road (p189) east out of town for panoramic views.

Heading for the Hills

More seasoned walkers have a choice of hikes rising to 2000m in altitude. On Lake Garda's Monte Baldo, you can hop off at the intermediate station of San Michele and hike back down to Malcesine. Hikers can

also scale Monte Altissimo (2053m). Likewise, you can hike up and/or down Monte Mottarone, Monte Brè, Monte San Salvatore, Cimetta or Cardada on Lake Maggiore.

In Lake Como's Triangolo Lariano, there are more challenging walking options that require some fitness and preparation. They include the two-day Dorsale hike, which takes you from Brunate to Bellagio.

Club Alpino Italiano (www.cai.it) trails are staked out in a web across northern Italy. You could search out little-known Romanesque churches like the Abbazia di San Pietro al Monte on Lake Como or drive up to Monte Bisbino and embark on some high-level walks. One of the best walks is the Via dei Monti Lariani, a six-day, 130km trail from Cernobbio to Sorico, which is part of the 6000km Sentiero Italia.

Serious hikes can be undertaken in the Val Brembana, north of Bergamo. Most of the area is covered by two parks, the Parco delle Orobie Valtellinesi and Parco delle Orobie Bergamasche (www.parks.it), of which the first is the most spectacular. The tourist office in Bergamo has details and you can find more information at www.sentierodelleorobie.it. Otherwise, behind

ALTERNATIVE ACTIVITIES

For those who aren't fans of hiking and biking, Milan and the lakes offer other more sedate pursuits, including long leisurely spa days, gentle river cruising and cooking classes.

Spa Towns

The Romans' favourite was lakeside Sirmione (p177), but art nouveau San Pellegrino Terme (p161) is now enjoying a renaissance. Bardolino (p193) on Lake Garda and Il Sereno on Lake Como are also popular spa spots, while Milan's Palazzo Parigi (p64) and Bulgari Hotel (p64) offer the ultimate in luxe spa experiences.

River Cruising

If you don't want to wrestle with sails and temperamental wind conditions, consider a canal cruise (p65) in Milan, a boat tour (p209) on Mantua's lakes or a cruise along the Mincio and Po rivers with **Avemaria Boat** (✆0444 127 84 30; www.avemariaboat. com; Via Conforto da Costozza 7, Vicenza; 7 days per person €990; ☎) ⚓.

Cookery Courses

You can learn a lot about Lombardy through its varied cuisine, so consider taking a few days off from the great outdoors with a food tour and cookery class at Teatro 7 (p65) in Milan or Bellagio Cooking Classes (p127) on Lake Como. Food tours with Sauce Milan (p73) and Try Verona (p198) are also a good eye-opener into the regional cuisine.

Ghiffa on Lake Maggiore, the Via delle Genti is a walking path that has connected Switzerland and northern Italy via the St Gotthard pass for centuries.

Top Walks

➡ **Greenway del Lago di Como** (p133) A 10km stroll on the west bank of Lake Como.

➡ **Monte Mottarone** (p87) Opt to hike all or part of the way up or down Monte Mottarone.

➡ **Cimetta** (p111) A gentle walk that leads to 360-degree views above Locarno.

➡ **Via dei Monti Lariani** A 130km trail along high ground above the west flank of Lake Como.

➡ **La Strada del Ponale** (p189) An easy 7km hike along the old Ponale Road from Riva del Garda to hilltop Pregasina.

➡ **Monte Altissimo** A demanding six-hour hike rising from Torbole to Monte Altissimo.

Water Sports

Sailing, windsurfing and kitesurfing have a cult following around Riva, Torbole, Gargnano, Toscolano-Maderno and Malcesine on Lake Garda, where schools and hire outlets abound along the lakefront. There's a smaller scene at the northern end of Lake Como around Gravedona, where waterskiing and wakeboarding are also popular. Likewise, Cannobio, at the northern end of Lake Maggiore, is a super windsurfing and sailing spot.

Various boat hire outlets on all the lakes will also rent out zodiacs and other small boats for a run-around, while Barindelli's (p126) in Bellagio offers tours in beautiful mahogany cigarette boats. On resort beaches, you can usually rent pedalos and kayaks.

Museo Nazionale della Scienza e della Tecnologia (p60), Milan

Plan Your Trip
Travel with Children

The Italian Lakes are a fabulous family-friendly destination, packed with outdoor activities, safely landscaped lakefront beaches and promenades, and two of Italy's largest theme parks. Even rides on turn-of-the-century trams, high-speed hydrofoils and cloud-scraping funiculars are bound to delight, while reasonably priced agriturismi (farm stay accommodation) and campgrounds abound.

VIKTOR GLADKOV / SHUTTERSTOCK ©

Best Regions for Kids

Milan

Home to Italy's best science museum, a castle and grand park, plus turn-of-the-century trams and canal cruises, Milan is more child-friendly than most imagine.

Lake Maggiore & Around

Whiz up funiculars with bikes and binoculars, traverse the 'Hundred Valleys' by rail, picnic in flower-filled gardens, bobsled high in the mountains and wander with white peacocks on the Borromean Islands.

Lake Como & Around

Head for the hills for walking and cycling trails or to Lenno and Villa Olmo near Como for *lido*-style lakeside swimming. To the north, in Gravedona, waterski or zip around in a zodiac.

Lake Garda & Around

Ringed with campsites, furnished with two theme parks and blessed with an endless number of exciting activities, Garda is the most family-friendly lake. Windsurf, hike, cycle and horse ride with specialist operators that provide classes and tours for all age groups.

The Italian Lakes for Kids

If you're looking for a family-friendly destination, the Italian Lakes certainly fit the bill. The variety of museums, adventure parks, gardens, beaches, activities and shopping means that there is truly something for everyone.

Lake Garda is an activity hot spot, offering rock climbing, canyoning and water sports. Lake Como's cloud-busting walking trails, funiculars, mountain biking (book in advance) and chichi *lidi* (beaches) offer family fun with a touch of glamour. Lake

Maggiore offers grand-slam sights and gardens within easy reach of Milan. And even in Milan and Verona, large parks and family-friendly attractions and dining keep everyone happy.

Your most important predeparture decisions will be accommodation and point of entry: Verona airport for Lake Garda; Milan's Malpensa or Bergamo's Orio al Serio airports for Lake Como; and Malpensa for Lake Maggiore. If you want to tour more than one lake, car hire is almost inevitable. However, think carefully about how much time you want to spend driving, particularly in summer when the roads are congested.

Children's Highlights
Cool Stuff

➡ **Museo Nazionale della Scienza e della Tecnologia** (p60) Let little Leonardos loose in Italy's best science museum in Milan.

➡ **Centovalli Train** (p111) Cross the vertiginous 'Hundred Valleys' on this historic train ride into Switzerland.

➡ **Museo Mille Miglia** (p169) Marvel at the vintage racing beauties in Brescia.

➡ **Rocca di Angera** (p103) Lake Maggiore's most imposing castle with one of the best doll and toy museums in Europe.

➡ **Sacro Monte di San Carlo** (p92) Climb the colossal statue of St Charles and peep through his eye holes.

➡ **Laveno Funivia** (p101) Lake Maggiore's funkiest funicular with open-air capsules.

Gardens to Explore

➡ **Parco Sempione** (p59) Rollerblade around Parco Sempione then take the lift up Torre Branca.

➡ **Il Vittoriale degli Italiani** (p184) Tour the wildly eccentric house then find the full-sized battleship in the garden.

➡ **Villa Taranto** (p95) Picnic and play amid rolling hillsides of rhododendrons, camellias and tulips.

➡ **Giardino Botanico Fondazione André Heller** (p184) Play eye-spy with world-class contemporary art amid the bamboo groves.

➡ **Villa Carlotta** (p136) Explore a fantastical floral landscape with a forest of ferns, a Zen garden and spectacular lookout point.

Outdoor Activities

➡ **Windsurfing & sailing** The lakefronts at Riva del Garda and Torbole are lined with schools.

➡ **Rock climbing** Check out one of the world's toughest rock-climbing festivals, the Rockmaster Festival (p188), then take a few lessons with Arco Mountain Guide (p189).

➡ **Canyoning** Jump, slide and abseil into crystal-clear waters with expert guides on Lake Ledro.

➡ **Cycling** Hire top-class off-road bikes from a national champion at Guti Bike Rent (p132) and Xtreme Malcesine (p190).

➡ **Kayaking** Take a spin on the glassy waters of Lake Como in kayaks from Bellagio Water Sports. (p126)

Theme Parks

➡ **Gardaland** (p194) One of Italy's top theme parks, with dinosaurs, pirate ships and roller coasters.

➡ **CanevaWorld** (p194) Medieval shows, an aqua park and Movieland Studios.

➡ **Parco della Villa Pallavicino** (☑0323 3 15 33; www.parcozoopallavicino.it; SS33/Via Sempione Sud; adult/reduced €9.50/6.50; ⊙9am-7pm mid-Mar–Oct) Animals and exotic birds roam free.

➡ **Alpyland** (p90) A 1.2km bobsled run with panoramic views.

Planning

Museum Discounts

Many museums and monuments are free for children – but there is no single rule about the age limit for free admission (often up to six years). In Milan, Bergamo and Verona state museums are free to EU passport holders aged under 18. Otherwise, museums offer a reduced admission fee – usually half the adult price – for children, usually six and over. Students and young adults between the ages of 18 and 26 also get discounted entry with the appropirate ID.

Dining

Lakeside towns have long been used to catering to Milanese and Veronese families on their summer vacations, and children are warmly welcomed in casual trattorias and *osterie* (taverns), although high-chairs are not always available. Menus always feature simple pasta dishes, cured ham as well as a varied selection of simply cooked fish and grilled meat. Restaurants in tourist hot spots like Stresa, Riva del Garda and Sirmione, as well as Milan and Verona, may have a *menù bambini* (children's menu), and are well served with pizzerias. If not, simply ask for a plate of pasta with butter or olive oil and Parmesan cheese.

Transport

Although having a car will allow you to move freely around the lakes, it is worth considering whether you really need one. Frequent trains from Milan connect with Stresa on Lake Maggiore and Como, while Sirmione on Lake Garda can be reached from Verona. What's more, once you're on the lakes it's far quicker (and more scenic) to travel across them on the efficient network of ferries and hydrofoils.

If you do decide to drive, you'll have more options on where to stay as the best-value accommodation is usually situated a little distance from the lake shore. Children under 150cm or 36kg must be attached in an appropriate child seat for their weight and are not allowed in the front. Car seats should be booked in advance.

On public transport, a seat on a bus costs the same for everyone (toddlers and babies on laps are free). Children under 12 pay half-fare on trains and ferries.

Regions at a Glance

Milan

Museums
Shopping
Nightlife

Old & New Masters

Milan is a city with a vibrant cultural life, which is on display in a diverse range of museums showcasing old masters, modern and contemporary art, rare historical artefacts and archaeology, pioneering science and technology, design, fashion and even toys.

Fashion City

Paris, New York and London may have equally influential designers but they can't compete with an industry town that lives and breathes fashion and takes retail as seriously as it does biotech or engineering. Shop Milan's Golden Quad for the cutting-edge scene.

Cocktails & Culture

Milan is home to Italy's major music producers and is on the international tour circuit of the best European and North American music acts, theatre and dance troupes. During the furniture and fashion trade fairs, the city hosts an endless round of stylish cocktail parties.

p52

Lake Maggiore & Around

Villas & Gardens
Scenery
Islands

Villa Taranto

Lake Maggiore's reputation for elegance is well earned with an A-list portfolio of villas (many of them upmarket hotels) surrounded by luxurious gardens. Verbania's Villa Taranto is considered by many to be the finest in Europe, with over 20,000 different species.

Panoramic Perches

Pretty towns strewn with art nouveau villas and framed by wooded hillsides are the glamorous ingredients of Italy's second-largest lake. For unforgettable views, whiz up the cable cars in Stresa, Laveno and Locarno.

Exclusive Hideaways

Aristocratic Isola Bella and Isola Madre harbour two of northern Italy's most fabulous palaces. Bijou Isola San Giulio, meanwhile, has an ancient frescoed basilica and San Pancrazio in the Isole di Brissago is covered in a luxurious botanical garden.

p86

Lake Como & Around

Towns
Scenery
Villas & Gardens

Urban Style

With its lakeside promenade, medieval lanes and fine, frescoed churches, Como is as beautiful as its chic inhabitants. Miniature Bellagio and Swiss Lugano offer more of the same with tumbling gardens, Visconti castles and mountaintop belvederes.

Extraordinary Views

Lake Como and the surrounding area has countless spectacular lookouts. Viewpoints, often accessible by funicular, are Brunate, Castello di Vezio, Monte Bisbino and Peglio, while further afield consider Cima Sighignola, Monte Brè and Monte San Salvatore.

Lakeside Living

Como's lakeside villas and gardens have attracted everyone from Pliny to George Clooney and even James Bond. The best examples are to be found at Como, Cernobbio, Bellagio and Varenna, although the most fabulous are Villa Carlotta and Villa Balbianello.

p116

Bergamo, Brescia & Cremona

Architecture
Scenery
Food & Wine

Medieval Marvels

Bergamo's Città Alta wonderfully evokes a medieval hilltop Italian city, but Cremona, with its grand piazza, and Brescia, with its extant Roman ruins, equally deserve your time.

Alpine Valleys

The valleys north of Bergamo serve as pathways into the Orobie Alps that rise like ramparts along Italy's northern border. Val Taleggio is the most scenic, closely followed by Valle Seriana, but on no account miss Cornello dei Tasso.

Culinary Excellence

The good burghers of Brescia, Bergamo and Cremona know a thing or two about hearty mountain cuisine and heritage Renaissance recipes. Join them for a blow-out meal or get on your bike and track down Italy's finest fizz in Franciacorta.

p150

Lake Garda & Around

Water Sports
Food & Wine
Art History

All Aboard!

Lake Garda has an unusual meteorological quirk – the winds that blow over its surface are almost as regular as clockwork. Their predictability has ensured Riva, Torbole, Gargnano and Malcesine are magnets for windsurfers and sailors.

Gourmet Garda

A fleet of ferries enables mini voyages of discovery in a landscape rich in food and wine. To the southwest are Valtenesi olive groves like Comincioli, while the vineyards of Valpolicella, Bardolino and Soave wow the palate with unusual regional wines.

Arty Itineraries

Trace a trail from Roman Verona to medieval Mantua for an eyeful of Romanesque and Renaissance art and architecture, a clutch of opulent churches and a marathon tour of Mantegna's masterly frescoes.

p176

On the
Road

Lake Maggiore & Around
p86

Lake Como & Around
p116

Bergamo, Brescia & Cremona
p150

Milan
p52
◉

Lake Garda & Around
p176

Milan

POP 1.35 MILLION / 🎵 02

Best Places to Eat

➜ Seta (p70)

➜ Cracco (p69)

➜ Alice Ristorante (p73)

➜ Ratanà (p73)

➜ Berberè (p72)

Best Tours

➜ Tickitaly (p60)

➜ Bike & the City (p65)

➜ Sauce Milan (p73)

➜ MilanoArte (p65)

Why Go?

Home of Italy's stock exchange, an industrial powerhouse and the internationally accepted arbiter of taste in fashion and design, Milan is a seething metropolis. At times it can seem brash, but beneath the veneer is a serious sense of history and place. The grand Gothic cathedral lies at the heart of this one-time imperial Roman capital, and expresses the love of beauty and power that still drives the city today. Art collections old and new, unparalleled shopping, sparkling nightlife, the prestige of opera at La Scala, the mark of Leonardo da Vinci's genius, a religious addiction to *calcio* (football) and endless opportunities to eat the best Lombard and Italian food make Milan much more than the puritanically work-obsessed city it is often portrayed as. Today the city leads the way with the largest postwar redevelopment in Italy, impressive, sustainable architecture and a futuristic skyline modelled by the late Zaha Hadid, Daniel Libeskind and César Pelli.

Road Distances (km)

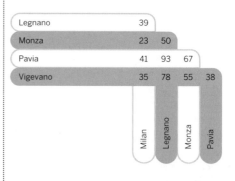

	Milan	Legnano	Monza	Pavia
Legnano	39			
Monza	23	50		
Pavia	41	93	67	
Vigevano	35	78	55	38

Milan Highlights

1 Duomo (p56) Climbing to the roof of Milan's marble cathedral for views of its sculpted spires.

2 The Last Supper (p59) Admiring centuries of invention in da Vinci's masterful mural, *Il Cenacolo*.

3 Pinacoteca di Brera (p58) Getting up close

with some of Italy's finest masterpieces.

4 Quadrilatero d'Oro (p59) Strutting your stuff on Planet Fashion's finest block.

5 Teatro alla Scala (p78) Mixing with old and new money at Italy's most famous opera house.

6 Castello Sforzesco (p58) Climbing ramparts and admiring the wealth of medieval artefacts amassed by Milan's dukes.

7 Salone Internazionale del Mobile (p68) Experiencing Milan's true Carnival – this week-long, world-class design fair.

NEIGHBOURHOODS AT A GLANCE

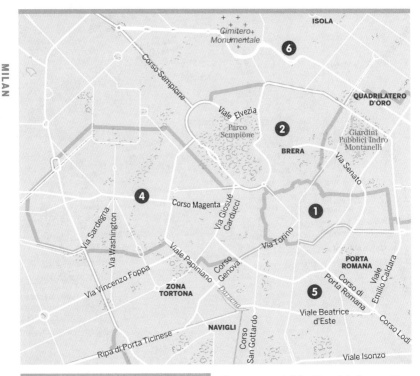

❶ Duomo & San Babila (p58)

Milan's centre is conveniently compact. The splendid cathedral sits in a vast piazza which throngs with tourists, touts and the Milanese themselves. From here, choose God or Mammon, art or music, or take in all four in the historic shopping arcade Galleria Vittorio Emanuele II, La Scala opera house and the museums of the Palazzo Reale and the Gallerie d'Italia.

❷ Brera & Parco Sempione (p58)

Brera's tight cobbled streets and ancient buildings are a reminder that Milan wasn't always a modern metropolis. At the heart of the neighbourhood is the 17th-century Palazzo di Brera, originally a Jesuit college,

though occupied by the city's famous Fine Art Academy since 1776. Around it are studios, galleries and some of the city's most fashionable restaurants. To the west, the grand Castello Sforzesco bookends the city's largest public park, Parco Sempione.

❸ Quadrilatero d'Oro & Porta Venezia (p59)

The Quadrilatero d'Oro (Golden Quad) sings a siren song to luxury-label lovers the world over. Boasting some of the most expensive real estate in the world, this 6000-sq-metre area is home to over 500 of the world's top fashion brands. Nestled in between the glittering windows you'll find historic palace museums, luxe spas and discreet, heritage restaurants. To the northeast is the pretty 19th-century public, pleasure garden framed by the Villa Reale and the gothic Natural History Museum.

❺ Navigli & Porta Romana (p61)

The Navigli neighbourhood is named after its most identifiable feature – the canals. Designed as the motorways of medieval Milan, they powered the city's fortunes until the railroads, WWII bombs and neglect brought about their closure in the 1970s. These days they provide a scenic backdrop to the boutiques and bars that make this Milan's most kicking bohemian 'burb. To the west, Porta Romana has a more up-and-coming vibe, its old warehouses and grand *palazzi* (mansions) slowly being converted into hip new apartment blocks, clubs and restaurants.

❻ Porta Garibaldi & Isola (p61)

Home to César Pelli's shardlike skyscraper, Herzog & de Meuron's contemporary *cascina* (farmhouse) and Stefano Boeri's high-rise apartment blocks festooned with hanging gardens, the shiny new area between Porta Garibaldi and Porta Nuova is Milan's mini-Manhattan. Swanky Corso Como seamlessly links Corso Garibaldi with the hip, multicultural neighbourhood of Isola, making this a hot spot for bars, restaurants and cutting-edge shops.

❹ Corso Magenta & Sant'Ambrogio (p59)

Leonardo da Vinci's *The Last Supper* and the Basilica di Sant'Ambrogio draw visitors to these leafy streets, but there's an equal mix of sacred and secular here. Milan's stock exchange sits on Piazza degli Affari, hence the chic shops on Corso Magenta and the *aperitivo* bars full of young bankers. To the south and west, the vibe grows more casual, influenced by students at the sprawling Università Cattolica, while families haunt friendly *rosticcerie* (rotisseries) along popular Corso Vercelli.

TOP SIGHT
DUOMO

A vision in pink Candoglia marble, Milan's cathedral aptly reflects the city's creative brio and ambition. Begun by Giangaleazzo Visconti in 1387, its design was originally considered unfeasible. Canals had to be dug to transport the vast quantities of marble to the city centre, and new technologies were invented to cater for the never-before-attempted scale. Now its pearly white facade rises like the filigree of a fairy-tale tiara, and wows the crowds with its extravagant details.

The Exterior & Roof Terraces

During his stint as king of Italy, Napoleon offered to fund the Duomo's completion in 1805, in time for his coronation. The architect piled on the neo-Gothic details, a homage to the original design that displayed a prescient use of fashion logic – ie everything old is new again. The petrified pinnacles, cusps, buttresses, arches and more than 3000 statues are almost all products of the 19th century.

Climb to the roof terraces, where you'll be within touching distance of the elaborate 135 spires and their forest of flying buttresses. In the centre of the roof rises the 15th-century octagonal lantern and spire, on top of which is the golden Madonnina (erected in 1774). For centuries she was the highest point in the city (108.5m) until the Pirelli skyscraper outdid her in 1958.

DON'T MISS

➡ The roof terraces

➡ Trivulzio candelabrum

➡ The crypt

➡ Scurolo di San Carlo

PRACTICALITIES

➡ Map p66

➡ ☑ 02 7202 3375

➡ www.duomomilano.it

➡ Piazza del Duomo

➡ adult/reduced Duomo €3/2, roof terraces via stairs €9/4.50, lift €13/7, archaeological area €7/3

➡ ☉ Duomo 8am-7pm, roof terraces 9am-7pm

➡ Ⓜ Duomo

The Interior

Initially designed to accommodate Milan's then population of around 40,000, the cathedral's elegant, hysterical and sublimely spiritual architecture can transport 21st-century types back to a medieval mindset. Once your eyes have adjusted to the subdued light and surreal proportions inside (there are five grandiose naves supported by 52 columns), stare up, and up, to the largest stained-glass windows in Christendom.

Before you wander among the cathedral's many treasures, look down and marvel at the polychrome marble floor that sweeps across 12,000 sq metres. The design was conceived by Pellegrino Tibaldi and took 400 years to complete. The pink and white blocks of Candoglia marble came from the cathedral's own quarries at Mergozzo (bequeathed in perpetuity by Giangaleazzo), and are inlaid with black marble from Varenna and red marble from Arzo.

Artworks

Bisecting the nave, the transept is especially rich in works of art. At either end there is an altar decorated with polychrome marbles, the most elaborate being the *Altar to the Virgin of the Tree* on the north side. In front of this stands the monumental, 5m-high Trivulzio candelabrum, a masterpiece of medieval bronze work, its seven branches inset with precious stones.

One of the cathedral's more unusual statues is the 1562 figure of St Bartholomew by Marco d'Agrate, a student of Leonardo da Vinci. It depicts St Bartholomew post-torture with his skin flayed from his flesh and cast about his neck like a cape. For 16th-century sculptors he was a favourite subject, enabling them to show off their anatomical knowledge as well as their technique.

The Crypt

From the ambulatory that encircles the choir are the stairs down to the crypt or Winter Choir. Designed by Tibaldi, this jewel-like circular chapel with its red porphyry pillars, polychrome marble floor and stucco ceiling contains a casket holding the relics of various saints and martyrs. A wooden choir stall encircles the room.

Through a gap in the crypt's choir stalls, a dark corridor leads to the Scurolo di San Carlo, a memorial chapel housing the remains of saintly Carlo Borromeo (cardinal archbishop of Milan; 1564–84), contained in a rock-crystal casket atop a silver altar.

MILAN SIGHTS

VENERANDA FABBRICA DEL DUOMO

The epic building of Milan's cathedral necessitated the creation of a 'factory' for operational activities and maintenance. The Fabbrica del Duomo oversaw construction from 1387 until the last gate was inaugurated in 1965. Today it continues the work of maintaining the cathedral. It's possible to visit the Fabbrica's marble quarries at Lago di Mergozzo, near Lago Maggiore.

There are three ticket offices. Most people queue at the one on the south side of the Duomo, but there are shorter queues at the ticket office in the Il Grande Museo del Duomo and at the main office (Piazza del Duomo 18).

SUNDIAL

On the floor by the main entrance you may notice a brass strip lined with signs of the zodiac. This is an 18th-century sundial. A hole in the vault of the south aisle casts a ray of sunlight at various points along its length at astronomical noon. The device is so precise that all the city's clocks were set by it up until the 19th century.

◎ Sights

◎ Duomo & San Babila

Palazzo Reale   MUSEUM, PALACE
(Map p66; ☑ 02 87 56 72; www.palazzorealemilano.
it; Piazza del Duomo 12; admission varies; ⊘ 2.30-
7.30pm Mon, 9.30am-7.30pm Tue, Wed, Fri & Sun,
to 10.30pm Thu & Sat; ⓜ Duomo) Empress Maria Theresa's favourite architect, Giuseppe
Piermarini, gave this town hall and Visconti
palace a neoclassical overhaul in the late
18th century. The supremely elegant interiors were all but destroyed by WWII bombs;
the **Sala delle Cariatidi** remains unreno-
vated as a reminder of war's indiscriminate
destruction. Now the once opulent palace
hosts blockbuster art exhibits, attracting serious crowds to shows as diverse as Escher,
Caravaggio and Arnaldo Pomodoro.

★**Museo del Novecento**   GALLERY
(Map p66; ☑ 02 8844 4061; www.museodel-
novecento.org; Via Marconi 1; adult/reduced €10/8;
⊘ 2.30-7.30pm Mon, 9.30am-7.30pm Tue, Wed, Fri
& Sun, to 10.30pm Thu & Sat; ⓜ Duomo) Overlooking Piazza del Duomo, with fabulous
views of the cathedral, is Mussolini's Arengario, from where he would harangue huge
crowds in his heyday. Now it houses Milan's
museum of 20th-century art. Built around a
futuristic spiral ramp (an ode to the Guggen-
heim), the lower floors are cramped, but the
heady collection, which includes the likes of
Umberto Boccioni, Campigli, de Chirico and
Marinetti, more than distracts.

**Galleria Vittorio
Emanuele II**   HISTORIC BUILDING
(Map p66; Piazza del Duomo; ⓜ Duomo) So much
more than a shopping arcade, the neoclassical Galleria Vittorio Emanuele II is a soaring iron-and-glass structure known locally
as *il salotto bueno,* the city's fine drawing
room. Shaped like a crucifix, it also marks
the *passeggiata* (evening stroll) route from
Piazza del Duomo to Piazza di Marino and
the doors of Teatro alla Scala (La Scala).

Gallerie d'Italia   MUSEUM
(Map p66; www.gallerieditalia.com; Piazza della
Scala 6; adult/reduced €10/8; ⊘ 9.30am-7.30pm
Tue-Wed & Fri-Sun, to 10.30pm Thu; ⓜ Duomo)
Housed in three fabulously decorated palaces, the enormous art collection of Fondazione Cariplo and Intesa Sanpaolo bank pays
homage to 18th- and 19th-century Lombard
painting. From a magnificent sequence of

bas-reliefs by Antonio Canova to luminous
Romantic masterpieces by Francesco Hayez,
the works span 23 rooms and document Milan's significant contribution to the rebirth
of Italian sculpture, the patriotic romanti-
cism of the Risorgimento (reunification period) and the birth of futurism at the dawn
of the 20th century.

**Biblioteca e Pinacoteca
Ambrosiana**   GALLERY, LIBRARY
(Map p66; ☑ 02 80 69 21; www.ambrosiana.it;
Piazza Pio XI 2; adult/reduced €15/10; ⊘ 10am-
6pm Tue-Sun; ⓜ Duomo) Europe's first public
library, built in 1609, the Biblioteca Ambrosiana was more a symbol of intellectual
ferment than of quiet scholarship. It houses more than 75,000 volumes and 35,000
manuscripts including Leonardo da Vinci's
priceless collection of drawings, the *Atlan-
tic Codex*. An art gallery – the Pinacoteca
– was added later. It exhibits Italian paintings from the 14th to the 20th century, most
famously Caravaggio's *Canestra di frutta*
(Basket of Fruit), which launched both his
career and Italy's ultrarealist traditions.

◎ Brera & Parco Sempione

★**Pinacoteca di Brera**   GALLERY
(Map p66; ☑ 02 72 26 31; www.pinacotecabrera.
org; Via Brera 28; adult/reduced €10/7; ⊘ 8.30am-
7.15pm Tue-Wed & Fri-Sun, to 10.15pm Thu; ⓜ Lanza,
Montenapoleone) Located upstairs from the
centuries-old Accademia di Belle Arti (still
one of Italy's most prestigious art schools),
this gallery houses Milan's impressive collection of Old Masters, much of it 'lifted' from
Venice by Napoleon. Rubens, Goya and Van
Dyck all have a place in the collection, but
you're here for the Italians: Titian, Tintoretto, Veronese and the Bellini brothers. Much
of the work has tremendous emotional
clout, most notably Mantegna's brutal *Lam-
entation over the Dead Christ.*

★**Castello Sforzesco**   CASTLE
(Map p66; ☑ 02 8846 3703; www.milanocastello.
it; Piazza Castello; adult/reduced €5/3; ⊘ 9am-
5.30pm Tue-Sun; ♿; ⓜ Cairoli) Originally a Visconti fortress, this iconic red-brick castle was
later home to the mighty Sforza dynasty, who
ruled Renaissance Milan. The castle's defences were designed by the multitalented da
Vinci; Napoleon later drained the moat and
removed the drawbridges. Today, it houses
seven specialised museums, which gather
together intriguing fragments of Milan's

cultural and civic history, including Michelangelo's final work, the *Rondanini Pietà*, now housed in the frescoed hall of the castle's Ospedale Spagnolo (Spanish Hospital).

Parco Sempione PARK
(Map p66; 6.30am-nightfall; ; Cadorna, Lanza) Situated behind Castello Sforzesco, Parco Sempione was once the preserve of hunting Sforza dukes. Then Napoleon came to town and set about landscaping. First the French carved out orchards; next they mooted the idea in 1891 for a vast public park. It was a resounding success and even today Milanese of all ages come to enjoy its winding paths and ornamental ponds. Giò Ponti's 1933 steel **tower** (Map p62; 02 331 41 20; €5; 3-7pm & 8.30pm-midnight Tue, Thu & Fri, 10.30am-12.30pm & 3pm-midnight Wed, 10.30am-2pm & 2.30pm-midnight Sat & Sun summer, closes 6.30pm winter; Cadorna), built for a Triennale exhibition, provides a fantastic 108m-high viewing platform over the park.

Triennale di Milano MUSEUM
(Map p66; 02 7243 4208; www.triennaledesign museum.it; Viale Emilio Alemanga 6; adult/reduced €10/6.50; 10.30am-8.30pm Tue-Sun; ; Cadorna) Italy's first Triennale took place in 1923 in Monza. It aimed to promote Italian design and applied arts, and its success led to the construction of Giovanni Muzio's **Palazzo d'Arte** in Milan in 1933. Since then, this exhibition space has championed design in all its forms, although the triennale formula has been replaced by long annual exhibits and international shows.

◉ Quadrilatero d'Oro & Porta Venezia

★Museo Poldi Pezzoli MUSEUM
(Map p66; 02 79 48 89; www.museopoldipezzoli. it; Via Alessandro Manzoni 12; adult/reduced €10/7; 10am-6pm Wed-Mon; Montenapoleone) Inheriting his fortune at the age of 24, Gian Giacomo Poldi Pezzoli also inherited his mother's love of art. During extensive European travels, he was inspired by the 'house museum' that was to become London's V&A and had the idea of transforming his apartments into a series of themed rooms based on the great art periods (the Middle Ages, early Renaissance, baroque etc.). Crammed with big-ticket Renaissance artworks, these **Sala d'Artista** are exquisite works of art in their own right.

★Galleria d'Arte Moderna GALLERY
(GAM; Map p66; 02 8844 5943; www.gammilano.com; Via Palestro 16; adult/reduced €5/3; 9am-5.30pm Tue-Sun; Palestro) Napoleon's temporary Milanese home, the 18th-century Villa Reale, now houses Milan's modern-art collection. Made up of bequests from leading Milanese families, the collection contains a stunning spread of 19th- and 20th-century Italian and international art, progressing from pieces by neoclassical sculptor Canova (in the ballroom) to futurist painters Giacomo Balla and Umberto Boccioni.

Villa Necchi Campiglio MUSEUM
(Map p62; 02 7634 0121; www.visitfai.it/ villanecchi; Via Mozart 14; adult/child €9/4; 10am-6pm Wed-Sun; San Babila) This exquisitely restored 1930s villa was designed by rationalist architect Piero Portaluppi for Pavian heiresses Nedda and Gigina Necchi, and Gigina's husband Angelo Campiglio. The trio were proud owners of one of Milan's only swimming pools, as well as terrarium-faced sunrooms and streamlined electronic shuttering. Portaluppi's commingling of art deco and rationalist styles powerfully evokes Milan's modernist imaginings while at the same time remaining anchored to a past that was rapidly slipping away.

Giardini Pubblici GARDENS
(Map p66; 6.30am-sunset; ; Palestro) A life story unfolds as you follow pebble paths past bumper cars and a carousel, onwards past games of football, kissing teens, a beer kiosk, babies in prams, jogging paths and shady benches. Jump in, or just stop and smell the roses. For grey days, the neo-Romanesque **Museo Civico di Storia Naturale** (Natural History Museum; Map p62; 02 8846 3337; www.comune.milano.it/museostorianaturale; Corso Venezia 55; adult/reduced €5/3; 9am-5.30pm Tue-Sun; ; Palestro) beckons families with quaint displays and dioramas of dinosaurs, fossils, fauna and the largest geology collection in Europe.

◉ Corso Magenta & Sant'Ambrogio

★The Last Supper ARTWORK
(Il Cenacolo; Map p62; 02 9280 0360; www. cenacolovinciano.net; Piazza Santa Maria delle Grazie 2; adult/reduced €10/5, plus booking fee €2; 8.15am-6.45pm Tue-Sun; Cadorna) Milan's

most famous mural, Leonardo da Vinci's *The Last Supper,* is hidden away on a wall of the refectory adjoining the Basilica di Santa Maria delle Grazie. Depicting Christ and his disciples at the dramatic moment when Christ reveals he's aware of his betrayal, it's a masterful psychological study and one of the world's most iconic images. To see it you must book in advance or sign up for a guided city tour.

When Leonardo was at work on the masterpiece, a star-struck monk noted that he would sometimes arrive in the morning, stare at the previous day's efforts, then promptly finish for the day. Your visit will be similarly brief (15 minutes to be exact), but the baggage of a thousand dodgy reproductions are quickly shed once standing face to face with the luminous work itself.

Centuries of damage have left the mural in a fragile state despite 22 years of restoration, which was completed in 1999. Da Vinci himself is partly to blame: his experimental mix of oil and tempera was applied between 1495 and 1498, rather than within a week as is typical of fresco techniques. The Dominicans didn't help matters when in 1652 they raised the refectory floor, hacking off a lower section of the scene, including Jesus' feet. But the most damage was caused by restorers in the 19th century, whose use of alcohol and cotton wool removed an entire layer. Yet the work's condition does little to lessen its astonishing beauty. Stare at the ethereal, lucent windows beyond the narrative action and you'll wonder if da Vinci's uncharacteristic short-sightedness wasn't divinely inspired.

English-language guided tours (€3.50 on top of the regular ticket price) take place at 9.30am and 3.30pm from Tuesday to Sunday – again, you'll need to book ahead.

---

❶ LAST SUPPER TOURS

Tickitaly (www.tickitaly.com; guided tours €44-70; ⊙ tours 7.15pm & 8pm) is the accredited ticketing website for Leonardo da Vinci's *Last Supper,* offering exclusive guided, after-hours tours, which allow an extended 30-minute visit. Some tours are followed by a wine tasting.

★ **Museo Nazionale della Scienza e della Tecnologia**   MUSEUM
(Map p62; ☎ 02 48 55 51; www.museoscienza.org; Via San Vittore 21; adult/child €10/7.50, submarine tours €8, flight simulator €10; ⊙ 9.30am-5pm Tue-Fri, to 6.30pm Sat & Sun; ♿; Ⓜ Sant'Ambrogio) Kids and would-be inventors will go goggle-eyed at Milan's science museum, the largest of its kind in Italy. It is a fitting tribute in a city where arch-inventor Leonardo da Vinci did much of his finest work. The 16th-century monastery where it is housed features a collection of more than 10,000 items, including models based on da Vinci's sketches, and outdoor hangars housing steam trains, planes and Italy's first submarine, *Enrico Toti.* More recently, the museum added a helicopter flight simulator, in which you can swoop over Milan in a real AW109 cockpit.

★ **Chiesa di San Maurizio**   CHURCH
(Map p66; ☎ 02 8844 5208; Corso Magenta 15; ⊙ 9.30am-7.30pm Tue-Sun; Ⓜ Cadorna) This 16th-century royal chapel and one-time Benedictine convent is Milan's hidden crown jewel, every inch of it covered in breathtaking frescoes, most of them executed by Bernardino Luini, who worked with Leonardo da Vinci. Many of the frescoes immortalise Ippolita Sforza, Milanese literary maven, and other members of the powerful Sforza and Bentivoglio clans who paid for the chapel's decoration.

Basilica di Sant'Ambrogio   BASILICA
(Map p66; ☎ 02 8645 0895; www.basilicasantambrogio.it; Piazza Sant'Ambrogio 15; ⊙ 10am-noon & 2.30-6pm Mon-Sat, 3-5pm Sun; Ⓜ Sant'Ambrogio) St Ambrose, Milan's patron saint and one-time superstar bishop, is buried in the crypt of this red-brick cathedral, which he founded in AD 379. It's a fitting legacy, built and rebuilt with a purposeful simplicity that is truly uplifting: the seminal Lombard Romanesque basilica. Shimmering altar mosaics and a biographical golden altarpiece (835), which once served as the cladding for the saint's sarcophagus, light up the shadowy vaulted interior.

Basilica di Santa Maria delle Grazie   BASILICA
(Map p62; ☎ 02 467 61 11; www.legraziemilano.it; Piazza Santa Maria delle Grazie; ⊙ 7am-noon & 3.30-7.30pm Mon-Sat, 7.30am-12.30pm & 4-9pm Sun; Ⓜ Cadorna, 🚋 16) Begun by Guiniforte Solari in 1463, with later additions by

Bramante, this handsome Lombard church encapsulates the magnificence of the Milanese court of Ludovico Sforza and Beatrice d'Este. Articulated in fine brickwork and terracotta, the building is robust but fanciful; its apse is topped by a masterful, drum-shaped dome attributed to Bramante, and its interior is lined with frescoed chapels decorated by the likes of Bernardo Zenale, Antonello da Messina, Bramantino and Paris Bordone, a student of Titian.

⊙ Navigli & Porta Romana

Fondazione Prada   GALLERY
(✉ 02 5666 2611; www.fondazioneprada.org; Largo Isarco 2; adult/reduced €10/8; ⊙10am-7pm Sun-Mon, Wed & Thu, to 8pm Fri & Sat; Ⓜ Lodi) Conceived by author and architect Miuccia Prada and Rem Koolhaas, this museum is as innovative and creative as the minds that gave it shape. Seven renovated buildings and three new structures have transformed a dilapidated former brandy factory into 19,000 sq metres of exciting, multilevel exhibition space. The buildings, including a four-storey Haunted House tower clad in gold leaf, work seamlessly together, presenting some stunning visual perspectives.

Armani Silos   MUSEUM
(Map p62; ✉ 02 9163 0010; www.armanisilos.com; Via Bergognone 40; adult/reduced €12/8.40; ⊙11am-7pm Wed-Sun; Ⓜ Porta Genova) Housed in a fiercely contemporary concrete building, Giorgio Armani's eponymous museum examines his love of elegant tailoring, which has made him such a staple of luxury businesswear. Although there are some 300 garments in the collection, most interesting, perhaps, is the floor dedicated to his highly crafted and colourful couture line. One for true fashion aficionados.

Basilica di Sant'Eustorgio   BASILICA
(Map p62; ✉ 02 8940 2671; www.santeustorgio.it; Piazza Sant'Eustorgio 3; chapel adult/reduced €6/3; ⊙10am-6pm; 🚋 3, 9) Built in the 4th century to house the bones of the Three Kings, Sant' Eustorgio is one of Milan's oldest churches. Its harmonious exterior belies its rabble-rousing past as Milan's Inquisition HQ, but the real draw is Pigello Portinari's private chapel. Representative of the Medici bank in Milan, Portinari had the cash to splash on Milan's finest Renaissance chapel, frescoed with masterpieces by Vicenzo Foppa.

⊙ Porta Garibaldi & Isola

★Cimitero Monumentale   CEMETERY
(Map p62; ✉ 02 8844 1274; Piazzale Cimitero Monumentale; ⊙8am-6pm Tue-Sun; Ⓜ Monumentale) **FREE** Behind striking Renaissance-revival black-and-white walls, Milan's wealthy have kept their dynastic ambitions alive long after death with grand sculptural gestures since 1866. Nineteenth-century death-and-the-maiden eroticism gives way to some fabulous abstract forms from mid-century masters. Studio BBPR's geometric steel-and-marble memorial to Milan's WWII concentration camp dead sits in the centre, stark and moving. Grab a map inside the forecourt.

★Fondazione Feltrinelli   ARCHITECTURE
(Map p62; ✉ 02 495 83 41; www.fondazionefeltrinelli.it; Viale Pasubio 5; Ⓜ Monumentale) Herzog & de Meuron's first public building in Italy is a combination of two elongated, slanted structures that look reminiscent of a greenhouse. That's not a coincidence as they are built on the site of a former nursery and take inspiration from Milan's historic *cascine* (farm buildings). With a steeply pitched roof and shark-tooth edge, they bring an awesome dose of modernity to the surrounding neighbourhood.

The Feltrinelli Foundation, which is home to one of its namesake bookshops (8am to 11pm Monday to Friday, 9.30am to 11pm Saturday and Sunday), an extremely good cafe, a reading room and a conference/events space, occupies one of the buildings while the other is home to Microsoft's Italian hub. Further shops, cafes and restaurants are expected to open in the ground-floor spaces in future.

Greater Milan

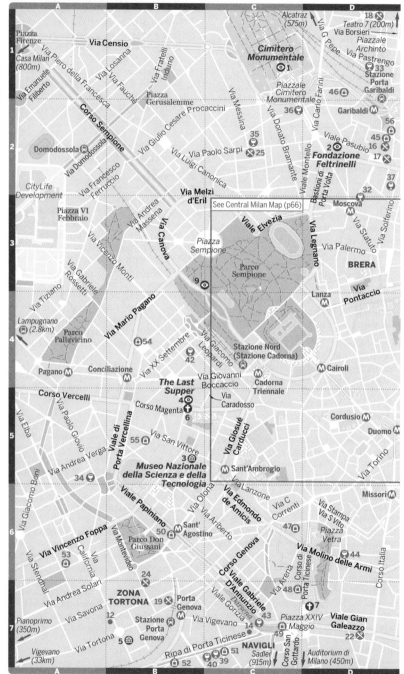

Alcatraz
(575m)

18

Teatro 7 (200m)

Via Borsieri

Piazza
Firenze

Via Censio

Casa Milan
(800m)

Via Emanuele
Filiberto

Via Piero della Francesca

Via Losanna

Via Fauché

Via Fratelli
Induno

Piazza
Gerusalemme

Corso Sempione

Via Giulio Cesare Procaccini

Via Messina

Cimitero
Monumentale

1

Piazzale
Cimitero
Monumentale

36

Via G Pepe

Piazzale
Archinto

Via Pastrengo

33

Stazione
Porta
Garibaldi

46

Garibaldi

56

Domodossola

Via Domodossola

Via Paolo Sarpi

35

25

Via Luigi Canonica

Via Donato Bramante

Via Carlo Farini

Via Montello

45

16

2

Fondazione
Feltrinelli

17

Viale Pasubio

CityLife
Development

Via Francesco
Ferruccio

Via Melzi
d'Eril

Bastioni di
Porta Volta

37

32

Piazza VI
Febbraio

Via Andrea
Massena

Via Vincenzo Monti

Via Canova

See Central Milan Map (p66)

Viale Elvezia

Moscova

Via Solferino

Via Statuto

Via Gabriele
Rossetti

Piazza
Sempione

Via Legnano

Via Palermo

BRERA

Via Tiziano

Parco
Sempione

9

Via
Pontaccio

Lampugnano
(2.8km)

Parco
Pallavicino

Via Mario Pagano

54

Via Giacomo
Leopardi

Lanza

Cairoli

Pagano

Conciliazione

Via XX Settembre

42

Stazione Nord
(Stazione Cadorna)

Cadorna
Triennale

Corso Vercelli

Via Paolo Giovio

The Last
Supper

Corso Magenta

Via Giovanni
Boccaccio

Via
Caradosso

4

6

Corso Vercelli

Via Elba

Viale di
Porta Vercellina

55

Via San Vittore

Via Giosuè
Carducci

Cordusio

Duomo

Via Andrea Verga

Sant'Ambrogio

Via Torino

34

3

Museo Nazionale
della Scienza e della
Tecnologia

Via Lanzone

Via C
Correnti

Missori

Via Giacomo Boni

Via Vincenzo Foppa

Viale Papiniano

Via Olona

Via Edmondo
de Amicis

Via Ariberto

47

Via Stampa
Via S Vito

Piazza
Vetra

44

53

Via
California

Parco Don
Giussani

50

Sant'
Agostino

Via Molino delle Armi

Corso Italia

Via Stendhal

Via Monteviedo

24

Corso Genova

Viale Gabriele
D'Annunzio

Via Arena

48

7

ZONA
TORTONA

19

Porta
Genova

Viale Gorizia

43

Piazza XXIV
Maggio

Viale Gian
Galeazzo

Pianoprimo
(350m)

Via Andrea Solari

Via Savona

12

Stazione
Porta
Genova

Via Vigevano

14

49

22

Vigevano
(33km)

Via Tortona

5

Ripa di Porta Ticinese

NAVIGLI

Corso San Gottardo

Auditorium di
Milano (450m)

52

40

39

51

Sadler
(915m)

Corso di
Porta Ticinese

MILAN

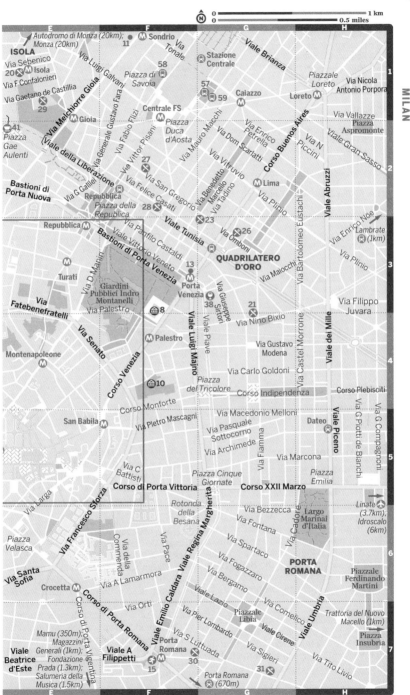

0 _____ 1 km
0 _____ 0.5 miles

ISOLA

Autodromo di Monza (20km);
Monza (20km)

Via Sebenico
20 Isola
Via F Confalonieri

Via Gaetano de Castillia
29

41
Piazza
Gae
Aulenti

Via Melchiorre Gioia

Viale della Liberazione

Bastioni di
Porta Nuova

11 Sondrio

Via Luigi Galvani

Via Generale Gustavo Fara

Piazza di
Savoia

Via Tonale

58

57
59

Stazione
Centrale

Viale Brianza

Piazzale
Loreto

Via Nicola
Antonio Porpora

Caiazzo

Loreto

Via Vallazze

Piazza
Aspromonte

Via Gran Sasso

Centrale FS

Gioia

Via Fabio Filzi

Via Vittor Pisani

27

Via San Gregorio

Via Felice Casati

Piazza
Duca
d'Aosta

Via Mauro Macchi

Via Dom Scarlatti

Via Enrico
Petrella

Via Vitruvio

Via Benedetto Marcello

Via Tadino

Corso Buenos Aires

Via N
Piccini

Lima

Via Plinio

Via Abruzzi

Via Enrico Noe

Lambrate
(1km)

Via Plinio

Repubblica

Via G Galilei

Piazza della
Repubblica

28

23

Viale Tunisia

26
Via Omboni

Via Bartolomeo Eustachi

Repubblica

Viale Vittorio Veneto

Viale Panfilo Castaldi

Bastioni di Porta Venezia

13

Porta
Venezia

**QUADRILATERO
D'ORO**

Via Malocchi

Turati

Via D Manin

Giardini
Pubblici Indro
Montanelli

Via Palestro

Bastioni di Porta Venezia

8

Via Giuseppe
Sirtori

38

21
Via Nino Bixio

Via Filippo
Juvara

Via
Fatebenefratelli

Palestro

Viale Piave

Via Gustavo
Modena

Viale dei Mille

Montenapoleone

Via Senato

Via Carlo Goldoni

Viale Luigi Majno

10

Piazza
del Tricolore

Corso Indipendenza

Corso Plebisciti

Corso Venezia

Corso Monforte

Via Castel Morrone

San Babila

Via Pietro Mascagni

Via Macedonio Melloni

Dateo

Viale Piceno

Via G Piotti de Bianchi

Via G Compagnoni

Via Pasquale
Sottocorno

Via Fiamma

Via Archimede

Via Marcona

Via C
Battisti

Piazza Cinque
Giornate

Piazza
Emilia

Linate
(3.7km);
Idroscalo
(6km)

Corso di Porta Vittoria

Corso XXII Marzo

Via Francesco Sforza

Rotonda
della
Besana

Via Bezzecca

Via Fontana

Largo
Marinai
d'Italia

Via Cadore

Piazza
Velasca

Viale Regina Margherita

Via Spartaco

**PORTA
ROMANA**

Piazzale
Ferdinando
Martini

Via Santa
Sofia

Crocetta

Corso di Porta Romana

Via della Commenda

Via A Lamarmora

Via Pace

Viale Emilio Caldara

Via Fogazzaro

Via Bergamo

Viale Lazio

Via Comelico

Via Cirene

Viale Umbria

Trattoria del Nuovo
Macello (1km)

Viale
Beatrice
d'Este

Mamu (350m);
Magazzini
Generali (1km);
Fondazione
Prada (1.3km);
Salumeria della
Musica (1.5km)

Corso di Porta Vigentina

Viale A
Filippetti

Via Orti

Via Pier Lombardo

Via S Luttuada

Piazzale
Libia

Viale Cirene

Porta
Romana

30

15

31
Via Sigieri

Via Tito Livio

Piazza
Insubria

Porta Romana
(670m)

E   F   G   H

Greater Milan

🏃 Activities

Palazzo Parigi Grand Spa   SPA
(Map p66; ☎ 02 62 56 25; www.palazzoparigi.com; Corso di Porta Nuova 1; Ⓜ Turati) This enormous, 1st-floor spa is one of the few in the city that has escaped the basement. As a result, light floods in to the marble interiors where a full-length pool, fitness club and hammam await. A hundred euros gets you all-day access to the facilities while the Royal Hammam (€130) includes an aromatic steam bath in your own pink marble pool.

Bulgari Spa   SPA
(Map p66; ☎ 02 805 80 51; www.bulgarihotel.com; Via Privata Fratelli Gabba 7/b; treatments from €80; ⊙ 7.30am-9pm; Ⓜ Montenapoleone) Antonio Citterio's lavishly designed spa at the Bulgari is one of Milan's most luxurious. The stream-lined modern design creates a soothing atmosphere, while the heated pool, lined with twinkling gold mosaic, is the height of decadence. Treatments utilise exclusive La Mer, Amala and Sothys products.

QC Terme Milano   SPA
(Map p62; ☎ 02 5519 9367; www.termemilano.com; Piazzale Medaglie d'Oro 2; day ticket weekdays/weekend €45/50; ⊙ 9.30am-midnight Mon-Fri, from 8.30am Sat & Sun; Ⓜ Porta Romana) Pad down the hallways of Milan's former public transport headquarters and make yourself comfortable in a pine-clad railway carriage for a bio sauna session. Such is the ingenuity of this remodelled spa, which has turned the art deco building into a luxurious wellness centre. Outside, the garden is dotted with Jacuzzi pools around which fatigued Milanese office workers snooze.

Navigli Lombardi BOATING
(Map p62; ☑02 667 91 31; www.naviglilombardi.
it; Alzaia Naviglio Grande 4; adult €14; ⊙Apr-Sep;
Ⓜ Porta Genova, ⌂3) Canals were once the
autostradas of medieval Milan, transporting
timber, marble, salt, oil and wine into town.
The largest of them, the Navigli Grande,
grew from an irrigation ditch to one of
the city's busiest thoroughfares by the 13th
century. Four cruises run from April to September; the most popular, the Conche Trail,
loops round the Naviglio Grande and Naviglio Pavese back through the dock.

🎓 Courses

Teatro 7 COOKING
(☑02 8907 3719; www.teatro7.com; Via Thaon di
Revel 7; classes from €75; ⊙10am-7pm; Ⓜ Zara)
Rock-star chef Rico Guarnieri is yours, as he
blurs boundaries between kitchen and table,
cook and diner. Make a meal with the best
local seasonal produce, using traditional
techniques in a dream contemporary kitch-
en. For details of culinary events, private
dinners and classes, check out the website.

👉 Tours

MilanoArte TOURS
(http://milanoarte.net; 1-/2-day 4-person tours
€300) High-end art, history and culture
tours by multilingual culture vultures An-
tonella Fuga and Giacomo Zavatteri. Not
only do they offer insightful, behind-the-
scenes tours of major museums like Brera
and La Scala, but for repeat visitors there are
in-depth tours on design (including the Furniture Fair) and fashion, with inputs from
scholars, researchers and working artisans.

Ad Artem CULTURAL
(Map p62; ☑02 659 77 28; www.adartem.it; Via
Melchiorre Gioia 1; adult/child €13/8; 🖈; Ⓜ Sondrio) Unusual cultural tours of Milan's
museums and monuments with qualified
art historians and actors. Highlight tours
include a walk around the battlements of
Castello Sforzesco; explorations of the castle's subterranean Ghirlanda passageway;
and family-friendly tours of the Museo del
Novecento, where kids are invited to build
and design their own artwork.

Bike & the City CYCLING
(Map p62; ☑393 8032968; www.bikeandthe
city.it; day/sunset tours €40/35; ⊙tours 10am,
3.30pm & 6.30pm; 🖈; Ⓜ Porta Venezia) Make
friends while you get the inside scoop on
city sights during these leisurely, four-hour
cycle tours. Tours start from Via Melchiorre
Gioia 73.

Autostradale Viaggi TOURS
(Map p66; ☑02 3008 9900; www.autostradale
viaggi.it; Passaggio Duomo 2; tours €75; ⊙9am-
6pm Mon-Fri, 9am-4pm Sat & Sun; 🖈; Ⓜ Duomo)
Offers coach tours around Milan (including
The Last Supper), as well as excursions to
the lakes and the Serravalle shopping outlet.
The main office is on Piazza Castello.

🎉 Festivals & Events

Corteo dei Re Magi RELIGIOUS
(⊙Jan) Legend says the remains of the three
wise men are buried in Milan. Be that as it
may, each year on 6 January the kings parade in costume from the Duomo to the Porta Ticinese.

MILAN COURSES

WORTH A TRIP

FOOTBALL MANIA

Unlike the Duomo, **San Siro Stadium** (Stadio Giuseppe Meazza; ☑02 4879 8201; www.
sansiro.net; Piazzale Angelo Moratti; tickets from €20; 🖈; Ⓜ San Siro Stadio) wasn't designed to hold the entire population of Milan, but on a Sunday afternoon amid 85,000
football-mad citizens, it can certainly feel like it. The city's two clubs, AC Milan and FC
Internazionale Milano (aka Inter), play on alternate weeks. Football fans may also want
to make the journey to **Casa Milan** (☑02 6228 4545; www.casamilan.com; Via Aldo Rossi 8;
adult/reduced €15/12; ⊙10am-7pm; 🖈; Ⓜ Portello) on Piazza Gino Valle, where AC Milan is
now headquartered. The huge glass wedge of a building was designed by Fabio Novembre and incorporates not only the club's admin, but the Mondo Milan Museum, a restaurant and a shop where you can kit yourself out in black and red. Inside the museum, the
club's 115-year history is explored through historic memorabilia, a holographic theatre, a
hall of fame and a glowing, golden trophy room.

Central Milan

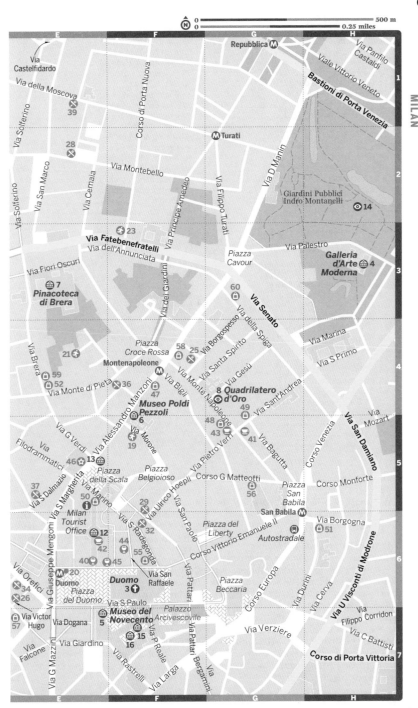

MILAN

Central Milan

Carnevale Ambrosiano   RELIGIOUS
(☺Feb) Lent comes late to Milan, with Carnevale sensibly held on the Saturday that falls after everyone else's frantic February Fat Tuesday.

Salone Internazionale del Mobile   FAIR
(International Furniture Fair; www.salonemilano.it; ☺Apr) The world's most prestigious furniture fair is held annually at **Fiera Milano** (www.fieramilano.it; Strada Statale del Sempione 28, Rho; Ⓜ Rho), with satellite exhibitions in Zona Tortona. Alongside the Salone runs the **Fuorisalone** (http://fuorisalone.it; literally, the outdoor lounge), which incorporates dozens of spontaneous design-related events, parties, exhibits and shows that animate the entire city.

MiArt   FAIR
(www.miart.it; ☺Apr) Milan's annual modern and contemporary art fair held in April may not be Basel, but it attracts more than 30,000 art lovers, more than 200 exhibitors and increasing amounts of international attention.

Cortili Aperti   CULTURAL
(www.adsi.it; ☺May) Over the last weekend in May, the gates to some of the city's most beautiful private courtyards are flung open. Print a map and make your own itinerary, or sign up for tours with **Città Nacosta Milano** (Map p66; ☏ 347 366 1174; www.cittanascostamilano.it; Via del Bollo 3; membership adult €20-40, under-28 €7; ☺9am-1pm & 2-6pm Mon-Fri; Ⓜ Duomo, Missori).

Estate Sforzesca CULTURAL
(Map p66; www.milanocastello.it; ⊘ Jun-Aug) Dozens of concerts, exhibitions, film screenings and family events are organised by the city council in a summer-long festival. The action takes place in and around the grounds of the castle. Ask at the tourist office for details.

Festa di Sant'Ambrogio &
Fiera degli Obej Obej RELIGIOUS
(⊘ Dec) The feast day of Milan's patron saint, St Ambrose, is celebrated on 7 December with the opening of the opera season at Teatro alla Scala (La Scala). In conjunction, a large Christmas Fair – Obej! Obej! (pronounced o-bay, o-bay) – sets up in Castello Sforzesco with stalls selling regional foods, sweets and seasonal handicrafts.

✖ Eating

✖ Duomo & San Babila

Luini FAST FOOD €
(Map p66; ☑02 8646 1917; www.luini.it; Via Santa Radegonda 16; panzerotti €2.70; ⊘10am-3pm Mon, to 8pm Tue-Sat; 🍴; Ⓜ Duomo) This historic joint is the go-to place for *panzerotti*, delicious pizza-dough parcels stuffed with a combination of mozzarella, spinach, tomato, ham or spicy salami, and then fried or baked in a wood-fired oven.

GB Bar SANDWICHES €
(Map p66; Via Agnello 18; sandwiches €4-5; ⊘6.30am-5.30pm Mon-Fri, 7am-6.30pm Sat; Ⓜ Duomo) Big, delicious and well priced, GB's *panini* are stuffed with gourmet fillings including smoked swordfish, pulled pork, top-quality Lombard cheeses and Asti truffles. There's some outdoor seating – and a regular queue, but service is fast.

Trattoria Milanese MILANESE €€
(Map p66; ☑02 8645 1991; Via Santa Marta 11; meals €35-45; ⊘noon-2.45pm & 7-10.45pm Mon-Sat; 🚊2, 14) Like an old friend you haven't seen in years, this trattoria welcomes you with generous goblets of wine, hearty servings of traditional Milanese fare and convivial banter over the vegetable buffet. Regulars slide into their seats, barely needing to order as waiters bring them their usual: meatballs wrapped in cabbage, minestrone or the sinfully good *risotto al salto* (refried risotto).

T'a Milano MILANESE €€
(Map p66; ☑02 8738 6130; www.tamilano.com; Via Clerici 1; meals €25-45; ⊘8am-midnight Mon-Fri, 11am-midnight Sat; 🛜; Ⓜ Cordusio) Chocolatiers Tancredi and Alberto Alemagna's Milanese outlet is an instagrammers dream. Aside from the counters crammed with delectable chocolates, the dining room is a delight to behold: huge marble floor tiles, sapphire-blue banquettes and glowing 1950s brass lamps. The crowd are equally chic. They come for king crab sandwiches, the fillet of San Pietro fish and, of course, the chocolate Duomo cake.

Peck Italian Bar ITALIAN €€
(Map p66; ☑02 869 30 17; www.peck.it; Via Cantù 3; meals €40-45; ⊘8am-10pm Mon-Fri, to 9pm Sat; ✳🛜; Ⓜ Duomo) The restaurant of heritage delicatessen Peck, this is the place to try Milanese specialities such as osso buco and *mondeghili* (meatballs) with chicory. The dishes let quality produce shine and come with just a smidgen of contemporary flair.

Cracco MODERN ITALIAN €€€
(Map p66; ☑02 87 67 74; www.ristorantecracco.it; Via Victor Hugo 4; meals €130-160; ⊘12.30-2pm & 7.30pm-12.30am Tue-Fri, 7.30-11pm Mon & Sat; Ⓜ Duomo) Two Michelin-star chef Carlo

---

DON'T MISS

FEELING PECKISH

Forget *The Last Supper:* gourmets head to the food and wine emporium **Peck** (Map p66; ☑02 802 31 61; www.peck.it; Via Spadari 9; ⊘3-8pm Mon, 9am-8pm Tue-Sat, 10am-5pm Sun; 🛜; Ⓜ Duomo). This Milanese institution opened its doors as a deli in 1883. The Aladdin's cave–like food hall is smaller than its reputation suggests, but what it lacks in space it makes up for in variety, with some 3200 variations of *parmigiano reggiano* (Parmesan) at its cheese counter, just for starters. Other treasures include an exquisite array of chocolates, pralines and pastries; freshly made gelato; seafood; caviar; pâtés; a butcher, and fruit and vegetable sellers; truffle products; olive oils and balsamic vinegar. Now you can even sample some of the goods at new in-store cafe, Piccolo Peck.

SUMMER ESCAPE

If you're wondering what the Milanese do to escape the stifling heat of summer in the city, look no further than **Idroscalo waterpark** (☑388 186 8575; www.idroscalomilano. com; Via Circonvallazione Idroscalonear, Linate Airport; adult/reduced Mon-Fri €8/5, Sat & Sun €12/10; ☉10am-8pm May-Sep; ⛵; ☐73). Located a quick 20-minute bus ride from the centre of town, this artificial lake was once the liquid landing strip for seaplanes, but has since been converted into a welcoming watery playground. Concerts regularly take place here, including indie-leaning festivals, and there's swimming and water sports, including wakeboarding and kitesurfing. Check the website for details and a weekly calendar of events. To get to Idroscalo, take bus 73 from San Babila to Linate Airport, then take the free shuttle.

Cracco keeps the Milanese in thrall with his off-the-wall inventiveness. The *risotto al sedano, rapa, tartufo nero e caffè* (risotto with celery, turnip, black truffle and coffee) is unlike any northern Italian rice dish you may have stumbled across elsewhere. Let the waiters do the thinking by ordering one of the tasting menus (€130 and €160).

✖ Brera & Parco Sempione

L'Orto di Brera   VEGETARIAN €
(Map p66; ☑02 8646 1056; www.ortodibrera.com; Via San Carpoforo 6; meals €5-10; ☉8.30am-7pm Mon-Sat; ⛱✎; Ⓜ Lanza) The colourful vegetables at this local grocers line the cobbled alley of San Carpoforo like floral displays at a high-end florist. Step inside and you'll find a surprising dining spot with fresh vegetal creations from chef Claudio Crotti ready to take away or snack on amid the baskets. There's also a range of freshly squeezed juices and biodynamic wines.

Al Politico   SANDWICHES €
(Map p66; Piazza Castello 5; sandwiches €3.50-5; ☉8am-8pm; Ⓜ Cairoli, Cadorna) This sandwich kiosk crammed with locals gives you a sense of Milan's sharp sense of humour. All the handsomely stuffed sandwiches are named after politicians, requiring diners to struggle between matching their political allegiances with their favourite stuffing. Table seating surrounds the kiosk.

Rovello 18   OSTERIA €€
(Map p66; ☑02 7209 3709; Via Tivoli 2; meals €35-50; ☉noon-3pm & 6-10.30pm Mon-Sat, 6-10.30pm Sun; Ⓜ Lanza) Take heart from the dresser stacked with venerable bottles of Barolo as you enter this unpretentious *osteria* (tavern). It's an indication of the smart, unfussy,

quality food that Gualtiero Panciroli serves up. Salt cod salad and marinated salmon are just as good as the homemade pasta with *guanciale* (pork cheek) and the rabbit stew. The latter pairs rather well with one of those Barolos.

Volemose Bene   OSTERIA €€
(Map p66; ☑02 3655 9618; www.volemosebene milano.it; Via della Moscova 25; meals €30-35; ☉noon-2.30pm & 7.30-11.30pm; Ⓜ Moscova) Deliberately kitsch, rustic interiors – checked tablecloths, strings of garlic, straw flagons – a loud crush of diners and stunningly good Roman cooking are the ingredients of this restaurant, which lives up to its name (roughly translated as 'caring for each other'). Don't miss Jewish-style artichokes, roast lamb with potatoes or fiery *pasta all'amatriciana,* pasta with spicy tomato sauce, *pecorino* (sheep's milk cheese) and bacon.

★Seta   GASTRONOMY €€€
(Mandarin Oriental; Map p66; ☑02 8731 8897; www.mandarinoriental.com; Via Andegari 9; meals €120; ☉12.30-2.30pm & 7.30-10.30pm Mon-Fri, 7.30-10.30pm Sat; P ❄ ⛱; Ⓜ Montenapoleone) Smooth as the silk after which it is named, Seta is Michelin-starred dining at its best: beautiful, inventive and full of flavour surprises. Diners sit on the edge of their teal-coloured velvet chairs in keen anticipation of Antonio Guida's inspired dishes such as plum-coloured roe deer with a dazzling splash of mango salsa. It's both solidly traditional and subtly daring, just like Milan.

Fioraio Bianchi Caffè   ITALIAN, FRENCH €€€
(Map p66; ☑02 2901 4390; www.fioraiobianchi caffe.it; Via Montebello 7; meals €45-60; ☉8am-midnight Mon-Sat; ⛱; Ⓜ Turati) This former florist's shop is great for a light French-

influenced lunch, or an excellent *aperitivo* (pre-dinner drink) among the flowers. Dinners are fresh and inventive with particularly delicious border-crossing desserts, from Provencal lavender brûlée to spice-inflected apple strudel.

Quadrilatero d'Oro & Porta Venezia

NÚN   KEBAB €
(Map p62; ☑ 02 9163 7315; www.nunmilano.com; Via Lazzaro Spallanzani 36; kebabs €4.50-6; ⊙ noon-11pm Tue-Sun; ☎ 🖍; Ⓜ Porta Venezia) Picking up on the demand for vegan, vegetarian and raw food, this clever contemporary kebab bar serves up hearty wraps stuffed with seasonal salads, aubergine, pomegranate and felafel. Meat eaters needn't worry though, as halal chicken is also served. Order at the counter, stipulating your preferred bread, filling and sauce, then wait to be called for collection.

Pavé   PASTRIES €
(Map p62; ☑ 02 9439 2259; www.pavemilano.com; Via Felice Casati 27; pastries €1.50-5.50, salads €6.50; ⊙ 8am-8pm Tue-Fri, 8.30am-7pm Sat & Sun; ☎ 🖍 🖳; Ⓜ Porta Venezia) Try not to argue over the *frolla al cacao,* an insanely good crumb tart filled with a sinfully good ganache and topped by raw chocolate nuggets. After all, it's just one of the temptations dreamed up by pastry maestros Diego, Luca and Giovanni. There's also San Franciscan sourdough, savoury brioche filled with ricotta and sundried tomatoes, and almond kipfel.

Gelato Giusto   GELATO €
(Map p62; ☑ 02 2951 0284; http://gelatogiusto.it; Via San Gregorio 17; 2/4 scoops €2.50/4.50; ⊙ noon-8.30pm; ❄ 🖳; Ⓜ Porta Venezia) 🍦 This gelateria is a temple to Lombardy's luxurious milk products: everything here is 100% natural, handmade and locally sourced. What's more, owner Vittoria is a Maître Chocolatier constantly in search of innovative and delightful flavours such as pistachio, cinnamon and blackcurrant, and ricotta with bitter orange.

Borgospesso 1   MILANESE €€
(Map p66; ☑ 02 3668 3500; www.borgospesso1.com; Via Borgospesso 1; meals €35-50; ⊙ 12.30-3pm & 7-11pm Mon-Sat; ❄; Ⓜ Montenapoleone) When the Quad's most historic restaurant, Bagutta, 1924 closed in 2014, residents were aghast. But now Bagutta is back as one of the offerings in this surprising new venue: the brick-vaulted crypt of a church. While Bagutta occupies a secluded, low-lit dining room of its own, the rest of the space is split between a marble-clad bar and bistro, and a deli selling gastronomic treats from Pasticceria Taveggia and Drogheria Parini.

Dim Sum   CHINESE €€€
(Map p62; ☑ 02 2952 2821; www.dimsummilano.com; Via Nino Bixio 29; meals €40-50; ⊙ noon-2.30pm & 7-11.30pm Tue-Sun; ❄; Ⓜ Porta Venezia) With Italy's largest Chinese population, it's surprising that until now Milan hasn't managed to conjure a gourmet Chinese restaurant. That is until the advent of this high-brow, blue-lit dim sum venue. Order broadly so you can sample the diversity of the menu, which includes Chianina beef and chives, pork and goji berries or seafood with a lime-flavoured rice wrap.

Corso Magenta & Sant'Ambrogio

★ Pasticceria Marchesi   PASTRIES €
(Map p66; ☑ 02 86 27 70; www.pasticceriamarchesi.it; Via Santa Maria alla Porta 11/a; ⊙ 7.30am-8pm Mon-Sat, 8.30am-1pm Sun; Ⓜ Cairoli, Cordusio) This wood-panelled *pasticceria* (pastry shop) has been baking since 1824 and turns out 10 different types of brioche alongside bignes, millefeuilles, croissants, pralines and more. The window displays have the wonky logic of a Hitchcock dream sequence, but with perfect-every-shot coffee, there's no shock ending. Don't overlook the fruit gels packaged together in

ANTICA BARBIERIA COLLA

Take a pew next to politicians, football stars and businessmen and let jovial Franco Bompieri steam, lather and close shave you into a state of bliss. Opened in 1904, this is the oldest barber shop (Map p66; ☑ 02 87 43 12; www.antica barbieriacolla.it; Via Gerolamo Morone 3; ⊙ 8.30am-12.30pm & 2.30-7pm Tue-Sat; Ⓜ Duomo, 🚋 1) in Europe – the brush used on Puccini is proudly displayed – and its range of own-brand shaving creams and colognes is second to none.

smartly contrasting flavours like green apple and prune.

De Santis
SANDWICHES €

(Map p66; ✏ 02 7209 5124; www.paninidesantis. it; Corso Magenta 9; sandwiches €6-8; ⊙ noon-11.30pm Sun-Thu, to 12.30am Fri & Sat; 🖪; Ⓜ Cadorna) Sandwiches here are so damn good you may eschew restaurant dining just to sample that *panini* with prosciutto, spicy goat cheese, pepperoni, aubergine and artichokes. There are 200 variations on the menu and De Santis' decades of experience are good reasons why punters are prepared to queue at this tiny venue. Beer is served on tap to the lucky few who find seating.

★ La Brisa
MODERN ITALIAN €€€

(Map p66; ✏ 02 8645 0521; www.ristorantelabrisa.it; Via Brisa 15; meals €50-70; ⊙ 12.45-2.30pm & 7.45-10.30pm Mon-Fri, 7.45-10.30pm Sun; ❄; Ⓜ Cairoli, Cordusio) Discreet, elegant and exquisitely romantic. Push open the screened door and the maître d' will guide you to a table beneath centuries-old linden trees in a secluded courtyard, where ivy climbs the walls and pink hydrangeas bob in the breeze. Chef Antonio Facciolo's seasonal menus are similarly elegant; his signature dish is a mouthwatering roast pork in a myrtle-berry drizzle.

✖ Navigli & Porta Romana

Gino Sorbillo
PIZZA €

(Map p62; ✏ 02 5810 4789; Via Montevideo 4; pizzas €8-12; ⊙ noon-3.30pm & 7-11.30pm; 🖪; Ⓜ Porta Genova) The king of Neapolitan pizza has taken Milan by storm with his organic, slow-levitation dough and divinely simple toppings of tomato, mozzarella, basil, broccoli, sweet peppers, spicy *'nduja* (salami) and Norcia ham. To reach perfection, the hand-kneaded dough is rested in wooden boxes first before being artfully twirled and baked in a giant wood-fired oven for that delicious crisp crust.

Gattullo
PASTICCERIA €

(Map p62; ✏ 02 5831 0497; www.gattullo.it; Piazzale di Porta Lodovico 2; pastries from €1.50; ⊙ 7am-9pm Tue-Sun; ❄🖪; 🚋 3, 9) Hailing from that great southern baking town, Ruvo di Puglia, in 1961, Joseph Gattullo built his small bakery into a pastry empire. The historic store and cafe is still located in its 1970s premises, resplendent with sci-fi Murano chandeliers and an elegant veneered

wooden bar. Come for breakfast, lunch or *aperitivo;* it's all fantastic.

★ Un Posto a Milano
MODERN ITALIAN €€

(Map p62; ✏ 02 545 77 85; www.unpostoamilano. it; Via Cuccagna 2; meals €15-35; ⊙ 12.30-3pm & 7.30-11pm; 🖋🖪; Ⓜ Porta Romana) A few years ago this country *cascina* (farmhouse) was a derelict ruin until a collection of cooperatives and cultural associations returned it to multifunctional use as restaurant, bar, social hub and hostel. Delicious salads, homemade foccacia, soups and snacks are served throughout the day at the bar, while the restaurant serves simple home cooking using locally sourced ingredients.

Trattoria Trippa
ITALIAN €€

(Map p62; ✏ 327 6687908; www.trippamilano.it; Via Giorgio Vasari 3; meals €30-40; ⊙ 7.30-11.30pm Mon-Sat; Ⓜ Porta Romana) Having honed his skills at the Bauer in Venice and Michelin-starred St Hubertus in the Dolomites, chef Diego Rossi and blogger Peter Caroli now have their own feted restaurant. As the name suggests, tripe features heavily on the menu alongside historic recipes using eel, wild greens, char, rabbit and even snails. The quality of the ingredients is superlative, and there's an interesting organic wine to match.

★ Basara
SUSHI €€€

(Map p62; ✏ 02 8324 1025; www.basaramilano.it; Via Tortona 12; meals €50-70; ⊙ 8.30am-3.30pm & 7pm-12.30am Mon-Sat; Ⓜ Porta Genova) Making a name for yourself in Milan's sophisticated sushi scene isn't easy, but chef Hiro's lobster maki roll sings a siren song that packs this place out for two sittings every evening. The raw-fish plates are superb, particularly the pretty block of red Sicilian shrimps served on a black slate slab with a sprinkle of sea salt.

Lunch is a good way to beat the dinner crowds, while the €12 *aperitivo* gives you a chance to sample the magic on a budget.

✖ Porta Garibaldi & Isola

★ Berberè
PIZZA €

(Map p62; ✏ 02 3670 7820; www.berberepizza. it; Via Sebenico 21; pizza €6.50-14; ⊙ 7-11.30pm Mon-Fri, 12.30-2.30pm & 7-11.30pm Sat & Sun; 🖪; Ⓜ Isola) Craft pizzas and craft beers is what Bolognese brothers Matteo and Salvatore promise you at this fantastically good pizzeria housed in an atmospheric 1950s cooperative. Everything from the Black Elk flour (they use variations of spelt, enkir and kamut, which give a lighter finish than wheat) to the Ponteré mozzarella, the Torre Guaceto tomatoes and Puglian *fiordilatte* (a semi-soft cheese) is sourced obsessively for the optimum flavour punch. Book ahead.

La Ravioleria Sarpi   CHINESE €
(Map p62; ☑331 8870596; Via Paolo Sarpi 27; dumplings €3-4.50; ☺9.30am-3pm & 4-9.30pm; ☑; ☐12, 14) This hole-in-the-wall Chinese takeaway has taken Milan by storm with its collaboration between a young Chinese economics student and one of the city's heritage DOC butchers belonging to Walter Sirtori, which is located next door. The result is a range of plump, Jiaozi dumplings inspired by Agie's grandmother, which are stuffed with just three fillings: beef and leek, pork and cabbage or rough-chopped vegetables.

Artico Gelateria   GELATO €
(Map p62; ☑02 4549 4698; www.articogelateria.com; Via Porro Lambertenghi 15; 2 scoops €2.20; ☺noon-11pm; ❄☝; Ⓜ Isola) All natural, hand-turned ice cream and sorbets in an interesting range of flavours, such as chocolate with chilli, and DOP pistachio with salt and pepper. Watch them being made behind the counter while you wait your turn in the eager queue. And for die-hard *gelato* fans there are now ice-cream-making courses with master Maurizio Poloni himself (half-day workshop €80).

★Ratanà   MILANESE €€
(Map p62; ☑02 8712 8855; www.ratana.it; Via Gaetano de Castillia 28; meals €35-45; ☺12.30-2.30pm & 7.30-11.30pm; Ⓜ Gioia) Located in a lovely Liberty building that once belonged to the railway, Cesare Battisti's neo-bistro turns out authentic Milanese flavours. Drawing his produce from Slow Food artisans, the menu offers up classics such as roasted pumpkin with robiola, risotto with turnip greens and crispy veal tongue with mash. There's a small bar, which locals mob at *aperitivo* time for tasty tapas and local wines.

Osteria del Treno   ITALIAN €€
(Map p62; ☑02 670 04 79; www.osteriadeltreno.it; Via San Gregorio 46; meals €35; ☺12.30-2.30pm & 8pm-midnight Mon-Fri, 8pm-midnight Sat & Sun; Ⓜ Centrale) This Slow Food *osteria* with its Liberty-style ballroom is a piece of Milanese

FOOD TOURS

Milan is a serious food town, as professional food writers Sara Porro, Simone Muzza and Jackie DeGiorgio will show you on **Sauce Milan's** (http://saucemilan.com; per person €95) convivial half-day tours of the city's finest cafes, markets, bars and street food stalls. More than just guides, Sara and Simone are grand drinking partners, contemporary Milanese cognoscenti and gelato connoisseurs. In fact, the perfect partners to show you around town.

history, built originally as a club for railway workers at the nearby Stazione Centrale. Self-service lunches showcase a variety of Presidio protected cheeses, cured meats and simple, authentic pasta dishes. Dinner is a more formal affair and on Sunday nights a *milonga* (tango dance) takes place in the ballroom.

★Alice Ristorante   MODERN ITALIAN €€€
(Map p62; ☑02 4949 7340; www.aliceristorante.it; Piazza XXV Aprile, Eataly; meals €40-50; ☺12.30-2pm & 7.30-10pm Mon-Sat; ❄☑; Ⓜ Moscova, Garibaldi) The one-Michelin starred restaurant of talented chef Viviana Varese and sommelier and fish expert Sandra Ciciriello is the pride of Eataly's foodstore. The artful furnishings and views over Piazza XXV Aprile are a match for the superlative food and the menu is full of humour, with dishes such as Polp Fiction (octopus with zucchini trumpets) and That Ball! (truffle ice cream with chocolate, *zabaglione* and cocoa).

10 Corso Como Café   CAFE €€€
(Map p62; ☑02 2901 3581; www.10corsocomo.it; Corso Como 10; meals €35-60; ☺10.30am-1am; ❄; Ⓜ Garibaldi) A picture-perfect courtyard space, draped in greenery, and world-class people-watching awaits at Corso Como. Sit pretty in the graphic, black-and-white chairs and enjoy goblets of fruit smoothies, crisp vegetable crudités, grilled shrimp and the most stylish cheese sandwich you're ever likely to see. Plus it offers the ultimate in afternoon tea: your choice of caviar and blinis (from €55) and a pot of Mariage Frères tea. The circular bar inside is a great place for a glass of wine.

1. Galleria Vittorio Emanuele II (p58)

This neoclassical masterpiece is home to Milan's finest shopping boutiques.

2. Castello Sforzesco (p58)

Once the residence of the Sforza dynasty, this magnificent castle was designed by Leonardo da Vinci.

3. Teatro alla Scala (p78)

Try to catch a performance at this world-famous opera house.

4. Duomo, Milan (p56)

Take a walk along the grand roof terrace of this exquisitely detailed cathedral.

🍷 Drinking & Nightlife

🍷 Duomo & San Babila

Camparino in Galleria   BAR
(Map p66; ☑02 8646 4435; www.camparino.it; Piazza del Duomo 21; drinks €12-24; ⊙7.15am-8.40pm Tue-Sun; Ⓜ Duomo) Open since the inauguration of the Galleria Vittorio Emanuele II arcade in 1867, this art nouveau bar has served drinks to the likes of Verdi, Toscanini, Dudovich and Carrà. Cast-iron chandeliers and huge mirrored walls trimmed with mosaics of birds and flowers set the tone for a classy Campari-based cocktail. Drink at the bar for one of the cheapest *aperitivo* in town.

Pasticceria Marchesi   CAFE
(Map p66; ☑02 9418 1710; www.pasticceria marchesi.it; Galleria Vittorio Emanuele II; ⊙7.30am-9pm; Ⓜ Duomo) With an 80% stake in the historic bakery, Prada has opened a luxurious new cafe on the 1st floor of its menswear store in the Galleria. Overlooking the mosaics down below, the lounge is decked out in green floral jacquard and velvet armchairs. Come for high tea or the excellent *aperitivo,* although expect a wait as service is snooze-inducing.

Straf Bar   BAR
(Map p66; ☑02 8050 8715; www.straf.it; Via San Raffaele 3; ⊙11am-midnight; 🛜; Ⓜ Duomo) A busy nightly *aperitivo* scene kicks on until pumpkin hour at the Straf's super-sexy hotel bar. The decor is along the now-familiar mod-exotic lines: wood, metal and stone played up against minimalist concrete. On Thursdays the bar hosts regular international DJs, while on Tuesdays there is live music.

Terrazza Aperol   BAR
(Map p66; ☑02 8633 1959; www.terrazzaaperol.it; Piazza del Duomo; cocktails €12-17; ⊙11am-11pm Sun-Fri, to midnight Sat; 🛜; Ⓜ Duomo) With its wacky moulded orange bar, orange bubble lights and low-slung '70s seats, this bar dedicated to the classic Aperol *spritz* (cocktail made with prosecco) channels a strong Austin Powers vibe. Still, the Duomo's extravagant exterior, which seems within arm's reach from the terrace, is more than a match for a paisley velvet suit.

🍷 Brera & Parco Sempione

Dry   COCKTAIL BAR
(Map p62; ☑02 6379 3414; www.drymilano.it; Via Solferino 33; cocktails €8-13, meals €20-25; ⊙7pm-1.30am; 🛜; Ⓜ Moscova) The brainchild of Michelin-starred chef Andrea Berton, Dry pairs its cocktails with gourmet pizzas. The inventive cocktail list includes the Corpse Reviver (London Dry gin, cointreau, Cocchi Americano and lemon juice) and the Martinez (Boompjes genever, vermouth, Maraschino liqueur and Boker's bitters), the latter inspired by French gold hunters in Martinez, the birthplace of barman Jerry Thomas.

Bulgari Hotel   BAR
(Map p66; ☑02 805 80 51; www.bulgarihotel. com; Via Privata Fratelli Gabba 7b; cocktails €22; ⊙7.30am-1am; 🛜; Ⓜ Montenapoleone) Whether experienced inside beneath the giant botanical sculptures at the earth-toned bar or outside on the terrace overlooking the brilliantly green garden, the *aperitivo* scene here is an intense slice of Milan life. The second-cheapest wine on the list may weigh in at €17 but it's cheap for the theatre, darling. The restaurant serves a refreshingly light Med menu.

Bento Bar   BAR
(Map p62; ☑02 659 80 75; www.bentobar.com; Corso Garibaldi 104; ⊙12.30-3pm & 6.30pm-midnight Mon-Sat, 6.30pm-midnight Sun; Ⓜ Moscova) Combining two of Milan's favourite things: *aperitivo* and sushi, Bento can't really go wrong. Which is why punters cram into this hip little bar to quaff endless variations on gin cocktails while grazing on an endless supply of octopus balls, salmon tataki and seared tuna sushi.

🍷 Quadrilatero d'Oro & Porta Venezia

Pasticceria Marchesi   CAFE
(Map p66; ☑02 7600 8238; www.pasticceria-marchesi.it; Via Montenapoleone 9; ⊙7.30am-9pm; 🛜; Ⓜ Montenapoleone) Decked out in pink, gold and green, Marchesi's Quad cafe is as easy on the eye as their pastries are on the taste buds. Inside you'll find a coffee bar and two large tearooms where brass-edged counters display a tantalising array of pralines, tarts, pastries and sweets. If you're visiting a Milanese home, a box bearing Marchesi's golden stamp will ensure a second invite.

HClub Diana COCKTAIL BAR
(Map p62; ☏ 02 2058 2004; www.sheraton.com/ dianamajestic; Viale Piave 42, Sheraton Diana Majestic; cocktails €13-15, brunch €38-43; ☉ 7am-1am; 🛜; Ⓜ Porta Venezia) Secreted behind a vast leather curtain at the back of the Sheraton, *aperitivo* at HClub Diana is one of Milan's most varied. Grab a freshly crushed peach bellini and lounge with the fashion pack around the low-lit garden pool in the shade of magnolia trees.

Pasticceria Cova CAFE
(Map p66; ☏ 02 7600 5599; www.pasticceriacova. com; Via Monte Napoleone 8; ☉ 7.45am-8.30pm Mon-Sat, 10am-7pm Sun; Ⓜ Montenapoleone) It can feel like feeding time at the zoo at Cova's ever-crowded bar, yet the relentlessly charming and attentive baristas won't overlook you, and the surroundings are soothingly pretty. The sweets case will tempt, but a thick-cut smoked salmon on rye is far more fortifying, along with a glass of Cova's own label *prosecco*.

🍷 Corso Magenta & Sant'Ambrogio

Ricerca Vini WINE BAR
(Map p62; ☏ 02 4819 3496; www.ricercavini.it; Via Vicenzo Monti 33; ☉ 10am-1pm & 3.30-10pm Tue-Sat, 4-10pm Mon; Ⓜ Cadorna) Sure, it's a wine shop, but it's a bar and a rather good restaurant, too. What better place to sample your options before committing to carry home one of the 2500 wines on offer here. It's one of the largest selections in the city, and the *aperitivo* platters of prosciutto and cheese are excellent. Some evenings it hosts tastings.

Bottiglieria Bulloni WINE BAR
(Map p62; ☏ 02 4800 3155; Via Lipari 2; ☉ 7am-9.30pm Mon-Fri, 8am-12.30pm & 5.30-9.30pm Sat; Ⓜ Sant'Agostino) Selling liquor and wine since 1933, this *bottiglieria* is the real-deal when it comes to *aperitivo* time. Forget new-fad dinner spreads, here it's strictly crostini, olives and gherkins, and a well-executed €6 *spritz*. Less than a dozen tables sit beneath the bottle-lined walls (glasses of wine cost €4 to €8), and behind the bar there's an original Futurist artwork by Enrico Prampolini.

🍷 Navigli & Porta Romana

★ **Rebelot del Pont** COCKTAIL BAR
(Map p62; ☏ 02 8419 4720; www.rebelotdelpont. com; Ripa di Porta Ticinese 55; ☉ 6pm-midnight Mon-Sat, noon-midnight Sun; 🚊 2, 9, 14, 19) *Rebelot* means 'pandemonium' in Milanese dialect and this place certainly pushes out the culinary and cocktail boat. Squired by top World Bartender Oscar Quagliarini, you can expect taste sensations such as the Marrakech Souk (blended whisky and spiced honey) and the Garden Sazerac (Monkey 47 gin, cherry liqueur, absinthe and a homemade 'perfume'). Pair with small plates of salted codfish and Tuscan black pork.

★ **VOLT** CLUB
(Map p62; ☏ 345 2285157; www.voltclub.it; Via Molino delle Armi 16; €15-20; ☉ 11.30pm-5am; 🚊 3) Milan's youngest club is also its hippest, and has its sights firmly set on the European Top Club's chart. Fully renovated, it now has a lighting and sound system designed in Berlin, a slick all-black interior and a line-up of top-notch DJs. Expect house music on Saturday, while other nights alternate different electronic-based genres, as well as hip-hop and dance.

Mag Café BAR
(Map p62; ☏ 02 3956 2875; Ripa di Porta Ticinese 43; cocktails €7-9, brunch €10; ☉ 7.30am-2am Mon-Fri, 9am-2am Sat & Sun; 🚊 2, 9) A Milanese speakeasy with wingback armchairs in whisky-coloured velvet, marble-topped tables, a patchwork of Persian rugs and huge lampshades that look like bird's nests. Like the decor, the drinks are creatively crafted, utilising interesting herbs and syrups, and served in vintage glassware. Mag also does a popular brunch on weekends.

Vista Darsena BAR
(Map p62; ☏ 02 4549 9470; Viale Gabriele d'Annunzio 20; cocktails €8-10; ☉ 8am-2am; 🍽; 🚊 3, 9, 14) Drinks with a view are the USP of this dock-side conservatory bar, which serves up breakfast, coffee, snacks and *aperitivo* from dawn until dusk. In winter, drinkers hunker down beneath the outdoor heaters, but in summer they grab their cocktails and sit beside the dock to watch the reflections corralled in the still water. *Aperitivo* runs from 6pm to 10pm.

MILAN DRINKING & NIGHTLIFE

🍴 Porta Garibaldi & Isola

★ Botanical Club
BAR

(Map p62; ☑ 02 3652 3846; www.thebotanicalclub. com; Via Pastrengo 11; meals €25-30; ⊙ 12.30-2.30pm & 6.30-10.30pm Mon-Fri, 6.30-10.30pm Sat; 🕾; Ⓜ Isola) This bar, bistro and gin distillery is Italy's first foray into the micro-distillery trend. Behind a bar festooned in greenery, mixologist Katerina Logvinova has over 150 gins to play with, including the house brand, Spleen & Ideal, which experiments with interesting botanicals such as Serbian juniper and tonka beans. To accompany divine concoctions like Chinese Dusk (London Dry Gin, sake, plum bitter and fruit liqueur) are contemporary plates of veal tartare and crab salad with green apple.

There's a second branch in Navigli on Via Tortona.

★ Cantine Isola
WINE BAR

(Map p62; ☑ 02 331 52 49; Via Sarpi 30; ⊙ 10am-10pm Tue-Sun; 🚇 12, 14) Only octogenarians make use of the table at the back – everyone else hovers near the beautiful old bar, balancing plates of bruschetta and holding glasses at the ready to sample a selection of wines from 400 exceptional vintners.

Ceresio 7
BAR

(Map p62; ☑ 02 3103 9221; www.ceresio7.com; Via Ceresio 7; aperitivo €15, meals €60-80; ⊙ 12.30pm-1am; 🕾; 🚇 2, 4) Heady views match the heady price of *aperitivo* at Milan's coolest rooftop bar, sitting atop the former 1930s Enel (electricity company) HQ. Two pools, two bars and a restaurant under the guidance of former Bulgari head chef Elio Sironi make this a hit with Milan's beautiful people. In sum-

mer you can book a whole day by the pool from €110, which includes food and drinks.

RED
CAFE

(Map p62; ☑ 02 6558 0153; Piazza Gae Aulenti 1; ⊙ 7.30am-11pm Mon-Fri, 10am-midnight Sat, 10am-11pm Sun; 🕾; Ⓜ Garibaldi) RED stands for Read, Eat, Dream and is the savvy idea of Italian publisher Feltrinelli. Aimed at attracting younger, iPad-toting customers, it is a concept cafe-cum-restaurant housed in a Feltrinelli bookstore stocked with some 5000 titles, located amid the skyscrapers on Piazza Gae Aulenti. At night, book browsers can enjoy the spectacularly lit landscape or challenge each other to games of table football.

☆ Entertainment

Teatro alla Scala
OPERA

(La Scala; Map p66; ☑ 02 7200 3744; www.teatroallascala.org; Piazza della Scala; tickets €30-300; Ⓜ Duomo) One of the most famous opera stages in the world, La Scala's season runs from early December through July. You can also see theatre, ballet and concerts here year-round (except August). Buy tickets online or by phone up to two months before the performance, or from the central box office. On performance days, tickets for the gallery are available from the box office at Via Filodrammatici 2 (one ticket per customer). Queue early.

Auditorium di Milano
CLASSICAL MUSIC

(☑ 02 8338 9401; www.laverdi.org; Largo Gustav Mahler; ⊙ box office 10am-7pm Tue-Sun; 🚇 3, 9, 10) Abandoned after WWII, the Cinema Massimo was transformed in 1999 into the state-of-the-art home of Milan's legendary Giuseppe Verde Symphonic Orchestra and Milan Chorus, as well as a venue for visiting international jazz acts and chamber music groups.

🛍 Shopping

🛍 Duomo & San Babila

Brian & Barry
DEPARTMENT STORE

(Map p66; www.brianandbarry.it; Via Durini 28; ⊙ 10am-7.30pm; 🕾; Ⓜ San Babila) From humble beginnings in Monza in 1924, Pietro and Maria Zaccardi built the Brian & Barry brand from scratch. Their impressive, 12-storey flagship store, designed by Giovanni Muzio, houses not only their good-value line but high-end fashion brands, accessories,

BEHIND THE SCENES AT LA SCALA

To glimpse the inner workings of La Scala visit the **Ansaldo workshops** (Map p62; ☑ 02 4335 3521; www.teatroallascala. org; Via Bergognone 34; ⊙ 9am-noon & 2-4pm Tue & Thu; Ⓜ Porto Genova) where the stage sets are crafted and painted, and where some 800 to 1000 new costumes are handmade each season. Tours on Tuesdays and Thursdays must be booked in advance and are guided in conjunction with the heads of each department.

cosmetics and food, including an outlet of Eataly. The top-floor bar, Terrazza12 (noon to 1am), is popular for business lunches and *aperitivo*.

Wait and See   FASHION & ACCESSORIES

(Map p66; ☑ 02 7208 0195; www.waitandsee.it; Via Santa Marta 14; ⊘ 3.30-7.30pm Mon, 10.30am-7.30pm Tue-Sat; M Duomo, Missori) With collaborations with international brands and designers such as Missoni, Etro and Anna Molinari under her belt, Uberta Zambeletti launched her own collection in 2010. Quirky Wait and See indulges her eclectic tastes and showcases unfamiliar brands alongside items exclusively designed for the store, including super-fun Lana Bi striped pant suits and Lisa C pop-art earrings.

Borsalino   FASHION & ACCESSORIES

(Map p66; ☑ 02 8901 5436; www.borsalino.com; Galleria Vittorio Emanuele II 92; ⊘ 3-7pm Mon, 10am-7pm Tue-Sat; M Duomo) Iconic Alessandrian milliner Borsalino has worked with design greats such as Achille Castiglioni, who once designed a pudding-bowl bowler hat. This outlet in the Galleria Vittoria Emanuele II shopping arcade stocks seasonal favourites. The main showroom is at **Via Sant'Andrea 5** (Map p66; ☑ 02 7601 7072; www.borsalino.com; Via Sant'Andrea 5; ⊘ 10am-7pm Mon-Sat; M Montenapoleone).

La Rinascente   DEPARTMENT STORE

(Map p66; ☑ 02 8 85 21; www.rinascente.it; Piazza del Duomo; ⊘ 9.30am-9pm Mon-Thu & Sun, to 10pm Sat; M Duomo) Italy's most prestigious department store doesn't let the fashion capital down – come for Italian diffusion lines, French lovelies and LA upstarts. The basement also hides a 'Made in Italy' design supermarket and chic hairdresser Aldo Coppola is on the top floor. Take away edible souvenirs from the 7th-floor food market (and peer across to the Duomo while you're at it).

Moroni Gomma   HOMEWARES

(Map p66; ☑ 02 79 62 20; www.moronigomma.it; Corso Matteotti 14; ⊘ 3-7pm Mon, 10am-7pm Tue-Sun; M San Babila) Stocked with irresistible gadgets and great accessories for the bathroom, kitchen and office, this family-owned design store is a one-stop shop for funky souvenirs and Milanese keepsakes. Who but the strongest will be able to resist the cuckoo clock shaped like the Duomo, a retro telephone in pastel colours or classic Italian moccasins in nonslip rubber?

🔒 Brera & Parco Sempione

Il Cirmolo   VINTAGE

(Map p66; ☑ 02 805 28 85; http://ilcirmoloanti-quariato.it; Via Fiori Chiari 3; ⊘ 3-7pm Mon, 10am-7pm Tue-Sat, 11am-7pm Sun; M Lanza) Sourcing antiques and funky vintage artefacts since the 1960s, Il Cirmolo is a little treasure trove of joy. You can spend a whole morning here picking through period signage, weird anatomical models, lamps, friezes and even the odd car fender or two. Don't be surprised if you leave with a life-sized Betty Boop. Every home should have one.

Cavalli e Nastri   FASHION & ACCESSORIES

(Map p66; ☑ 02 7200 0449; www.cavallienastri.com; Via Brera 2; ⊘ 10.30am-7.30pm Mon-Sat, noon-7.30pm Sun; M Montenapoleone) This gorgeously colourful shop is known for its vintage clothes and accessories. It specialises in lovingly curated frocks, bags, jewellery and even shoes, sourced from early- and mid-20th-century Italian fashion houses, and priced accordingly. You'll find its **menswear store** (Map p62; ☑ 02 4945 1174; www.cavallienastri.com; Via Gian Giacomo Mora 3; ⊘ 10.30am-7.30pm Mon-Sat, noon-7.30pm Sun; 🚋 2, 14) at Via Mora 3.

Rigadritto   GIFTS & SOUVENIRS

(Map p66; ☑ 02 8058 2936; www.rigadritto.com; Via Brera 6; ⊘ 10.30am-7.30pm Mon-Sat, 11am-7pm Sun; 🚻; M Montenapoleone) Loads of little stickers, clips, pencils and decorated stationery fill this graphic, colourful space. Cat and dog T-shirts that turn humans into pets are delightful.

Triennale Bookstore   BOOKS

(Map p66; ☑ 02 8901 2117; Viale Emilio Alemagna 6; ⊘ 10.30am-8.30pm Tue-Sun; 🔊; M Cadorna) Designed by Studio Urquiola, the Triennale's bookshop stocks beautifully produced architecture, design, fashion and photography books as enthralling as the exhibitions themselves. In addition, you can pick up some excellent objects from some of the best names in contemporary Italian design.

🔒 Quadrilatero d'Oro & Porta Venezia

Pellini   JEWELLERY, ACCESSORIES

(Map p66; ☑ 02 7600 8084; www.pellini.it; Via Manzoni 20; ⊘ 9.30am-7.30pm Tue-Sat, 2.30-7.30pm Mon; M Montenapoleone) For unique, one-off costume jewellery pieces, bags and hair pieces, look no further than the boutique of Donatella Pellini, granddaughter of famous costume designer Emma Pellini. The Pellini women have been making their trademark resin jewellery for three generations, and their fanciful creations incorporating flowers, sand and fabric are surprisingly affordable.

Aspesi   FASHION & ACCESSORIES

(Map p66; ☑02 7602 2478; www.aspesi.com; Via Monte Napoleone 13; ⊗10am-7pm Mon-Sat; Ⓜ San Babila, Montenapoleone) The size of this Antonio Citterio–designed shop is a clue to just how much Italians love this label – Aspesi outerwear is de rigueur for mountain and lake weekends. The arty industrial sprawl is ironically at odds with an essentially practical marque: sportswear at its most understated.

Sermoneta   FASHION & ACCESSORIES

(Map p66; ☑02 7631 8303; www.sermonetagloves. com; Via della Spiga 31; ⊗9.30am-7pm Mon-Sat; Ⓜ Montenapoleone) A hole in the wall on chic Via della Spiga, Sermoneta's boutique store sells standards such as hand-stitched calfskin gloves alongside more unique styles made of pony skin or peccary hide.

Alessi   HOMEWARES

(Map p66; ☑02 79 57 26; www.alessi.com; Via Manzoni 14-16; ⊗10am-2pm & 3-7pm Mon, 10am-7pm Tue-Sat; Ⓜ Montenapoleone) Established in Omegna in 1921, Alessi has gone on to transform our homes with more than 22,000 crafted utensils, many of which have been designed by the world's leading architect-designers. Some of them now reside in the V&A in London and New York's MoMA, but you can find everything ever done at this flagship store.

🏠 **Corso Magenta & Sant'Ambrogio**

⭐ **Spazio Rossana Orlandi**   HOMEWARES

(Map p62; ☑02 467 44 71; www.rossanaorlandi. com; Via Matteo Bandello 14; ⊗10am-7pm Mon-Sat; Ⓜ Sant'Ambrogio) Installed in a former tie factory in the Magenta district, this iconic interior design studio is a challenge to find. Once inside, though, it's hard to leave the dream-like treasure trove stacked with vintage and contemporary limited-edition pieces from young and upcoming artists.

Galleria L'Affiche   ART

(Map p66; ☑02 8645 0124; www.affiche.it; Via Nirone 11; ⊗2.30-8pm Mon, 10am-8pm Tue-Sat; 🚌16) A treasure trove of vintage posters, fine-art prints, playbills and photographs, Galleria L'Affiche has a cult following and loyal stable of artists who entrust it with some of their finest work. Invest a few euros in some kitsch vintage postcards or spend several hundreds on a collectible; either way, you'll have hours of fun here.

Pupi Solari   CHILDREN'S CLOTHING

(Map p62; ☑02 46 33 25; www.pupisolari.it; Piazza Tommaseo 2; ⊗10am-7.30pm Tue-Sat; 🚻; Ⓜ Conciliazione, 🚌29, 30) Many Milanese from a certain kind of family will recall regular Pupi Solari visits for shoe fittings and picking out exquisitely decorated party dresses or tweed jackets just like daddy's. This flagship store, opened in 1978, and originally dedicated to trendsetting kidswear, has now expanded to include a women's department, a menswear branch (Host) and a small tearoom.

🏠 **Navigli & Porta Romana**

⭐ **NonostanteMarras**   FASHION & ACCESSORIES

(Map p62; ☑393 8934340; Via Cola di Rienzo 8; ⊗10am-7pm Mon-Sat, noon-7pm Sun; 🚌14) Brainchild of Sardinian fashion designer Antonio Marras, this eccentric concept store hidden in an ivy-draped courtyard is full of magpie artefacts, books and Marras' creative, colourful clothes. Come here to find something unique, have a cup of tea or simply to enjoy the magical space.

Mamu   MUSIC

(☑02 3668 6303; www.magazzinomusica.it; Via Francesco Soave 3; ⊗11am-7.30pm Tue-Fri, from 10am Sat & Sun; 📞; 🚌24) Taking a leaf out of the concept store book, Nicola Kitharatzis has created this classical music wonderland, a huge 350-sq-metre space where enthusiasts (professional and amateur) can come to buy music, drink coffee, repair and buy instruments, read essays and themed novels and, of course, listen to a program of weekly concerts and events. Check out the website for information on events.

Nipper   VINTAGE

(Map p62; ☑02 837 69 47; www.nipper.it; Via Ripa di Porta Ticinese 69; ⊗2-8pm Wed-Sat; Ⓜ Porta Genova) With a focus on vintage technology, Nipper feels like a mix between a period newsroom and a games arcade. The shop is

NAVIGLI MARKETS

Overlooking the Darsena, once the city's main port where the confluence of two canals linking the city with the Ticino and Po rivers, converged, is the Mercato Comunale (Map p62; Piazza XXIV Maggio; ☉8.30am-1pm & 4-7.30pm Tue-Sat, 8.30am-1pm Mon; ☐3, 9, 10, 14). Open Tuesday to Saturday, it is the city's main covered market, selling fresh fruit, vegetables and cheese. Northwest, Viale Gabriele d'Annunzio merges into Viale Papiniano, where the city's largest flea market (Map p62; Viale Papiniano; ☉7.30am-2pm Tue, to 6pm Sat; ⓂSant'Agostino) operates. It's at its best on Saturday morning.

On the last Sunday of the month, the city's most scenic market, the Mercatone dell'Antiquariato (Map p62; www.navigliogrande.mi.it; Naviglio Grande; ☉last Sun of month; ⓂPorta Genova), sets up along a 2km stretch of the Navigli Grande. With over 400 well-vetted antique and secondhand traders, it provides hours of treasure-hunting pleasure.

the brainchild of Alfonso and Chantal, who not only lovingly curate the collection, but also spend considerable time renovating bakelite radios, neon signs and American jukeboxes. Smaller pieces, like the model airplanes and desk clocks, make great gifts.

Mauro Leone SHOES
(Map p62; ☑02 5810 5041; www.mauroleone. com; Corso di Porta Ticinese 103; ☉3-7.30pm Mon, 10am-7.30pm Tue-Sat; ☐3) A firm favourite with fashionistas on a budget, Mauro Leone's handmade-in-Italy footwear offers style for between €50 and €80 per pair. Pick from a range that spans mid-heeled ankle boots in cobalt blue to ballerina pumps in Ferrari red with a peek of toe cleavage; it's no wonder Milanese love Mauro's shoes.

🏠 Porta Garibaldi & Isola

⭐ **Eataly** FOOD
(Map p62; ☑02 4949 7301; www.eataly.net/it_it/ negozi/milano-smeraldo/; Piazza XXV Aprile 10; ☉8.30am-midnight; 🛜🚻; ⓂMoscova, Garibaldi) A cult destination dedicated to Italian gastronomy, this 5000-sq-metre emporium showcases the best, locally sourced products over four huge floors, including small craft beer producers, specialist gelato from Làit and mozzarella from Miracolo a Milano. In addition, there are 19 different eateries, rooms for food workshops and a Michelin-starred restaurant, Alice. It's housed in the revamped Teatro Smeraldo so live music, readings and recitals are a part of the experience.

Zaini CHOCOLATE
(Map p62; ☑02 6949 14449; www.zainimilano. com; Via de Cristoforis 5; ☉7.30am-10pm Tue-Fri, to 8pm Mon, 9am-10pm Sat, 9am-7pm Sun; 🚻; ⓂGaribaldi) In 1913 Luigi Zaini opened his first chocolate factory and this sweet-filled store is located where it once stood. Although you're welcome to wrap your chops around the unctuous hot chocolate laced with rosebuds served at the bar, the big seller here is 'Emilia', a dark-chocolate delight named after the family nanny who tested many of the recipes in the family kitchen.

10 Corso Como FASHION & ACCESSORIES
(Map p62; ☑02 2900 2674; www.10corsocomo. com; Corso Como 10; ☉10.30am-7.30pm Fri-Tue, to 9pm Wed & Thu; ⓂGaribaldi) This might be the world's most hyped 'concept shop', but Carla Sozzani's selection of desirable things (Lanvin ballet flats, Alexander Girard wooden dolls, a demicouture frock by a designer you've not read about *yet*) makes 10 Corso Como a fun window-shopping experience. There's a bookshop upstairs with art and design titles, and a hyper-stylish bar and restaurant in the main atrium and picture-perfect courtyard.

Bargain hunters take note: the outlet store (Map p62; ☑02 2901 5130; www.10corso como.com; Via Tazzoli 3; ☉11am-7pm; ⓂGaribaldi) nearby sells last season's stock at a discount.

ℹ️ Information

EMERGENCY

Police Station (Questura; ☑02 6 22 61; http://questure.poliziadistato.it/milano; Via

DAY TRIPS FROM MILAN

MONZA

Known to many as the home of a classic European Formula One track where high-speed races have been held annually in September since 1950. Aside from the racetrack, which you can actually drive on most days in winter, history and architecture buffs will also be amply rewarded with an excursion to this elegant provincial town.

☆ Best Things to See/Do

☉ **Duomo** (www.duomomonza.it) The Gothic *duomo* (cathedral) contains the **Corona Ferrea** (Iron Crown), fashioned according to legend with one of the nails from the Crucifixion. Charlemagne, Frederick I (Barbarossa) and Napoleon had themselves crowned with it. It's on show in the chapel from Tuesday to Sunday.)

☉ **Museo e Tesoro del Duomo** (www.museo duomomonza.it) The cathedral museum contains one of the finest collections of religious art in Europe.

☉ **Villa Reale** (www.villarealedimonza.it) Villa Reale was modelled on Vienna's Schönbrunn Palace. It served as the summer home for Italian royalty, but was abandoned following the murder of Umberto I. Years of restoration have revived its glorious 3500-sq-metre frescoed, stuccoed and gilded interior.

🏃 **Autodromo Nazionale Monza** (www. monzanet.it) This is one of the most famous racetracks in the world. In addition to glitzy race days, the track hosts year-round events including cycle races, bike fests and even marathons. In winter, you can drive your own vehicle around it; or take a spin in a Ferrari (www.puresport.it).

☆ How to Get There

Ride the M1 metro line (red line) to Sesto 1st Maggio from where it's just one stop on the suburban rail network. Other frequent trains connect from Milan's Stazione Centrale (€2.20 to €9.90, 10 to 30 minutes).

PAVIA

Pavia is an important university city, with previous alumni including explorer Christopher Columbus, physicist Alessandro Volta and poet and revolutionary Ugo Foscolo. Pavia's historic centre preserves a clutch of worthwhile sights while, to the north of the city, is the fabulous Carthusian monastery Certosa di Pavia.

☆ Best Things to See/Eat

☉ **Certosa di Pavia** (www.certosadipavia. com) One of the Italian Renaissance's most notable buildings is the splendid Certosa di Pavia. Intended as a companion piece to Milan's Duomo, the final result, completed more than a century later, is a unique hybrid between late-Gothic and Renaissance styles.

☉ **Museo per la Storia dell'Università di Pavia** (http://musei.unipv.eu/msu) Pavia's university is one of the oldest in Europe. Within the stately campus a museum tells the story of the institute's long history and harbours relics like the preserved head of pioneering anatomist Antonio Scarpa.

✕ **Antica Osteria del Previ** (www.antica osteriadelprevi.com)The menu at this rustic *osteria* is well-rooted in the territory. Expect superlative risotto, soused trout, goose salami and Pavian-style salt cod.

☆ How to Get There

Pavia and the Certosa di Pavia are connected to Milan via the S13 suburban railway service, which stops at Porta Venezia and Stazione Centrale (€4 to €9, 25 to 40 minutes). Frequent buses link Pavia bus station and Certosa di Pavia (€1.80, 15 minutes, every 30 minutes).

OLTREPÒ PAVESE

To escape the urban bustle of Milan, consider hiring a car for the day and heading to Oltrepò Pavese. Oltrepò is the Tuscany of the north and riots broke out in the Middle Ages when Milanese markets were cut off from the region's wineries. These days the area is a picture of tranquillity; medieval villages perch on hilltops, and there's nary a tourist in sight anywhere.

☆ **Best Things to See/Do/Eat**

◉ **Montesegale** This fortified town dates from the 11th century and overlooks the almond and chestnut forests of the Ardivestra valley. It is dominated by a vast castle. During the summer it hosts cultural festivals and you can visit the modern-art collection by appointment.

◉ **Fortunago** One of Italy's most beautiful medieval villages and its 390 residents continue their centuries-old way of life. A path through the village, the Sentiero della Rocca, winds up to the church of San Giorgio from where you can enjoy a stunning panorama.

🍴 **Strada del Vino e dei Sapori dell' Oltrepò Pavese** (www.viniesaporioltrepo.it) Follow this food and wine route through 1100km of vineyards along the southern bank of the river Po. It is the largest wine region in Lombardy.

✖ **Ristorante Sasseo** (www.sasseo.com) The 18th-century home and restaurant of Elena Grigoroi and chef Giorgio Lutrini serves two affordable tasting menus informed by its garden produce and local culinary traditions. Dishes include braised guinea fowl ravioli, grilled char and Carmagnola rabbit with wild mustard leaves.

☆ **How to Get There**

It's necessary to hire a car to get around Oltrepò Pavese.

Escape the city and day-trip out to atmospheric Monza, Pavia and Oltrepò Pavese for car racing, historic splendour, and fine regional food and wine.

Fatebenefratelli 11; ⊙8am-2pm & 3-6pm Mon-Fri; Ⓜ Turati) Milan police headquarters.

MEDICAL SERVICES

American International Medical Centre
(AIMC; ☑ 02 5831 9808; www.aimclinic.it; Via Mercalli 11; ⊙9am-5.30pm Mon-Fri; Ⓜ Crocetta) Private, international health clinic with English-speaking staff.

Farmacia Essere Benessere (☑ 02 669 07 35; 2nd fl, Stazione Centrale; ⊙7am-10pm Mon-Thu, to 10.45pm Fri & Sat, 8am-10.45pm Sun; Ⓜ Centrale FS) Large, well-stocked pharmacy with late hours located on the 2nd floor of Stazione Centrale.

Lloyds Farmacia (☑ 02 498 4165; www.lloydsfarmacia.it; Piazza de Angeli 1; ⊙24hr; Ⓜ Angeli) Convenient, 24-hour pharmacy near the De Angeli metro stop.

Ospedale Maggiore Policlinico (☑24hr 02 5 50 31; www.policlinico.mi.it; Via Francesco Sforza 35; Ⓜ Crocetta) Milan's main hospital; offers an outpatient service.

Pronto Farmacia (☑ 800 801 185; ⊙24hr) Free phone helpline with details of open pharmacies in Lombardy. It also assists those in need of urgent prescriptions and general information. The toll-free number is only accessible on local lines.

TOURIST INFORMATION

Milan Tourist Office (Map p66; ☑ 02 8845 5555; www.turismo.milano.it; Galleria Vittorio Emanuele II 11-12; ⊙9am-7pm Mon-Fri, to 6pm Sat, 10am-6pm Sun; Ⓜ Duomo) Centrally located in the Galleria with helpful English-speaking staff and tonnes of maps and brochures.

Teatro alla Scala Box Office (☑ 02 7200 3744; Galleria del Sagrato, Piazza del Duomo; ⊙noon-6pm; Ⓜ Duomo) The central box office for La Scala is in the metro station under Piazza del Duomo.

USEFUL WEBSITES

Cenacolo Vinciano (www.cenacolovinciano.org) Booking for *The Last Supper,* which is handled by Vivatickets.

Hello Milano (www.hellomilano.it) English-language website with information on events, exhibitions and concerts.

Lonely Planet (www.lonelyplanet.com/milan) Destination information, hotel bookings, traveller forum and more.

Milan Tourism (www.turismo.milano.it) Milan's excellent official tourism portal.

Vivi Milano (www.vivimilano.it) Restaurant and cultural listings from *Corriere della Sera.*

❶ Getting There & Away

AIR

Aeroporto Malpensa (MXP; ☑ 02 23 23 23; www.milanomalpensa-airport.com; ᠗ Malpensa Express) Northern Italy's main international airport is about 50km northwest of Milan city. Services include car rental, banks, a VAT refund office and free wi-fi with the ViaMilano app.

Aeroporto Linate (LIN; ☑ 02 23 23 23; www.milanolinate-airport.com) Located 7km east of Milan city centre; domestic and European flights only.

BUS

Lampugnano Bus Terminal (Via Giulia Natta; Ⓜ Lampugnano) is 5km west of central Milan, and is located next to the Lampugnano metro stop, which you can arrive at on M1 (red line).

Autostradale (Map p66; ☑ 02 3008 9300; www.autostradale.it) is the main national operator. Tickets can be purchased at its offices or at the tourist office.

Eurolines (☑ 0861 199 1900; www.eurolines.it), a consortium of European coach companies, also operates services out of the terminal.

CAR & MOTORCYCLE

The A1, A4, A7 and A8 motorways converge on Milan from all directions.

Before entering the city centre inform yourself of the Area C, controlled traffic zone, which restricts both cars and bikes. Information on it and congestion charges can be found at www.muoversi.milano.it. Tickets can be bought online.

TRAIN

Milan is a major European rail hub. High-speed services arrive from across Italy, and from France, Switzerland and Germany. An overnight sleeper train also runs from Barcelona (Spain). For train timetables and fares, check out www.trenitalia.com, www.sbb.ch and www.bahn.de.

Stazione Centrale (www.milanocentrale.it; Piazza Duca d'Aosta; ⊙4am-1am; Ⓜ Centrale) Milan's Central Station is a masterpiece of rationalist architecture. International high-speed trains serve Switzerland and France, while national and regional trains serve Mantua, Venice, Turin, Rome and Naples.

Milano Porta Garibaldi (www.centostazioni.it; Piazza Sigmund Freud; Ⓜ Garibaldi) The main Centostazioni hub for national and commuter

---

❶ **TICKETS & PASSES**

There are several good money-saving passes available for public transport:

One-day ticket Valid for 24 hours; €4.50

Two-day ticket Valid for 48 hours; €8.25

Carnet of 10 tickets Valid for 90 minutes each; €13.80

Evening ticket Valid from 8pm until the end of service; €3

rail services. The bulk of trains to towns north and west of Milan depart from here, as well as high-speed services to Rome, Paris and Munich. You can also catch the Malpensa Express here. The station is served by two metro lines, M2 (green line) and M5 (lilac line).

ℹ Getting Around

TO/FROM THE AIRPORT

Aeroporto Malpensa Malpensa Express (☏ 02 7249 4949; www.malpensaexpress. it; one way €13) trains run to the city centre (50 minutes) every 30 minutes from 5.40am to 10.40pm; the **Malpensa Shuttle** (Map p62; ☏ 02 5858 3185; www.malpensashuttle.it; one way/return €10/16; Ⓜ Centrale) continues a limited services between 10.45pm and 5.30am. Taxis are a €90 set fare (50 minutes).

Aeroporto Linate Airport Bus Express (Map p62; ☏ 02 3391 0794; www.airportbusexpress. it; one way/return €5/9; Ⓜ Centrale) coaches run to Stazione Centrale (25 minutes) every 30 minutes between 5.30am and 10pm; ATM city bus 73 departs to Piazza San Babila (€1.50, 25 minutes) every 10 minutes between 5.35am and 12.35am. Taxis cost between €20 and €30, depending on your destination.

BICYCLE

BikeMi (☏ 02 4860 7607; www.bikemi.it; 🚲) is a public bicycle system with stops all over town.

Get passes online or by dropping into the **ATM Info Point** (p85) at the Duomo, Cadorna or Centrale metro stops.

CAR & MOTORCYCLE

It simply isn't worth having a car in Milan. Many streets have restricted access and parking is a nightmare.

A congestion zone, Area C, is now enforced in the city centre between 7.30am and 7.30pm Monday to Wednesday and Friday (to 6pm on Thursday). To enter you need to buy a daily pass costing €5. You can purchase it online at www. muoversi.milano.it.

In the centre, street parking costs between €1.50 and €3 per hour. Underground car parks charge between €25 and €40 for 24 hours.

PUBLIC TRANSPORT

ATM (Azienda Trasporti Milano; ☏ 02 4860 7607; www.atm.it) runs Milan's public transport network, including trams, buses and the metro. Services operate between 5.40am and 12.20am (from 6.15am on Sunday). Night services run every half-hour between 12.20am and 5.40am, when the metro is closed.

A ticket costs €1.50 for all modes of transport and is valid for one metro ride or 90 minutes on trams and buses. It must be validated when boarding. Tickets are sold at electronic ticket machines in the station, or at tobacconists and newsstands.

Route maps are available from ATM info points, or download the IATM app.

Lake Maggiore & Around

Best Places to Eat

➜ Casabella (p95)

➜ Il Sole (p102)

➜ Ristorante Milano (p96)

➜ Ristorante Locanda Locarnese (p113)

➜ Cucchiaio di Legno (p109)

➜ Grotto Sant'Anna (p100)

Best Gardens

➜ Isola Bella (p93)

➜ Isola Madre (p94)

➜ Villa Taranto (p95)

➜ Villa della Porta Bozzolo (p101)

➜ Giardino Botanico Alpinia (p90)

Why Go?

Italy's second-largest lake, Maggiore is one of Europe's more graceful corners. Arrayed around the lake shore are a series of pretty towns (Stresa, Verbania, Cannobio and, on the Swiss side of the border, Locarno) and these serve as gateways to gorgeous Maggiore islands. Behind the towns, wooded hillsides rise, strewn with decadent villas, lush botanical gardens and even the occasional castle.

Further still from the lakeshore, but not as far as you might think, the snow-capped peaks of Switzerland provide the perfect backdrop, and idyllic vantage points over the lake are many, from the breakfast terrace of your lakeside hotel to the eyries reached by cable car from Locarno, Laveno and Stresa. And fabulous detours await, whether into the high valleys from the northern end of the lake or to Orta San Giulio to the southwest, one of the region's most beguiling villages.

Road Distances (km)

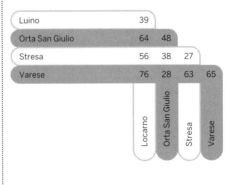

	Locarno	Orta San Giulio	Stresa	Varese
Luino	39			
Orta San Giulio	64	48		
Stresa	56	38	27	
Varese	76	28	63	65

If Lake Maggiore is your first impression of Italy, you're in for a treat. By train or by road, travellers traversing the Alps from Switzerland at the Simplon Pass wind down from the mountains and sidle up to this enormous finger of blue beauty. The star attractions are the Borromean Islands, which, like a fleet of fine vessels, lie at anchor at the Borromean Gulf's (Golfo Borromeo) entrance, an incursion of water between the lake's two main towns, Stresa and Verbania.

More than its siblings to the east, Lake Como and Lake Garda, Lake Maggiore has retained a belle époque air. All three have mesmerised foreign visitors down the centuries but Lake Maggiore became a popular tourist destination in the late 19th century after the Simplon Pass was opened.

ⓘ Getting There & Away

BOAT

Navigazione Lago Maggiore (☑ 800 551801; www.navigazionelaghi.it) Operates passenger ferries and hydrofoils around the lake; its ticket booths are next to embarkation quays. Services include those connecting Stresa with Arona (€6.20, 40 minutes), Angera (€6.20, 35 minutes) and Verbania Pallanza (often just called Pallanza; €5, 35 minutes). Day passes include a ticket linking Stresa with Isola Superiore, Isola Bella and Isola Madre (€16.90). Services are drastically reduced in autumn and winter.

The full Como-to-Colico run happens only two to four times a day (and only on the high-speed ferry) from November to March. There's still service from Cernobbio and Moltrasio to Como every 40 minutes from 7am to 8pm.

The only car ferry connecting the western and eastern shores sails between Verbania Intra (often just called Intra) and Laveno. Car ferries run every 20 to 30 minutes; one-way transport costs from €8 to €13 for a car and driver; €5 for a bicycle and cyclist.

BUS

SAF (☑ 0323 55 21 72; www.safduemila.com) The daily Verbania Intra–to–Milan service links Stresa with Arona (€2.70, 20 minutes), Verbania Pallanza (€2.70, 20 minutes), Verbania Intra (€2.70, 25 minutes) and Milan (€10.50, 1½ hours).

SAF also runs the Alibus, a pre-booked shuttle bus linking the same towns with Malpensa airport (€15).

CAR

The SS33 hugs the western shore of Lake Maggiore, intersecting with the SS34 just north of Baveno. On the eastern shore the SP69 travels up most of the lakeside, though it morphs into the SS394 around Luino. A key gateway to the lake is Angera, 68km northwest of Milan (via the E62 and the SS33) and 26km west of Varese (via the SP36 and SP69).

TRAIN

Trains run the length of the east bank and up the west bank to Stresa before continuing on to Domodossola. Trains from both Milano Centrale and Porta Garibaldi run regularly to Arona (€6.10, one hour) and Stresa (€8.60, 70 minutes). FNM trains from Milan (Cadorna station) arrive in Laveno via Varese.

LAKE MAGGIORE WEST BANK

Stresa

☑ 0323 / POP 5000

Perhaps more than any other Lake Maggiore town, Stresa, with a ringside view of sunrise over the lake, captures the lake's prevailing air of elegance and bygone decadence. This is most evident in the string of belle époque confections along the waterfront, a legacy of the town's easy access from Milan, which has made it a favourite for artists and writers since the late 19th century.

People still stream into Stresa to meander along its promenade and explore the little hive of cobbled streets in its old centre (especially pleasant for a coffee break is shady Piazza Cadorna).

⊙ Sights

Monte Mottarone   MOUNTAIN
The cable-car trip up Monte Mottarone (1492m) from the northwestern end of Stresa offers pretty views over Lake Maggiore, including Isola Bella and Isola Superiore. From the summit on a clear day you can see Lake Orta, several other smaller lakes and Monte Rosa, on the Alpine border with Switzerland.

The 20-minute cable-car journey on the **Funivia Stresa–Mottarone** (☑ 0323 3 02 95; www.stresa-mottarone.it; Piazzale della Funivia; return adult/reduced €19/12, to Alpino station €13.50/8.50; ⊙ 9.30am-5.40pm

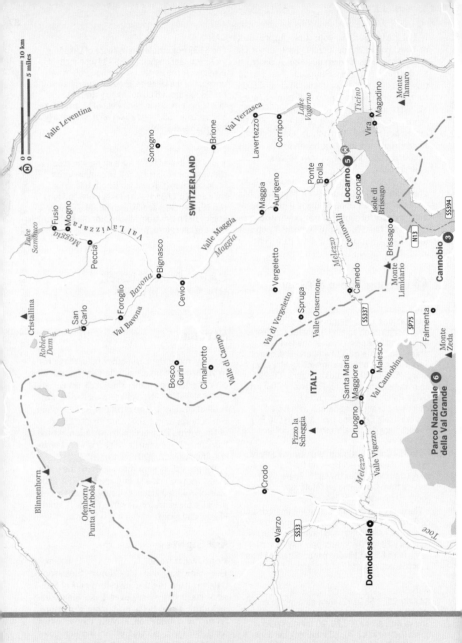

Lake Maggiore & Around Highlights

❶ Borromean Islands (p93)
Spending the day wandering lavish villas and colourful gardens, stopping for lunch at a picturesque island fishing village.

❷ Orta San Giulio (p108) Exploring a tiny island, lunching on a lakeside piazza and climbing the sacred mountain for captivating scenery.

❸ Cannobio (p97)
Taking a serene riverside walk, followed by a meal in one of Maggiore's most charming villages.

❹ Varese (p103)
Seeing some of the region's best art exhibitions, then visiting Lombard ruins

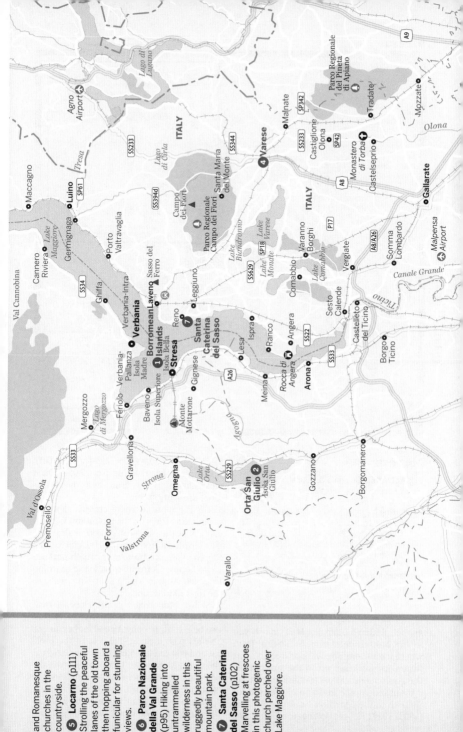

and Romanesque churches in the countryside.

5 Locarno (p111)
Strolling the peaceful lanes of the old town then hopping aboard a funicular for stunning views.

6 Parco Nazionale della Val Grande
(p95) Hiking into untrammelled wilderness in this ruggedly beautiful mountain park.

7 Santa Caterina del Sasso (p102)
Marvelling at frescoes in this photogenic church perched over Lake Maggiore.

Agno Airport

Maccagno

Lago di Lugano

Parco Regionale del Pineta di Apiano

A9

Mozzate

Tradate

SP342

Luino

SP61

Tresa

ITALY

Malnate

SS233

Olona

Germignaga

Porto Valtravaglia

SS233

Lago di Ghirla

SS394d

Santa Maria del Monte

Castiglione Olona

SP42

Monastero di Torba

Gallarate

Cannero Riviera

Lake Maggiore

SS34

Ghiffa

Campo dei Fiori

Parco Regionale Campo dei Fiori

SS344

4 Varese

A8

Castelseprio

Val Cannobina

Verbania-Intra

Sasso del Ferro

ITALY

Lake Biandronno

Lake Varese

Varano Borghi

P17

Vergiate

A8/A26

Malpensa Airport

Somma Lombardo

Verbania **Verbania**

Borromean Laveno

Islands

1

Reno

7 Santa Caterina del Sasso

Leggiuno

SP18

SS629

Lake Monate

Comabbio

Lake Comabbio

Canale Grande

Ticino

Mergozzo

Lago di Mergozzo

Verbania-Pallanza

Isola Madre

Stresa

Isola Bella

Isola Superiore

Gignese

Lesa

Ispra

Ranco

Sesto Calende

Castelletto del Ticino

Ferriolo

Baveno

A26

Meina

Angera

SS22

Borgo Ticino

Gravellona

SS33

Strona

Monte Mottarone

Agogna

Lesa

Rocca di Angera

Arona

SS33

Premosello

Val d'Ossola

Forno

Valstrona

Omegna

SS229

Orta San Giulio 2

Isola San Giulio

Lake Orta

Gozzano

Borgomanero

Varallo

Borgomanero

Stresa

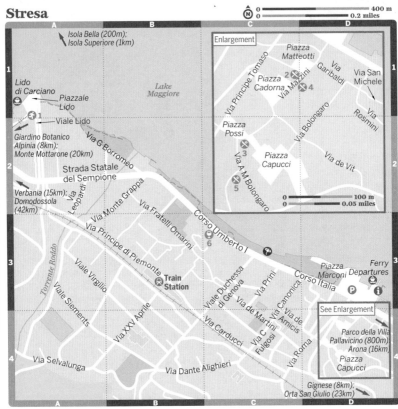

Stresa

🟢 Activities, Courses & Tours
1 Funivia Stresa–Mottarone...............A1

✖ Eating
2 La Botte...C1
3 Osteria degli Amici.........................C2
4 Piemontese....................................D1
5 Ristorante Il Vicoletto....................C2

🟡 Drinking & Nightlife
6 Grand Hotel des Iles
  Borromées...................................C3

Apr-Oct, 8.10am-5.20pm Nov-Mar) takes you to the Mottarone station at 1385m, from where it's a 15-minute walk or free chairlift (when it's working) up to the summit. At the Alpino midstation (803m) more than a thousand Alpine and sub-Alpine species flourish in the Giardino Botanico Alpinia (📞 0323 92 71 73; Viale Mottino 26; adult/reduced

€4/3.50; ☺ 9.30am-6pm mid-Apr–early-Oct), a botanic garden dating from 1934. On a clear day, the views from here over Maggiore are truly special.

For the more active, there are plenty of good hiking trails on the mountain. Walkers can ask at the cable-car station or the tourist office for a free copy of *Trekking on the Slopes of Mount Mottarone*, which outlines a two-hour walk from Stresa to the Giardino Botanico Alpinia and a four-hour walk to the top of Mottarone.

Skiing Mottarone's gentle slopes (www.mottaroneski.it) is limited to five green and two blue runs, making it good for beginners. The ski pass includes the cost of the cable car and you can hire gear from the station at the top of Mottarone. The ski pass costs €17 per adult per day (€24 on weekends) while equipment costs extra.

Also possible from the summit is Alpyland (📞 0323 199 10 07; www.alpyland.com;

adult/child €5/4; ⊙10am-5pm Mon-Fri, to 6pm Sat & Sun Apr-Oct, weekends only Dec-Mar, closed Nov; 📷), a 1200m-long bobsled descent with adjustable speeds that makes it ideal for families.

🎊 Festivals & Events

Stresa Festival   MUSIC
(📞0323 3 10 95; www.stresafestival.eu; ⊙mid-Jul–early Sep) A prestigious festival that dates back more than half a century, with classical concerts, as well as midsummer jazz performances.

🍴 Eating & Drinking

★Ristorante Il Vicoletto   RISTORANTE €€
(📞0323 93 21 02; www.ristorantevicoletto.com; Vicolo del Pocivo 3; meals €30-45; ⊙noon-2pm & 6.30-10pm Fri-Wed) One of the most popular restaurants in Stresa, Il Vicoletto has a delectable regional menu including lake trout, wild asparagus, and traditional risotto with radicchio and Taleggio (cheese). The dining room is modestly elegant with bottle-lined dressers and linen-covered tables, while the local clientele speaks volumes in this tourist town. Reservations essential.

Osteria degli Amici   ITALIAN €€
(📞0323 3 04 53; Via Anna Maria Bolongaro 33; pizzas €5-10, meals €30-35; ⊙noon-2.30pm & 7-11pm Thu-Tue, closed Jan) You may need to queue here, but it's worth it to dine under vines on one of Stresa's prettiest terraces in the centre of town, just off pedestrianised Via Mazzini. If it's a little cool for sitting outside, the airy dining room is an equally fine setting for enjoying risotto with saffron, grilled *branzino* (sea bass), and myriad other selections, including pizzas.

La Botte   TRATTORIA €€
(📞0323 3 04 62; Via Mazzini 6; meals €25-35; ⊙noon-2.05pm & 6.50-10pm Thu-Tue) Regional dishes are at the heart of this tiny trattoria's business, so expect grilled lake fish, boar fillets and plenty of polenta (the version with sauteed mushrooms is superb). The decor is old-style *osteria* (casual tavern or eatery presided over by a host) with dark timber furniture and decades of accumulated knick-knacks.

Find it just back from the lake front in the depths of the old town.

LAKE MAGGIORE EXPRESS

The Lago Maggiore Express (📞091 756 04 00; www.lagomaggioreexpress.com; adult/child 1-day tour €34/17, 2-day tour €44/22) is a picturesque day trip you can do under your own steam. It includes train travel from Arona or Stresa to Domodossola, from where you get the charming Centovalli (Hundred Valleys) train to Locarno in Switzerland, before hopping on a ferry back to Stresa. Tickets are available from the Navigazione Lago Maggiore (p87) ticket booths at each port.

The two-day version is better value if you have the time.

Piemontese   PIEDMONTESE €€€
(📞0323 3 02 35; www.ristorantepiemontese.com; Via Mazzini 25; meals €40-55; ⊙noon-3pm & 7-11pm Tue-Sun) The name gives a huge clue as to the focus of this refined dining room. Regional delights include gnocchi with gorgonzola and hazelnuts, and baked perch with black venere rice. The Lake Menu (€39) features carp, trout, perch and pike, while the *menù degustazione* (€55) takes things up a notch with a decadent spread of *lumache* (snails), *capesante* (scallops) and foie gras.

Grand Hotel des Iles Borromées   COCKTAIL BAR
(📞0323 93 89 38; www.borromees.it; Corso Umberto I 67; ⊙6pm-late) Following his WWI stint on the Italian front, Ernest Hemingway checked in here to nurse his battle scars, and to write *A Farewell to Arms*. The passionate antiwar novel featured this sumptuous hotel. You might baulk at room prices (guests have included Princess Margaret and the Vanderbilts) but you can still slug back a Manhattan on the terraces with cinematic views.

ℹ️ Information

Stresa Tourist Office (📞0323 3 13 08; www.stresaturismo.it; Piazza Marconi 16; ⊙10am-12.30pm & 3-6.30pm summer, closed Sat afternoon & Sun winter) Has brochures and tips on activities in the area. Located at the ferry dock.

ⓘ Getting There & Away

BOAT

Boats depart from the **ferry dock** on Piazza Marconi and connect Stresa with Arona (one way adult/child €6.20/3.10, 40 minutes, seven daily), Angera (€6.20/3.10, 35 minutes, six daily), Baveno (€3.90/2, 20 minutes, every half hour) and Verbania Pallanza (€5/2.50, 35 minutes, every 30 to 60 minutes).

If you're just visiting the Borromean Islands, private taxi boats offer speedy transfers every half hour between **Lido di Carciano** and the islands (2-island/3-island return ticket €10/13).

BUS

Buses leave from Piazza Marconi on the waterfront at Stresa for destinations around the lake and elsewhere, including Milan, Novara and Lake Orta. The daily Verbania–Milan intercity bus service operated by **SAF** (p87) links Stresa with Arona (€2.70, 20 minutes), Verbania Pallanza (€2.70, 20 minutes) and Verbania Intra (€2.70, 25 minutes) and Milan (€10.50, 1½ hours).

CAR

Coming from Milan, take the A8/A26 motorway, following signs for Gravellona Toce. To follow the lake road, exit the autostrada at Castelletto Ticino. From there, the SS33 hugs the shore to Arona, Stresa and Baveno. From Feriolo, the SS34 continues the lakeside run to the Swiss border (where it becomes route 13 to Locarno and beyond).

Parking in Stresa can require patience and is mostly metered. Free spaces can be found near the train station, and the streets further uphill from the lake.

TRAIN

Stresa is 1¼ hours from Milan (from €8.60; trains every 30 to 90 minutes) on the Domodossola–Milan train line. Domodossola (€4.15 to €9.90), 30 minutes northwest, is on the Swiss

border, from where seven trains daily head to Brig – with four trains continuing on to Geneva.

Arona

📞 0322 / POP 14,200

Some 20km south of Stresa, Arona is a lively lakeside town whose lanes are lined with shops and eateries, and its picturesque piazzas draw a wide cross section of Maggiorean society in the evenings. Arona was the birthplace of the son of the Count of Arona and Margherita de' Medici, who would go on to be canonised San Carlo Borromeo (1538–84). Arona's biggest attraction is a massive statue of San Carlo that looms on a hilltop north of town.

◉ Sights

Sacro Monte di San Carlo   LANDMARK
(📞 0322 24 96 69; www.statuasancarlo.it; Piazza San Carlo; €6, to exterior only €3.50; ⏰ 9am-12.30pm & 2.30-6.15pm mid-Mar–mid-Oct, to 4.30pm Sun Nov-Dec and Mar 1-15, closed Jan & Feb) When Milan's superstar bishop San Carlo Borromeo (1538–84) was declared a saint in 1610, his cousin Federico ordered the creation of a *sacro monte* in his memory, featuring 15 chapels lining a path to a church. The church and three of those chapels were built, along with a special extra: a hollow 35m bronze-and-copper statue of the saint. Commonly known as the Sancarlone (Big St Charles) you can climb up inside it to discover spectacular views through the giant's eyes (and even ears).

It's a bit of a vertiginous ascent (up a long ladder-like staircase) and children under six years old are not allowed up. There's a small garden surrounding the statue, with panels explaining key episodes of Borromeo's life.

ZIPLINING ABOVE LAKE MAGGIORE

For a pure adrenaline rush, take a high-speed ride on the **Lago Maggiore Zipline** (📞 333 9467147; www.lagomaggiorezipline.it; Via Giulio Pastore, Alpe Segletta; one ride €39, two-person ride €70; ⏰ 10am-9pm May-Aug, to 6pm Sep & Oct, 11am-4pm Sat & Sun Nov-Mar, 11am-6pm Apr). The line, which runs for 1850m, gives grand views over the lake, though it's over all too quickly as you make the descent in some 90 seconds or so, reaching speeds at up to 120km/h. You can go down solo or in pairs.

Call ahead to reserve a space or book online, with a small added commission fee. It's located about 22km from Intra (a 40-minute drive). Check the website for driving instructions. You can also arrange horse riding, rock climbing, mountain biking and other adventures here (all by advance booking). Or you can simply enjoy the view at a more tranquil speed (sitting down) while having a meal at the on-site restaurant.

To reach this hill, with nice views over the south end of Lake Maggiore and across to the Rocca di Angera, walk or drive about 2km west from Piazza del Popolo.

🍴 Eating

Taverna del Pittore　　　　RISTORANTE €€€
(☑ 0322 24 33 66; www.ristorantetavernadel-pittore.it; Piazza del Popolo 39; meals €50-70; ⊙ noon-2.30pm & 7.30-10pm Fri-Wed) What is possibly Largo Maggiore's most romantic restaurant has a waterside terrace and views of the illuminated Rocca di Angera fortress (p103) at night. The refined food is no less fabulous, with squid, duck and octopus transformed into exquisitely arranged dishes featuring ravioli, broth, risotto and gnocchi.

Despite the fine-dining quality, the atmosphere is charmingly relaxed and the staff is friendly and knowledgeable.

ℹ Information

Arona Tourist Office (☑ 0322 24 36 01; www.comune.arona.no.it; Piazzale Duca d'Aosta; ⊙ 9.30am-12.30pm & 3.30-6.30pm) Located opposite the train station, near the waterfront.

Borromean Islands

Forming Lake Maggiore's most beautiful corner, the Borromean Islands (Isole Borromee) can be reached from various points around the lake, but Stresa and Verbania offer the best access to them. Three of the four islands – Bella, Madre and Superiore (aka Isola dei Pescatori) – can all be visited, but tiny San Giovanni remains off limits. The Borromeo family, a noble family from Milan, has owned these islands (they own six of the lake's nine islands) since the 17th century.

Isola Bella

The grandest and busiest of the islands – the crowds can get a little overwhelming on weekends – Isola Bella is the centrepiece of the Borromeo Lake Maggiore empire. The island took the name of Carlo III's wife, the bella Isabella, in the 17th century, when its centrepiece, Palazzo Borromeo, was built for the Borromeo family.

It's difficult to imagine that prior to its construction the island was little more than

ℹ VISITING THE ISLANDS

Ferries chug to the Borromean Islands from **Stresa** (the main dock), **Lido di Carciano** (by the Stresa–Mottarone cable car) and Verbania Pallanza. Services connect them all but more regular half-hourly runs connect Stresa, Isola Bella, Isola Superiore and Baveno. If you plan to visit all three islands from either Verbania or Stresa, you're better off buying a day ticket for €17 – it's a round-trip ticket that includes stops in Verbania, Stresa, Baveno and the three islands.

Smaller, slightly cheaper taxi boats (around €15) run between Stresa and the islands; these depart from private docks along the Stresa waterfront.

a chunk of rock inhabited by a handful of hardy fishing families. To this day, only 16 people live year-round on the island, but in summer the place looks like a scene from the Normandy landings of 1944, with countless vessels ferrying battalions of visitors to and fro. Construction of the villa and gardens was thought out in such a way that the island has the vague appearance of a vessel, with the villa at the prow and the gardens at the rear.

⊙ Sights

Palazzo Borromeo　　　　　　PALACE
(☑ 0323 3 05 56; www.isoleborromee.it; Isola Bella; adult/child €16/8.50, incl Palazzo Madre €21/10; ⊙ 9am-5.30pm mid-Mar–mid-Oct) Presiding over 10 tiers of spectacular terraced gardens roamed by peacocks, this baroque palace is arguably Lake Maggiore's finest building. Wandering the grounds and 1st floors reveals guestrooms, studies and reception halls. Particularly striking rooms include the Sala di Napoleone, where the emperor Napoleon stayed with his wife in 1797; the grand Sala da Ballo (Ballroom); the ornate Sala del Trono (Throne Room); and the Sala delle Regine (Queen's Room). Paintings from the 130-strong Borromeo collection hang all around.

Highlights of the art works are pieces by several old masters, including Rubens, Titian, Paolo Veronese, Andrea Mantegna, Van Dyck and José Ribera (Spagnoletto). You'll also find Flemish tapestries, sculptures by Antonio Canova and – in the Salone Grande – a

200-year-old wooden model of the palace and island.

Below the ground floor, a 3000-year-old fossilised boat is displayed in the cool palace grottoes, which are studded with pink marble, lava stone and pebbles from the lake bed. White peacocks, whose fanned feathers resemble bridal gowns, strut about the gardens, which are considered one of the finest examples of baroque Italian landscaping.

In summer, the family that owns Palazzo Borromeo moves in and occupies the 2nd and 3rd floors (off-limits to visitors), totalling a mere 50-odd rooms.

You can also purchase a combined ticket to Palazzo Madre on nearby Isola Madre, and Rocca di Angera (p103) in Angera.

✖ Eating

Elvezia   ITALIAN €€
(☎ 0323 3 00 43; Via de Martini 35; meals €32-42; ⊙ 9am-6pm Tue-Sun Mar-Oct, Fri-Sun only Nov-Feb) With its rambling rooms, fish-themed portico and upstairs pergola and balcony dining area, this is the best spot on Isola Bella for home cooking. Dishes include ricotta-stuffed ravioli, various risottos and lake fish such as *coregone alle mandorle* (lake whitefish in almonds).

Elvezia also opens on Saturday nights (from 7pm) during the summer. Reservations essential.

Isola Madre

The largest island in the Borromean archipelago, Isola Madre covers 7.8 hectares entirely devoted to a delightful botanical garden – one of the oldest in Italy. The island's benign microclimate favours the growth of wisteria, rare sub-tropical plants, and exotic flowers and trees, the oldest being the enormous Kashmir cypress, which is over 200 years old.

◉ Sights

Isola Madre   ISLAND
(☎ 0323 3 05 56; www.isoleborromee.it; adult/child €13/6.50, incl Palazzo Borromeo €21/10; ⊙ 9am-5.30pm mid-Mar–mid-Oct) The closest of the three islands to Verbania, Isola Madre is entirely taken up by the Palazzo Madre and the lovely gardens that surround it. The 16th- to

18th-century Palazzo Madre is a wonderfully decadent structure crammed full of all manner of antique furnishings and adornments. Highlights include Countess Borromeo's doll collection, a neoclassical puppet theatre designed by a scenographer from Milan's La Scala, and a 'horror' theatre with a cast of devilish marionettes.

Outside the palazzo, the English-style botanic gardens are dazzling with colourful azaleas, rhododendrons, camellias, eucalypts, banana trees, hibiscus, fruit orchards, an olive grove and much more. In fact, the Isola Madre gardens are even more lavish than those of Palazzo Borromeo on Isola Bella. Exotic birdlife, including white peacocks and golden pheasants, roam the grounds.

A combined ticket also covers admission to Palazzo Borromeo (p93) on Isola Bella.

Isola Superiore (Isola dei Pescatori)

Tiny 'Fishermen's Island,' with a permanent population of around 50, retains much of its original fishing-village atmosphere. Apart from an 11th-century apse and a 16th-century fresco in the charming Chiesa di San Vittore, there are no real sights. Many visitors make it their port of call for lunch, but stay overnight and you'll fall in love with the place. Restaurants cluster around the boat landing, all serving grilled fish fresh from the lake (from around €15). On some days in spring and autumn, heavy rain can lift the lake's level a fraction, causing minor flooding on the island. The houses are built with this in mind, with entrance stairs facing internal streets and they're high enough to prevent water entering the houses.

✖ Eating

La Pescheria   ITALIAN €€
(☎ 0323 93 38 08; www.la-pescheria.it; Via Lungolago 6; meals €30-40; ⊙ noon-2pm & 6-9pm Feb-Nov) Choose between a vine-covered terrace overlooking the lake and the terracotta-hued interior dining rooms at this friendly restaurant. Start things off with *misto di filetti di lago* (a combination of lake fish) and follow it up with *ravioli di pesce di lago con zafferano e pistacchi* (lake fish ravioli with saffron and pistachio nuts).

★ **Casabella** RISTORANTE €€€
(☑ 0323 3 34 71; www.isola-pescatori.it; Via del Marinaio 1; meals €30-50, five-course tasting menu €55; ☺ noon-2pm & 6-8.30pm Feb-Nov) The setting is bewitching – right by the shore – and the food is acclaimed. The admirably short menu might feature home-smoked beef with spinach, blanched squid with ricotta or perfectly cooked lake fish. Leave room for dessert; the pear cake with chocolate fondant is faultless.

If you don't want to leave after dinner (likely) there are two snug **bedrooms** on-site (doubles from €110).

Verbania

☑ 0323 / POP 30,800

Verbania, the biggest town on Lake Maggiore, makes a good base for exploring the west bank. The town is strung out along the lakeshore and consists of three districts. Verbania Pallanza, the middle chunk, is the most interesting of the three, with a pretty waterfront and a ferry stop.

Running north from Pallanza, the waterfront road, Via Vittorio Veneto, has a jogging and cycling path that follows the lakefront, which is especially pretty around the little port and the nearby Isolino San Giovanni, a wooded islet just offshore. It connects Pallanza with Villa Taranto and Verbania Intra, which has handy car ferries to Laveno on the lake's east bank.

◉ Sights

Villa Taranto GARDENS
(☑ 0323 55 66 67; www.villataranto.it; Via Vittorio Veneto 111, Verbania Pallanza; adult/reduced €10/5.50; ☺ 8.30am-6.30pm Apr-Sep, 9am-4pm Oct; ℗) The grounds of this late-19th-century villa are one of Lake Maggiore's highlights. A Scottish captain, Neil McEacharn, bought the Normandy-style villa from the Savoy family in 1931 after spotting an ad in the *Times*. He planted some 20,000 plant species over 30 years, and today it's considered one of Europe's finest botanic gardens. Even the main entrance path is a grand affair, bordered by lawns and a cornucopia of

---

OFF THE BEATEN TRACK

PARCO NAZIONALE DELLA VAL GRANDE

A wooded wilderness set amid a little-visited stretch of the Italian Alps, the Parco Nazionale della Val Grande (☑ 0324 8 75 40; www.parcovalgrande.it) is far removed from the more domesticated beauty of the lakes only a short distance away (Verbania is 10km from its southeastern edge). Declared a park in 1992, it covers 150 sq km and is claimed to be Italy's largest wilderness area.

Never more than sparsely inhabited by farmers in search of summer pastures for cattle or loggers, the area has been largely free of human inhabitants since the 1940s. The last of them were partisans who fought the Germans in the latter half of WWII. (In June to October 1944, 5000 German troops moved against 500 partisans holed up in the Val Grande, killing 300 of them and destroying farms across the area.)

The lower Val Grande is dominated by chestnut trees, which give way to beech trees further up. Milan's Duomo had a special licence to log here from the 14th century. Wood was needed in the Candoglia marble quarries, to float the marble on canals to Milan and for use in scaffolding. The absence of humans in the park today has allowed wildlife to proliferate. Most numerous is the chamois, and peregrine falcons and golden eagles can be spotted. Wolves are also believed to be present, although seeing one is highly unlikely.

Information centres are located in four villages surrounding the park. The handiest for those staying around Lake Maggiore are Intragna and Cicogna (both near Verbania), the latter actually inside the park boundary. They tend to open only in spring and summer – call the main park number for their opening hours.

Walks into the park will bring you to some majestic locations but as a rule should be done with local guides. Extremely basic, unstaffed refuges where you can sleep (if you have your own sleeping bag) dot the park. They come with a stove and wood for heating, and little else. Otherwise, there are *sentieri natura* (nature paths). Routes are available at the information centres and on the park's website.

colourful flowers. It's a short walk from the Villa Taranto ferry stop.

What you'll see changes with the seasons: the winding dahlia path shows off blooms from more than 300 species from June to October; in April and May, the dogwood and related flowers run riot. In the hothouses you can admire extraordinary equatorial water lilies.

The villa itself is not open to the public as it houses the offices of the local prefecture.

Museo del Paesaggio
MUSEUM

(📞 0323 55 66 21; www.museodelpaesaggio.it; Via Ruga 44, Verbania Pallanza; €5; ⊙10am-6pm Tue-Fri, to 7pm Sat, Sun & holidays) Set in a stately 17th-century palazzo tucked down one of Pallanza's back lanes, this museum houses an exquisite collection of works by the sculptor Paolo Troubetzkoy. Though not well known today, Troubetzkoy, who was born nearby in 1866, was celebrated as one of the great artists of the 20th century, and he created vivid works of luminaries such as Toscanini, Tolstoy and George Bernard Shaw among others.

Villa Giulia
HISTORIC SITE

(📞 339 2124340; www.barvillagiulia.it; Corso Zanitello 8, Verbania Pallanza; ⊙grounds 9am-7pm) Theatrical Villa Giulia, with its towering lemon-yellow facade and colonnaded balconies, has a photogenic setting on the lakeside. Originally the home of Bernardino Branca (who invented one of Italy's most famous liqueurs, Fernet), today the villa hosts periodic exhibitions; it also has a res-taurant and bar (meals around €30) with seating overlooking the lake.

🎉 Festivals & Events

Mostra Nazionale della Camelia
FLOWERS

(www.camelieinmostra.it) Twice a year, in spring and winter, a splash of extra floral colour comes to Verbania Pallanza with a display of more than 200 varieties of camellia in the gardens of Villa Giulia or Villa Rusco-ni-Clerici (📞 335 6011486; www.villarusconiclerici.it; Via Vittorio Veneto) or both. Dates vary, but you are looking at a weekend in late March or early December.

Settimana del Tulipano
FLOWERS

In the last week of April, tens of thousands of tulips erupt in magnificent multicoloured bloom in Verbania's Villa Taranto.

🍴 Eating

⭐ Osteria Castello
OSTERIA €€

(📞 0323 51 65 79; www.osteriacastello.com; Piazza Castello 9, Verbania Intra; meals €25-35; ⊙11am-2.30pm & 6pm-midnight Mon-Sat) Its 100-plus years of history run like a rich seam through this enchanting osteria, where archive photos and bottles line the walls. Order a glass of wine from the vast selection; sample some ham; or tuck into the pasta or lake fish of the day.

When enjoyed on the vine-shaded terrace alongside locals the meal tastes even better.

Osteria dell'Angolo
PIEDMONTESE €€

(📞 0323 55 63 62; Piazza Garibaldi 35, Verbania Pallanza; meals €32-42; ⊙noon-2.30pm & 7-9.30pm Tue-Sun) Greenery drapes a terrace dotted with only eight tables at this osteria, and well-presented dishes showcase creative Piedmontese cuisine. The lake fish is particularly fine (try the trout carpaccio), while the well-chosen wine list means it could turn into a very long lunch indeed.

Osteria dell'Angolo is less than 50m from the Verbania Pallanza ferry jetty.

Bolongaro
TRATTORIA €€

(📞 0323 50 32 54; Piazza Garibaldi 9, Verbania Pallanza; meals €25-35; ⊙noon-3pm & 6.30-11pm) A terrace overlooking Pallanza's ferry jetty and a wildly ornate interior help make this largely unremarkable eatery a perennially popular choice. As do the big pizzas, wide range of primi (first courses) and mains with local flourishes: a trio of smoked fish, thinly sliced game and gnocchetti with cheese from nearby Monte Mottarone.

⭐ Ristorante Milano
MODERN ITALIAN €€€

(📞 0323 55 68 16; www.ristorantemilanolago maggiore.it; Corso Zanitello 2, Verbania Pallanza; meals €68-80, menus €55-75; ⊙noon-2pm & 7-9pm Wed-Mon; ❄) The setting really is hard to beat: Milano directly overlooks Pallanza's minuscule horseshoe-shaped harbour (200m south of the ferry jetty), with a scattering of tables sitting on lakeside lawns amid the trees. It's an idyllic spot to enjoy lake fish, local lamb and some innovative Italian cuisine, such as pigeon with paté and red-currant reduction.

🍷 Drinking & Nightlife

**La Bottiglieria
del Castello** WINE BAR
(☑ 0323 51 65 79; www.osteriacastello.com; Piazza Castello 5, Verbania Intra; ⊙ 11am-2.30pm & 6pm-midnight Mon-Sat) Sample mountain cheeses with a glass of Dolcetto in the pretty piazza at Intra Verbania. If you do you'll be upholding a proud tradition, started in 1905 when sister restaurant Osteria Castello (just next door) served tumblers of wine to mill workers and fishers who came here to drink and catch up on the daily news.

ℹ Information

Verbania Tourist Office (☑ 0323 50 32 49; www.verbania-turismo.it; Via Ruga 44, Verbania Pallanza; ⊙ 9.30am-12.30pm & 3-5pm Mon-Sat) The tourist office is located in the same complex as the **Museo del Paesaggio** (p96).

ℹ Getting There & Away

Verbania Pallanza is on the S34 that runs along the lake's western shore. It is well-connected to other lakeside towns by **ferry** (p87). Ask at Verbania's boat landing for various deals on ferry and hydrofoil tickets for market days in the lakeside towns. Otherwise, a hop-on-hop-off round trip taking in Isola Madre, Isola Superiore,

Isola Bella and Stresa costs €17. Further afield, one-way/return tickets to Cannobio cost €6.80/12.60.

Cannobio

☑ 0323 / POP 5200

Just 5km south of the Swiss border, Cannobio's toy-town cobblestone streets are delightfully quaint. Nicely set apart from the busier towns to the north and south, it's a dreamy place that makes for a charming lake base. There's a public beach at the north end of town, which is also the departure point for a scenic walk along the Cannobino River.

⊙ Sights & Activities

Most beguiling of all is Cannobio's east-facing waterfront promenade. Its central stretch, the elongated **Piazza di Vittorio Emanuele III** (closed off at its northern end by the Bramante-style Santuario della Pietà church), has pastel-hued houses that overlook the pedestrian-only flagstone square across to the hills of the east shore. A series of restaurants and cafes occupy the houses' ground floors and spill on to the square. Otherwise, meandering the small web of lanes that makes up the old town is a pleasant way to while away your time, although specific sights are few and far between.

OFF THE BEATEN TRACK

WALKING TO ORRIDO DI SANT'ANNA

The 3km walk to Orrido di Sant'Anna is a splendid way to see some of Cannobio's natural beauty. From the beach just north of the centre, follow the Cannobino River inland, crossing the second bridge (a bouncy pedestrian-only suspension bridge), and take the well-marked trail along the northern bank. This passes besides woods (meandering paths lead closer to the rushing mountain stream), and finally to tranquil shallows at the base of a cliff topped by a small church (the 17th-century Chiesa di Sant'Anna). The rocky beach here makes a fine spot for a dip on warm days. Just past the church is the Orrido di Sant'Anna, a tight ravine where the rushing water has carved a path through the mountains on its descent to the lake. From here, you can retrace your steps back to town, or loop back to Cannobio by taking the road from here. Take the trail leading uphill off to the right near the Camping Valle Romantica, which offers pretty views on the return to Cannobio.

Allow about two hours for the walk – though it's worth timing your arrival to Orrido di Sant'Anna to allow a lunchtime stop at the Grotto Sant'Anna, right next to the ravine (reserve ahead). Though the trail is easy to follow, you can pick up a map and get other walking suggestions at the tourist office (p100).

ROAD TRIP: LAKES & MOUNTAINS

• •

Despite centuries of fame as a tourist destination, there are still corners of the Italian Lakes that seem untouched by time. This picturesque drive starting in the lovely, unspoilt hamlet of Cannobio takes you high into the mountains around the Parco Nazionale della Val Grande before dropping you down to picturesque Lake Orta. While half a day is ample, this drive could easily fill a most pleasurable day in your life.

❶ Cannobio

Sheltered by a high mountain and sitting at the foot of the Cannobino valley, the medieval, lakeside hamlet of **Cannobio** (p97) is located 5km from the Swiss border. It is a dreamy place. Piazza di Vittorio Emanuele III, lined with pastel-hued houses, is the location of a huge Sunday market that attracts visitors from across the border. You can hire

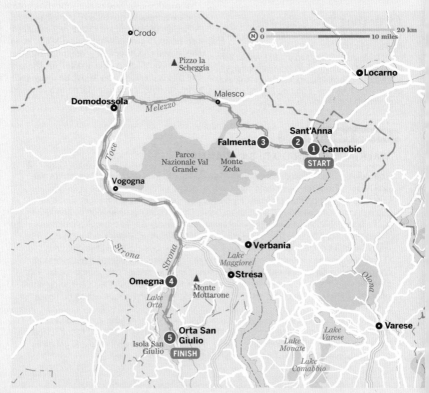

Half a day 110km/68 miles

Great for.... Outdoors, For Families

Best Time to Go Summer, when the weather is fine

● ●

small **sailing boats** here and nip across to the ruined Castelli della Malpaga, marooned on a rocky islet in the lake.

❷ Sant'Anna

From Cannobio, take the scenic P75 which leads high into the heavily wooded hills of the Val Cannobino. Just 2.5km along the valley from Cannobio, in Sant'Anna (p97), the Torrente Cannobio forces its way powerfully through a narrow gorge known as the Orrido di Sant'Anna, crossed at its narrowest part by a cute Romanesque bridge. If you've started the journey just before lunch, consider pausing for a meal at **Grotto Sant'Anna** (p100), a Ticino-style grotto that overlooks the thundering gorge.

❸ Falmenta

About 7km further up the valley, a steep 3km side road consisting of hairpin bends leads up to the central valley's main town, Falmenta (666m – they say the town's priest would like to have 1m added to or subtracted from the official figure). It's pleasant to wander around and you can drop in for coffee at the friendly, family-run Circolo ACLI San Lorenzo. At the top of the valley in Malesco, turn left (west) towards Domodossola. If you haven't eaten by the time you arrive, take the 33km round trip detour to the village of Crodo which hides **Ristorante Marconi** (⌨ 0324 61 87 97; www.ristorantemarconi .com; Via Pellanda 21; meals €36-48; ☺ noon-2.30pm & 7-9.30pm Thu-Sun Mar-Oct) where, in a simple but welcoming stone house, you'll be welcomed with fine food from the kitchen of chef Denis Croce. Be sure to call ahead.

❹ Omegna

Forsake the autostrada and follow the S33 past Domodossola to Vogogna where a 14th-century castle keeps watch over the town. With the forested hillsides of the wilderness Parco Nazionale della Val Grande visible away to the north, continue east then southeast, following the signs for Omegna at the head of Lake Orta. Here you can drop into **Alessi's** (⌨ 0323 86 86 48; www.alessi. com; Via Privata Alessi 6; ☺ 9.30am-6pm Mon-Sat, 2.30-6pm Sun) fabulous factory. Established in Omegna in 1921, these kitchen gadget pioneers went on to transform modern kitchens with humorous, ultracool utensils designed by a pantheon of great-name architect-designers, including Achille Castiglioni, Philippe Starck, Massimiliano Fuksas and Zaha Hadid. You'll find the whole range here alongside special offers and end-of-line deals.

❺ Orta San Giulio

From Omegna it's a quick 10.5km lakeside drive into charming Orta San Giulio (p108) along the SP229. This captivating medieval village is the focal point of pretty Lake Orta, which is separated from Lake Maggiore by Monte Mottarone (1492m) and enveloped by thick, dark-green woodlands. And, you can finish the trip with with a quick boat trip to Isola San Giulio, where you can see the frescoed 12th-century **Basilica di San Giulio** (p108).

**Orrido di
Sant'Anna**   NATURAL FEATURE
A picturesque ravine located 3km from Cannobio. You can drive here, though the best way to come is by taking a scenic walking path that follows the rushing Cannobino River.

**Tomaso
Surf & Sail**   WATER SPORTS
(☑ 333 7000291; www.tomaso.com; Via Nazionale 7; ⊙ 9.30am-7pm Jun-Sep, 11am-6pm Oct-May) This recommended outfitter has all the essentials for a day out on the water. You can hire SUP boards (per one/two hours €25/40), windsurfing gear (per one/four hours from €25/80), sailing dinghies (two hours €65), catamarans and motorboats. If you lack the know-how, Tomaso also offers lessons in windsurfing (per hour €80), sailing (per hour from €110) and waterskiing (per half-hour €85).

Cicli Prezan   CYCLING
(☑ 0323 7 12 30; www.cicliprezan.it; Viale Vittorio Veneto 9; per hr/day €10/20; ⊙ 8am-noon & 3-7pm Mon-Sat, 8.30am-noon Sun) Rents out both road and mountain bikes.

✖ Eating & Drinking

Outdoor cafes on Cannobio's lakeside piazza make a fine setting for an afternoon drink. During the summer, the bar and lounge beside the beach is the liveliest place for cocktails and DJs.

★ Grotto Sant'Anna   ITALIAN €€
(☑ 0323 7 06 82; Via Sant'Anna 30, Orrido Sant'Anna; meals €35-45; ⊙ noon-1.45pm & 7-9.45pm Tue-Sun Apr-Oct) This Ticino-style *grotto* (traditional inn) overlooks the thundering gorge that is the Orrido di Sant'Anna. Granite tables and benches located under a thick-leafed pergola provide a ringside seat to this natural phenomenon. If you can take your eyes off the water, dig into a dish of *trota al forno* (oven-baked trout) or *costolette di agnello al timo* (lamb chops with thyme).

L'Imbuto   ITALIAN €€
(☑ 0323 7 00 26; www.ristorantelimbuto.it; Piazza Maggio 27-28 12; meals €35-42; ⊙ noon-2.30pm & 7-10pm) Praised by locals, L'Imbuto is a modern, convivial lakeside restaurant that serves up creative, expertly prepared dishes

that are excellent value for the money. Creative antipasti like *polpo con mozzarella, pomodorini e olive* (octopus with mozzarella, cherry tomatoes and olives) to *ravioli alla trota* (trout ravioli), *costine di maiale* (pork ribs) and the seafood-loaded *spaghetti ai frutti di mare*. Perfect pizzas are also available.

Lo Scalo   MODERN ITALIAN €€€
(☑ 0323 7 14 80; www.loscalo.com; Piazza Vittorio Emanuele III 32; meals €45-55; ⊙ noon-2.30pm & 7-11pm Wed-Sun, 7-11pm Tue) Cannobio's best restaurant, Lo Scalo serves cuisine that is sophisticated and precise, featuring dishes such as a suckling pig with spring onions and black garlic, and ricotta and tomato gnocchi with clams. The two-course lunch (€25) and five-course *menù degustazione* (€55) are both great-value treats, best enjoyed at a table on the waterfront promenade.

❶ Information

Tourist Office (☑ 0323 7 12 12; www.pro-cannobio.it; Via Giovanola 25; ⊙ 9am-noon & 4-7pm Mon-Sat, 9am-noon Sun) Hands out brochures and provides town info. Located next to the Romanesque bell tower.

❶ Getting There & Away

Boat services (p87) connect Cannobio with most other Lake Maggiore towns. Cannobio is located along the SS34, about 5km south of the Swiss border, and 22km north of the lakeside town of Verbania. A parking area (per hour €1) is signposted off the main road through town; from here it's a short walk down through the old town.

LAKE MAGGIORE EAST BANK

Lake Maggiore's eastern shore has less to detain you than does the west, but there are still enough worthwhile sights for at least a half-day's detour, although you'll need your own vehicle. If you can, make it a Wednesday to coincide with **Luino's enormous weekly market** (⊙ 8.30am-4.30pm) where you can bargain hunt everything from local cheese to vintage furniture.

Laveno

☑ 0332 / POP 8900

Laveno is a pleasant lakeside town, with a tiny cobblestone centre, a picturesque marina and striking views of jagged peaks to the north. It's also a fine base for walks through sleepy villages and woodlands in the heights high above the lake. A funicular provides speedy access up the slopes.

◉ Sights & Activities

Laveno Funivia   FUNICULAR

(☑ 0332 66 80 12; www.funiviedellagomaggiore.it; adult one way/return €7/10, child €5/7; ☉ 11am-5pm Mon-Fri, to 6pm Sat, 10am-6pm Sun Apr-Oct, shorter hours rest of year) A highlight of Laveno is the Funivia, which whisks passengers up to a panoramic spot 949m above sea level, in the shadow of the **Sasso del Ferro** peak (1062m). The views over the lake and beyond to the Alps are breathtaking.

From there, you can head off on longer walks into the hills. Stop by the tourist office for suggested itineraries.

Icaro 2000   ADVENTURE SPORTS

(☑ 335 6938992; www.icaro2000.com; tandem hang-gliding €100) For a pure adrenaline rush, sign up for a tandem hang-gliding flight with Icaro 2000. The price includes transport, all equipment and a short movie of the flight. The airborne adventure lasts around 15 to 20 minutes. Book at least a few days in advance.

❶ Information

Laveno Tourist Office (☑ 0332 66 72 23; www.stradasaporivallivaresine.it; Piazzale Europa 1; ☉ 10.30am-4pm Tue-Fri, to 5.30pm Sat & Sun) Just outside the train station, this helpful office is a great source of info on walks in the area. You can also buy a few local products – honey, ceramics, grappa, and lotions made from, uh, donkey milk.

❶ Getting There & Away

Laveno is located along the SP69 near the lake's midpoint. It's a 20km drive south to Angera, and 24km southeast to Varese. Trains run every hour or so from Milan's Porta Garibaldi to **Laveno-Mombello Nord station** (Via Giuseppe Garibaldi; one way €6.70, 90 minutes) – an easy stroll to the centre.

Frequent vehicle ferries connect Laveno with Intra across the lake (one way €3.40, 20 minutes). Laveno isn't on the main north-south ferry run, meaning you'll have to cross to Intra first, then catch an onward boat.

Casalzuigno

In the unassuming town of Casalzuigno, about 9km east of Laveno, generations of nobles have swanned about the magnificent gardens of **Villa della Porta Bozzolo** (☑ 0332 62 41 36; www.fondoambiente.it; Viale Senatore Camillo Bozzolo 5; adult/child €7/4; ☉ 10am-6pm Wed-Sun Mar-Sep, to 5pm Wed-Sun Oct & Nov, closed Dec-Feb), completed in 1690. The grand two-storey building, surrounded by various outbuildings, has a calm,

LAKE MAGGIORE & AROUND LAVENO

LOCAL KNOWLEDGE

TOP FRESCOES

Among the best-kept secrets of the Lake Maggiore area are the fabulous frescoes, artistic remnants with centuries of history, in some cases remarkably well preserved. The best range from pre-Romanesque to wonderful Florentine Renaissance. Our favourites include the following:

Basilica di San Giulio (p108) The 12th-century church on Lake Orta's island is jammed with vibrant frescoes depicting saints.

Museo della Collegiata (p106) Florentine master Masolino da Panicale carried out a series on the life of St John the Baptist in 1435.

Chiesa di Santa Maria Foris Portas (p107) A modest Lombard church contains extraordinary pre-Romanesque frescoes that may date to the 7th century.

Santa Caterina del Sasso The church in this former monastery is filled with well-preserved frescoes.

self-assured feel. Inside, the ballroom and upstairs gallery are richly decorated with frescoes. Don't miss the cool, dark library with *stile liberty* (Italian art nouveau) chandeliers and 18th-century walnut book cabinets.

Outside, fine Italianate gardens with viewpoints and statuary add to the grandeur, particularly the thousand species of roses – one of the most important collections of its kind. There's a decent restaurant with terrace seating.

Santa Caterina del Sasso

One of northern Italy's most spectacularly sited monasteries, Santa Caterina del Sasso (www.santacaterinadelsasso.com; Via Santa Caterina 13; ⊙9am-noon & 2-6pm Apr-Oct, to 5pm Mar, closed weekdays Nov-Feb) FREE clings to the high rocky face of Lake Maggiore's southeast shore. The buildings span the 13th and 14th centuries; the porticoes and chapels are packed with frescoes; the views from the tiny courtyards are superb. The monastery is reached either by climbing up 80 steps from the Santa Caterina ferry quay, or by clattering down a 268-step staircase from the car park (there's also a lift for €1 each way).

Dominican friars founded the monastery in the 13th century, and bits were tacked on subsequently down the decades. Enter by the portico overlooking the lake, then pass through the south monastery and a small courtyard (with an 18th-century wine press), which leads into another Gothic portico. A 16th-century fresco series depicting the *Danza macabra* (Dance of Death) can still be made out on its upper level.

Finally you reach the church, which is fronted by a four-arch portico. A curious affair, the church is actually the cobbling together of a series of 13th- and 14th-century chapels that form an oddly shaped whole. Inside, the carnival of frescoes includes the Christ Pantocrator in the Cappella di San Nicola, the first chapel on the right upon entering.

Ferries from Stresa (adult/reduced return €6.80/5.60) stop here regularly. Otherwise, by car or bus it's 6.5km south of Laveno (watch for the signs for Leggiuno and then a sign for the convent, 1km in off the main road).

Ranco
📞 0331 / POP 1400

Perched on the edge of Lake Maggiore, the tranquil village of Ranco has a laid-back vibe that draws travellers who want to escape the bigger crowds of Stresa and other west bank destinations. Aside from the lakeside promenade, there aren't many attractions in town – especially since the closure of the eccentric European transportation museum in Ranco.

✖️ Eating & Drinking

⭐ Il Sole   CONTEMPORARY ITALIAN €€€
(📞 0331 97 65 07; www.ilsolediranco.it; Piazza Venezia 5; meals €55-80, tasting menu €100; ⊙noon-2.30pm & 7-10pm Wed-Sun) Aside from relax along the waterfront, the main thing to do in Ranco is call by this fantastic restaurant, with its lake views, beautiful garden and even better cooking. Some local critics consider it among the best in Italy.

It's difficult to choose: a carpaccio of white asparagus with salmon? Ricotta and walnut ravioli with prawns? Or perhaps the heavenly light *fritto misto* (mixed fried fish and seafood)? Leave the thinking up to staff and opt for one of the tasting menus.

Il Sole is also a fine place to overnight (doubles €190 to €350).

Il Molo   CAFE
(📞 0331 97 51 90; Via Lungolago; ⊙8am-10pm Mon-Thu, to 1am Fri & Sat, 9am-9pm Sun; 📶) You can't get much closer to the lake than Il Molo, the liveliest eating and drinking spot in Ranco. Grab an open-air table and join locals and day trippers over drinks and tasty snacks, sandwiches and daily specials (including vegetarian options), against a backdrop of sparkling waterfront and groovy beats.

Angera
📞 0331 / POP 5600

Overlooking the narrow southern reaches of Maggiore, Angera has a leafy waterfront speckled with villas and old fishing families' houses and there are good views from the grassy shoreline to Arona across the lake. Angera's star attraction is its massive 15th-century hilltop castle, though pleasant parks and quaint back lanes packed with history make for some rewarding exploring.

◉ Sights

Rocca di Angera   CASTLE
(www.isoleborromee.it; Via Rocca Castello 2; adult/
child €9.50/6, combined ticket incl Isola Bella & Isola Madre €25/13.50; ⊙ 9am-5.30pm) The chunky
medieval Rocca di Angera fortress lords it
over the town of Angera in no uncertain
terms. From a distance, it is the first thing
one sees. Inside is the 12-room Museo della
Bambola, displaying the Borromeo family's
priceless collection of dolls. What better
place for them than this towering, fairy-tale
castle with its high, crenellated walls atop
a rocky outcrop? Modest vineyards cling to
the slopes around it.

The Borromeo clan bought the castle from Milan's Visconti family in 1449.
Various rooms and halls open on to the
courtyard, among them the awe-inspiring
Sala della Giustizia (Hall of Justice), with
its overarching vault and lively 13th-cen-
tury frescoes. From the tower there are
breathtaking views. The doll collection
counts more than a thousand items, while
a separate collection of French and German
mechanical dolls and figurines (dating from
1870 to 1920) perform highly amusing actions (including a monkey playing the violin
and a granny urinating in a chamber pot)
– don't miss the videos showing the dolls in
action.

The easiest way up is by car (signposted
from the centre of Angera). By foot, follow
the signs from Piazza Garibaldi on the wa-
terfont (1.5km walk).

Oasi della Bruschera   NATURE RESERVE
(Via Sandro Pertini; ⊙ 24hr) FREE One of the
last remaining wooded wetlands in Lombardy, this 400-hectare site has several trails
including a lakeside path with fine views
across the reed beds to Angera. The reserve
is an important nesting site for waterbirds,
including moorhens, mallards and king-
fishers. Just off shore is Isola Partegora, a
protected island that's home to a colony of
cormorants.

The park is located about 1.3km east of
the ferry dock, with an entrance near Via
Arena and Via Sandro Pertini.

✗ Eating

Hotel Lido Angera   ITALIAN €€
(☑ 0331 93 02 32; www.hotellido.it; Viale della
Libertà 11; meals €35-48; ⊙ noon-2.30pm & 7.30-
10pm Tue-Sun) If you like fresh lake fish then
this is the place to come. Set right on the

lake and surrounded by greenery, this hotel-restaurant serves up a mix of classical
local dishes with a contemporary spin, especially in the pleasing presentation. Grab
a table by the large windows, gaze over the
lake and enjoy. It's signposted along the road
into Angera from Ranco.

The wine list is broad, including products
from all over the country, and they'll ensure
you choose the best wines to go with each
dish.

❶ Information

Tourist Office (☑ 0331 93 19 15; www.angera.
it; Piazza della Vittoria; ⊙ 10am-1pm & 2-5pm
Tue & Thu-Sun mid-Apr–Sep) Useful info on the
area, located near the ferry dock.

❶ Getting There & Away

Angera is located off the SP69, located roughly
26km southwest of Varese. Ferries run several
times a day between Arona and Stresa (€6.20,
50 to 80 minutes).

VARESE REGION

Though often overlooked by visitors travelling between the big lakes, Varese and the
surrounding countryside make for some
fascinating exploring. Lombard ruins, early
Christian artistic treasures and a lofty *sacro monte* (sacred mountain) are among the
highlights of a day's ramble. Varese itself has
a quaint pedestrianised centre and several
excellent museums.

Varese

☑ 0332 / POP 80,600
Spread out to the south of the Campo dei
Fiori hills, between the provinces of Lake
Maggiore and Lake Como, Varese is a
prosperous provincial capital with a pretty old town and some grand villas worth
exploring.

◉ Sights

North off Piazza Monte Grappa, the delightful pedestrianised Corso Matteotti signals
the western boundary of Varese's tiny historic centre, at whose heart rises the baroque
Basilica di San Vittore (Piazza San Vittore;
⊙ 9am-noon & 3-6pm). The interior is a lavish affair, while the exterior is watched over

Varese

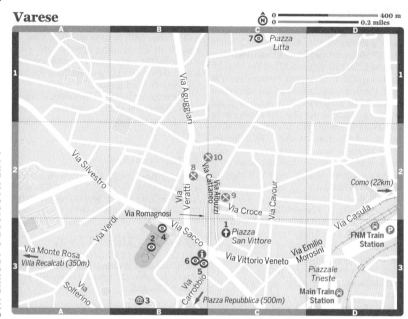

N 0 ——————— 400 m
0 ——————— 0.2 miles

by the muscular, freestanding **Torre Campanaria** (Bell Tower), which dates from the 17th and 18th centuries.

Villa Panza   ARCHITECTURE, MUSEUM
(☑ 0332 28 39 60; www.fondoambiente.it; Piazza Litta 1; adult/reduced €13/6; ⊙ 10am-6pm Tue-Sun) On a rise north of Varese's centre, where the high walls of private residences enclose narrow, winding lanes, Villa Panza enjoys beautiful views of the Alps from its extensive gardens. The villa was donated to the nation in 1996 and part of that donation was an art collection, mostly monochrome

canvases by American post-WWII artists, scattered about the opulent rooms and halls of the villa.

One of the finest rooms is the 1830 Salone Impero (Empire Hall), with heavy chandeliers and four canvases by American David Simpson (born 1928). More can be seen in the outbuildings (*rustici*), which are also used for temporary art exhibitions. The gardens, a combination of 18th-century Italianate and early-19th-century English style make for a lovely meander before or after the art.

Admission is slightly cheaper on Tuesday and Wednesday (€10).

Museo Castiglioni   MUSEUM
(☑ 0332 169 24 29; www.museocastiglioni.it; Viale Vico 46, Parco Toeplitz; adult/reduced €7/5; ⊙ 10am-1pm & 2-6pm Thu-Sun) Set in the lush grounds of the Toeplitz estate, the Museo Castiglioni houses a surprising collection of ethnographic works. The Castiglioni brothers devoted their lives to archaeological research, and their travels among the Maasai, the Tuareg and the Nubians led to the creation of this small but fascinating museum. Exhibitions touch on the social customs, rituals, and lifestyles of often overlooked peoples, and photos,

tools and headdresses help bring the displays to life.

Piazza Monte Grappa   PIAZZA

Piazza Monte Grappa, on the cusp of Varese's old town, is fascinating for history and architecture buffs. The square was completely remade in grand Fascist fashion in the early 1930s. Most extraordinary is the Torre Civica, an enormous and somehow menacing clock tower; at the base flowers an *arengario* (a balcony from which Mussolini and co could harangue the populace). It has an almost sci-fi quality about it.

Palazzo Estense   ARCHITECTURE

(off Via Montebello) From the 17th century, nobles and the rich, many from Milan, began to build second residences around Varese's historic centre. Of these, the most sumptuous is the Palazzo Estense, completed in 1771 for Francesco III d'Este, the Austrian-appointed governor of the Duchy of Milan.

From Via Sacco, the main entrance is surprisingly understated as the main graceful facade actually looks south onto the Italianate Giardini Estensi (www.comune. varese.it/palazzo-e-giardini-estensi; Via Luigi Sacco; ⊙8am-dusk; FREE). The building now belongs to the town hall and cannot be visited, but anyone may swan through the entrance into the gardens, punctuated by ponds and, hidden on a rise behind Villa Mirabello (Piazza della Motta 4, off Viale Sant'Antonio; adult/child €4/2; ⊙10am-12.30pm & 2-6pm Tue-Sun Jun-Oct, 9.30am-12.30pm & 2-5.30pm Nov-May), is a giant cedar of Lebanon.

From Palazzo Estense, villa fans could round off by walking half a kilometre from Via Sacco to the 17th-century Villa Recalcati (Via Francesco Daverio), now seat of the provincial government. You can wander around the outside of the building.

✗ Eating

Ristorante Bologna   ITALIAN €€

(✆0332 23 21 00; www.albergobologna.it; Via Broggi 7; meals €30-35; 🖘) The ever popular Bologna has a loyal local following for its well-executed but uncomplicated dishes that won't break the budget. Start off with a creamy mushroom risotto, followed perhaps by breaded veal cutlets or a tender grilled sea bass. The cosy dining room is plastered with photos (and jerseys) of Italian basketball greats.

Vecchia Trattoria della Pesa   CONTEMPORARY ITALIAN €€

(Da Annetta; ✆0332 28 70 70; www.daannetta.it; Via Cattaneo 14; meals €38-45; ⊙noon-2.30pm & 6.30-10pm) New York–style decor meets Italian trattoria at this attractive place in the old town. The owners have a number of well-regarded restaurants around the Varese area, including Da Annetta where it all began in 1928, and this in-town option is a bit like the decor – a mix of the traditional staples with contemporary riffs on the theme in a menu that changes regularly.

Da Annetta   ITALIAN €€€

(✆0332 49 02 30; www.daannetta.it; Via Fé 25, Capodilago; meals €60-75; ⊙noon-2.30pm & 7-10pm Thu-Mon, noon-2.30pm Tue Sep-Jul) When this place opened in 1928, its owners couldn't have guessed it would have such a long life. The broad menu offers all sorts of tempting goodies, starting with the *fagottini di pasta rossa, ricotta, pesto, olive e crema di burrata* (red pasta bundles stuffed with ricotta, pesto, olives and mozzarrella-style cream).

Ristorante Teatro   ITALIAN €€€

(✆0332 24 11 24; www.ristoranteteatro.it; Via Croce 3; meals €50-60; ⊙12.20-2pm & 7.20-10pm Wed-Mon) A Varese stalwart for fine cooking, Ristorante Teatro serves up fresh local specialities with an emphasis on the best ingredients rather than frilly elaborations – think local truffles, mushrooms and fresh fish.

ℹ Information

Varese Tourist Office (✆0332 28 19 44; www.vareseturismo.it; Piazza Monte Grappa 5; ⊙9.30am-1pm & 2-5.30pm Mon-Sat) Just outside the old centre, this helpful office can give tips and advice on exploring Varese and the surrounding region.

ℹ Getting There & Away

BUS

Local buses depart from outside the **train station** and fan out from Varese to most towns around the province. Every half-hour local city bus C (€1.40) runs from various stops around central Varese to the *sacro monte*.

CAR

The fastest way to Varese is via the A8 motorway from Milan. If you're driving into central Varese,

LAKE MAGGIORE & AROUND VARESE

follow the signs to the parking station at Piazza Repubblica.

TRAIN

Regular but sluggish trains leave from Milan's Porta Venezia and Porta Garibaldi stations for **Varese's main station** (Piazzale Trieste, €6.10, 55 to 80 minutes). Some of these continue to Laveno on Lake Maggiore. For around the same price and taking around the same duration, FNM trains (www.ferrovienord.it) run from Milan's Stazione Nord to **Varese Nord** and one to Laveno, via Voltorre and Gemonio. Both train stations are an easy walk to the centre.

Santa Maria del Monte

The medieval hamlet of Santa Maria del Monte (880m), 8km north of Varese, has long been a destination for pilgrims, with its historic chapels leading up to a sanctuary offering sweeping views over the countryside. The *sacro monte* is inside the Parco Regionale Campo dei Fiori, a patch of thickly wooded hills. After taking in the views, the hamlet and its tangle of medieval streets are worth exploring.

◉ Sights

Casa Museo
Lodovico Pogliaghi   MUSEUM
(🖉 328 8377206; www.casamuseopogliaghi.it; Viale del Santuario; €5; ☺ 10am-6pm Sat, Sun & holidays mid-Mar–May & Sep–mid-Nov, 6.30-10.30pm Fri Jun-Aug) Up on Santa Maria del Monte, this beautiful villa and its surrounding gardens house a small but dazzling repository of artworks, with paintings, sculptures and textiles spanning more than 2000 years of human history. Among the treasures is the original plaster cast of the main door of Milan's Duomo, Greco-Roman carvings and Egyptian sarcophagi.

Sacro Monte
del Rosario   CHRISTIAN SITE
(🖉 0332 28 46 24; www.sacromonte.it; Viale del Santuario) This hilltop north of Varese had long been a pilgrimage site for the faithful. But at the beginning of the 17th century, the Church and Lombardy's Spanish rulers came up with the idea of creating a sacred way to lead up to this sacred mount, Sacro Monte del Rosario, one of a dozen or so built in the 16th and 17th centuries in Lombardy and Piedmont. The result is

a cobbled 2km climb (the starting point is at 585m).

Fourteen chapels dotted along the way are representative of the mysteries of the Rosary (hence the name). At the end of the climb you can drink in the magnificent views with a well-deserved beer on the terrace of Ristorante Monforte.

✗ Eating & Drinking

Al Borducan   ITALIAN €€
(🖉 0332 22 29 16; www.borducan.com; Via Beata Caterina Moriggi 43; meals €38-45; ☺ noon-2pm & 7.30-10pm Thu-Tue) Many folks make the sacrifice of climbing up in the evening for a romantic evening meal at the *stile liberty* Al Borducan. Inside is a fine dining room with tapered candles, fresh-cut flowers and splendid views – an elegant setting for nicely prepared *orecchiette* with broccoli and foie gras, Lake Maggiore scallops and herb-crusted lamb chops.

Don't bypass the restaurant's namesake liqueur – an orange-infused digestive made from a recipe that's been handed down over the generations.

ⓘ Getting There & Away

Funicolare di Varese (one way €1; ☺ 10am-7.30pm Sat & Sun mid-Mar-late Oct, 9am-7.30pm daily late-Jul–late-Aug, 10am-6.10pm Sun late Oct–mid-Mar, closed Jan) The funicular to the *sacro monte* runs every 10 minutes.

Castiglione Olona

The nondescript modern town of Castiglione Olona, 8km south of Varese off the SP42 road, contains a quite extraordinary gem. The old centre was largely rebuilt under the auspices of its most favoured son, Cardinal Branda Castiglioni (1350-1443), in Florentine Renaissance style. Via Branda leads from the central square up to the **Museo della Collegiata** (www.museocollegiata.it; Via Cardinal Branda 1; adult/reduced €6/4; ☺ 10am-1pm & 3-6pm Tue-Sun Apr-Sep, 9.30am-12.30pm & 2.30-5.30pm Tue-Sat & 10am-1pm & 3-6pm Sun Oct-Mar), a church that contains the town's masterpiece.

Inside its baptistery, Florentine master Masolino da Panicale carried out a series of frescoes on the life of St John the Baptist in 1435. Also in the complex is a church with exquisite 15th-century frescoes by three Tuscan painters and a small museum with ecclesiastical treasures, including 15th-century tomes with illuminated lettering.

Castelseprio & Torba

Several of Lombardy's most important historic sites lie scattered among woodlands 14km south of Varese. Here you can peer back through the centuries while walking amid fragments of a Lombard settlement at Castelseprio, contemplate the lives of medieval nuns at the Monastero di Torba, and gaze at mystifying 1400-year-old frescoes at the Chiesa di Santa Maria Foris Portas. The trio (along with four farther flung places) comprise a Unesco World Heritage Site entitled the 'Longobards in Italy, Places of Power'.

◉ Sights

**Parco Archeologico
di Castelseprio**   RUINS
(☑ 0331 82 04 38; www.simarch.org; Via Castelvecchio 1513; ⊙ 8.30am-7pm Tue-Sat, 9.45am-6pm Sun & holidays Feb-Nov, shorter hours Nov-Jan) FREE Spread out in peaceful woods about 1.5km outside the village of Castelseprio, around 20km south of Varese, is the ancient archaeological site of Sibrium, a Lombard *castrum* (fortified settlement) with remains of fortress walls, various churches and towers. As long ago as the 5th or 6th century AD, the Lombards began erecting a fort on this site. By the 7th century it was a small town, with its Basilica di San Giovanni, houses and watchtowers.

**Chiesa di Santa Maria
Foris Portas**   CHURCH
(Holy Mary Outside the Gates; Castelseprio; ⊙ 8.30am-7pm Tue-Fri, 8.30am-2.30pm & 5.30-7pm Sat, 9.45am-2.30pm & 5.30-6pm Sun Feb-Nov, shorter hours Dec & Jan) FREE Just outside the archaeological site of Sibrium, the small pre-Romanesque Chiesa di Santa Maria Foris Portas was built around the 7th century. Inside in the apse are some remarkable frescoes depicting scenes from the infancy of Jesus Christ and dominated by an image of Christ Pantocrator.

Art historians tend to think the frecoes were painted in Lombard times but some believe they are from the Carolingian pe-riod (8th or 9th century). Either way, they are a rare and vivid ray of pre-Romanesque artistic beauty. The realism, life and colour of the human figures seem to owe something to the classical art of ancient times, not at all like the stiff and, to some eyes, childlike religious art of the Romanesque period, still several centuries away. The church is usually kept locked; ask at the information office at Sibrium for staff to open it.

**Monastero
di Torba**   MONASTERY
(☑ 0331 82 03 01; www.fondoambiente.it; adult/child €6.50/free; ⊙ 10am-6pm Wed-Sun Mar-Sep, to 5pm Wed-Sun Oct, Nov & 2nd half of Feb, closed Dec & Jan) Dating back to the 5th century, the Monastero di Torba started life as a forward watchtower for the Lombard *castrum* of Sibrium; and it was the only one to remain intact. It was then turned into the centrepiece of a Benedictine convent and adorned with rare 8th-century frescoes.

The Monastero di Torba has a **restaurant** (mains around €12) with simple pastas and baked dishes.

ℹ Getting There & Away
The historical area is situated some 14km south of Varese. To get to the **archaeological park** take a leafy 1.5km drive from Castelseprio village. The **church** is 200m from the parking area and information office. **Torba** is about 1.5km drive northeast from the village. It is not practical to visit these sites by public transport.

LAKE ORTA

Enveloped by thick, dark-green woodlands, tranquil Lake Orta (aka Lake Cusio) could make a perfect elopers' getaway. Measuring 13.4km long by 2.5km wide, it's separated from its bigger and better-known eastern neighbour, Lake Maggiore, by Monte Mottarone. The focal point of the lake is the captivating medieval village of Orta San Giulio, which is often referred to simply as Orta.

If it's romance you want, come during the week and you'll have the place largely to yourself. On spring and summer weekends, good-natured groups of day trippers from Milan and beyond descend on the place, creating plenty of atmosphere, but crowding the town. You can't blame them: it's perfect for a day out and a long Sunday lunch.

Orta San Giulio

📞 0322 / POP 1200

There's a very northern Italian magic about Orta San Giulio, one of the prettiest old lakeside towns you'll find anywhere. Aside from its lovely architecture and tangle of narrow lanes, it also serves as the gateway to the lovely Isola San Giulio and is watched over by a forested hillside strewn with chapels. As you can imagine, it's a great place to spend a few days, particularly during the week when it's likely to be just you and the locals.

◉ Sights

Isola San Giulio   ISLAND

Anchored barely 500m in front of Piazza Mario Motta is Isola San Giulio. The island is dominated by the 12th-century Basilica di San Giulio (☉9.30am-6pm Tue-Sun, 2-5pm Mon Apr-Sep, 9.30am-noon & 2-5pm Tue-Sun, 2-5pm Mon Oct-Mar), full of vibrant frescoes that alone make a trip to the island worthwhile. The frescoes mostly depict saints (and sometimes their moment of martyrdom – St Laurence seems supremely indifferent to his roasting on a grate). Step inside after mass, when the air is thick with incense and the frescoes seem to take on a whole new power.

The church, island and mainland town are named after a Greek evangelist, Giulio, who's said to have rid the island of snakes,

---

ANELLO AZZURO

It is possible to circle Lake Orta on foot. Known locally as the **Anello Azzurro** (Blue Ring), the circuit walk of the entire lake takes about three days at a leisurely pace. Starting at Orta and heading south, you are looking at about 14km to Pella, about 13km the following day to Omegna and another 14km from Omegna back to Orta. The recommended kick-off point is *sacro monte* in Orta. Readers of Italian can get a closer route description at www.lagodorta.net, which offers all sorts of other ideas on walks in the area.

---

dragons and assorted monsters in the late 4th century. His remains lie in the crypt of the Basilica di San Giulio.

The footpath encircling the island makes for a peaceful stroll, hence its popular name of Via del Silenzio. Indeed, a series of aphorisms on the wonders of silence (all very fine when screaming school groups have the run of the place) have been placed along the way. You can walk the so-called Via della Meditazione in either direction, with multilingual signs to inspire you on your search for inner peace.

Regular ferry services (return €3.15) run from Orta San Giulio's waterfront. More-expensive private launches (return €9) also run, departing when there are sufficient passengers to warrant the five-minute crossing.

Piazza Mario Motta   PIAZZA

Here's a picture of how life really should be lived: rise early and head for a coffee on Piazza Mario Motta, gazing across at the sun-struck Isola San Giulio in the early morning quiet. From your vantage point, contemplate the Palazzotto, a squat, fresco-enlivened structure sitting atop pillars like giant stilts at the northern end of the square.

Once the seat of a local council, the Palazzotto now occasionally opens for temporary exhibitions, but climb the stairs anyway for good views. The square burbles with local life on market day (Wednesday).

Sacro Monte di San Francesco   CHAPEL, PARK

Beyond the lush gardens and residences that mark the hill rising behind Orta is a kind of parallel 'town' – the *sacro monte,* where 20 small chapels dedicated to St Francis of Assisi dot the hillside. The views down to the lake are captivating, and meandering from chapel to chapel is a wonderfully tranquil way to pass a few hours.

From Piazza Mario Motta, Salita della Motta leads up a cobbled hill between centuries-old houses to the baroque-fronted Chiesa dell'Assunta (Via San Bernardino; ☉9am-6pm) and then bends right (south) to the cemetery and back right up the sacred mountain. The 20 chapels are scattered about, each dedicated to recounting a part of St Francis' life. Some boast wonderful frescoes while others are more modest affairs. If you're driving, a road also leads up from near the tourist office.

Orta San Giulio

0   200 m
0   0.1 miles

🎊 Festivals & Events

Orta Jazz Festival MUSIC
(www.facebook.com/ortajazzfestival) Against the backdrop of lovely Lake Orta, the Piazza Mario Motta becomes an open-air stage for free jazz concerts during the summer. One jam a month is held from June to September. Check the Facebook page or contact the tourist office for upcoming times.

🍴 Eating

Enoteca Al Boeuc PIEDMONTESE €
(☑ 339 5840039; http://alboeuc.beepworld.it; Via Bersani 28; meals €18-25; ⏱ 11.30am-3pm & 6.30pm-midnight Wed-Mon) This candlelit stone cavern has been around since the 16th century. These days it offers glasses of fine wines (try the velvety Barolo) and snacks including mixed bruschette with truffles and mushrooms, meat and cheese platters, and that Piedmontese favourite:

Orta San Giulio

◎ Sights

✖ Eating

bagna caüda (a hot dip of butter, olive oil, garlic and anchovies in which you bathe vegetables).

⭐**Cucchiaio di Legno** AGRITURISMO €€
(☑ 339 5775385; www.ilcucchiaiodilegno.com; Via Prisciola 10, Legro; set menu €30; ⏱ 6-9pm Thu-Sun, noon-2.30pm Sat & Sun; P ❄ 🛜) Delicious home cooking emerges from the kitchen of this honest-to-goodness *agriturismo*

(farm-stay accommodation); expect fish fresh from the lake, and salami and cheese from the surrounding valleys. When eating al fresco on the vine-draped patio it feels rather like you're dining at the house of a friend. Bookings required.

There's a clutch of bright, snazzy **rooms**, too (doubles €80). It's located in tiny Legro, 800m south of the Orta–Miasino train station.

Ristoro Olina   ITALIAN €€
(☑ 0322 90 56 56; Via Olina 40; meals €35-40; ◔ noon-2pm & 7-9.30pm Thu-Tue; ☑) A modern, laid-back alternative to your typical low-lit trattoria, this place offers a broad range of thoughtfully prepared dishes that combine creativity with excellent products. Try whole fish baked with herbs and vegetables, braised artichokes with truffle, or pork belly with horseradish and wild arugula. The changing menu has decent vegetarian options, including a vegan dish or two.

Venus   TRATTORIA €€
(☑ 0322 9 03 62; www.venusorta.it; Piazza Motta 50; meals €30-45; ◔ noon-3pm & 6-10pm Tue-Sun) Although the food doesn't quite match the views, this lakeside charmer always draws a crowd. The menu of hearty local dishes features rich plates of creamy risotto with scallops, lamb chops in a pistachio crust and fillet of perch with a butter, spinach and citrus reduction.

And you can eat it all beside the beached boats, which are situated just metres from the lake.

★ Locanda di Orta   MODERN ITALIAN €€€
(☑ 0322 90 51 88; www.locandaorta.com; Via Olina 18; meals €55-80, menus €75-90; ◔ noon-2.30pm & 7.30-9pm) Some of Orta's most creative cooking is served up in the wisteria-draped Locanda di Orta, squeezed into the heart of the old town. It's a supremely stylish, intimate affair (it only seats around 17 people) where culinary alchemy converts traditional Lake Orta ingredients into works of foodie art.

❶ Information

Pro Loco (☑ 339 5267436; Via Bossi 11; ◔ 11am-1pm & 2-4pm Mon, Tue & Thu, 10am-1pm & 2-4pm Fri-Sun) In the town hall, this is a handy office for all things Lake Orta related.

The small public garden behind the office has pretty lake views.

Main Tourist Office (☑ 0322 91 19 72; www.distrettolaghi.it; Via Panoramica; ◔ 10am-1pm & 2-6pm Wed-Mon) This small info house on the road into Orta San Giulio can provide information on the whole of Lake Orta.

❶ Getting There & Away

BOAT

Navigazione Lago d'Orta (☑ 345 5170005; www.navigazionelagodorta.it) run boat services to numerous lakeside spots from its **landing stage** at Piazza Mario Motta, including Isola San Giulio (return €3.15, five minutes, every half hour), Omegna (€7.35, 50 minutes, two to three daily), Pella (€4.90, 20 minutes, every half-hour) and Ronco (€4.90, 30 minutes, two to three daily). A day ticket entitles the holder to unlimited travel on the whole lake costs €8.90.

BUS

Only intermittent buses serve Lake Orta's west bank towns. From June to September, three buses a day run between Stresa and Orta (€4, 45 minutes).

CAR

Orta San Giulio is just off the SP229, which follows the lake's eastern shore. Nearby cities include Milan (86km), Stresa (25km) and Varese (62km). From Milan take the A8 and E62 tollway, exit at SP142 toward Borgomanera, then take the SP229 up to Orta San Giulio.

There are two parking areas where the road dips down into town, one outdoor with parking meters, the other under cover. At both you pay €2/10 per hour/day.

TRAIN

Orta–Miasino train station (Via Stazione) is a 3km walk from the centre of Orta San Giulio. Five to nine trains run to Novara (€4.40, 50 minutes) in the north and Domodossola (€4.60, one hour) in the south. From Milan, there are trains from Stazione Centrale (change at Novara) every two hours or so (from €9, two hours).

Between March and October, a little **tourist train** (☑ 339 5313589; www.treninodiorta.it/ita; one way/return €3/5; ◔ 9am-7pm May-Sep, 9am-5.30pm Mar, Apr & Oct) shuttles services between the town centre, *sacro monte* and the train station, running approximately every half hour.

LOCARNO (SWITZERLAND)

POP 15,968

With its palm trees and much-hyped 2300 hours of sunshine a year, visitors have swooned over Locarno's near-Mediterranean setting since the late 19th century. Switzerland's lowest-altitude town is quite special, for sure, with an air of chic insouciance, a promenade strung along its mountain-facing lakefront and botanical gardens bristling with subtropical flowers and foliage. Beyond the lake, there's a pretty Renaissance Old Town to roam, which fans out from the Piazza Grande, host of a renowned music and film festival in summer.

For an eyrie-like view over the lake and an escape from the crowds, hitch a ride up to the forested peaks of Cardada and Cimetta. Or do as centuries of pilgrims have done before you and hike up the many steps to the Santuario della Madonna del Sasso.

⊙ Sights

You can feel just how close you are to Italy exploring Locarno's hilly Città Vecchia (Old Town), an appealing jumble of piazzas, arcades, churches and tall, shuttered Lombard houses in ice-cream colours. At its centre sits the **Piazza Grande**, with narrow lanes threading off in all directions, while **Castello Visconteo** guards its southwestern fringes.

★ Santuario della Madonna del Sasso   CHURCH

(www.madonnadelsasso.org; Via Santuario 2; ⊙7.30am-6pm) Overlooking the town, this sanctuary was built after the Virgin Mary supposedly appeared in a vision to a monk, Bartolomeo d'Ivrea, in 1480. There's a highly adorned church and several rather rough, near-life-size statue groups (including one of the Last Supper) in niches on the stairway. The best-known painting in the church is *La fuga in egitto* (Flight to Egypt), painted in 1522 by Bramantino.

A **funicular** (one way/return adult Sfr4.80/7.20, child Sfr2.20/3.60; ⊙8am-10pm May, Jun & Sep, to midnight Jul & Aug, to 9pm Apr & Oct, to 7.30pm Nov-Mar) runs every 15 minutes from the town centre past the sanctuary to Orselina, but a more scenic, pilgrim-style approach is the 20-minute walk up the chapel-lined Via Crucis (take Via al Sasso off Via Cappuccini).

Castello Visconteo   MUSEUM, CASTLE

(Piazza Castello; adult/child Sfr7/free; ⊙10am-noon & 2-5pm Tue-Sun Apr-Oct) Named after the Visconti clan that long ruled Milan, this fortified 15th-century castle's nucleus was raised around the 10th century. It now houses a museum with Roman and Bronze Age exhibits and also hosts a small display (in Italian) on the 1925 Locarno Treaty. Locarno is believed to have been a glass-manufacturing town in Roman times, which accounts for the many glass artefacts in the museum.

The castle changed hands various times and was occupied by the Milanese under Luchino Visconti in 1342. Taken by French forces in 1499, the castle and town of Locarno eventually fell to the Swiss confederation in 1516.

Parco Muralto   GARDENS

(Viale Verbano) Locarno's climate is perfect for lolling about the lake. Bristling with palms and ablaze with flowers in spring and summer, these gardens are a scenic spot for a picnic or swim, and tots can let off steam in the adventure playground.

Pinacoteca Casa Rusca   GALLERY

(http://museocasarusca.ch; Piazza Sant'Antonio; adult/child Sfr12/free; ⊙10am-noon & 2-5pm Tue-Sun) This gallery occupies a beautifully restored 18th-century townhouse, Casa Rusca. The permanent collection zooms in on 20th century paintings, sculpture and graphic works, and features a sizeable number of originals by German-French sculptor, painter and abstract artist Jean Arp (1886–1966).

⚡ Activities

Cimetta   CABLE CAR

(www.cardada.ch; return adult one way/return from Orselina Sfr30/36, child Sfr15/18; ⊙9.15am-12.30pm & 1.30-4.50pm daily Mar-Nov)

OFF THE BEATEN TRACK

THE CENTOVALLI

The **Centovalli train** (☎0324 24 20 55; www.centovalli.ch; Via Geremia Bonomelli; one way from €18), which trundles across numerous viaducts past villages along the deep valley between Locarno and Domodossola, is a scenic thrill. The train has roughly hourly departures and takes a little under two hours.

Locarno (Switzerland)

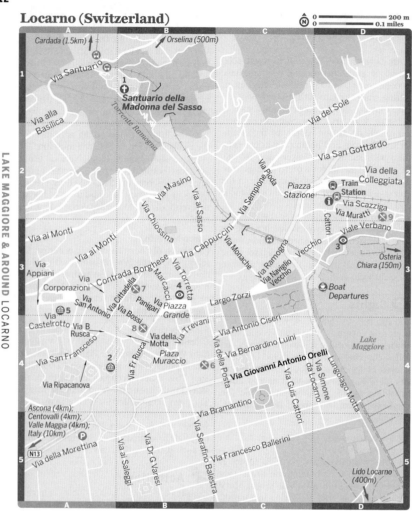

Locarno (Switzerland)

On clear days, the panorama that opens up at the 1671m Cimetta is out of this world – below you is the blue glitter of Lake Maggiore and beyond the Alps seem to ripple into infinity. Look carefully and you might be able to make out Switzerland's highest peak, the 4634m Dufourspitze, with its hat of snow.

The mountain is sliced up by walking trails (paths are marked) that can have you stomping along from 1½ to four or so hours, depending on which you choose. Longer routes lead into the Valle Maggia and Val Verzasca. In winter, skiers carve up the same slopes. A one-day ski pass costs Sfr38/22 for adults/children.

Cimetta is also a popular launch spot for paragliders. If you fancy taking flight, check out the offer of **Mountaingliders** (☑079 761 51 06; www.mountaingliders.com; tandem flights Sfr180).

Cardada HIKING
(www.cardada.ch; adult one way/return Sfr24/28, child Sfr12/14; ☺9.15am-6.15pm) From the Orselina funicular stop, a cable car rises every 30 minutes to 1332m Cardada, where a chairlift soars to Cimetta at 1671m. Make for the promenade suspended above the trees, at the end of which is a lookout point with 180-degree views over the city, Lake Maggiore and the valleys beyond. Cardada attracts hikers, mountain bikers and families.

Lido Locarno SWIMMING
(www.lidolocarno.ch; Via Respini 11; adult/child Sfr13/7, incl waterslides Sfr18/11; ☺8.30am-9pm) 🏊 Locarno's *lido* has several pools, including an Olympic-size one, children's splash areas and waterslides, and fabulous lake and mountain views. The huge complex uses solar and hydropower.

✨ Festivals & Events

Moon and Stars MUSIC
(https://moonandstars.ch; ☺mid-Jul) The stars shine at this open-air music festival in mid-July. Sting, Jamiroquai and Amy Macdonald were among recent headliners. Check the website for the full line-up and tickets.

Locarno Festival FILM
(www.pardo.ch; ☺early Aug) Locarno has hosted this 11-day film festival in August since 1948. At night, films are screened on a giant screen in **Piazza Grande**.

🍴 Eating

Caffe dell'Arte CAFE €
(www.caffedellarte.ch; Via Cittadella 9; light dishes Sfr15-20; ☺noon-8pm; 🛜) This classy, light-filled cafe is right at home in Locarno's old town with some outdoor tables on the lane, free wi-fi and a small but light menu that includes plates of local cheeses or lasagna.

Locanda Locarnese ITALIAN €€
(☑091 756 87 56; www.locandalocarnese.ch; Via Bossi 1; mains Sfr40-45; ☺noon-2.30pm & 7pm-midnight Mon-Sat) Elegant rusticity sums up this smart restaurant, with a beamed ceiling, crisp white tablecloths and an open fire, as well as a smattering of pavement seating. It's a romantic and intimate choice for season-driven dishes such as bresaola with artichokes and wild sea bass with chanterelle sauce and peaches.

Osteria Chiara ITALIAN €€
(☑091 743 32 96; www.osteriachiara.ch; Vicolo dei Chiara 1; mains Sfr34-45; ☺10am-2.30pm & 6.30-11pm Wed-Sun) Hidden up a flight of steps, Osteria Chiara has all the cosy feel of a grotto. Sit at granite tables beneath the pergola or at timber tables by the fireplace for homemade pasta and hearty meat dishes such as veal osso buco with saffroninfused risotto. From the lake, follow the signs uphill.

Bottega del Vino ITALIAN €€
(☑091 751 82 79; www.anceda.ch; Via Bernardino Luini 13; mains Sfr27-39; ☺10am-2pm & 5.30pm-midnight Mon-Fri, 6pm-midnight Sat) One for oenophiles, this bottle-lined wine bar and bistro has a convivial vibe and simple but spot-on dishes such as asparagus salad with parmesan, steak tartare and Sicilian-style tuna with tomatoes, capers and olives. These pair well with the carefully selected Ticinese wines on the list. The two-course lunch represents good value at Sfr25.

Osteria del Centenario FUSION €€€
(☑091 743 82 22; Viale Verbano 17; mains Sfr41-62, lunch Sfr25-45, dinner tasting menu Sfr126; ☺11.30am-3pm & 6.30pm-midnight Tue-Sat) Down by the lake, this is a top culinary address, turning out creative fusion dishes like pigeon served two ways with green curry and lime, and panna cotta with adzuki beans, matcha-tea sauce and vanilla. Service is attentive, the ambience discreetly elegant and many ingredients hail from Ticino.

ℹ️ Information

Tourist Office (☑0848 091 091; www.ascona-locarno.com; Piazza Stazione; ☺9am-6pm

LAKE MAGGIORE & AROUND LOCARNO

Mon-Fri, 10am-6pm Sat, 10am-1.30pm & 2.30-5pm Sun) Conveniently located at Locarno's train station, this tourist office has stacks of information about Locarno and the surrounding region. Ask about the Ticino Discovery Card and the Lago Maggiore Guest Card and its discounts.

❶ Getting There & Away

BUS
Postal buses to the surrounding valleys leave from outside the train station, and **boats** from the lakefront. There is cheap street parking along Via della Morettina.

CAR
If you're driving, Locarno is just off the main A13 road that links to Ascona, 2km southwest, and heads east to Bellinzona, 23km away.

TRAIN
Hourly trains run direct to/from Lucerne (Sfr59, two hours). There's also roughly hourly service to/from Brig (Sfr56, 2¾ hours), passing through Italy (bring your passport, and change trains at Domodossola). Most trains to/from Zürich (Sfr64, 2¼ hours) go via Bellinzona. There are twice-hourly train connections from Lugano (Sfr15.20, 58 minutes).

ASCONA (SWITZERLAND)

POP 5439

If ever there was a prize for the 'most perfect lake town', Ascona would surely win hands-down. Palm trees and pristine houses in a fresco painter's palette of pastels line the promenade, overlooking the glassy waters of Lake Maggiore to the rugged green mountains beyond. Michelin-starred restaurants, an 18-hole golf course and the Old Town's boutiques, galleries and antique shops attract a good-living, big-spending crowd.

◉ Sights & Activities

Isole di Brissago ISLAND
(www.isolebrissago.ch; adult/child Sfr8/2.50; ⊙9am-6pm Apr-late Oct) Marooned in the glimmering waters of Lake Maggiore, this speck of an island is famous for its botanic gardens that were designed in the 19th century. Magnolias, orchids, yuccas and agaves are among the 1700 species that flourish here.

Navigazione Lago Maggiore boats (Sfr16.80, 25 minutes) run regularly between Ascona and Brissago.

Museo Comunale d'Arte Moderna MUSEUM
(www.museoascona.ch; Via Borgo 34; adult/child Sfr10/free; ⊙10am-noon & 2-5pm Tue-Sat, 10.30am-12.30pm Sun Mar-Dec) Housed in the late-16th-century Palazzo Pancaldi, this museum showcases paintings by artists connected with the town, among them Paul Klee, Ben Nicholson, Alexej von Jawlensky and Hans Arp. But its pride and joy is the Marianne von Werefkin collection, comprising 90 paintings and 170 sketch books by the avant-garde Russian-Swiss Expressionist painter. Temporary exhibitions often home in on different aspects of the permanent collection.

Lido Ascona SWIMMING
(https://lidoascona.ch; Via Lido 81; adult/child Sfr6/3; ⊙lido 8.30am-5.30pm Jun–mid-Sep, bar to 1am) If you are itching to jump into that aqua-blue lake, head to this *lido* with a beach, diving platform, volleyball court and slides for the kids. The lounge bar is a cool spot to linger over a sundowner.

AscoNautica WATER SPORTS
(☑091 791 51 85; www.asconautica.ch; Via Albarelle 6) This reputable outfit arranges water sports including sailing, waterskiing and wakeboarding, and rents out sailing boats. See the website for prices.

⚑ Festivals & Events

Jazz Ascona MUSIC
(www.jazzascona.ch; ⊙late Jun) With the weather warming up in the second half of June, Ascona grooves into summer with local and international jazz acts.

Settimane Musicali MUSIC
(www.settimane-musicali.ch; ⊙early Sep–mid-Oct) Settimane Musicali is an international classical music festival that has been held annually in Ascona since 1946 from early September to mid-October.

✗ Eating

Antica Osteria Vacchini TICINESE €€
(☑091 791 13 96; www.osteriavacchini.ch; Via Contrada Maggiore 23; mains Sfr30-40; ⊙9am-2pm & 5-11pm Mon-Sat) Sizzling and stirring since

1685, this restaurant stays true to the best of Ticinese traditions, with a rustic, vaulted interior and a large terrace for warm-weather dining. The house special is *piodadella della Vallamaggia,* a set of three kinds of cold meats with three matching sauces, salad and fried potatoes – a filling and tasty summer option.

Grottino Ticinese   SWISS €€
(📋 091 791 3230; http://grottino-ticinese.ch; Via S Materno 10, Losone; mains Sfr20-40; 🕑 11.30am-2pm & 5.30-11pm Thu-Tue; 🎤) If you're craving the rustic warmth and simplicity of a Ticinese grotto, this is your place. There's an attractive garden for summer day dining and a menu jam-packed with local faves like polenta, *brasato* (beef braised in red wine) and osso buco. The lunch menu is a snip at Sfr14.50.

★**Ecco**   FUSION €€€
(📋 091 785 88 88; www.giardino.ch; Via del Segnale 10; tasting menus Sfr180-230; 🕑 7pm-midnight Wed-Sun & noon-2pm Sun mid-Apr–late Oct)

Super-chic Ecco flaunts two Michelin stars and dining here is an event. Chef Rolf Fliegauf runs the stove and works wonders with carefully selected seasonal ingredients to create dishes that are richly aromatic, edible works of art – be it Norway lobster with apricot and avocado, or meltingly tender bison fillet with bone marrow and celery.

ℹ Information

Tourist Office (📋 0848 091 091; www.ascona-locarno.com; Via B Papio 5; 🕑 9am-6pm Mon-Fri, 10am-6pm Sat, 10am-2pm Sun)

ℹ Getting There & Away

Ascona is on the main A13 road that leads along Lake Maggiore's northern shore, linking to Locarno, 2km northeast, and runs all the way to Bellinzona, 25km east.

Bus 1 from Locarno's **train station** (Piazza Staggione) and Piazza Grande stops at Ascona's post office with departures every 15 minutes (Sfr2.10, 18 minutes). Boat services on Lake Maggiore stop at Ascona.

LAKE MAGGIORE & AROUND ASCONA

Lake Como & Around

Best Places to Eat

➡ Crotto del Sergente (p121)

➡ Materia (p129)

➡ Il Cavatappi (p140)

➡ Antica Trattoria del Risorgimento (p136)

➡ Locanda dell'Isola (p133)

➡ Osteria Sale e Tabacchi (p138)

Best Places to Escape

➡ Valtellina (p141)

➡ Correno Plinio (p138)

➡ Valsassina (p140)

➡ La Dorsale del Triangolo Lariano (p44)

Why Go?

Set in the shadow of the snow-covered Rhaetian Alps and hemmed in on both sides by steep, verdant hillsides, Lake Como (aka Lake Lario) is perhaps the most spectacular of the three major lakes. Shaped like an upside-down Y, measuring around 160km in squiggly shoreline, it's littered with villages, including exquisite Bellagio and Varenna. Where the southern and western shores converge is the lake's main town, Como, an elegant, prosperous Italian city.

Among the area's siren calls are some extraordinarily sumptuous villas, often graced with paradisiacal gardens. The mountainous terrain means that opportunities for taking bird's-eye views of the lake and its towns are numerous. And with a fraction of the visitors drawn here compared to Lake Maggiore or Lake Garda, Lake Como and its surrounding area offer the traveller the chance to enjoy a real sense of discovery.

Road Distances (km)

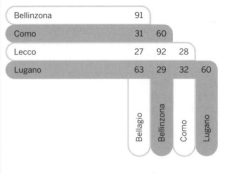

	Bellagio	Bellinzona	Como	Lugano
Bellinzona	91			
Como	31	60		
Lecco	27	92	28	
Lugano	63	29	32	60

COMO

📋 031 / POP 84,500

With its charming historic centre, the town of Como sparkles year-round. Within its remaining 12th-century city walls, the beautiful people of this prosperous city whisk about from shop to cafe, sweeping by the grandeur of the city's cathedral, villas and the loveliness of its lake shore with admirable insouciance. The town is a lovely spot for an aimless wander, punctuated with coffee and drink stops, especially in Piazzas Cavour, Alessandro Volta and San Fedele.

Como built its wealth on the silk industry and it remains Europe's most important producer of silk products.

⊙ Sights

★ **Basilica di San Fedele**   BASILICA
(Piazza San Fedele; ⊙ 8am-noon & 3.30-7pm) With three naves and three apses, this evocative basilica is often likened to a clover leaf. Parts of it date from the 12th century while the facade is the result of a 1914 revamp. The 16th-century rose window and 16th- and 17th-century frescoes enhance the appeal. The apses are centuries-old and feature some eye-catching sculpture on the right.

A craft and antiques **market** (Craft & Antiques Market; ⊙ 9am-7pm Sat) fills the piazza in front of the basilica on Saturdays.

Villa Olmo   HISTORIC BUILDING
(📋 031 25 23 52; www.villaolmocomo.it; Via Cantoni 1; gardens free, villa entry varies by exhibition; ⊙ villa during exhibitions 10am-6pm Tue-Sun, gardens 8am-11pm Apr-Sep, to 7pm Oct-Mar) Set facing the lake, the grand creamy facade of neoclassical Villa Olmo is one of Como's biggest landmarks. The extravagant structure was built in 1728 by the Odescalchi family, related to Pope Innocent XI. If there's an art exhibition showing, you'll get to admire the sumptuous *stile liberty* (Italian art nouveau) interiors. Otherwise, you can enjoy the Italianate and English gardens.

At press time, parts of the grounds and sections of the villa were closed for long-term restoration and garden improvements.

★ **Duomo**   CATHEDRAL
(Cattedrale di Como; 📋 031 3 31 22 75; Piazza del Duomo; ⊙ 10.30am-5pm Mon-Sat, 1-4.30pm Sun) Although largely Gothic in style, elements of Romanesque, Renaissance and baroque can also be seen in Como's imposing, marble-clad *duomo*. The cathedral was built between the 14th and 18th centuries, and is crowned by a high octagonal dome.

Villa Sucota   HISTORIC BUILDING
(📋 031 338 49 76; www.fondazioneratti.org; Via Cernobbio 19; ⊙ gardens 10am-6pm Sun year-round, daily in Aug; museum hours vary) A grand villa overlooking the lake, northwest of the centre, Villa Sucota was built in the late-19th and early-20th centuries. It has been home to various aristocratic families over the years, including Metternich, Napoleon's doctor. These days it serves as the headquarters for the Antonio Ratti Foundation, with a focus on textiles and contemporary art. Changing exhibitions are held inside (some free), and there's usually public art in the gardens.

Museo della Seta   MUSEUM
(Silk Museum; 📋 031 30 31 80; www.museoseta como.com; Via Castelnuovo 9; adult/reduced €10/7; ⊙ 10am-6pm Tue-Fri, to 1pm Sat) Lake Como's aspiring silk makers still learn their trade in the 1970s-built Istituto Tecnico Industriale di Setificio textile technical school. It's also home to the Museo della Seta, which draws together the threads of the town's silk history. Early dyeing and printing equipment features amid displays that chart the entire fabric production process.

Basilica di Sant'Abbondio   BASILICA
(Via Regina; ⊙ 8am-6pm summer, to 4.30pm winter) About 500m south of Como's city walls

LAKE COMO & AROUND COMO

LOCAL KNOWLEDGE

OPEN GARDENS

On Sundays, the interconnected grounds of three Como villas open to the public (from about 10am to 6pm). Dotting the shore just northwest of the centre, a 1km promenade connects the **Villa Olmo**, the **Villa del Grumello** (www.villadelgrumello.it; Via Cernobbio 11; ⊙ grounds 10am-7pm Sun year-round, daily in Aug) and the **Villa Sucota**. Sometimes referred to as the Chilometro della Conoscenza (Kilometre of Knowledge), this scenic stroll takes in lush trails, fragrant gardens and hilltop views with lovely Lake Como ever in the background. Be sure to stop in the Villa Olmo and the Villa Sucota, which often host temporary art exhibitions.

Lake Como & Around Highlights

1 Como (p117)
Exploring the bustling plazas and hidden medieval lanes of Lake Como's best-known destination.

2 Castello di Vezio (p139) Wandering the scenic waterfront of Varenna then climbing to this hilltop fortress for superlative views.

3 Villa Carlotta (p136) Imagining how 19th-century aristocrats lived overlooking the gorgeous gardens of this fabled *palazzo*.

4 Bellagio (p125) Staying on after the crowds have left and having the picturesque lanes of this lakeside village all to yourself.

5 Brunate (p120) Taking the funicular to this clifftop village for panoramic lake views.

6 Lugano (p142) Riding the funiculars and ambling along the waterfront of Switzerland's easy-going lakeside beauty.

7 Bellinzona (p147) Stepping back into medieval times by visiting the three Unesco World Heritage–listed castles.

8 Ossuccio (p132) Walking the old pilgrim's path above the lake, followed by a visit to archaeologically rich Isola Comacina, Como's only island.

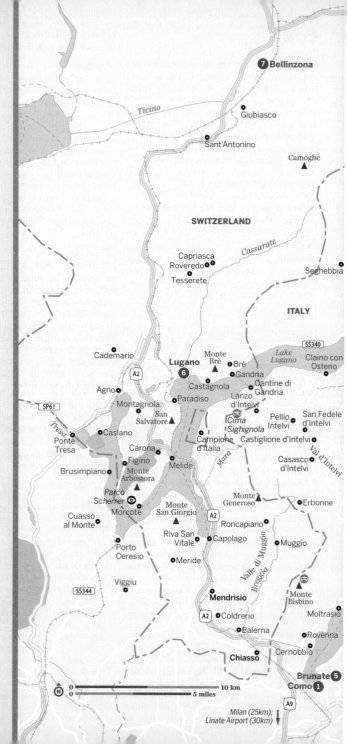

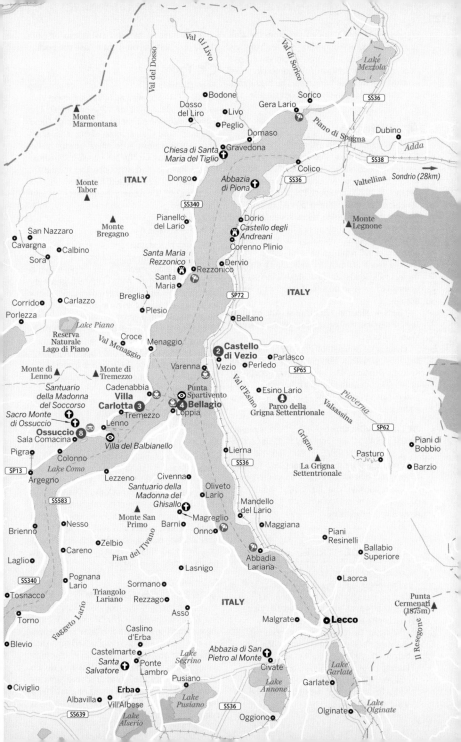

is the remarkable 11th-century Romanesque Basilica di Sant'Abbondio. Aside from its proud, high structure and impressive apse decorated with a beautiful geometric relief around the outside windows, the highlights are the extraordinary frescoes inside the apse.

🏃 Activities

Funicolare Como–Brunate CABLE CAR
(☑ 031 30 36 08; www.funicolarecomo.it; Piazza de Gasperi 4; adult one way/return €3/5.50, reduced €2/3.20; ☺ half-hourly departures 6am-midnight summer, to 10.30pm winter) Prepare for some spectacular views. The Como–Brunate cable car (built in 1894) takes seven minutes to trundle up to the quiet hilltop village of **Brunate** (720m), revealing a memorable panorama of mountains and lakes. From there a steep 30-minute walk along a stony mule track leads to **San Maurizio** (907m), where 143 steps climb to the top of a light-house.

The San Maurizio lighthouse was built in 1927 to mark the centenary of Alessandro Volta's death.

The Como tourist office (p124) can provide a map with a range of suggested walks around Brunate. It's best to book a return ticket. The meandering path between Como and Brunate is narrow, steep and poorly signed.

★ Lido di Villa Olmo SWIMMING
(☑ 031 3 38 48 54; www.lidovillaolmo.it; Via Cernobbio 2; adult/reduced €9/5; ☺ 9am-7pm mid-May–Sep) What a delight: a compact *lido* (beach) where you can plunge into open-air pools, sunbathe beside the lake, rent boats, sip cocktails at the waterfront bar and soak up mountain views. Bliss.

A LAKESIDE STROLL

One of Como's most charming walks is the lakeside stroll west from Piazza Cavour. Passeggiata Lino Gelpi leads past the **Monumento ai Caduti** (Viale Puecher 9), a 1931 memorial to Italy's WWI dead. Next you'll pass a series of mansions and villas, including **Villa Saporiti** (Via Borgovico 148) and **Villa Gallia**, both now owned by the provincial government and closed to the public, before arriving at the garden-ringed **Villa Olmo** (p117).

You'll have to bring a swim cap or purchase one here if you want to use the pool.

☞ Tours

Aero Club Como SCENIC FLIGHTS
(☑ 031 57 44 95; www.aeroclubcomo.com; Viale Masia 44; 30min flight for 1/2 people €180) For a true touch of glamour, take one of these seaplane tours and buzz about the skies high above Como. The often-bumpy take-off and landing on the lake itself is thrilling, as are the views down onto the miniature villas and villages dotted far below. Flights are popular; in summer book three or four days ahead.

🍴 Eating

★ Cascina Respaù ITALIAN €
(☑ 031 52 36 62; www.cascinarespau.it; Via Santa Brigide e Respaù; meals €15-25; ☺ noon-3pm & 7-10pm Sat & Sun) 🍴 Amid the lush greenery high above Como, this small rustic eatery feels like an idyllic escape from the sometimes maddening crowds along the lake. Charming hosts, delicious home-made dishes and a cosy setting (with outdoor seating on warm days) add to the appeal – as does the attention to locally sourced ingredients, like fall-off-the-bone pork and organic wines from small producers.

Call ahead to let them know you're coming. There's also a delightful **hostel** (dorm/double from €19/55) here.

La Vita è Bella ITALIAN €
(☑ 031 30 26 67; Piazza Croggi 4; meals €20-30; ☺ noon-3pm & 7-10.30pm; 🌱) For something a little different, head to this congenial, easy-going spot near Como's waterfront. Famed far and wide for bountiful, creatively topped salads, La Vita also serves up good pastas, grilled meats and seafood, and a fine paella. The small space (and glassed-in terrace in front) fills up nightly, so it's best to reserve a table in advance.

Gelateria Ceccato GELATO €
(☑ 031 2 33 91; Lungo Lario Trieste 16; gelato €2-4; ☺ noon-midnight summer, hours vary winter) For generations *comaschi* (Como residents) have turned to Ceccato for their Sunday-afternoon gelato and then embarked on a ritual *passeggiata* (stroll) with their dripping cones along the lake shore. You can do no better than imitate them: order a creamy *stracciatella* (chocolate chip) or perhaps a mix of fresh fruit flavours and head off for a relaxed promenade.

★**Crotto del Sergente**   TRATTORIA €€
(☑031 28 39 11; www.crottodelsergente.it; Via Crotto del Sergente 13; meals €35-45; ☺noon-2pm & 7.30-10pm Sun-Fri, 7.30-10pm Sat) Although it's a bit of a trek (4km southeast of Como's centre), the delectable Slow Food cooking at this rustic eatery makes it well worth the effort. Set in a barrel-vaulted brick dining room, Crotto del Sergente serves excellent grilled meats and seafood (including a flavoursome bouillabaisse), best matched with a fine glass of Nebbiolo. Reserve ahead.

★**Natta Café**   CAFE €€
(☑031 26 91 23; www.facebook.com/nattacafecomo; Via Natta 16; meals €20-35; ☺12.30-3pm & 7.30-11pm Tue-Sun; ☏) 🅿 In an atmospheric stone-arched dining room, this *osteria* (tavern) has a proud focus on superb local ingredients and classic wines, while also remaining remarkably warm and inviting. It's a particularly good spot for a light meal, with delectable cheese platters, creative bruschetta and *piadine* (flat-bread sandwiches) and excellent salmon tartare – though pastas and daily specials provide more filling options.

★**Osteria del Gallo**   ITALIAN €€
(☑031 27 25 91; www.osteriadelgallo-como.it; Via Vitani 16; meals €26-32; ☺12.30-3pm Mon, to 10pm Tue-Sat) An ageless *osteria* that looks exactly the part. In the wood-lined dining room, wine bottles and other goodies fill the shelves, and diners sit at small timber tables to tuck into traditional local food. The menu is chalked up daily and might include a first course of *zuppa di ceci* (chickpea soup), followed by lightly fried lake fish.

Pane e Tulipani   CAFE €€
(☑031 26 42 42; www.pane-e-tulipani.com; Via Lambertenghi 3; meals €28-45; ☺10am-11pm Tue-Sun) With its vast number of grappa bottles, shabby-chic furniture and huge vases of flowers, this sweet eatery – which is part-cafe, part-bistro and part–flower shop – has a bohemian air. This means you get to sample creative twists on Italian standards (don't expect big portions) or linger in the afternoon over drinks and snacks surrounded by a profusion of blooms.

Ristorante da Rino   TUSCAN €€
(☑031 27 30 28; www.ristoranterino.com; Via Vitani 3; meals €35-45; ☺12.30-2pm & 7.30-10pm Tue-Sat, 12.30-2pm Sun) When the (acclaimed) specialities of the house all involve truffles, you tend to be onto a good thing. There's a stellar range of *primi* and *secondi*, and you'll find truffles with *tagliolini* (thin ribbon pasta), risotto and eggs. The pick is *filetto alla medici* – a tender beef fillet steeped in truffles and red wine.

Ristorante Sociale   ITALIAN €€
(☑031 26 40 42; www.ristorantesociale.it; Via Rodari 6; meals €26-36; ☺noon-2pm & 7-10.30pm Wed-Mon) A workaday street round the back of the *duomo* is an unlikely spot for such a bewitching restaurant. The menu is packed with local meat and lake produce, and might feature perch and porcini mushrooms. Tuck in under the red-brick barrel ceiling, or in the charming courtyard.

It's the perfect spot for a great-value two-course lunch (€18, includes water, coffee and wine).

Osteria Angolo del Silenzio   ITALIAN €€
(☑031 337 21 57; www.osterialangolodelsilenzio-como.com; Viale Lecco 25; meals €38-45; ☺noon-3pm & 7-10pm Tue-Sun) The 'Corner of Silence' lives up to its name with a succession of dining rooms and a fine rear garden. Locals mix with the occasional celeb hoping to pass off unobserved while digging into the succulent *filetti di pesce persico con risotto* (perch fillets with risotto).

🍷 Drinking & Nightlife

Brothers Cafe   CAFE
(☑031 225 45 25; Via Paolo Carcano 2; ☺7am-9pm) There's no sign and the space is tiny, but the charm factor is high in this hip little cafe and drinking den. Stop by in the morning for fresh pastries and espresso, then pop back in the evening for cocktails (jaunty suspender-wearing baristas whip up a mighty fine spritz). There's also a lunch plate or two for the midday crowd.

Vintage Jazz Food & Wine   BAR
(☑031 414 13 46; www.vintagejazzcomo.com; Via Olginati 14; ☺9.30am-midnight Tue-Thu, to 1.30am Fri & Sat, 3.30pm-midnight Sun) Flickering candles, walls covered with bric-a-brac and a jazzy soundtrack make a fine setting for an evening drink at this rambling eating and drinking space on Piazza Mazzini. This place gets packed, especially around *aperitivo* (pre-dinner drink) time, so go early (or late) to beat the crowds.

Como

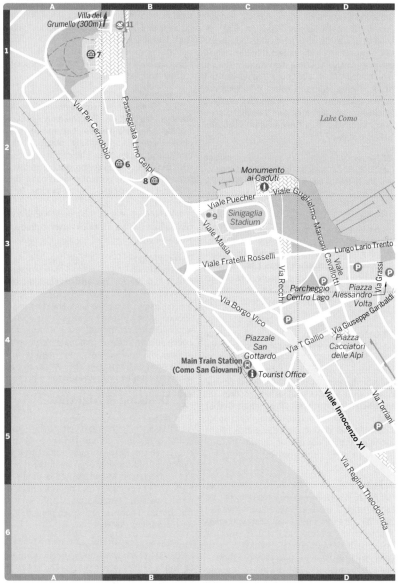

Enoteca Castiglioni WINE BAR
(📞 031 26 18 60; www.castiglionistore.com; Via Rovelli 17; ⏰10am-8pm Mon-Fri, to 9pm Sat) If you are lucky you will bag one of the clutch of tiny tables situated beside the ranks of shelves lined with wine bottles. It is a smart, modern setting in which to sample top-quality deli produce along with first-rate vintage wines.

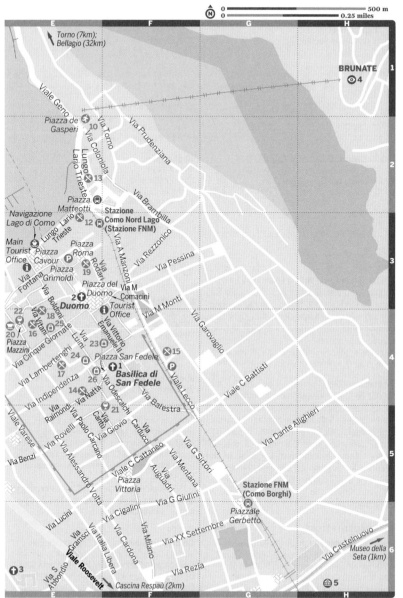

LAKE COMO & AROUND COMO

Shopping

Lopez Vintage FASHION & ACCESSORIES
(031 24 20 43; Via Vitani 32; 10am-12.30pm &
3.30-7pm Tue-Sat) On Como's most atmospheric street, Lopez Vintage lures you in with its whimsical window displays of curios from a bygone era. Inside, the tiny jewel box of a shop has elegant vintage pieces – slim-fitting dresses, oversized sunglasses, hats, accessories and other eye candy. Prices can be high, but you'll discover unique apparel you won't find elsewhere.

Como

A Picci   GIFTS & SOUVENIRS
(☑ 031 26 13 69; Via Vittorio Emanuele II 54; ⊙ 3-7.30pm Mon, 9am-12.30pm & 3-7.30pm Tue-Sat) First opened in 1919, this is the last remaining silk shop in town dedicated to selling Como-designed-and-made silk ties, scarves, throws and sarongs. Products are grouped in price category (starting at €15 for a tie), reflecting the skill and work involved.

Enoteca da Gigi   WINE
(☑ 031 26 31 86; www.enotecagigi.com; Via Luini 48; ⊙ 11am-1.30pm & 2.30-8pm Mon, 9am-8pm Tue-Fri, to 9pm Sat) Wines, vintage whiskies and grappas, along with olive oils and balsamic vinegars, line the walls of this sociable wine shop and bar. Drop by in the evening for a glass of *prosecco* (sparkling wine) or a sauvignon blanc (from around €3) and enjoy the free, freshly prepared bruschetta.

ℹ Information

Main Tourist Office (☑ 031 26 97 12; www.visitcomo.eu; Piazza Cavour 17; ⊙ 9am-1pm & 2.30-6pm Mon-Sat year-round, 9.30am-1pm Sun Jun-Sep) Como's main tourist office.

Tourist Office (☑ 342 0076403; www.visitcomo.eu; Como San Giovanni, Piazzale San Gottardo; ⊙ 9am-5pm summer, 10am-4pm Wed-Mon winter) Inside the San Giovanni train station.

Tourist Office (☑ 031 26 42 15; www.visitcomo.eu; Via Comacini; ⊙ 10am-6pm) Beside the *duomo*.

ℹ Getting There & Away

BUS
ASF Autolinee (SPT; ☑ 031 24 72 49; www.sptlinea.it) ASF Autolinee operates buses around Lake Como. Key routes include Como–Menaggio (€6.10, 1¼ hours, three to five daily) via the west shore; Como–Bellagio (€3.40, 70 minutes, roughly hourly); and Como–Erba–Lecco (€3.40, one hour, almost hourly). Further afield, buses link Como with Bergamo (€6.10, 2¼ hours, up to six daily).

CAR
Traffic in and around Como can be busy in summer. From Milan, take the A9 motorway and turn off at Monte Olimpino. The SP342 leads east to Lecco and the SS342 goes west to Varese. The roads around the lake are narrow and can be hair-raising.

Most parking is metered in Como. **Parcheggio Centro Lago** (Via Sant'Elia 6; per hr €2.40) is a handy central car park.

TRAIN
Como San Giovanni (Via Corrado e Giulio Venini) Como's main train station has services from Milan's Stazione Centrale or Porta Garibaldi (€4.80 to €13.50 depending on type of train, 37 to 90 minutes, at least hourly) that continue into Switzerland.

Como Nord Lago (Stazione FNM; Via A Manzoni) Como's lakeside train station (aka Stazione FNM) is an easy stroll to the centre. Trains from Milan's Stazione Nord (€4.80, one hour, hourly) use this station.

BOAT

Navigazione Lago di Como (☎800 551801; www.navigazionelaghi.it; Lungo Lario Trento) Operates year-round lake-wide ferries and hydrofoils, which in Como depart from the jetties beside Piazza Cavour. Single fares range between €2.50 (to Cernobbio) and €12.60 (to Lecco). Return fares cost double. The faster hydrofoil services cost €1.40 to €4.90 extra. Car ferries link Menaggio on the west shore of Lake Como with Varenna on the east and Bellagio to the south.

Ferries operate year-round, but services are reduced in winter. Zonal passes (per day €6.90 to €28; per six days €20.70 to €84) allow unlimited journeys and can work out cheaper than buying single or return tickets.

TRIANGOLO LARIANO

They call the stretch of territory between Como and Lecco in the south and Bellagio in the north the Triangolo Lariano (Lake Lario Triangle), a mountainous and crumpled territory jammed with a surprising variety of landscapes. From the high and exhilarating 32km lakeside road between Como and Bellagio to quiet inland villages, there's plenty to discover.

The pearl is Bellagio, suspended like a pendant on the promontory where the lake's western and eastern arms split and head south. Hidden from view along the Como–Bellagio road are enchanting lakeside villages, like Torno and Careno (which get no direct sunlight in winter). The sunnier 22km eastern branch, between Bellagio and Lecco, is also a pretty drive.

Activities

Jungle Raider Park Xtreme   ADVENTURE SPORTS
(☎346 508 82 64; www.jrpxtreme.com; Viale Campoè, Caglio; €30; ⏰10am-3.30pm Sat & Sun Apr-Jun & Sep-Oct, 10am-5.30pm Tue, Thu, Sat & Sun Jul & Aug) This new adventure park offers adrenaline-fueled adventures thanks to its ziplines that take you on a course through the lush hillsides high above Lake Como. The whole course, featuring seven different stages, takes about two hours to complete.

There's also a smaller family-friendly section for rope-bridge walks amid the treetops (admission for these €8 to €15). The park is about 20km south of Bellagio (a 40-minute drive). Call ahead to reserve a spot before making the trip.

Bellagio

☎031 / POP 3100
It's impossible not to be smitten by Bellagio's waterfront of bobbing boats, its maze of steep stone staircases, red-roofed and green-shuttered buildings, dark cypress groves and rhododendron-filled gardens. Like the prow of a beautiful vessel, it sits at the crux of the inverted Y that is Lake Como;

LAKE COMO & AROUND BELLAGIO

OFF THE BEATEN TRACK

HIKING THE TRIANGOLO LARIANO

Hiking options abound in the Triangolo Lariano. The classic trail is known as the **Dorsale** (Ridge) and zigzags for around 30km across the interior of this mountainous country from the **Brunate** (p120) funicular station to Bellagio. The standard trail takes about 12 hours and is usually done in two stages, stopping in mountain huts along the way. The standard route follows mule trails, presents no particular difficulties to moderately fit ramblers and is also ideal for **mountain biking**.

The more adventurous can follow the **Dorsale Creste** trail, which follows a series of mountain crests. Several mountain huts (*rifugi*) are dotted along the way, and you'll find a couple of accommodation options at **Pian del Tivano**, roughly halfway along the trail. You can do a little **cross-country skiing** (*sci di fondo*) here in winter. From the 17th century until the early 1900s, when the lakeside road from Como to Bellagio was completed, travellers used the 32km **Strada Regia** (Royal Way), a partly stone-paved path that links various villages on the west shore of the Triangolo Lariano from Torno to Lezzeno. The easiest stretch connects Torno and Pognana Lario (about five hours), while the stage from Pognana to Lezzeno via Nesso (or Careno) branches into mountainous back country between villages. Other walking trails abound.

Ask at the main Como **tourist office** for the fine *Carta dei Sentieri* (Trail Map; 1:25,000) produced by the Comunità Montana Triangolo Lariano.

the Como and Lecco arms of the lake wash off to port and starboard. Wander out of the old town centre to Punta Spartivento and gaze north up the third arm towards the Alps. In Roman times, Pliny had one of his favourite villas here.

Bellagio is hardly a secret. On summer weekends, foreign tourists are overwhelmed by hordes of day trippers up from Milan. Try to come midweek if you want a modicum of peace. It makes a nice base for ferry trips to other locations on the lake, in particular Varenna, on Lake Como's east shore.

◉ Sights

Villa Melzi d'Eril   GARDENS
(☑ 339 4573838; www.giardinidivillamelzi.it; Lungo Lario Manzoni; adult/reduced €6.50/4; ⊙ 9.30am-6.30pm Apr-Oct) The grounds of neoclassical Villa Melzi d'Eril are a highlight among Lake Como's (many) delightful places. The villa was built in 1808 for one of Napoleon's associates and is coloured by flowering azaleas and rhododendrons in spring. The statue-studded gardens was the first English-style park on the lake.

The walk to Villa Melzi, south along the lake shore from the Bellagio ferry jetties, reveals views of ranks of gracious residencies stacked up on the waterside hills.

Villa Serbelloni   GARDENS
(☑ 031 95 15 55; Piazza della Chiesa 14; adult/child €9/5; ⊙ tours 11.30am & 3.30pm Tue-Sun mid-Mar–Oct) The lavish gardens of Villa Serbelloni cover much of the promontory on which Bellagio sits. The villa has been a magnet for Europe's great and good, including Austria's emperor Maximilian I, Ludovico il Moro and Queen Victoria. The interior is closed to the public, but you can explore the terraced park and gardens, by guided tour only. Numbers are limited; tickets are sold at the Promo-Bellagio (p128) information office near the church.

🏃 Activities

Lido di Bellagio   SWIMMING
(☑ 031 95 11 95; www.lidodibellagio.com; Via Paolo Carcano 1; per half-/full day €6/10; ⊙ 10.30am-6.30pm Tue-Sun May, Jun & Sep, daily Jul & Aug) With its sand-covered decking, diving platforms and gazebos, Bellagio's *lido* is a prime place to laze on a sun lounger or plunge into the lake.

🧭 Tours

Bellagio Water Sports   WATER SPORTS
(☑ 340 394 93 75; www.bellagiowatersports.com; Pescallo Harbour; rental per 2/4hr €18/30, tours €35; ⊙ 8.30am-4.30pm Mon-Sat, to 2.30pm Sun) You can hire sit-on-top kayaks and SUP boards at this experienced outfitter based in Pescallo, on the east side of the Bellagio headland. Bellagio Water Sports also offers five different kayaking tours, from a one-hour paddle taking in nearby historical villas to a 3½-hour trip to scenic Varenna.

Barindelli's   BOATING
(☑ 338 211 03 37; www.barindellitaxiboats.it; Piazza Mazzini; tours per hour €150) For a touch of film-star glamour, take a tour in one of Barindelli's chic mahogany cigarette boats.

WORTH A TRIP

MADONNA DEL GHISALLO

In the high-country village of **Magreglio** (497m), 7km south of Bellagio, stands a simple 17th-century church known as the **Santuario della Madonna del Ghisallo** (Via Campolungo 2; ⊙ 9.30am-5.30pm Apr-Oct). But this is not just any old high-mountain chapel.

The road up has frequently been included as a classic stage of the Giro d'Italia cycle race, and is known to professional and amateur cyclists alike. The sanctuary long ago became a symbolic finishing line for cyclists, who began leaving mementoes there. The place's importance for two-wheel enthusiasts was such that Pope Pius XII declared the Madonna del Ghisallo the patron of cyclists.

The gifts and tokens left at the sanctuary down the years became so numerous that it was decided to open the nearby **Museo del Ciclismo** (☑ 031 96 58 85; www.museo delghisallo.it; Via Gino Bartali 4; €6; ⊙ 10am-6pm Sat & Sun Apr, Tue-Sun May-Oct) to contain the overflow. The museum is devoted to all aspects of the business of cycling, with a hundred film clips of great moments in Italian cycling, memorabilia (including many bicycles) and temporary exhibitions – ample reward for the punishing climb.

The group offers hour-long sunset tours around the Bellagio headland and can also tailor-make outings around the lake.

🥾 Courses

⭐ **Bellagio Cooking Classes** COOKING
(☑ 333 7860090; www.gustoitalianobellagio.com; Salita Plinio 5; per person €90) A wonderful way to really get to know Bellagio, these cooking classes have a personal touch – they take you to the village shops to buy the food and then local home-cooks lead the sessions. Classes are small (a minimum of three, maximum of seven). Payment in cash only.

🍴 Eating

⭐ **Ristorante Silvio** ITALIAN €€
(☑ 031 95 03 22; www.bellagiosilvio.com; Via Carcano 12; meals €28-38; ⊙ noon-3pm & 6.30-10pm Mar–mid-Nov & Christmas week) Operating since 1919, this place must be getting something right to achieve the seemingly unanimous acclaim. Simple food at reasonable prices combine with lovely views over the lake. You might start with a *riso e filetto di pesce* (rice with lemon juice and Parmesan, topped by fillets of the day's lake catch), followed by a *frittura leggera di luccio* (fry-up of pike chunks).

From the pergola garden outside, you can also espy the Romanesque Chiesa di Santa Maria of Loppia in among the cypresses. It's 1km south of the centre of Bellagio above Loppia, which you can walk down to from here along an overgrown stairway.

⭐ **Ittiturismo da Abate** SEAFOOD €€
(☑ 031 91 49 86; www.ittiturismodabate.it; Frazione Villa 4, Lezzeno; meals €28-38; ⊙ 7-10.30pm Tue-Sun, noon-2.30pm Sun; P ♿) Most dishes at Slow Food–focused Da Abate feature fish that's been caught that day in the lake (the restaurant will only open if they've caught enough), so you can sample *lavarello* (white fish) in balsamic vinegar, linguine with perch and black olives, and the robust *missoltino* (fish dried in salt and bay leaves).

Da Abate is 8km south of Bellagio. Booking advised.

Terrazza Barchetta ITALIAN €€
(☑ 031 95 13 89; www.ristorantebarchetta.com; Salita Mella 13; meals €37-54; ⊙ noon-2.30pm & 7-10.15pm) This intimate terrace just above a meeting of laneways in Bellagio's old town is a fine place for a meal. The restaurant has been around since 1887, which is plenty

of time to perfect dishes such as boneless lake trout with an almond crust or grilled lamb chops with mint sauce. Pizzas are also top-notch.

Ristorante Antico Pozzo ITALIAN €€
(☑ 339 873 61 88; www.bellagioanticopozzo.eu; Salita Mella 26; meals €32-48; ⊙ noon-10pm) They do the simple things well here – think pizza, pasta and other Italian staples served on an agreeable open courtyard.

🍷 Drinking & Nightlife

⭐ **Enoteca Cava Turacciolo** WINE BAR
(☑ 031 95 09 75; www.cavaturacciolo.it; Salita Genazzini 3; ⊙ 10.30am-1am Thu-Tue Apr-Oct, shorter hours Nov, Dec & Mar, closed Jan & Feb) A contender for Bellagio's most charming address, this cosy wine bar occupies a candlelit, stonewalled space tucked down a lane near the waterfront. The encyclopedic wine list covers every region in Italy, and there's excellent charcuterie and cheese boards on offer – as well as a few pasta and fish plates.

Bar Rossi BAR
(☑ 031 95 01 96; Piazza Mazzini 22; snacks €4-8; ⊙ 6.30am-11pm Apr-Sep, to 8pm Oct-Mar) All gleaming walnut wood, glinting mirrors and regiments of bottles, the art nouveau Bar Rossi is one cafe not to miss. Revel in the elegant interior or take a seat outside under the arches and watch the ferries come and go.

🛍 Shopping

Alimentaria Gastronomia FOOD
(Via Bellosio 1; ⊙ 7.30am-9pm) The smells wafting out from this deli will surely tempt you to step inside. Among the piled-high Larian goodies are dried porcini mushrooms, DOP Laghi Lombardi-Lario olive oil, *missoltini* (dried fish) and some rather irreverently shaped bottles of limoncello.

There's an excellent cheese and meat counter, and staff can happily assemble sandwiches with your ingredients of choice.

Atelier ART
(☑ 031 95 13 96; www.atelierbellagio.it; Salita Mella 27; ⊙ 10am-1pm & 2-5pm) Lili Barone and Gabriel Kantor turn out exquisite etchings, engravings and other design products from their studio high in Bellagio's old town. Opening hours can be a bit hit-or-miss.

Carmen Como Silk CLOTHING
(☑ 031 95 01 01; Salita Serbelloni 8; ⊙ 10am-6.30pm) Como's renowned silk manufacturing

industry sends ties, scarves and other accessories up the road to this small Bellagio shop.

Magda Guaitamacchi CERAMICS
([☎]031 95 14 62; www.bellagio.co.nz/magdaguaitamacchi; Salita Serbelloni 27; ⊘10am-12.45pm & 2.30-6.45pm) Magda Guaitamacchi turns out gorgeous ceramic and porcelain pieces that have gone on show around the world.

ℹ Information

Tourist Office ([☎]031 95 02 04; www.bellagio lakecomo.com; Piazza Mazzini; ⊘9am-1pm & 2-6pm Mon-Sat, 10.30am-12.30pm & 1.30-5.30pm Sun, reduced hours winter) Bellagio's official tourist office, next to the boat landing stage is quite helpful. Can provide information on walks in the area, water sports, mountain biking and other activities.
PromoBellagio ([☎]031 95 15 55; www.bellagio lakecomo.com; Piazza della Chiesa 14; ⊘9.30am-1pm Mon, 9-11am & 2.30-3.30pm Tue-Sun Apr-Oct) A consortium of local businesses that provides useful information. This is also the place to book guided tours to visit **Villa Serbelloni** (p126).

ℹ Getting There & Away

Bellagio Bus Stop (Lunco Lario Manzoni) The Bellagio bus stop is located in front of the embarkation point for the car ferry.

Torno

POP 1200

Spread around a point in Lake Como's jagged shore, Torno is a lovely stop just 7km from Como – it's easy to understand why Hermann Hesse fell in love with it when he visited in 1913. The lakeside Piazza Casartelli, fronted by several restaurants and the **Chiesa di Santa Tecla** (a baroque remake of the Romanesque original), the tiny port and shady trees complete the picture of this front-row seat on the lake.

✖ Eating

Hotel Ristorante Vapore ITALIAN €€
([☎]031 41 93 11; www.hotelvapore.it; Via Plinio 20; meals €37-47; ⊘12.15-2.30pm & 7-10pm Thu-Tue; ☏) At the north end of Torno's lakeside square, this family-run hotel-restaurant has an elegant dining room and an even lovelier lakeside terrace. Both make fine settings for lake fish and beautifully executed pastas and steaks.

If you need a break from the heaving crowds of Como (city), you can also overnight in one of the hotel's peaceful rooms (doubles around €130)

LAKE COMO WEST BANK

By not having the mountains block the light, the western shore gets the most sunshine on Lake Como. For this reason, it's lined with the most lavish villas, where high-fliers from football players to film stars reside. The shore stretches 75km from Como north to Sorico at the lake's tip; from here you can continue north along an Alpine valley to Chiavenna and, 40km further, cross into Switzerland.

Between May and September, watch out for musical concerts at some of Lake Como's lakeside villas as part of the Lake Como Festival (www.lakecomofestival.com).

Cernobbio

POP 7100

The shoreline of Cernobbio, a graceful town 5km north of Como (and now melded to it with residential districts), is laced with a series of fine villas fronting the water. It's probably true that half of Cernobbio's visitors come by in the hope of spotting George Clooney at one of its central cafes (he lives about 10km up the road in Laglio), especially since scenes from *Ocean's 12* were shot here.

◉ Sights

Villa Bernasconi HISTORIC BUILDING
(Via Regina 7) One of the most outstanding *stile liberty* (Italian art nouveau) villas in the lakes area, Villa Bernasconi was built by successful textile merchant Davide Bernasconi in 1906. It bears all the classic elements, with use of ceramics, stained class, wrought iron and, a comparative novelty, cement. The floral relief decoration on the exterior displays silkworms, moths and mulberry leaves – a direct advertisement of where Bernasconi's wealth came from.

The local town hall has restored the long-abandoned interior of the building, which opens periodically for exhibitions – including shows related to *stile liberty* architecture. Ask for the latest at the tourist office (p129), handily located next door.

MONTE BISBINO

Following signs out of central Cernobbio, take the scenic drive that winds 17km up through the residential villages behind Cernobbio to Monte Bisbino (1325m), a fabulous lookout spot. You won't need to wait to reach the mountain for great views – at every turn on the way up, you look back down on the lake from a different angle.

After a seemingly endless series of switchbacks on an increasingly narrow road that, in its latter stages, is enclosed by a canopy of thick woods, you emerge at the top. Climb the stairs to where the TV antennas are and then take in views of the Como end of the lake, the Lombard plain to Milan and as far off as the Swiss Alps (including the Jungfrau) on a clear day.

Trattoria La Vignetta (☑031 334 70 55; www.lavignetta.it; Via Monte Grappa 32; meals €32-42; ⊗noon-3pm & 7-10pm Wed-Mon) A five-minute uphill walk from the waterfront along a jasmine-perfumed residential lane, this hotel restaurant sits atop a little rise. Inside, the timber-panelled dining room with its antique wooden tables is a lovely setting for perfectly oven-cooked fish, perhaps preceded by a creamy risotto. On a balmy evening, take a table in the gravel garden outside and admire the surrounding greenery.

Upstairs from the restaurant, La Vignetta offers a handful of simple but cheerfully decorated **guestrooms** (s/d from €50/95).

Materia (☑031 207 55 48; www.ristorantemateria.it; Via Cinque Giornate 32; meals €45-55, menus €50-90; ⊗noon-2.30pm Wed-Sun & 7-10.30pm Tue-Sun) The talk of the town is this enticing Zen-like space, a 10-minute walk from the waterfront. Materia sources many herbs (including unusual varieties) and vegetables from its own greenhouse, and its daring menu pushes flavour notes you won't find elsewhere. Think marinated trout with horseradish and fermented kiwi; pearl barley with sage, bacon and potatoes; and lamb with wild garlic.

Gatto Nero (☑031 51 20 42; www.ristorantegattonero.it; Via Monte Santo 69, Rovenna; meals €50-70; ⊗12.30-2pm & 7-10.30pm) The jet set loves this elegant eatery high above Cernobbio, and for good reason. Book a front-row table and you'll have unobstructed views of the lake stretching out far below. Inside, dark-tile floors, plenty of timber and low lighting continue the romantic theme. The food, meanwhile, is strictly modern Italian, well presented and packed with flavour.

Tourist Office (☑345 9979943; Via Regina 7; ⊗10am-1pm & 2-5pm) This new tourist office is an excellent source of info on Cernobbio and the surrounding area.

Giardino Della Valle GARDENS
(Via Montesanto 5; ⊗24hr) On the east side of Cernobbio, this small but lush garden makes a fine setting for a stroll. What was once an illegal refuse site has been dramatically transformed into narrow pathways meandering among azaleas, roses and irises, with little wooden bridges, peonies and birdsong.

Moltrasio & Laglio

The lower lakeside road skirts the lake shore out of Cernobbio and past a fabulous row of 19th-century villas (all private property) around Moltrasio. Winston Churchill holidayed in one (Villa Le Rose) just after WWII and another is owned by the Versace fashion dynasty. Gianni Versace, who was murdered in Miami Beach, Florida, in 1997, is buried in the village cemetery. Near **Villa Passalacqua** (www.thevillapassalacqua.com; Via Regina 28), which is sometimes used for events, is the lovely **Chiesa di Sant'Agata** (Via Bresana, Moltrasio; ⊗irregular hours), which houses some intriguing frescoes (if you get lucky and find it open). A few kilometres north, the villa-lined hamlet of Laglio is home to *Ocean's* star George Clooney (he lives in Villa Oleandra). In both villages, stop anywhere, clatter down the cobblestone lanes and stairs to the lake, gawp at the villas as best you can and dream about how making it big in Hollywood could transform your life.

Eating

Trattoria del Fagiano TRATTORIA €€
(☑031 29 00 00; www.trattoriadelfagiano.it; Via Roma 54, Tosnacco; meals €30-35; ⊗12.30-2.30pm

ROAD TRIP: HIGH INTO THE HILLS

Writers from Goethe to Hemingway have lavished praise on Lake Como, dramatically ringed by snow-powdered mountains and garlanded by grand villas. While lakeside towns count Hollywood movie stars among their residents, this trip takes you high above the shore for a glimpse into a quieter rural lifestyle and sensational views from Cima Sighignola, otherwise known as the 'Balcony of Italy'.

❶ Menaggio

Leave **Como** and drive along the lake's west bank, as far as gorgeous **Villa Carlotta** (p136) in the town of **Cadenabbia** 33km north of Como. The villa was once the home of a Prussian princess and its salons are filled with pearly-white sculptures by Antonio Canova, while the 8-hectare gardens include a rolling fern valley, a grove of magnificent

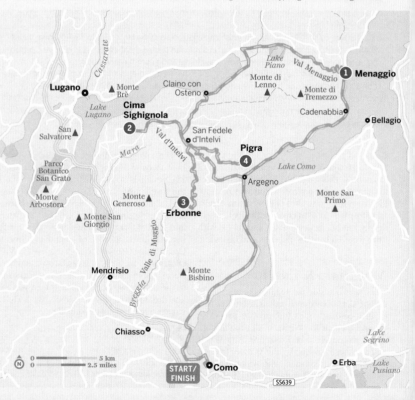

Half a day 145km/90 miles

Great for.... Outdoors, History & Culture

Best Time to Go Spring, when the hills are covered in flowers

• •

cedars and one of the finest collections of rhodedendrons and camellias in Europe.

Continue on for another 3km to Me-naggio (p137), which has a cute cobblestone old centre, a useful **tourist office** (p137) and a ferry stop. The central square overlooking the lake has a couple of cafes that are perfect for lake-gazing and people-watching.

❷ Cima Sighignola

From Menaggio, follow the signs inland towards Lugano, but instead of heading for Switzerland, pass Lake Piano and then take the south (left) turn after 12km and follow the shore of Lake Lugano for Claino con Osteno, a pretty lakeside village with a photogenic stone church.

The road climbs steeply for 11km to San Fedele d'Intelvi, which stands at the crossroads of some intriguing roads. For the first of these, follow the signs for Lanzo d'Intelvi (6km), from where there are signs to glorious Cima Sighignola, also known as the Balcone d'Italia (1320m), a further 6km on. Below lies all of Lugano, its lake and mountain peaks and, beyond, you can make out part of Lake Maggiore, Varese, the Alps and the Lombard plains.

❸ Erbonne

Return to San Fedele d'Intelvi, but only to follow the signs for the lovely, quiet country road to Erbonne (963m), a frontier hamlet that was a key crossing point for smugglers until the 1970s. The former barracks of the Guardia di Finanza (customs police) house possibly the smallest museum in Italy (the

Museo della Guardia di Finanza e del Contrabbando) – you simply peer in through the glass door.

Consider lunching at the **Osteria del Valico** (☑ 031 83 01 74; meals €27-35; ⊙ 10am-6.30pm & 7-10pm Wed-Mon Jun-Sep, Sat, Sun & holidays Oct-May), the only eatery in Erbonne for the last 100 years. It has moved from house to house, snaking up to its present charming location in 2000, and serves simple local fare including *pizzoccheri* followed by polenta served with pork, liver or local cheeses. When you've had your fill, ask for a grappa (a huge bottle hangs from the ceiling at the bar) or an Amaro Gratta il Culo (Scratch Your Arse Amaro, a herbal liquor) to digest it all.

❹ Pigra

Return to San Fedele d'Intelvi (9km), and follow the signs to Pigra (7km; p132) for more stunning views, this time of Lake Como's southern end.

Back in San Fedele d'Intelvi drive for 9km down to Argegno, a tiny village with a tangle of medieval lanes situated on the shores of Lake Como. From here it's a 21km lakeshore drive back to Como.

& 6.30-9.30pm Wed-Sun) A short climb above the SS340 road and Moltrasio, you'll stumble across this easygoing, family affair. 'The Pheasant' serves no-nonsense local food (fish features highly, but several meat dishes are on offer, too) in a good-natured, rambunctious atmosphere. Booking is strongly advised for Friday, Saturday and Sunday nights.

Argegno

Argegno is a small village nestled on Lake Como's edge, with a tangle of medieval streets and a picturesque stone bridge (also from the Middle Ages) over the Telo River which flows into the lake here. The busy highway (SS340) cutting right through town somewhat detracts from the charm as does Argegno's popularity. During the summer and on holiday weekends, the tourist crowds can overwhelm the small village.

Argegno is the access point for trips to the **Val d'Intelvi**, with jaw-dropping views from its lofty peaks.

◎ Sights & Activities

Guti Bike Rent   CYCLING
(☑ 389 5539775; www.gutibikerent.com; Via Spluga 5, Argegno; bike hire per half-day €25-35, full day €35-50; ◎ 9am-12.30pm & 2-7pm) This new outfit hires out quality mountain and road bikes (Giant brand) as well as essential gear (GPS Garmin, GoPro, bike seats for kids). All bikes have assist electric batteries, handy for getting up those big hills. The owner Iván Álvarez Gutiérrez, a 15-time Spanish national team-cyclist, can advise you on great routes both on- and off-road in the area.

Funivia Argegno-Pigra   FUNICULAR
(☑ 031 81 08 44; SS340; adult one way/return €3.40/4.50, child €2/2.80, bicycle €7.90; ◎ 8am-noon & 2.30-7pm, shorter hours in winter) This cable car (about 300m north of Argegno's Piazza Roma) makes the five-minute climb to the 860m-high village of tiny Pigra every 30 minutes. From the square where the cable car arrives and from the grounds of the tiny Chiesa di Santa Margherita, the views back down over the lake are quite striking.

Pigra itself warrants some wandering along its centuries-old lanes and stairways.

✗ Eating

Barchetta   ITALIAN €€
(☑ 031 82 11 05; www.ristorantebarchetta.it; Piazza Roma 2; meals €30-38; ◎ noon-2.30pm & 7-9.30pm Tue-Sun) The 'Little Boat', appropriately enough, specialises in lake fish and, come autumn, dishes using mushrooms and truffles. A few tables are scattered along the footpath, but dining inside is a more refined experience. The food is fabulous. Whichever pasta you start with, leave room for the abundant *misto pesce di lago* (a mixed grill of lake fish).

Ossuccio & Isola Comacina

Overlooking a tranquil stretch of Lake Como, the tiny village of Ossuccio has much history in its narrow lanes, with a few Romanesque vestiges and an archaeological museum that peers back through the centuries. There are also two star attractions nearby. The first is the Isola Comacina, a tiny island just offshore with medieval ruins and a human history that predates the Romans. Ossuccio's other attraction lies 1km uphill from the lakefront – the Sacro Monte di Ossuccio (the Sacred Mountain of Ossuccio), a chapel-lined walking route that has been a pilgrimage destination for centuries.

◎ Sights

Isola Comacina   ISLAND
(www.isola-comacina.it/en; adult/reduced €6/5; ◎ 10am-5pm mid-Mar–Oct, to 6pm Jul–mid-Sep) Once the site of a Roman fort and medieval settlement, Lake Como's only island forms its own little bay with the mainland, just offshore from Ossuccio. When the Lombards invaded northern Italy, the island held out as a Byzantine redoubt, and slowly filled with houses and churches, the whole known as Cristopolis. They even say the Holy Grail was deposited here for a time. Purchase admission tickets from the **Antiquarium** (☑ 0344 5 63 69; www.isola-comacina.it; Via Somalvico; €2, incl island visit €6; ◎ 10am-5pm closed Mon & Thu, mid-Mar–Oct); boat tickets to the island are sold separately by taxi boat and ferry operators.

Santuario della Madonna del Soccorso   CHURCH
(Via al Santuario; ◎ 8am-7pm) On the heights above Ossuccio, this lavish sanctuary is the destination for devoted pilgrims who make

LAKE COMO WALKS

The west bank of Lake Como offers widely diverse walking possibilities. For one suggested strolling route of 10km between Cadenabbia and Colonno, to the south, have a look at **Greenway del Lago di Como** (www.greenwaydellago.it).

For something altogether more challenging, you could head inland and get onto the **Via dei Monti Lariani**, a 130km trail from Cernobbio in the south to Sorico in the north. Keeping largely to high ground well above the lake, the journey is punctuated by *rifugi* (mountain huts) and the occasional village where you can find accommodation. Reckon on six days to do the walk comfortably. The trail is part of the 6000km Sentiero Italia marked out by the Club Alpino Italiano, and it's one of the most popular hikes in Lombardy.

It's best to travel with a map. Kompass produces some of the best maps to the area, including *Kompass Map 91 Lago di Como - Lugano*.

---

the steep 30-minute climb, passing a series of chapels (built from 1635 to 1714) along the way. The climb up the so-called **Sacro Monte di Ossuccio** affords matchless views over olive groves, the Isola Comacina and the lake beyond. At the top, you reach the Santuario della Madonna del Soccorso, which houses a 14th-century marble sculpture of Our Lady to which miraculous powers were long attributed.

✕ Eating

Trattoria del Santuario   ITALIAN €
(☑ 0344 5 63 11; Via al Santuario 50; meals €22-28; ⊘ 9am-7pm Wed-Mon) This cafe and restaurant is a fine spot for a bit of refreshment after the steep climb to the sanctuary next door. Arrive at lunch time for regional dishes like polenta with porcini mushrooms, cured meats and *pizzoccheri* (buckwheat pasta with cheese).

Taverna Bleu   ITALIAN €€
(☑ 0344 5 51 07; www.tavernableu.it; Via Puricelli 4, Sala Comicina; meals €30-45; ⊘ noon-2.30pm & 7-9.30pm Wed-Mon Mar-Nov) Known for its fine fish dishes, the Blue Tavern is in a lovely spot down from the main road at lake level in Sala Comacina (located 1.5km southwest of Ossuccio). Sit in the shady gravel-and-grass garden by the canary-yellow building that hosts indoor dining and a charming hotel.

Eat à la carte or opt for a set menu that includes a tasty mixed-vegetable dish, risotto and a melt-in-the-mouth fillet of lake perch. Taverna Bleu also has 15 **guestrooms** (doubles €150 to €280), the best with sparkling lake views.

Locanda dell'Isola   ITALIAN €€€
(☑ 0344 5 50 83; www.comacina.it; Via Spluga 5; set menu €75; ⊘ noon-2pm & 7-9.30pm Wed-Mon mid-Mar–Oct) Since 1948, the Locanda dell'Isola has been serving the same abundant set menu on the south side of the island, characterised by a round of nine vegetables, cold meats, trout, chicken, cheese and dessert. To finish off, brandy is burned in a huge pot to ward off the excommunication of the island declared by the Bishop of Como back in the 12th century. Doesn't accept credit cards.

Lenno
☑ 0344 / POP 1900

It may not look like much from the main road, but it's well worth dropping down into lakeside Lenno. Aside from a pretty main square, Lenno is home to one of Lake Como's most celebrated villas and has a lovely lake-shore promenade.

⊙ Sights

★ **Villa Balbianello**   VILLA, GARDENS
(☑ 0344 5 61 10; www.fondoambiente.it; Via Comoedia 5, Località Balbianello; villa & gardens adult/reduced €20/10, gardens only adult/reduced €10/5; ⊘ gardens 10am-6pm Tue & Thu-Sun mid-Mar–mid-Nov) A 1km walk along the (partially wooded) lake shore from Lenno's main square, Villa Balbianello has cinematic pedigree: this was where scenes from *Star Wars Episode II* and the 2006 James Bond remake of *Casino Royale* were shot. The reason? It is one of the most dramatic locations anywhere on Lake Como, providing a genuinely stunning marriage of architecture and lake views.

STEFANO EMBER / SHUTTERSTOCK ©

1. Chiesa di Santa Maria degli Angioli (p142), Lugano
Marvel at Bernadino Luini's frescoes depicting the crucifixion of Christ.

2. Castelgrande, Bellinzona (p147)
The castle's iconic tower rises high above Bellinzona's Old Town.

3. Villa Olmo (p117)
Statues adorn the lavish gardens of this neoclassical villa.

4. Menaggio (p137)
This pretty cobblestoned town offers breathtaking views of Lake Como.

Though the grounds are lovely, it's well worth joining a guided tour to see the villa's interior. Here you'll see the exquisite collections of the villa's last resident, Guido Monzino, who purchased the estate in 1974. Monzino was an entrepreneur, art collector and explorer, who filled the 18th-century mansion with artwork and mementoes from his adventures in Africa, the Himalayas and the polar regions, among other places.

Built by Cardinal Angelo Durini in 1787, Villa Balbianello was used for a while by Allied commanders at the tail end of WWII. The sculpted gardens, which were restored to Renaissance glory by Monzino, are the perfect place for hopelessly romantic elopers to spend a day. You can access the villa by a 1km path (amid vegetation so florid as to seem Southeast Asian) or take a taxi boat from Lenno.

Lido di Lenno　　　　　　　　BEACH
(✒ 0344 5 70 93; www.lidodilenno.com; Via Comoedia 1; beach access €5; ⊙ 10am-1.30am daily May-Sep) Summer evenings in Lenno take on a hedonistic hue at the Lido di Lenno. People from near and far converge on this artificial sandy beach, located virtually next to the path and boat pier for Villa Balbianello (p133), to enjoy food from the grill, cocktails (€6 to €10) and a (bracing) dip in the chilly, clear waters of the lake.

✖ Eating

★ Antica Trattoria del Risorgimento　　　　　　ITALIAN €€
(✒ 0344 4 17 89; Via San Abbondio 8, Mezzegra; meals €30-38; ⊙ 7-10.30pm Tue-Sun & noon-2.30pm Sat & Sun; 🎅 ✎) Tucked down a narrow lane in the tiny village of Mezzegra, this charming spot cooks up beautifully prepared regional dishes. The small menu, which changes by

---

LAKE COMO BY MOTORBIKE

If travelling by motorbike through Lake Como's cinematic scenery sounds irresistible, rent a Ducati from Lake Como Motorbike (✒ 349 427 75 42; www. lakecomomotorbike.com; Via Statale 60, Mandello del Lario), who offer guided day trips (€130 for the guide) and bike hire for experienced riders (per day €135 to €180). Helmet, jacket and gloves are provided. If you've not driven a bike before don't worry – you can ride pillion on the back of the guide's bike (€50).

---

day, features three different starters, three first courses and three second courses, and might include delicacies like lake trout cooked on a stone, risotto with wild nettle, and roast suckling pig. Reserve ahead.

ℹ Getting There & Away

Taxi Boat (✒ 333 4103854; www.taxiboatlecco. com; one way/return €5/7) Shuttles regularly from Lenno to the picturesque **Villa Balbianello** (p133). For a bit more DIY adventure, the same company hires out 40hp boats (one/two/three hours from €70/110/150). Boats hold up to six passengers and no licence is required. Boats depart from beside the **Lido di Lenno**.

Tremezzo
✒ 0344 / POP 1260

Tremezzo is worth visiting for the 17th-century Villa Carlotta, one of Como's loveliest villas, whose art-packed interior is slightly overshadowed by the sprawling gardens surrounding it. Aside from Villa Carlotta, Tremezzo has pretty views across the lake, though there isn't much of a village centre, and the main road goes right along the lake shore (so you'll need to watch your step given the sometimes heavy traffic).

◉ Sights

★ Villa Carlotta　　　　HISTORIC BUILDING
(✒ 034 44 04 05; www.villacarlotta.it; Via Regina 2; adult/reduced €10/8; ⊙ 9am-7.30pm Apr-Sep, 9.30am-5pm mid-Mar & Oct) Waterfront Villa Carlotta sits high on Como's must-visit list. The botanic gardens are filled with colour from orange trees interlaced with pergolas, while some of Europe's finest rhododendrons, azaleas and camellias bloom. The 8-hectare gardens also contains a lush fern valley, a bamboo grove, a Zen-style rock garden, towering cedars and a high-up lookout fringed by olive trees. The 17th-century villa, strung with paintings, sculptures (some by Antonio Canova) and tapestries adds an artful element to the beauty.

The name of the villa comes from the Prussian princess who was given the place in 1847 as a wedding present from her mother. Upstairs, rooms with period furniture provide an irresistible insight into the royal lifestyle. You, too, can swan from the Salotto Impero (Empire Room) to Carlotta's bedroom and wonder just what it must have been like to hit the hay after a hard day at the lake. Villa Carlotta has its own ferry stop.

✖ Eating

★ **Al Veluu** RISTORANTE €€€
(☏0344 4 05 10; www.alveluu.com; Via Rogaro 11; meals €45-75; ☺noon-2.30pm & 7-10pm Wed-Mon; ⓐ) Situated on a steep hillside with panoramic lake views from its terrace, this excellent restaurant serves up home-cooked dishes that are prepared with great pride. They also reflect Lake Como's seasonal produce, so expect butter-soft, milk-fed kid with rosemary at Easter or wild asparagus and polenta in spring.

ℹ Information

Tremezzo Tourist Office (☏0344 4 04 93; Via Statale Regina; ☺9am-noon & 3.30-6.30pm Wed-Mon Apr-Oct) By the boat jetty.

Menaggio & Val Menaggio

POP 3200

One of the prettiest villages on Lake Como's western shore, Menaggio has much going for it. Its compact cobblestone centre adjoins the riverside promenade, and is dotted with shops and outdoor cafes. This is also a fine departure point for walks into the craggy heights around Val Menaggio.

🏃 Activities

Menaggio Water Taxi BOATING
(☏333 6520699; www.menaggiowatertaxi.com; Via Mazzini; tours from €45) This professionally run boating operator offers various boating excursions, including a three-hour tour taking in the grand villas around Como, and a sunset tour – glass of bubbly included. Contact in advance for upcoming tour dates; tours run daily in July and August and several times weekly at other times.

If you prefer to go it alone, MWT also hires out smaller 40hp boats (no licence required).

AC Boat BOATING
(☏345 9010694; Lungolago Castelli; kayak hire per hour s/d €12/20; ☺9am-7pm Mar-Oct) For a DIY adventure, hire a boat from this outfit for a trip out on Lake Como. For smaller six-person 40hp vessels, no special licence is required. Prices start at €65 for one hour and €220 for four hours, and includes fuel. You can also hire kayaks.

ANTICA STRADA REGINA

A narrow cobblestone lane that was once part of a Roman road along the western side of Lake Como has been preserved in sections. The **Antica Strada Regina** traverses wooded greenery, passes through age-old villages and offers fine views over the shoreline – at times from 150m heights. One of the best sections to walk is the 7km stretch (about three hours' walk) between Menaggio and Rezzonico. The **tourist office** has info and can advise on worthwhile detours along the way.

If you don't want to walk back, catch the C10 bus on the return (22 minutes).

✖ Eating & Drinking

Cafe del Pess CAFE €€
(☏0344 3 20 53; Piazza Garibaldi 8; meals €20-30; ☺9am-8pm) The liveliest meeting spot in Menaggio is this eating and drinking den on Piazza Garibaldi, with tables spilling onto the cobblestones – perfect for people watching and contemplating the watery, mountain-backed horizon. Pizzas and pastas are well-executed, though it's also the go-to spot for a morning espresso or an afternoon spritz.

Il Gabbiano BAR
(☏0344 3 26 08; www.barilgabbiano.com; Viale Benedetto Castelli 23; ☺1am-10pm, closed Wed; ⓐ) The lakeside terrace here provides some of the most expansive views of Como's glittering waters. Set 300m northeast of Menaggio's cute cobblestone centre, it's the perfect spot to order gelato or a glass of wine and sit back to enjoy the laid-back vibe.

ℹ Information

Tourist Office (☏0344 3 29 24; www.menaggio.com; Piazza Garibaldi 3; ☺9am-12.30pm & 2.30-6pm Apr-Oct, closed Wed & Sun Nov-Mar) Menaggio's helpful tourist office has brochures on walking and biking, and has suggestions for activities for each day of the week, taking advantage of weekly markets and other events.

Rezzonico

POP 1080

Beyond Menaggio, the northern stretch of Lake Como is known as the Alto Lario (Upper Lario). It's far less touristed than other

WORTH A TRIP

OSTERIA SALI E TABACCHI

Tucked away in the hamlet of Maggiana, signposted 3km uphill from lakeside Mandello del Lario (home to the legendary Moto Guzzi motorcycle manufacturer), this **osteria** (☑ 0341 73 37 15; www.osteriasalietabacchi.it; Piazza San Rocco 3, Maggiana; meals €30-40; ⊙ noon-2.30pm & 7-10pm Wed-Sun,) has appeared in countless Italian good-food guides. The post office, bar and tobacco store has a modest dining room situated off to one side, filled with dark timber tables.

In the summer months, lake fish dominates the menu. Try the perch risotto. Just behind the restaurant is a medieval watchtower, where they say Holy Roman Emperor Frederick Barbarossa stayed in 1158 – too soon for him to try the risotto.

more famous points along the lake, but still holds some enticing secrets. The biggest draw to the region is Rezzonico, a small, delightful village that sees only a handful of visitors. Here you'll find a quiet pebble **beach** with wooden fisherfolks' seats lined up along it. Rezzonico is also the starting/ending point of a picturesque walk to Menaggio along the old Roman road known as the Antica Strada Regina (p137).

🍴 Eating

Hotel Lauro Ristorante   ITALIAN €
(☑ 0344 5 00 29; www.hotellauro.com; Località Rezzonico; meals €22-28; ⊙ 12.30-2.15pm & 7.15-9.15pm Tue-Sun; 🛜) On the steps leading down to Rezzonico's waterfront, this simple family-run *locanda* (inn) has been serving up serving up Como specialities since the 19th century. You'll find good, honest cooking in a decidedly untouristy corner of Lombardy, with tasty pastas, grilled meats and lake fish. Don't overlook the home-made desserts.

If you fall under the spell of Rezzonico, you can overnight in one of Lauro's eight simple **guestrooms** (doubles €55 to €80).

Gravedona, Peglio & Domaso

Gravedona and neighbouring Domaso (1.5km to the east) stretch along a gently curved bay on the lake. Often overlooked by Como visitors, these two towns make a pleasant escape from thicker crowds to the south. Gravedona also makes a fine base for forays out onto the water, with motorboats and sailboats available for hire.

High above Gravedona, the plateau town of Peglio (650m) offers wonderful views of the lake and plains around Gravedona.

Chiesa di Santa Maria del Tiglio   CHURCH
(Via Roma; ⊙ 9am-5pm) This square-based, late-12th-century church has an unusual bell tower (probably added later), which is octagonal at the top and rises from the centre of the facade. Inside, high arched galleries allow in sunlight at the top of the church. Colourful remnants of frescoes dating to the 14th and 15th centuries depict, among other things, the Last Judgment. The heavy wooden crucifix is a fine example of Romanesque carving.

Como Lake Boats   BOATING
(☑ 333 401 49 95; www.comolakeboats.it; Via Antica Regina 26; ⊙ 9am-noon & 1-6pm) Hires out a range of motorboats, including 40hp boats – no licence required – for up to five adults (€80 for two hours), smaller rubber dinghies (€65 for two hours) as well as bigger vessels for licenced boat operators. For those who prefer quieter journeys, sailboats are available (with or without a skipper).

Como Lake Boats also organises waterskiing and wakeboarding (€70 for 30 minutes). Novices can also sign up for lessons (€40 for instruction with 15 minutes in the water).

LAKE COMO EAST BANK

Lake Como's eastern shore has a wilder feel to it than the more illustrious west. Less touristed, it hides numerous gems that alone justify the effort. Back-country drives take you still further off the beaten track.

Correno Plinio

Located about 6km north of Bellano, Correno Plinio is a bite-sized taste of another era. With striking architecture and an idyllic shoreline, the village is a fascinating place to explore. Among the highlights are a picturesque main square which is surrounded by imposing medieval structures.

◉ Sights

Piazza Garibaldi   SQUARE
(off Via 4 Novembre) Piazza Garibaldi is roughly cobblestoned and it's plain from its time-warped nature that nothing much has changed here down the centuries. Many of the deep-grey, stone houses are still occupied, their inhabitants carefully tending garden plots that give the huddled hamlet flashes of bright colour.

The highlight of the square, the 14th-century **Chiesa di Tommaso Beckett** competes for attention with the neighbouring **Castello degli Andreani**, built around the same time. Frescoes inside the church were uncovered during restoration work in 1966. Two stout, crenellated towers stand guard over the castle, which is closed to visitors. A series of uneven stone stairways tumble between the tightly packed houses to the shoreline, one ending up at a tiny port (with space for nine motorboats and a family of ducks).

Varenna

☑ 0341 / POP 780

Varenna, a beguiling village bursting with florid plantlife, exotic flowery perfumes and birdsong, is a short ferry ride away from its rival in postcard beauty, Bellagio. A great way to get the lay of the land is to walk up to Castello di Vezio, which offers panoramic views over Varenna and the lake.

The SP65 road beyond makes for a pretty drive into the Val d'Esino, through the villages of Perledo, Esino Lario and Parlasco (which has tarted itself up with more than a dozen frescoes on the walls of its stone houses), where it runs into Valsassina.

◉ Sights

Villa Monastero   HISTORIC BUILDING
(☑ 0341 29 54 50; www.villamonastero.eu; Via IV Novembre; villa & gardens adult/reduced €8/5, gardens only €5/3; ⊙ 9.30am-7pm May-Aug, 10am-6pm Apr & Sep, to 5pm Mar & Oct, 11am-5pm Sun only Jan & Feb) At Villa Monastero elegant balustrades and statues sit amid exotic shrubs; spiky yucca trees frame lake and mountain views. The villa itself is a former convent that was turned into a private residence in the 18th century – which explains the giddy opulence of some of the 11 rooms.

Villa Cipressi   GARDENS
(☑ 0341 83 01 13; www.hotelvillacipressi.it; Via IV Novembre 22; adult/child €4/2; ⊙ 10am-6pm Mar-Oct) In Villa Cipressi's gardens cypress trees, palms, magnolias and camellias fill terraces that descend to the lake. Even getting here is picturesque: from the square next to the boat jetty (Piazzale Martiri della Libertà), follow the narrow lakeside promenade around the shore then bear left (inland) up the steps to central Piazza San Giorgio. The villa is signposted from there.

Castello di Vezio   CASTLE
(☑ 348 8242504; www.castellodivezio.it; Vezio, near Varenna; adult/reduced €4/3; ⊙ 10am-6pm Apr-Sep, to 5pm Mar & Oct) High above the terracotta rooftops of Varenna, the imposing Castello di Vezio offers magnificent views over Lake Como. The 13th-century building was once part of a chain of early-warning medieval watchtowers. Get there by taking a steep cobblestone path (about a half-hour hike) from Olivedo (the northern end of Varenna) to Vezio. You can also take a path (around 40-minutes' walk) along the Sentiero Scabium, reached by taking the uphill ramp just opposite the Villa Monastero.

You can clamber up the stairs to check out temporary exhibitions – a curious

---

ABBAZIA DI PIONA

The Cistercian **Abbazia di Piona** (Piona Abbey; ☑ 0341 94 03 31; www.cistercensi.info/piona; Via Abbazia di Piona; ⊙ 9.30am-noon & 2.15-5pm) has a magnificent setting on a promontory stretching out into Lake Como. There's evidence that a small chapel was built here as far back as the 7th century. The present Romanesque church and its medieval frescoes are attractive, but the star is the irregularly shaped 13th-century cloister – a rich example of transitional style from Romanesque to Gothic, it's an oasis of peace.

The monks who live here today enjoy incomparable views west over the lake to Gravedona and the snowcapped peaks behind it and to the north. A small shop on the grounds sells honey and liqueurs – including limoncello – made by the abbey. The turn-off to the abbey is located 3km south of Colico. Take the part-cobbled side road off the SP72 road for 2km.

VALSASSINA

It doesn't occur to too many people to follow this 33km back-valley route between Lecco to Bellano. If you've driven up or down the coast one way, this drive along the Valsassina is an alternative for the return trip. From Lecco, the SP62 road switches back and forth, affording priceless views of the Lecco end of Lake Como over your shoulder.

These views are finally cut off by the Grigne mountain range, whose highest peak is **La Grigna Settentrionale** (2408m). The core of this area constitutes the **Parco della Grigna Settentrionale** (www.parks.it/parco.grigna.settentrionale; Cortenova) **FREE**. From Lecco, you cannot fail to notice the jagged crest of **Il Resegone**, a broad-spined mountain with what look like dangerously pointy teeth (the highest of which is Punta Cermenati, at 1875m). About 9km northeast of Lecco, at Ballabio Superiore, a turn-off west sees you ascend about 8km of switchbacks through wooded country to **Piani Resinelli**, the starting point for several hikes.

display on the lariosaurus, a diminutive dinosaur that once resided in the area, was on display when we were there. Today's animal residents are birds of prey. The castle hosts regular falconry displays in the afternoons – daily except Tuesdays and Fridays. Call for times (usually between 2.30 and 4.30pm, depending on the day and season).

A few steps from the castle, the tiny hamlet of Vezio is thought to have Etruscan origins. It's worth having a poke about its narrow lanes.

✖ Eating

Il Cavatappi ITALIAN €€
(☑ 0341 81 53 49; www.cavatappivarenna.it; Via XX Settembre 10; meals €30-40; ⊘ noon-2pm & 6.30-9pm Thu-Tue, closed Jan & Feb; ☑) Set along a narrow pedestrian lane in the upper part of the Varenna, Il Cavatappi is an intimate spot with just seven tables set amid arched ceilings and stone walls, as opera plays quietly in the background. The cooking is outstanding, with creative twists on traditional recipes.

Osteria Quatro Pass ITALIAN €€
(☑ 0341 81 50 91; www.quattropass.com; Via XX Settembre 20; meals €28-42; ⊘ noon-2pm & 7-10pm, closed Mon-Wed winter) Places that don't have a lake view in Varenna are at a distinct disadvantage, which is why this place works just that extra bit harder with the food and service. Cured meats, lake fish and other local specialities are perfectly prepared and presented.

Ristorante La Vista ITALIAN €€
(☑ 0341 83 02 98; www.varenna.net; Hotel Milano, Via XX Settembre 35; meals €42-50; ⊘ 7-10pm

Wed-Sat & Mon mid-Mar–late Oct) The fabulous views from the terrace high in Varenna's old town are only half the story here. The fresh, inventive food is from a menu that changes with the seasons; service rarely misses a beat.

Cavallino TRATTORIA €€
(☑ 0341 81 52 19; www.cavallino-varenna.it; Piazza Martiri della Libertà 5; meals €32-42; ⊘ noon-2.30pm & 7-9.30pm Thu-Tue; ☑) Lake-fish specialities pack the menu of this Slow Food eatery set on Varenna's quay. Among the highlights are *crostoni* topped with a fish and calvados pâté; ravioli filled with *lavarello* (white fish) in a creamy radicchio sauce; and a risotto of perch, Parmesan, butter and sage.

The restaurant also organises a special evening featuring a 40-minute boat trip (during which you sip complementary *prosecco*), a lakeside stroll and a waterside, candle-lit four-course dinner (€75).

🍷 Drinking & Nightlife

Il Molo BAR
(☑ 0341 83 00 70; www.barilmolo.it; Via Riva Garibaldi 14; ⊘ 9am-1am Apr-Oct) The tiny terrace of Bar Il Molo is Varenna's most sought-after *aperitivi* spot. It's raised above the water with cracking views north right up the lake.

It's also a fine spot for pizzas, salads, hot sandwiches and other light fare.

ℹ Information

Tourist Office (☑ 0341 83 03 67; www.varenna italy.com; Via 4 Novembre 3; ⊘ 10am-3pm Mon, 10am-1pm & 2-6pm Tue-Sun Jul, shorter hours rest of year) Varenna's tourist office can provide information on the lake's entire eastern shore. Located on the main road in town, just west of Villa Monastero.

Valtellina

From the northern end of Lake Como, the Valtellina cuts a broad swathe of a valley (at whose centre runs the Adda river) eastward between the Swiss mountain frontier to the north and the Orobie Alps to the south. Much of its steep northern flank is carpeted by the vineyards (mostly the Nebbiolo grape variety) that produce such coveted drops as Sforzato (Sfurzat). You can largely skip the valley towns, but a detour to the hillside wine villages is worthwhile. Two points of reference are **Ponte**, 8km east of Sondrio, and **Teglio** (with a cute Romanesque church), 8km further east. The brisk climb up among the vineyards affords sweeping views across the valley. And what better way to taste Valtellina reds than by calling into any local trattoria?

◎ Sights & Activities

Tirano   AREA
The prettiest town along the valley floor is Tirano, terminus for trains arriving from Milan via Lake Como and others arriving from Switzerland. At its east end is the quiet old town, with winding lanes next to the gushing Adda. About 1.5km west of the centre stands the proud **Renaissance Santuario della Madonna** church.

**Trenino Rosso
del Bernina**   RAIL
(☑0342 70 62 63; www.treninorosso.it; Via Giuseppe Mazzini; adult/child return €61/15) Travelling along a gravity-defying narrow-gauge rail track, the bright red train known as the Trenino Rosso del Bernina leaves Tirano then crests Europe's highest Alpine pass at 2253m on the way to St Moritz in Switzerland. It leaves about ten times daily from mid-May to October; travel time is around 2½ hours.

Arpepe   WINE
(☑0342 21 41 20; www.arpepe.com; Via Buon Consiglio 4, Sondrio) Book two weeks in advance to visit the cellars of this famous Valtellina producer. Run by a winemaking family for five generations, Arpepe has been making rich Nebbiolo wines since 1860.

✖ Eating

★Altavilla   GASTRONOMY €€
(☑0342 72 03 55; www.altavilla.info; Via ai Monti 46, Bianzone; meals €30-40; ◎noon-2.30pm & 7-10pm Tue-Sun, daily Aug; ℙ🛜♿🐕) In this charming Alpine guesthouse and restaurant you'll find one of the region's gastronomic treats. Owner and Slow Food connoisseur Anna Bertola spreads a culinary feast for her guests with traditional mountain dishes like *sciàtt* (buckwheat fritters stuffed with Bitto cheese) and *pizzoccheri* (buckwheat pasta). The artisanal salami, mountain venison and aged Bitto cheese are particular highlights, as is the 500-label wine list.

Reserve a **room** (s/d €48/78) for the night and you can sleep it all off afterwards.

❶ Information

Valtellina Tourist Office (☑0342 21 92 46; www.valtellina.it; Via Tonale 13, Sondrio; ◎7.45am-6.30pm Mon-Fri, to 1pm Sat) In Sondrio, this office provides information about the whole valley.

LAKE LUGANO

Spilling over into northern Italy, Lake Lugano is a sparkling blue expanse at Ticino's southernmost tip. Less overrun than many of the lakes over the border, it is bewitching. On clear days the views are spectacular, with the pleats of wooded peaks fading into the hazy distance – among them the highest of the high, 1704m Monte Generoso.

❶ Information

Ticino Tourism (www.ticino.ch) This website gives the inside scoop on regional attractions, activities, itineraries, transport, accommodation, food and events. It's a great first port of call and brochures can be downloaded online. Search by region and/or theme.

❶ Getting There & Away

Società Navigazione del Lago di Lugano (☑091 971 52 23; www.lakelugano.ch; Viale Castagnola 12, Lugano) Boats are operated by the Società Navigazione del Lago di Lugano. Examples of return fares from Lugano are Melide (Sfr27.40), Morcote (Sfr38) and Ponte Tresa (Sfr45.60). If you want to visit several places, buy a pass: one, three or seven days cost Sfr49, Sfr59 or Sfr76 respectively. There are reduced fares for children.

Lugano (Switzerland)

POP 63.583

The largest city in the Swiss canton of Ticino is also the country's third-most-important banking centre. Suits aside, Lugano is a vivacious city, with posh designer boutiques, bars and pavement cafes huddling in the maze of cobblestone streets that untangle at the edge of the lake. The recent opening of its LAC arts centre has bumped it up in the cultural stakes, too. Popping up above the lake are the twin peaks of Monte Brè and Monte San Salvatore, both commanding astonishing views deep into the Alps and attracting hikers and mountain bikers in the warmer months.

◎ Sights

Take the stairs or the funicular (p145) from Lugano's train station down to the centre, a patchwork of interlocking *piazze*.

MASI - Museo d'Arte
della Svizzera Italiana   GALLERY
(www.masilugano.ch; LAC Lugano Arte e Cultura, Piazza Bernardino Luini 6; adult/child Sfr15/free; ◎10am-6pm Tue-Sun, to 8pm Thu) The showpiece of Lugano's striking new LAC (p145) cultural centre, the MASI zooms in predominantly on 20th century and contemporary art – from the abstract to the highly experimental, with exhibitions spread across three spaces. There is no permanent collection on display at present, but there is a high-calibre roster of rotating exhibitions. Recent focuses have included the work of Swiss Surrealist Meret Oppenheim and the epic, thought-provoking photography of British artist Craigie Horsfield.

Chiesa di Santa Maria degli Angioli   CHURCH
(St Mary of the Angel; Piazza Luini; ◎7am-6pm) This simple Romanesque church contains two frescoes by Bernardino Luini dating from 1529. Covering the entire wall that divides the church in two is a grand didactic illustration of the crucifixion of Christ. The power and vivacity of the colours are astounding.

Parco Ciani   GARDENS
(Viale Carlo Cattaneo; ◎6am-11pm) **FREE** This lakefront promenade necklaces the shore of glassy Lago di Lugano, set against a backdrop of rugged mountains. Notice the distinctive profiles of cone-shaped twin peaks Monte Brè and Monte San Salvatore. Linden and chestnut trees provide welcome shade in summer, while tulips, camellias and magnolias bloom in spring.

Monte Brè   MOUNTAIN
(www.montebre.ch; funicular one way/return Sfr16/25; ◎9.10am-6.45pm) Rising dramatically above the lake, the conical peak of Monte Brè (925m) is the trailhead for hiking and mountain-biking trails that afford wide-reaching views of the lake and stretch all the way to the Bernese and Valais Alps. Mountain bikes can be hired near the summit for Sfr24/32 for a full/half day. A funicular from Cassarate whisks you up to the mountain. If you don't fancy walking, take bus 2 from central Lugano.

Monte San Salvatore   MOUNTAIN
(www.montesansalvatore.ch; funicular one way/return Sfr23/30; ◎9am-6pm) Lugano's very own Sugarloaf Mountain, the 912m peak of Monte San Salvatore has riveting 360-degree views over the lake and southern Ticino to the Alps beyond. A turn-of-the-century funicular hauls you up to Monte San Salvatore, operating from mid-March to early November. The panorama at the top is tremendous, reaching over lakes, rippling mountains to Italy in the south and the high Alps in the west. For more fabulous views, the walk to Paradiso or Melide is two hours well spent.

Cattedrale di San Lorenzo   CATHEDRAL
(St Lawrence Cathedral; Via San Lorenzo; ◎6.30am-6pm) Freshly renovated in 2016, Lugano's early-16th-century cathedral conceals some fine frescoes and ornate baroque statues behind its Renaissance facade. Out front are far-reaching views over the Old Town's jumble of terracotta rooftops to the lake and mountains.

🏃 Activities

Lugano Guided Tours   TOURS
(◎mid-Mar–Oct) Departing from the tourist office (p145), Lugano's brilliant guided tours include a free spin of the city centre on Mondays (10am to noon). Other tours are available for a small contribution of Sfr10/5 per adult/child, including the peak of Monte San Salvatore on Wednesdays (10am to 1pm), an architectural highlights tour on Thursdays (10am to noon) and Monte Brè on Fridays (1.10pm to 5.30pm).

Lido   SWIMMING
(Viale Castagnola; adult/child Sfr11/6; ◎9am-7pm May & Sep, to 7.30pm Jun-Aug; 👧) Right on the lake and with glorious views across to the mountains, this *lido* has beaches, volleyball,

splash areas for kids and an Olympic-size swimming pool.

Società Navigazione del Lago di Lugano
BOATING

(☑ 091 971 52 23; www.lakelugano.ch; Riva Vela; ☺ Apr-Oct) A relaxed way to see the lake's highlights is on one of these cruises, including bay tours (one hour, Sfr27.40), 'lake and mountain' tours taking in Capo Lago and Monte Generoso (two hours, Sfr31.40) and 'magic' tours (90 minutes, Sfr41.40) via Gandria, Melide and Morcote. Visit the website for timetables and crossings.

★☆ Festivals & Events

LuganoMusica
MUSIC

(www.luganomusica.ch) Lugano takes in some classical tunes during this festival from mid-April to June in the Palazzo dei Congressi.

Estival Jazz
MUSIC

(www.estivaljazz.ch) Lugano swings into summer at this free open-air concert that occurs in early July (plus two days in Mendrisio the week before).

Blues to Bop Festival
MUSIC

(www.bluestobop.ch) A host of international blues stars take to the stage on Lugano's piazzas at this open-air music festival, which is held over four days in late August. See the website for the line-up.

✕ Eating

Pasta e Pesto
ITALIAN €

(☑ 091 922 66 11; Via Cattedrale 16; pasta Sfr10.50-15, menus Sfr15-19.50; ☺ 9.30am-5.30pm Mon-Sat) Doing pretty much what it says on the tin, this cute little place near the cathedral has a pocket-size terrace for digging into fresh home-made pasta with a variety of toppings.

La Tinèra
SWISS

(☑ 091 923 52 19; Via dei Gorini 2; ☺ 11.30am-3pm & 5.30-11pm Mon-Sat) Huddled down a back-street near Piazza di Riforma, this convivial, rustic restaurant rolls out extremely tasty Ticinese home cooking. You might begin, say, with homemade *salumi*, moving on to polenta with porcini mushrooms or meltingly tender osso buco. Simply pair with a good merlot from the region.

Bottegone del Vino
ITALIAN €€

(☑ 091 922 76 89; Via Magatti 3; mains Sfr20-42; ☺ 11.30am-midnight Mon-Sat) Favoured by Lugano's downtown banking brigade, this place has a season-driven menu, with ever-

changing lunch and dinner options scrawled on the blackboard daily. Expect specialities such as ravioli stuffed with fine Tuscan Chianina beef, accompanied by a wide selection of local wines. Knowledgeable waiters fuss around the tables and are only too happy to suggest the perfect Ticino tipple.

Arté al Lago
SEAFOOD €€€

(☑ 091 973 48 00; www.villacastagnola.com; Piazza Emilio Bossi 7; mains Sfr51-56, menus Sfr110-120; ☺ noon-2pm & 7-9.30pm Tue-Sat) This Michelin-starred restaurant at the exclusive lakefront Villa Castagnola is Lugano's culinary star. Chef Frank Oerthle does remarkable things with fish and seafood, with ingredient-focused, deceptively simple-sounding specialities such as marinated grouper with spring herbs, and veal with morels and sweet peas. Gaze out across the lake through the picture windows or up to the contemporary artworks gracing the walls.

Metamorphosis
MEDITERRANEAN €€€

(☑ 091 994 68 68; http://metaworld.ch; Riva Paradiso 2; mains Sfr45-52, tasting menus Sfr85-120; ☺ 9am-3pm Mon-Tue, 9am-midnight Wed-Fri, 10.30am-midnight Sat) One for special occasions, Metamorphosis is housed in Lugano's futuristic Palazzo Mantegazza, right by the lake shore. Chef Luca Bellanca walks the culinary high-wire, bringing simple, natural Mediterranean flavours to life with imagination and flair in dishes such as red-mullet sandwich with spinach and raspberry, and glazed piglet with puffed potatoes and Greek yoghurt. Bus 431 to Paradiso stops nearby.

🍷 Drinking

Al Lido
LOUNGE

(http://allidobar.com; Viale Castagnola 6; ☺ 9am-9.30pm Mar-Dec, shorter hrs in winter) Partygoers flock to this cool summertime beach lounge for DJ beats, drinks, snacks and flirting by

Lugano (Switzerland)

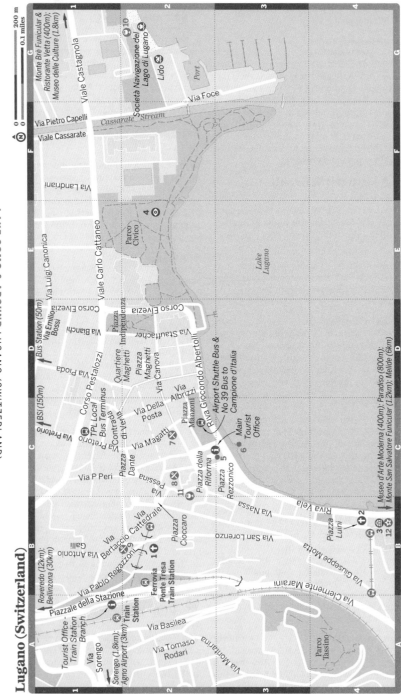

Lugano (Switzerland)

◎ **Sights**
  1 Cattedrale di San Lorenzo B2
  2 Chiesa di Santa Maria degli
    Angioli B4
  3 MASI - Museo d'Arte della
    Svizzera Italiana B4
  4 Parco Ciani E2

◆ **Activities, Courses & Tours**
  5 Lugano Guided Tours C3
  6 Società Navigazione del Lago di
    Lugano C3

✖ **Eating**
  7 Bottegone del Vino C2
  8 La Tinèra C2
  9 Pasta e Pesto B2

◎ **Drinking & Nightlife**
  10 Al Lido G2
  11 Grand Café Al Porto C2

◎ **Entertainment**
  12 LAC - Lugano Arte e Cultura B4

the lakefront. It's right next to Lugano's lido (p142) if you fancy a dip before or after.

Grand Café Al Porto   INTERNATIONAL
(☑091 910 51 30; www.grand-cafe-lugano.ch; Via Pessina 3; ⊗8am-6.30pm Mon-Sat) Going strong since 1803, this cafe is the vision of old-school grandeur with its polished wood panelling and pineapple-shaped chandeliers. The tortes, pastries and fruit cakes are irresistible, as is the hot chocolate.

☆ Entertainment

**LAC - Lugano
Arte e Cultura**   ARTS CENTRE
(☑058 866 42 22; www.luganolac.ch; Piazza Bernardino Luini 6) Lugano is justifiably proud of its cutting-edge new cultural centre, which has given the city its artistic mojo back. It brings together contemporary art (at the MASI; p142), music, theatre, poetry recitals, workshops and more. For listings and tickets, visit the website.

ⓘ Information

Main Tourist Office (☑058 866 66 00; www. lugano-tourism.ch; Piazza Riforma, Palazzo Civico; ⊗9am-6pm Mon-Fri, 9am-5pm Sat, 10am-4pm Sun) Guided tours of Lugano begin here. There is also a tourist information (☑091 923 51 20; Piazzale della Stazione; ⊗9am-7pm Mon-Fri, 9am-1pm Sat) booth at the main railway station.

ⓘ Getting There & Away

AIR

Lugano airport is served by a handful of Swiss-Italian carriers including Swiss, Silver Air and **Etihad** (www.etihadregional.com). Flights to Geneva and Zurich operate year-round.

A **shuttle bus** runs to Lugano's airport from Piazza Manzoni (one-way/return Sfr10/18) and

the train station (one way/return Sfr8/15, 20 minutes). See timetables on www.shuttle-bus.com. A taxi to the airport costs around Sfr30 (20 min).
Lugano Airport (☑091 610 12 82; www. lugano-airport.ch) Lugano airport is served by a handful of Swiss-Italian carriers including Swiss, Silver Air and Etihad Regional. Flights to Geneva and Zurich operate year-round.

BUS

The easiest way to reach St Moritz from Lugano is to take the train to Bellinzona and switch to a postal bus via Thusis (Sfr84, four hours, hourly). Local buses depart from the **TPL Terminus** (☑058 866 72 24; www.tplsa.ch; Corso Pestalozzi; ⊗8am-6.30pm Mon-Fri, 9am-noon Sat).

Bus 1 runs from Castagnola in the east through the centre to Paradiso, while bus 2 runs from central Lugano to Paradiso via the train station. A single trip costs Sfr2.50 or it's Sfr7.50 for a one-day pass.

CAR

The main artery running north-south through Ticino is the A2 motorway, which links Lugano to Bellinzona, 37km north, and Chiasso on the Italian border, 26km south.

In Lugano, you can hire cars at **Avis** (☑091 913 41 51; Via Clemente Maraini 14; ⊗8am-noon & 2-6.30pm Mon-Fri, 8am-3pm Sat) and **Hertz** (☑091 912 40 60; www.hertz.ch; Via San Gottardo 13; ⊗7.30am-12.30pm & 1.30-6.30pm Mon-Fri, 8am-12.30pm & 1.30-5pm Sat).

TRAIN

Lugano has very frequent **train connections** (Piazzale della Stazione) to Bellinzona (Sfr11, 30 minutes), with onward connections to destinations further north. Getting to Locarno (Sfr15.20, one hour) involves a change at Giubiasco. Note that the train station can be reached by foot or **funicular** (Piazzale della Stazione; Sfr1.30; ⊗5am-midnight).

Around Lake Lugano

The villages that cling tightly to Lake Lugano's shores and tumble haphazardly down its slopes, such as Gandria, Meride and Morcote, are among Switzerland's most beguiling, with hidden back alleys, pastel-painted houses and botanical gardens to explore.

Gandria

POP 275 / ELEV 327M

Looking as though it will topple off its terraced hillside with the merest puff of breath, lakeside Gandria is ludicrously pretty, with pastel-coloured houses stacked on top of one another like children's building blocks, narrow stairwells, arcades, courtyards and terraced gardens. At the foot of Monte Brè, it is the last Swiss village before reaching Italy on the SS340, and it was once renowned for its production of olive oil (notice the traditional press in front of the town hall). It's perfect for an aimless amble, with hidden corners aplenty and 16th- and 17th-century houses festooned with frescoes.

◉ Sights & Activities

**Museo delle
Dogane Svizzere** MUSEUM
(Swiss Customs Museum; www.zollmuseum.ch; Riva delle Cantine; adult/child Sfr3/1.50; ☺1.30-5.30pm Apr–mid-Oct) FREE Across the lake from Gandria is the Museo delle Dogane Svizzere, accessible by boat. It tells the history of customs (and, more interestingly, smuggling) in this border area. On display are confiscated smugglers' boats that once operated on the lake.

Sentiero di Gandria WALKING
The 5km, one-and-a-half hour Gandria Trail hugs the shore of Lago di Lugano, taking you from Gandria to Lugano, or vice-versa, and passing through glorious gardens where century-old olive trees and Mediterranean flowers grow. The views out across the lake and up to the slopes of Monte Brè and Monte San Salvatore are outstanding.

✖ Eating

Ristorante le Bucce di Gandria ITALIAN €€
(Via Cantonale; mains Sfr22-32; ☺7pm-midnight Wed-Thu, noon-3pm & 7pm-midnight Fri-Sun) Climb the steps of Gandria's old town and you'll be rewarded with gorgeous lake views from this hillside restaurant. The menu keeps things regional and seasonal, adding a dash of creativity in dishes such as ravioli of salt cod with onion-cardamom cream and venison fillet with fondant potatoes and cinnamon pear. It's all delicious and served with a smile.

Morcote

POP 769 / ELEV 272M

Spilling photogenically down a hillside, the one-time fishing village of Morcote, huddling below Monte Abostora, is a joy to explore on foot, with its botanical gardens and dazzling lake and mountain views. It was voted Switzerland's most beautiful village in 2016 and lives up to the hype with its adorable maze of narrow cobbled lanes, passageways, arcaded patrician houses and hilltop church.

◉ Sights

Parco Scherrer GARDEN, ARCHITECTURE
(Riva di Pilastri 20; adult/child Sfr7/2; ☺10am-5pm Mar-Jun, Sep & Oct, 10am-6pm Jul-Aug) Set in sub-

---

DON'T MISS

MONTE GENEROSA

Popping up between Italy and Switzerland, the 1704m peak of Monte Generoso has far-reaching views across a patchwork of lakes and mountains. It's best visited as a day trip from Lugano or one of the nearby lake towns, such as Meride. The rack-and-pinion railway that departs from Capolago roughly hourly has been trundling to the top since 1890. Some 51km of marked footpaths fan out from the summit, among them an hour-long nature trail that gives you a handle on local wildlife, which includes a sizeable chamois colony. The mountain also attracts climbers, mountain bikers and paragliders.

While you're up there, you can dine in style at Mario Botta's attention-grabbing **Fiore di Pietra** (☎091 630 51 11; www.montegeneroso.ch; mains Sfr32-55; ☺11.30am-2.30pm). The 'Flower of Stone' houses a restaurant where chef Luca Bassan creates dishes with a seasonal touch to the table – from polenta–Alpine cheese ravioli with thyme to rabbit with cep mushrooms, all expertly paired with local wines. There are magnificent 360-degree views from the terrace.

tropical parkland, Parco Scherrer, 400m west of the boat stop in Morcote, is the dream come true of textile merchant and art enthusiast Hermann Arthur Scherrer, who bought the land sloping down to the lake in 1930. Inspired by his travels, the gardens have a dash of the exotic, bristling with palms and oleanders, camellias and azaleas, cypresses and bamboo. Hidden among the foliage are replicas of grand buildings – from the Temple of Nefertiti to a Siamese teahouse.

Chiesa di Santa Maria del Sasso   CHURCH
(Sentée da la Gesa; ⊙9am-8pm) It's a stiff 15-minute climb up a seemingly endless flight of steps to this church, lifted on a hilltop above the lake and easily identified by its prominent bell tower. Originally built in Romanesque style in the 15th century and later given a baroque makeover, it houses some attractive frescoes. More striking still are the views over Morcote's higgledy-piggledy old town to the lake and mountains beyond.

🍴 Eating

Ristorante della Torre   ITALIAN €€
(☑091 996 26 36; http://ristorantetorre.ch; Riveta da la Tor; mains Sfr22-35; ⊙9.30am-midnight) A rustic, beamed dining room with an invitingly old-fashioned air sets the scene at this restaurant, with a lovely terrace right by the lake. Service is super-friendly and the food, though not imaginative, is bang on the money – whether you go for pizza, pasta, risotto or grilled fish and meat.

Meride

POP 314 / ELEV 583M

Rimmed by vineyards and slumbering at the foot of Monte San Giorgio, Meride is a pipsqueak of a village with postcard looks. Its medieval centre is woven with cobbled alleys and lined with stone-built, shuttered houses redolent of neighbouring Italy. Anyone with even a passing interest in paleontology will love its fossil museum, while others will appreciate its quaint, off-the-radar charm.

◉ Sights

Monte San Giorgio   MOUNTAIN
Rising in a pyramid above Lake Lugano, 1097m Monte San Giorgio has become Ticino's mountain of myth thanks to its rich stash of Triassic marine-life fossils, which have won it Unesco World Heritage status. A four-hour, 12km circular trail takes you

up from Meride. An old mule track wends through thick forest to the summit, commanding fine lake views, then you'll descend on a path with panels detailing the fossils and their excavation sites.

Museo dei Fossili   MUSEUM
(Fossil Museum; www.montesangiorgio.ch; Via Bernardo Peyer 9; adult/child Sfr12/6; ⊙9am-5pm Tue-Sun) Revamped and expanded by Ticinese starchitect Mario Botta, Meride's Fossil Museum showcases vestiges of the first creatures to inhabit the region – reptiles and fish dating back more than 200 million years. It may sound dry but the finds are important enough to warrant Unesco recognition of the area around Monte San Giorgio (where they were uncovered) as a World Heritage Site. You're welcomed by a 2.5m long replica of a *Ticinosuchus*.

Bellinzona

POP 18,700 / ELEV 230M

Rearing up at the convergence of several valleys amid lovely Alpine scenery, Bellinzona is Ticino's head-turning capital. Its three hulking medieval fortresses have enthralled artists and poets for centuries, including that greatest of Romantic painters, William Turner. Yet Bellinzona keeps a surprisingly low profile considering that its hat-trick of castles form one of only 12 Unesco World Heritage Sites in Switzerland.

◉ Sights

★Castelgrande   CASTLE
(www.bellinzonese-altoticino.ch; Via Salita Castelgrande; ⊙grounds 10am-6pm Mon, 9am-10pm Tue-Sun; Murata 10am-7pm) Rising dramatically above the Old Town, this medieval stronghold is Bellinzona's most visible icon. Head up Salita San Michele from Piazza Collegiata, or take the lift, buried deep in the rocky hill in an extraordinary concrete bunker-style construction, from Piazza del Sole. After wandering the grounds and the museum (adult/child Sfr5/2; ⊙10am-6pm Apr-Oct, 10am-5pm Nov-Mar), stroll west along the Murata, the castle's snaking ramparts, with photogenic views of vine-streaked mountains and castle-studded hills.

★Castello di Montebello   CASTLE
(www.bellinzonese-altoticino.ch; Salita al Castello di Montebello; castle free, museum adult/child Sfr5/2; ⊙10am-6pm Apr-Oct, 10.30am-4pm Nov-Mar) **FREE** On cloudless days, you can see Lake

Bellinzona (Switzerland)

Bellinzona (Switzerland)

◎ Top Sights

1 Castelgrande	B2
2 Castello di Montebello	C3
3 Castello di Sasso Corbaro	D4

◎ Sights

Museo di Castelgrande	(see 1)

✕ Eating

4 Casa del Popolo	D1
5 Grotto Castelgrande	B2
6 Locanda Orico	A2
7 Osteria Mistral	A3
8 Trattoria Cantinin dal Gatt	B3

◎ Drinking & Nightlife

9 Il Fermento	B2

Maggiore from this 13th-century hilltop fortification. The fortress is one of Bellinzona's most impressive with its drawbridges, ram-

parts and small **museum** catapulting you back to medieval times.

★ **Castello di Sasso Corbaro** CASTLE
(www.bellinzonese-altoticino.ch; Via Sasso Corbaro; castle free, museum & tower adult/child Sfr5/2; ☉10am-6pm Apr-Oct, 10.30am-4pm Nov-Mar) From central Bellinzona, it's a 3.5km hike south to the Castello di Sasso Corbaro. Perched high on a wooded hillside, the castle has an austere beauty with its impenetrable walls and sturdy towers.

Chiesa di San Biagio CHURCH
(Piazza San Biagio; ☉7am-noon & 2-5pm) This 14th-century church is one of Bellinzona's most evocative with its original frescoes of the medieval Lombard-Siena school.

Villa dei Cedri GALLERY
(www.villacedri.ch; Via San Biagio 9; adult/child Sfr10/7; ☉2-6pm Wed-Fri, 11am-6pm Sat & Sun) Housed in a handsome 19th-century villa,

this gallery presents mostly local and northern Italian works of the 19th and 20th centuries. Just as appealing are the palm-studded gardens. See the website for details of temporary exhibitions.

✿ Festivals & Events

Rabadan   CARNIVAL
(www.rabadan.ch; ⊘late Feb) Costumed parades, street theatre, jangling jesters and marching bands infuse Bellinzona with carnival fever seven-and-a-half weeks before Easter Sunday.

La Bacchica   CULTURAL
(www.labacchica.ch) A traditional vintners' festival in September, with wine-tasting, folk processions, plays and music aplenty.

✗ Eating & Drinking

Osteria Mistral   ITALIAN €€
(🖉 091 825 60 12; www.osteriamistral.ch; Via Orico 2; 2-/3-course lunch menu Sfr33/40, 3-/4-/6-course dinner menu Sfr68/82/115; ⊘11.45am-3pm Mon-Fri & 6.45pm-midnight Mon-Sat) Luca Braghelli takes pride in local sourcing and makes the most of whatever is in season at this smart, intimate *osteria*. Be it home-made pasta or autumn venison, everything is cooked to a T and expertly matched with regional wines.

Trattoria Cantinin dal Gatt   ITALIAN €€
(🖉 091 825 27 71; www.cantinindalgatt.ch; Vicolo al Sasso 4; lunch menus Sfr18-28, mains Sfr25-36; ⊘11am-3pm & 6pm-midnight Tue-Fri, 9am-3pm & 6pm-midnight Sat; ☕) Slip up a cobblestone side-street to find this cracking little trattoria, brimming with warmth and bonhomie. The brick-vaulted interior is an inviting spot for digging into big Italian flavours courtesy of Tuscan chef Luca. Begin, say, with home-made gnocchi with lobster bisque, shrimp and black olive tapenade, followed perhaps by mains such as roasted rabbit with sweet pepper salsa.

Grotto Castelgrande   ITALIAN €€
(🖉 091 814 87 81; www.castelgrande.ch; Via Salita Castelgrande; mains Sfr29-39, 2-/3-course menu Sfr25/31; ⊘9.30am-midnight Tue-Sat) For the best view of Bellinzona's illuminated castles, book a table on the vine-strewn terrace of this atmospheric vaulted cellar for dishes such as fillet of beef served with porcini mushrooms and Grana cheese.

Casa del Popolo   ITALIAN €€
(🖉 091 825 29 21; https://casadelpopolo.ch; Viale Stazione 31; mains Sfr24-33, pizza Sfr10-18; ⊘7am-11pm Mon-Thu, 7am-midnight Fri, 8am-midnight Sat, 8am-11pm Sun; ☕) Taking pride in local sourcing and keeping things as seasonal as possible, this buzzy bistro is a good option close to the train station. Besides pizza, there are plenty of well-prepared classics on the menu, from mushroom risotto to *vitello tonnato* (sliced veal in a creamy sauce), including several options for vegetarians and kids.

Locanda Orico   ITALIAN €€€
(🖉 091 825 15 18; www.locandaorico.ch; Via Orico 13; mains Sfr40-65, lunch menu Sfr48, dinner menus Sfr110-125; ⊘11.45am-2pm & 6.45pm-midnight Tue-Sat) Seasonality is the name of the game at this Michelin-starred temple to good food, housed in a slickly converted *palazzo* in the old town. Creations such as pumpkin gnocchi in jugged chamois meat, and wild turbot with fettuccine and basil butter are served with finesse.

Il Fermento   BREWERY
(www.ilfermento.ch; Via Codeborgo 12; ⊘11am-9pm Mon-Wed, to 1pm Thu-Fri, to 9pm Sat) For one of the top craft beers in town, swing across to this hip new urban microbrewery. Sip hoppy amber ales, zesty IPAs and malty bitters in the industro-cool interior or out on the pavement terrace if the sun's out.

ⓘ Information

Tourist Office (🖉 091 825 21 31; www.bellinzona turismo.ch; Piazza Nosetto; ⊘9am-6.30pm Mon-Fri, 9am-2pm Sat, 10am-2pm Sun Apr-Oct, shorter hours rest of year) In the restored Renaissance Palazzo del Comune (town hall).

ⓘ Getting There & Away

The gateway to Ticino, Bellinzona is a major transport hub. The A2 motorway blazes through, linking it to Lugano in the south and running all the way north to Basel. The A13 motorway connects up to Chur, capital of Graubünden, 116km north.

Bellinzona has frequent **train connections** (Viale della Stazione) to Locarno (Sfr8.80, 27 minutes) and Lugano (Sfr10.20, 30 minutes). It is also on the Zürich–Milan route. **Bus** 171 runs roughly hourly northeast to Chur (Sfr59.40, 2¼ to three hours), departing from beside the train station. There is an underground car park on **Piazza del Sole** (Piazza del Sole; per hour Sfr2).

Bergamo, Brescia & Cremona

Best Places to Eat

➡ Da Vittorio (p157)

➡ Cascina Valentino (p174)

➡ Due Colombe (p165)

➡ Noi (p157)

➡ La Vineria (p169)

➡ Locanda al Lago (p164)

Best Escapes

➡ Val Taleggio (p160)

➡ Lake Iseo (p163)

➡ Orobie Alps (p161)

➡ Franciacorta Wine Region (p166)

Why Go?

Medieval towns, gentle lakes hemmed in by steep hillsides, vast plains, prehistoric rock art and mighty mountains make this part of the Lombard region one of northern Italy's most underrated corners. You'd need a couple of weeks to cover the area well, so you need to make choices. Bergamo, with its medieval Città Alta (Upper Town), is a must, and it's an inspired choice if this is your point of arrival in Italy. Townies and church lovers might concentrate on the main centres (Brescia, Cremona, Crema and Lodi), which all have fascinating medieval cores. An alternative tour of plains settlements will turn up palaces, castles and forts. Wine buffs may prefer touring the Franciacorta, south of Lake Iseo. North of Bergamo, several valleys lead deep into the picturesque Orobie Alps.

Road Distances (km)

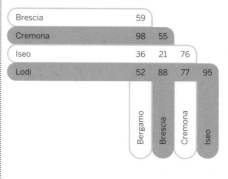

	Bergamo	Brescia	Cremona	Iseo
Brescia	59			
Cremona	98	55		
Iseo	36	21	76	
Lodi	52	88	77	95

BERGAMO

📱 035 / POP 121,000

This eastern Lombard city offers a wealth of art and medieval Renaissance and baroque architecture, a privileged position overlooking the southern plains, breathtaking views and some fine dining. Bergamo is one of northern Italy's most beguiling cities.

The city's defining feature is a double identity. The ancient hilltop Città Alta (Upper Town) is a tangle of tiny medieval streets, embraced by 5km of Venetian walls. It lords it over the largely (but not entirely) modern Lower Town (Città Bassa). A funicular connects the two.

👁 Sights

The best way to explore Bergamo's old town is to simply wander without haste. Via Bartolomeo Colleoni and Via Gombito are lined with all sorts of curious shops and eateries. Wander along the perimeter streets of the old town too, for rewarding panoramas from the city's Venetian-era defensive walls.

★ Accademia Carrara   GALLERY
(📱 035 23 43 96; www.lacarrara.it; Piazza Carrara 82; adult/reduced €10/8; ⏰ 10am-7pm May-Nov, 9.30am-5.30pm Dec-Apr) Just east of the old city walls is one of Italy's great art repositories. Founded in 1780, it contains an exceptional range of Italian masters. Raphael's *San Sebastiano* is a highlight, and other artists represented include Botticelli, Canaletto, Mantegna and Titian.

The collection was started by local scholar Count Giacomo Carrara (1714–96) and has now swelled to 1800 paintings dating from the 15th to 19th centuries. Reopened after a seven-year renovation, the gallery's displays revolve around 28 rooms. Highlights include the sections on Giovanni Bellini, Florence and the major local artists Lorenzo Lotto and Giovanni Battista Moroni.

★ Torre del Campanone   TOWER
(📱 035 24 71 16; Piazza Vecchia; adult/reduced €3/free; ⏰ 9.30am-6pm Tue-Fri, to 8pm Sat & Sun Apr-Oct, reduced hours winter) Bergamo's colossal, square-based Torre del Campanone soars 52m above the city. It still tolls a bell at 10pm, the legacy of an old curfew. Taking the lift to the top of the tower reveals sweeping views down onto the town, up to the pre-Alps and across to the Lombard plains.

Piazza Vecchia   PIAZZA
(Old Square) The Upper Town's beating heart is the cafe-clad Piazza Vecchia, lined by elegant architecture that is a testament in stone and brick to Bergamo's long and colourful history. Its highlights include the Palazzo Nuovo, Palazzo del Podestà, Palazzo della Ragione and the Torre del Campanone. Tucked in behind the secular buildings of Piazza Vecchia, **Piazza del Duomo** is the core of Bergamo's spiritual life

Le Corbusier apparently described Piazza Vecchia as the 'most beautiful square in Europe' – good thing they didn't let him try out any of his ideas on it. Had he done so, he'd have been following a certain precedent. The Renaissance square was created by levelling the huddle of medieval housing that once stood there.

The white porticoed building on Via Bartolomeo Colleoni, which forms the northern side of the piazza, is the **Palazzo Nuovo** (Angelo Mai Library). Designed in 1611 by a brilliant architectural mind from Vicenza, Vincenzo Scamozzi (1548–1616), it was not actually completed until 1928. Long the seat of the town hall, it has been a library since 1873. Diagonally opposite, on the northwest side of the square, the **Palazzo del Podestà** (Museo Storico dell'Età Veneta; 📱 035 24 71 16; www.palazzodelpodesta.it; adult/reduced €7/5; ⏰ 9.30am-1pm & 2.30-6pm Tue-Sun) was long home to Venice's representative in Bergamo.

Looming overhead, the massive, square-based Torre del Campanone tolls the old 10pm curfew. Originally raised in the 12th century and partly used as a jail in the 14th, it has undergone numerous alterations. In 1486, cheerful citizens lit a bonfire atop the tower to celebrate a religious holiday. Oddly, they didn't foresee that this would lead to the timber roof catching and burning to a crisp, leading to one of many renovations. Lighting fires is no longer allowed but you can take a wheelchair-accessible lift to the top, from where there are splendid views.

Turn south and you face the imposing arches and columns of the **Palazzo della Ragione**, built in the 12th century. The lion of St Mark is a reminder of Venice's long reign here. It's an early 20th-century replica of the 15th-century original, which was torn down when Napoleon took over in 1797. Note the sun clock in the pavement beneath the arches, and the curious Romanesque and Gothic animals and busts decorating

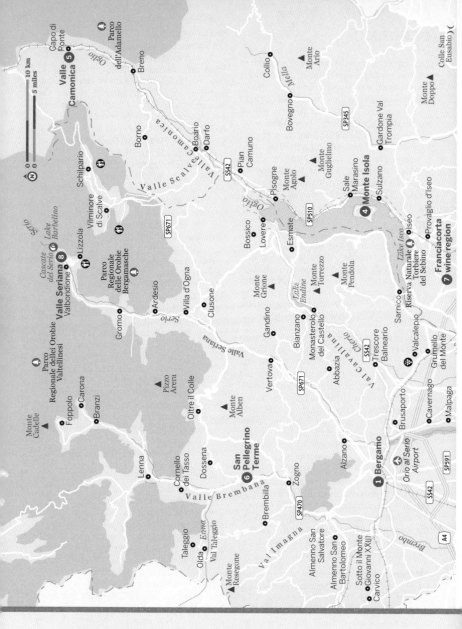

Bergamo, Brescia & Cremona Highlights

1 Bergamo (p151) Wandering endlessly through the medieval lanes of the Città Alta, beginning in the cinematic Piazza Vecchia.

2 Brescia (p167) Stepping back in time while visiting ancient Roman ruins, a hilltop castle and a museum packed with historical treasures.

3 Cremona (p170) Strolling past instrument workshops and visiting the Museo del Violino in this pretty town of violin makers.

4 Monte Isola (p44) Going for a scenic walk around a village-dotted island on one of Lombardy's least-known Italian lakes.

5 **Valle Camonica**
(p166) Discovering Unesco World Heritage–listed rock art north of Lake Iseo.

6 **San Pellegrino Terme** (p161) Soaking in the famed mineral water that's known across the world.

7 **Due Colombe**
(p165) Touring the Franciacorta wine region then stopping for lunch at this award-winning dining room.

8 **Valle Seriana**
(p162) Heading into the valleys north of Bergamo for jaw-dropping views.

Bergamo

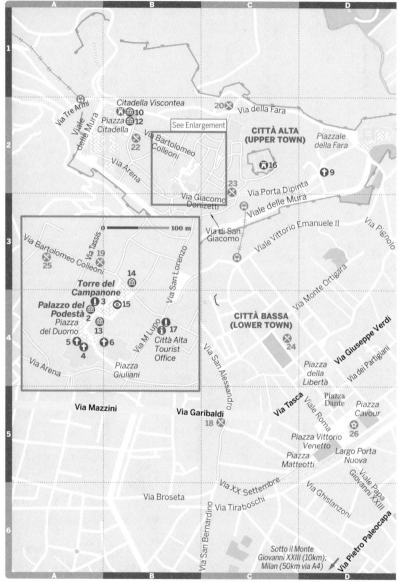

Citadella Viscontea

20

Via della Fara

Via Tre Armi

10

Piazza 12
Citadella

22

Via Arena

Via Bartolomeo
Colleoni

See Enlargement

CITTÀ ALTA
(UPPER TOWN)

Piazzale
della Fara

16

9

23

Via Porta Dipinta

Via Giacomo
Donizetti

Viale delle Mura

0   100 m

Via Bartolomeo Colleoni

Via Tassis

19

25

14

Torre del
Campanone

Palazzo del
Podestà

3   15

2

Piazza
del Duomo

13

5   4   6

Via Arena

Via M.Lupo

17

Città Alta
Tourist
Office

Piazza
Giuliani

Via di San
Giacomo

Via San Lorenzo

Viale Vittorio Emanuele II

Via Pignolo

Viale delle Mura

Via Monte Ortigara

CITTÀ BASSA
(LOWER TOWN)

24

Piazza
della
Libertà

Via Giuseppe Verdi

Via dei Partigiani

Via Tasca

Piazza
Dante

Piazza
Cavour

26

Via Mazzini

Via Garibaldi

18

Via San Alessandro

Viale Roma

Piazza Vittorio
Venetto

Piazza
Matteotti

Largo Porta
Nuova

Viale Papa
Giovanni XXIII

Via Broseta

Via San Bernardino

Via Tiraboschi

Via XX Settembre

Via Ghislanzoni

Via Pietro Paleocapa

Sotto il Monte
Giovanni XXIII (10km);
Milan (50km via A4)

---

the pillars of the arches. Today the Palazzo houses temporary exhibitions.

Basilica di Santa Maria Maggiore BASILICA
(Piazza del Duomo; ⊙ 9am-12.30pm & 2.30-6pm Mon-Fri, 9am-6pm Sat & Sun Apr-Oct, shorter hours

Nov-Mar) Bergamo's most striking church, begun in 1137, is quite a mishmash of styles. To its whirl of Romanesque apses (on which some external frescoes remain visible), Gothic additions were added. Influences seem to come from afar, with dual-colour

0   400 m
N   0   0.2 miles

Bergamo

tomb of the great Bergamo-born composer Gaetano Donizetti.

According to legend, the people of Bergamo begged for protection from the Virgin Mary during a terrible outbreak of the plague in the early 1100s. When the town was spared, Bergamo made good on its word and began construction on the massive Basilica di Santa Maria Maggiore.

Cappella Colleoni   CHAPEL
(Piazza Duomo; ⊙9am-12.30pm & 2-6.30pm Mar-Oct, 9am-12.30pm & 2-4.30pm Tue-Sun Nov-Feb) The Cappella Colleoni was built between 1472 and 1476 as a magnificent mausoleum-cum-chapel for the Bergamese mercenary commander Bartolomeo Colleoni (c 1400–75), who led Venice's armies in campaigns across northern Italy. He lies buried inside in a magnificent tomb.

banding (black and white, and rose and white) typical of Tuscany and an interesting *trompe l'œil* pattern on part of the facade. Highlights include wooden marquetry designed by Lorenzo Lotto and the funerary

---

LOCAL KNOWLEDGE

IN SEARCH OF LORENZO LOTTO

One of the great names of the late Venetian Renaissance, Lorenzo Lotto worked for 12 years in and around Bergamo from 1513. Today, three of his works remain in situ in three churches scattered about the city. Seeing them is largely a matter of luck, as finding these churches open is a hit-and-miss affair. Just off Via Porta Dipinta at the eastern end of the Città Alta, the diminutive **Chiesa di San Michele al Pozzo** (St Michael at the Well; Via Porta Dipinta; ⊗9am-noon & 2-6pm) is home to a chapel filled with a cycle of paintings known as the *Storie della vergine* (Stories of the Virgin Mother), starting with her birth and culminating with the scene of her visiting Elisabeth (her cousin and soon-to-be mother of St John the Baptist). In two churches in the Città Bassa, the **Chiesa del Santo Spirito** (Church of the Holy Spirit; Via Tasso 100; ⊗8-11am & 3-6pm Thu-Tue) and **Chiesa di San Bernardino** (Via Pignolo 59; ⊗9.30-10.30am Sun), you can observe how Lotto treats the same subject in quite different fashion in altarpieces dedicated to the *Madonna in trono e santi* (Madonna Enthroned with Saints). The latter is done with great flair and freedom, full of vivid colour, while the former seems more subdued.

Venetian rococo master Giambattista Tiepolo (1696–1770) did some of the frescoes below the central dome.

Rocca   FORTRESS
(☑035 24 71 16; Piazzale Brigata Legnano; museum €3, grounds free; ⊗9.30am-1pm & 2.30-6pm Tue-Sun) This impressive fortress is dominated by a round tower that dates from Bergamo's days as a Venetian outpost. La Rocca houses part of the city's history museum, and is surrounded by a park with lovely views over lower Bergamo. The views are even better from the castle's tower.

Galleria d'Arte Moderna e Contemporanea   GALLERY
(GAMeC; ☑035 27 02 72; www.gamec.it; Via San Tomaso 53; Permanent/temporary exhibition free/€6; ⊗10am-1pm & 3-6pm Wed-Mon) The modern works by Italian artists displayed here include pieces by Giacomo Balla, Giorgio Morandi, Giorgio de Chirico and Filippo de Pisis. A contribution from Vassily Kandinsky lends an international touch.

Temporary exhibitions stay open for longer hours (Wednesday to Monday from 10am to 7pm).

Torre di Gombito   TOWER
(☑035 24 22 26; Via Gombito 13; ⊗by reservation 10am-4pm Mon Apr-Sep) **FREE** For a wonderful view from one of the highest points in the old town, climb the 12th-century Gombito Tower. Visits must be reserved in advance at the tourist office (p160), which is at the base of the tower, and leave at 10am, 10.45am, 11.30am, 2.30pm, 3.15pm and 4pm on Mondays. Keep in mind it's 263 steps to the top and there's no lift.

Cattedrale di Bergamo   CATHEDRAL
(☑035 21 02 23; www.cattedraledibergamo.it; Piazza del Duomo; ⊗7.30am-noon & 3-6.30pm Mon-Fri, 7am-6.30pm Sat & Sun) Roman remains were discovered during renovations of Bergamo's baroque cathedral, with an interior dating to the 17th century. A rather squat building, it has a brilliant white facade (completed in the 19th century). Among the relics in a side chapel is the one-time coffin of the beatified Pope John XXII. The church also contains paintings by Moroni and Tiepolo.

Citadella Viscontea   FORTRESS
Built by the powerful Visconti clan in 1355, Bergamo's fortress has some imposing features, including a medieval postern gate, a 14th-century portico and Romanesque arcades. Today the citadel houses the **Civico Museo Archeologico di Bergamo** (☑035 28 60 70; www.museoarcheologicobergamo.it; Piazza Cittadella 9; incl Museo Civico Scienze Naturali €3; ⊗9am-12.30pm & 2.30-6pm Tue-Sun) and the **Museo Civico Scienze Naturali** (www.museoscienzebergamo.it; incl Civico Museo Archeologico di Bergamo €3; ⊗9am-12.30pm & 2.30-5.30pm Tue-Fri, from 10am Sat & Sun).

☞ Tours

Guide Turistiche Città di Bergamo   TOURS
(☑328 6123502; www.bergamoguide.it; tour 3/6hr €125/200) This outfit offers historical guided walks through the old streets, food and wine-focussed tours and Donizetti-themed tours, plus tours further afield (Lake Iseo, the Brembana Valley). Prices for half- and full-day tours are for up to 15 people.

Eating

Il Coccio
ITALIAN €

(☑035 093 23 38; www.trattoriailcoccio.it; Via Sant'Alessandro 54; meals €12-20; ⊘11.30am-2.30pm & 6.30-9.30pm Tue-Sat, 11.30am-2.30pm Sun; 🖉) A local favourite in the lower town is Il Coccio, a tiny eatery that whips up a few tasty dishes each day, served counter-style with a smile. The menu changes daily and features the likes of lasagna, chick peas with rosemary, grilled asparagus with pancetta and roasted veal. Leave room for dessert (including apple and cinnamon tarts).

Il Fornaio
PIZZA, BAKERY €

(Via Bartolomeo Colleoni 1; pizza slices around €3-4; ⊘8am-9pm) Join the crowds that mill around this local favourite for coffee that packs a punch and pizza slices that drip with delicious ingredients: spinach laced with creamy mozzarella or gorgonzola studded with walnuts. Take it away or compete for a table upstairs.

Polentone
ITALIAN €

(☑348 8046021; Piazza Mercato delle Scarpe 1; polentas €6-9; ⊘11.30am-3.30pm & 6.30-10.30pm Mon-Fri, 11.30am-1am Sat, to 10pm Sun; 🖉) Styling itself as Italy's first polenta takeaway, Polentone serves up steaming bowls of polenta in the sauce of your choice, including wild boar or vegetarian. Choose between *gialla* (simple corn polenta) or *taragna* (with Taleggio cheese and butter).

It's under the arches, opposite the Città Alta funicular stop, with a few wooden stools strewn around.

La Tana
ITALIAN €€

(☑035 21 31 37; www.tanaristorante.it; Via San Lorenzo 25; meals €32-42) In the upper town, but just off the beaten path, La Tana remains exceptionally popular for painstakingly prepared Bergamesque dishes served in a sun-drenched interior of exposed brick and colourful artwork, or out on the small front terrace.

Osteria della Birra
OSTERIA €€

(☑035 24 24 40; www.elavbrewery.com; Piazza Mascheroni 1; meals €25-30; ⊘noon-3pm & 6pm-2am Mon-Fri, noon-2am Sat & Sun) Being the official *osteria* (tavern) of craft brewers, this convivial eatery ensures there's a top selection on tap; the tangy Indie Ale tastes particularly fine. Squeeze in at a tiny table or lounge in the courtyard and chow down on platters piled high with local meats, or polenta stuffed with Taleggio (cheese) and porcini mushrooms.

Enoteca Zanini
WINE BAR, RESTAURANT €€

(☑035 22 50 49; www.enotecazanini.com; Via Santa Caterina 90a; meals €32-42; ⊘12.30-2.15pm & 7.30-10.15pm Tue-Sun) Run by two accredited wine sommeliers who have worked for Gualtiero Marchesi in Erbusco, this is a great place to sample regional wine by the glass. The red-brick interior makes for a cosy atmosphere and the menu features original dishes such as roasted octopus with chickpea purée and candy tomatoes, and home-made dumplings with braised beef tail.

Vineria Cozzi
ITALIAN €€

(☑035 23 88 36; www.vineriacozzi.it; Via Bartolomeo Colleoni 22, Città Alta; meals €37-45; ⊘10.30am-3pm & 6.30pm-midnight) Things have changed little since the original wine dealer started here in 1848. Elegant tables with delicate wrought-iron-backed chairs, globe lamps and red-and-white-checked floors make a charming setting for bruschetta with goat cheese and smoked aubergine, or home-made ravioli with bacon, butter and sage. Start off with a delectable cheese fondue with poached egg and black truffle.

★ Da Vittorio
GASTRONOMY €€€

(☑035 68 10 24; www.davittorio.com; Via Cantalupa 17, Brusaporto; set menu lunch €70, dinner €180-280; ⊘12.30-2.30pm & 7-10pm Thu-Tue Sep-Jul)

DON'T MISS

NOI

Thirty-something chef Tommaso Spagnolo learned his craft at celebrated restaurants in London and New York (including the top-rated Eleven Madison Park) before returning to his hometown to open his creative *osteria*, Noi (☑035 23 77 50; www.noi-restaurant.it; Via Alberto Pitentino 6; meals €35-45; ⊘7.30pm-midnight Mon, 12.30-2.30pm & 7.30pm-midnight Tue-Sat; 🖃), in 2016. The seasonally driven menu features beautifully prepared dishes, including tender grilled octopus with sweet potato and radicchio, sashimi with horseradish, and the juiciest rib-eye for miles around.

Five- and eight-course tasting menus (€35 and €50 respectively) are the way to go. Noi is located just a short walk southeast of the Accademia Carrara.

ROAD TRIP: CASTLE CIRCUIT

• •

Towers, castles and strongholds characterise the rich agricultural plains south of Bergamo, which for centuries lay in the path of the warring powers in Milan and Venice, who held Bergamo between 1428 and 1797. This tour covers some of the areas most impressive castles along with unusual destinations such as the pilgrimage site of Caravaggio and the Unesco Heritage 'workers' town of Crespi d'Adda.

❶ Cavernago

Take the SS42 east out of Bergamo, or drop south to the A4 motorway and head a short way east, turning south onto the SP498 for

Cavernago, a village presided over by one of several forts built by the mercenary commander Bartolomeo Colleoni. **Castello Colleoni** (Via Castello di Cavernago) was raised in the Middle Ages but substantially overhauled in

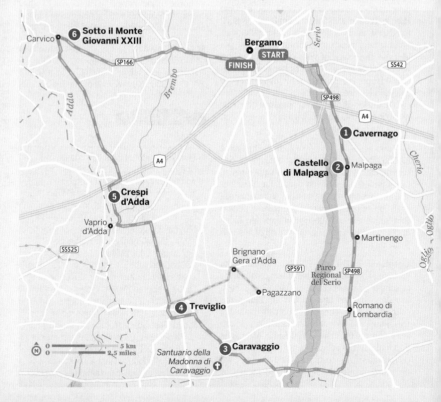

the 17th and 18th centuries. You can peek through slits at the entrance to see the frescoed gallery around the courtyard.

❷ Castello di Malpaga

Barely 3km southwest, on a farming estate, lies the crenellated brickwork of **Castello di Malpaga** (☑ 035 840 00 03; www.castellomalpaga. it; Piazza Marconi, Malpaga; €6, with guided tour €9; ⊙ 10am-6pm Sat & to 5pm Sun Mar-Nov), another Colleoni residence. He had the original 14th-century castle expanded, turning the original defensive walls into a kind of interior courtyard. Some original frescoes still remain in place.

❸ Caravaggio

Picking up the SP498 again head to Romano di Lombardia and the A35 autostrada. When you reach the A35 turn west to Treviglio and after 12km exit for Caravaggio. Aside from the impressive **Chiesa dei Santi Fermo e Rustico** (Piazza San Fermo; ⊙ 7am-noon & 3-6.30pm) and its claim to fame as the birthplace of the like-named artist, the town's main attraction lies along a tree-lined boulevard about 1.5km southwest of the centre. The **Santuario della Madonna di Caravaggio** (☑ 0363 35 71; www.santuariodicaravaggio.org; Viale Papa Giovanni XXIII; ⊙ 6.30am-noon & 2-6pm) is a grandiose building started on the orders of Filippo Maria Visconti, Duke of Milan, after an alleged sighting on this spot of the Virgin Mary in 1432. With its richly decorated 18th-century interior, it remains an object of pilgrimage today.

❹ Treviglio

A short hop northwest brings you to Treviglio (pop 25,000), at whose centre rises the **Basilicata di San Martino** (Piazza Luciano Manara; ⊙ 7.30-11.30am & 2.30-6pm). A minor country road leads northeast out of Treviglio for Brignano Gera d'Adda, home to the Palazzo Visconti (Via Vittorio Emanuele II), one of several Visconti castles in the area. Now a baroque residence jammed with frescoes it has just reopened after a 40-year closure. Barely 3km southeast, in Pagazzano, stands another Visconti castle, the **Castello di Pagazzano** (☑ 0363 81 46 29; www.castellodipagazzano.it; Piazza Castello; adult/child €7/free; ⊙ 9am-noon & 2-6pm 1st & 3rd Sun of month Mar-Nov), this one surrounded by a moat.

❺ Crespi d'Adda

Crespi d'Adda (www.villaggiocrespi.it) some 20km northwest, is a perfect example of a 19th-century workers' town built. Here, the Crespi textile dynasty built cotton mills (which closed in 2004), modest housing for employees, and a boisterous castle for the family. The town was declared a World Heritage Site in 1995. If hunger strikes, make for **Osteria da Mualdo** (☑ 02 9093 7077; www.osteriadamualdo.it; Via Privata Crespi 6, Crespi d'Adda; meals €30-45, 5-/7-course menu €50/70; ⊙ noon-2pm & 7-10pm Tue-Sat, noon-2pm Sun) (Via Privata Crespi 6).

❻ Sotto il Monte Giovanni XXIII

From Crespi, follow the Adda river north on the SP170 15km to Carvico. Two kilometres east is Sotto il Monte Giovanni XXIII. Angelo Roncalli was born in this hamlet in 1881. In 1958, he become Pope John XXIII. In his five years as pontiff, he changed the face of the Catholic Church through the Vatican II Council reforms. You can visit his humble birthplace in the centre of town and a small museum set up in a house he used on summer holidays as cardinal. From here, it is an 18km drive east back into Bergamo along the SP166 road.

Bergamo's acclaimed Vittorio is set in a country house 9km east of town and is up there with the best restaurants in Italy, thanks to the celebrated talents of Bergamo-born chef Enrico Cerea. The guiding thought behind the cuisine is the subtle use of the freshest possible seasonal products to create local dishes with inventive flair.

The multicourse decadence that can easily stretch into three hours and will cost a fortune – but for foodies, this triple-Michelin-starred restaurant is the Holy Grail.

**Ristorante
Roof Garden** MODERN ITALIAN €€€
(☑ 035 36 61 59; www.roofgardenrestaurant.it; Piazza della Repubblica 6; meals €50-80; ◉ 12.30-2pm Mon-Fri & 7.45-10pm Mon-Sat) The rooftop restaurant of the Hotel San Marco offers exquisitely prepared dishes against a sweeping panoramic view over Bergamo. Dine on black ink tagliatelli with sea urchins and cuttlefish tartare or braised beef in Valcalepio red wine with polenta.

☆ Entertainment

Teatro Donizetti PERFORMING ARTS
(☑ 035 416 06 11; www.teatro.gaetano-donizetti.com; Piazza Cavour 15; ◉ box office 1-8pm Tue-Sat) Named after the famed composer who was born in Bergamo, this is one of Lombardy's grand opera houses and dates back to the 18th century. The dazzling, horseshoe-shaped theatre hosts a wide range of fare, including ballet, jazz and symphonic music, in addition to lavish opera productions.

The box office also opens on Sundays on performance days (from 2pm to 3.30pm).

❶ Information

ASST Papa Giovanni XXIII (☑ 035 26 71 11; Piazza OMS 1; ◉ 24hr) Located about 4km west of central Bergamo, this modern, state-of-the-art hospital has excellent facilities.

Città Alta Tourist Office (☑ 035 24 22 26; www.visitbergamo.net; Via Gombito 13; ◉ 9am-5.30pm) Helpful multilingual office in the heart of the Upper Town.

Città Bassa Tourist Office (☑ 035 21 02 04; www.visitbergamo.net; Viale Papa Giovanni XXIII 57; ◉ 9am-12.30pm & 2-5.30pm) Near the train and bus stations, in the Lower Town. Office will likely move across the street to Piazzale Marconi (just outside the train station) in the future.

❶ Getting There & Away

AIR
Orio al Serio (☑ 035 32 63 23; www.sacbo.it), 4km southeast of Bergamo train station, has regular flights to/from the UK and other European destinations, as a result of which Bergamo is increasingly one of the most popular entry points into northern Italy.

BUS & FUNICULAR
The main **bus station** (☑ 800 139392; www.bergamotrasporti.it) for provincial services is across Piazzale Marconi from the train station. **SAB** (☑ 035 28 90 11; www.arriva.it) operates regular bus service to Brescia, Mantua and the lakes.

ATB bus 1 connects the train station with the **funicular** (☑ 035 23 60 26; www.atb.bergamo.it; ◉ 7.30am-11.45pm) to the Upper Town and Colle Aperto (going the other way not all buses stop right at the station but at the Porta Nuova stop). From Colle Aperto, either bus 21 or a **funicular** continues uphill to San Vigilio. Buy tickets, valid for 75 minutes' travel on buses, for €1.30 from machines at the train and funicular stations or at newspaper stands.

OFF THE BEATEN TRACK

VAL IMAGNA & VAL TALEGGIO

North of Bergamo, the little visited **Val Imagna** and **Val Taleggio** make a dramatic setting for a scenic drive. Forested hillsides, age-old villages and flower-covered plains are just a few reasons to make the journey. Other highlights include the 900-year-old Romanesque church of **San Tomè** (◉ 10am-noon & 2.30-5.30pm Tue-Sun) and rustic inns well off the beaten path, such as **La Collina** (☑ 035 64 25 70; www.ristorantecollina.it; Via Capaler 5, Almenno San Bartolomeo; meals €45-50; ◉ noon-2pm & 7-10pm Wed-Sun) in Almenno San Bartolomeo and **Il Borgo Zen** (☑ 0345 4 70 06; www.albergodellasalute.it; Via Roma 110, Olda; meals €30-38; ◉ 12.30-2.30pm & 6.30-9.30pm Tue-Sun; ☑) in Olda. The latter is situated halfway along the wild and woolly Val Taleggio and serves excellent home-cooked dishes featuring the local Taleggio cheese. Try the *strozzapreti ai spinaci con crema di Taleggio*, a kind of spinach gnocchi bathed in a thick, creamy Taleggio sauce.

CAR

From Milan or Brescia, take the A4 motorway and follow the Bergamo exits.

Traffic is restricted in the Città Alta, although you can approach and find limited parking outside the city walls. Otherwise, use metered parking or car parks in the Lower Town. There's free parking on the streets south of the train station.

TRAIN

One or two trains run every hour between Milan (not all stop at Stazione Centrale) and Bergamo's **train station** (☎ 035 24 79 50; Piazza Marconi) (€5.50, 50 to 65 minutes). Every 30 to 60 minutes a train runs to/from Brescia (€4.80, one to 1½ hours). Change there for Cremona or Mantua. There's a taxi rank at the train station.

BERGAMO'S VALLEYS

The series of tranquil valleys that works its way like a hand of bony fingers into the mountains north of Bergamo rank among the region's best-kept secrets. Here the hills rise to the status of mountains in the Orobie Alps, which throw up a mix of jagged peaks, gentler, snow-covered slopes, thickly wooded dales and open high-country pasture.

Valle Brembana

Named after the Brembo river that winds its way through the mountains, the peaceful Valle Brembana has all sorts of gems awaiting discovery. You can soak in the famed waters of San Pellegrino Terme, explore medieval stone hamlets like Cornello dei Tasso or go hiking against the backdrop of the Orobie Alps.

From golden-hued **Cornello dei Tasso**, the valley road proceeds north and splits delta-like into a series of valleys, some of which culminate in small winter ski towns, such as Foppolo, in the Orobie Alps. Hikers should note Branzi and Carona, which can make bases for walks or to a series of glacial lakes. Scenic-drive enthusiasts might opt for a different route: a minor road linking the Valle Brembana with the Valle Seriana via the villages of Dossena and Oltre il Colle. Territory ranges from dense forest to fine open views north to the Orobie Alps from around Oltre il Colle.

❶ Getting There & Away

From Bergamo's bus station, **SAB** (p160) operates services to just about every village in the valleys, albeit not with great frequency. Timetables are available at the station.

Your own vehicle makes touring the valleys a great deal easier. The SS470 road heads north from Bergamo along the Valle Brembana.

San Pellegrino Terme

☎ 0345 / POP 4800

Best known today for its sparkling mineral waters, San Pellegrino Terme has a picturesque riverside setting that makes a fine base for exploring the Valle Brembana. It also has some lovely architecture, and a newly opened spa, where visitors can enjoy a soak in some of Europe's best-known springs.

Lightly sparkling mineral water was first bottled in San Pellegrino Terme, 25km north of Bergamo along the Valle Brembana, at the beginning of the 19th century.

Thermal baths tourism began late that century, and local investors decided to spend big on new facilities in the early 1900s, creating the massive, seven-storey Grand Hotel (1904) and the exuberant Casinò di San Pellegrino Terme (1907). They face each other over the Brembo river and together form a treasure chest of *stile liberty* architecture (Italian art nouveau).

◎ Sights & Activities

QC Terme   THERMAL BATHS

(☎ 0345 2 01 02; www.qcterme.com; Viale della Vittoria 53; €38-50; ☺10am-11pm Mon-Fri, from 9am Sat & Sun) Next to the Casinò, these new thermal baths offer a decadent day of relaxation amid saunas, salt chambers, aromatherapy rooms, Vichy showers, relaxation lounges with fireplaces, a restaurant, and myriad pools and tubs for immersing in those mineral-rich San Pellegrino waters. The sleek modern building has fine vantage points of the mountainous surrounds, and the outdoor pool has the loveliest view of all.

Prices vary depending on what day and hour you go; admission must be booked online. It's worth having a meal (fresh healthy cuisine served buffet-style) in the restaurant – if you don't mind dining in your bathrobe.

**Casinò di
San Pellegrino Terme**   ARCHITECTURE

(☎ 0345 2 10 20; www.associazioneoter.com/casino-teatro; Via Bartolomeo Villa 16; ☺irregular hours) Built in 1907, the striking Casinò di San Pellegrino Terme is full of whimsical detail. The *stile liberty* facade bears reliefs and sculptures of mythological figures and naturalistic forms (from laurel leaves to beetles), as well as two giant wrought-iron lamp holders. If you can't make it in person, you'll find an image of the belle epoque beauty on a logo of San Pellegrino bottled sparkling water.

Recently restored, the building opens occasionally to the public, with guided tours (admission €7) offered roughly three or four times a month. Visit the website for upcoming tours.

✕ Eating

Cà Bigio BERGAMESE €€

(☑0345 2 10 58; www.bigio.info; Viale Papa Giovanni XXIII 60, San Pellegrino Terme; meals €35-43; ◷noon-2pm & 7-10pm; 🐾) The Bigio family invented the archetypal Bergamese dessert, *polenta e osei* (cakes filled with jam and cream, topped with sweet polenta and chocolate birds). At their restaurant, though, it's the savouries that will win you over.

Grab a table at the back for views up through the garden to the Casinò di San Pellegrino Terme and order meaty dishes like lamb with artichokes, alpine cheese and thyme or duck tortelli with black truffles for a true taste of the mountains.

Valle Seriana

Northeast of Bergamo, the Valle Seriana is a lure for travellers wanting to get off the beaten path. Quiet beauty reigns supreme in the lush green mountains near Ardesio, with charming medieval villages like Gromo and fresco-covered churches far from the teeming crowds. This is also a fine place for getting out into nature, with superb hiking outside of Valbondione. There's more great scenery 7km east of Valbondione at Lizzola, another hiking base at 1256m, with magnificent views of the surrounding mountains and back south down the valley.

◉ Sights

Cascate del Serio WATERFALL

From Valbondione, it's a three-hour (one-way) hike to Cascate del Serio, a triple cascade of 300m that constitutes one of Europe's tallest waterfalls.

Basilica di Santa Maria Assunta CHURCH

(Piazza della Emancipazione; ◷8am-noon & 3-6pm) Some 25km northeast of central Bergamo, the town of Gandino is well worth a stop for its impressive Basilica di Santa Maria Assunta, a baroque beauty with a richly decorated interior atop a sloping square.

ℹ Getting There & Away

You'll need a car to properly visit the area. From Bergamo, take SP35 northeast, then hop on the SP671 and the SP49. It's 53km (about an hour's drive) from Bergamo to Valbondione.

Val Cavallina

The broad Val Cavallina follows the Cherio river east of Bergamo towards forest-lined Lake Endine, with the medieval village of Monasterolo del Castello on its southeastern bank. Other highlights in this region include the hidden Lorenzo Lotto masterpieces of Trescore Balneario, and Bianzino with its splendid views over the lake. For scenic walks, both the Riserva Naturale Regionale Valle del Freddo and Esmate provide fine vantage points from lofty heights.

◉ Sights

Lake Endine LAKE

Lovely, mirror-still Lake Endine is surrounded by woods and reed banks. Tranquillity is assured on this lake where motorboats are banned. Lakeside paths provide a fine vantage point for soaking up the views, particularly from Monasterolo del Castello, a quiet medieval village on the south bank of the lake. The Monasterolo castle, turned into a country mansion in the 16th century, is just outside the village to the southwest.

Riserva Naturale Regionale Valle del Freddo PARK

(☑035 4 34 98 17; www.parks.it/riserva.valle.del.freddo; off SS442) Around 2km northeast of Lake Endine, the Cold Valley Reserve has a unique microclimate, with a particularly chilly subsoil (stick your hands into some of the holes in the ground) that allows 24 species of Alpine flowers (including edelweiss) and plants to flourish at an altitude of just 360m. The reserve has a short loop trail and lies near another trail leading to tiny Lake Gaiano.

Oratorio di Suardi CHURCH

(Capella di Villa Suardi; ☑035 94 47 77; info@prolocotrescore.it; Via Suardi 20, Trescore Balneario;

€8; ⏱ 3-3.45pm Sun Mar-Nov or by appointment) The highlight of this small atmospheric chapel is the collection of vibrant frescoes by Lorenzo Lotto depicting stories of St Barbara and St Brigid. Lotto even snuck in his own self-portrait above the main door, depicting a hunter carrying an owl and a bundle of branches over his shoulder. The church stands in the luxuriant grounds of Villa Suardi, just off the SS42.

❶ Information

Trescore Balneario Tourist Office (☑ 035 94 47 77; www.prolocotrescore.it; Via Suardi 16; ⏱ 8.30am-12.45pm Mon-Sat) Contact this tourist office to arrange a guided tour of the Oratorio di Suardi (four person minimum). The office also sells hiking maps for the surrounding area and nearby Lake Endine.

❶ Getting There & Away

It's impractical to attempt to explore this region without a car. The SS42 road takes you through the valley's highlights, and connects the north of Lake Iseo with Bergamo.

LAKE ISEO & AROUND

Less than 100km from both Bergamo and Brescia, Lake Iseo (aka Sebino) is one of the least known Lombard lakes. Shut in by soaring mountains, it's a magnificent sight. About halfway along the lake, a mountain soars right out of the water.

With the exception of the south shore and a series of tunnels at the northeast end of the lake, the road closely hugs the water on its circuit around Lake Iseo and is especially dramatic south of Lovere. Various back roads also lead high up behind Lovere for magnificent views.

To the lake's north stretches the Valle Camonica, famed for its Stone Age rock carvings. To the south stretches the rolling Franciacorta wine country and, to the west, the picture-book-pretty Lake Endine.

❶ Getting There & Away

BOAT

Navigazione sul Lago d'Iseo (☑ 035 97 14 83; www.navigazionelagoiseo.it) ferries zigzag their way along the length of the lake with stops around Monte Isola. There are also fairly regular runs between Lovere and Pisogne in the north.

There are only two daily services that run the whole way from Sarnico to Pisogne (a trip that can take two to three hours depending on stops, €5.50) and vice versa. Small boats make the quick crossing (10 minutes, every half-hour) from Sale Marasino and Sulzano, on the east shore, respectively to Carzano and Peschiera Maraglio on Monte Isola (one-way/return €3/5 one way/return).

BUS

From Bergamo, **SAB** (☑ 035 28 90 11; www. arriva.it) operates services (line E) to Sarnico (€3.80, 50 minutes) and Tavernola Bergamasca. Line D also goes to Sarnico, while line C runs via Lake Endine to Lovere and on to Boario in the Valle Camonica. The same company also has a service along the Valle Camonica.

CAR

From Bergamo or Brescia you can take the A4 motorway then turn north to Sarnico. Otherwise, the SS42 road east out of Bergamo leads past Lake Endine to Lovere, while the SP510 from Brescia follows the eastern shore of the lake. They merge north of the lake as the SS42 and proceed up the Valle Camonica.

TRAIN

Trains run from Brescia to Iseo (€3.30, 30 minutes, hourly), up the east shore of the lake, and on up the Valle Camonica as far as Edolo, 56km north of the lake (up to 2½ hours).

Monte Isola

The towering island at the south end of Lake Iseo is easily the lake's most striking feature and merits an effort to get to know. Francesco Sforza granted the people of Monte Isola special fishing rights in the 15th century. Its people, whose ancestors may have lived here in Roman times, were also known for their handmade fishing nets. Perched on Europe's biggest lake island (4.28 sq km), they were

DON'T MISS

VIEWS FROM ESMATE

The hamlet of **Esmate** provides a scenic vantage point over the northern end of Lake Iseo. The views are good from the churchyard but breathtaking if you follow Via Cerrete about 2.5km from the church (it changes names several times). Where it narrows amid thick woods, several brief trails (20m or so) lead out to magnificent, wild viewpoints high above the lake.

largely self-sufficient in basic land produce. A handful of villages are scattered around the island. From **Carzano**, in the northeast (where many boats land), you can climb rough stairs to scattered rural settlements and follow a path to the top of the island (599m). The town hall is in **Siviano**, on the northwest shore. A 15km trail allows you to walk or cycle right around the island.

✗ Eating

★ **Locanda al Lago**   ITALIAN €€
(☑ 030 988 64 72; www.locandaallago.it; Località Carzano 38, Monte Isola; meals €27-37; ☉ noon-2.30pm & 7-9pm Wed-Sun) The Soardi family has been serving up local dishes since 1948, perfecting deceptively simple treatments of lake fish. It means you can sit on their waterside terrace and feast on trout carpaccio or the day's catch combined with *trenette* (a flat pasta) and lashings of extra virgin Monte Isola olive oil. It's near the quay where ferries from Sale Marasino stop.

Residenza Vittoria Ristorante   ITALIAN €€
(☑ 030 988 62 22; www.monteisola.com; Località Sensole 22; meals €30-35; ☉ noon-3.30pm & 7-9pm) On the southern shore of the island, this perfectly located spot serves a mouthwatering plate of mixed grilled lake fish as well as trout ravioli with Monte Isola olive oil, tender perch fillets and other fine selections. The outdoor tables are just metres from the water – a nice place to linger over a meal (which is just as well as service can be slow).

Ferries stop nearby at Sensole, though it's a pleasant 20-minute walk to the dock at Peschiera Maraglio, which has more frequent service.

Iseo

☑ 030 / POP 9200

The sun sets directly in front of the lakefront promenade in Iseo, at the lake's southeast edge. The squares just behind the waterfront are wonderful places in which to hang about in cafes and people-watch.

About 500m west of the old centre, you can hire canoes and pedalos for about €6 an hour. Located in a campground near town, **Iseobike** (☑ 340 3962095; www.iseobike.com; Via per Rovato 26; bike rental per 2hr/day €5/20, helmet €3; ☉ 9.30am-12.15pm & 2.30-7pm Apr-Sep) rents bikes and can put together tailor-made cycling tours around the lake and

amid the vineyards of the Franciacorta wine area immediately to the south.

✗ Eating & Drinking

One block in from the lake, Piazza Mazzini is the go-to spot for an *aperitivo* (pre-dinner drink) at cafe tables on the cobblestones.

Forno di Porta del Campo   PIZZA €
(☑ 333 2193800; Via Campo 15; pizza €7-12; ☉ 11am-midnight, shorter hours winter) When peckish in Iseo you could always do what the locals do: grab a huge but supremely thin and crispy pizza from this bustling takeaway, then stroll a few metres to eat it sitting beside the lake.

La Tana dell'Orso   RISTORANTE €€
(☑ 030 982 16 16; Vicolo Borni 19; meals €32-42; ☉ 7-9.30pm Mon, Tue & Thu, noon-2pm & 7-9.30pm Fri-Sun) For an intimate ambience and fine local fare head to this excellent eatery where a barrel ceiling sits above rough stone walls. 'The Bear's Den' is hidden away down a cobbled *vicolo* off Piazza Garibaldi. The gnocchi with mussels and clams, beef with polenta, and *casoncelli* (stuffed pasta) are all crowd-pleasers.

Gös   TRATTORIA €€
(☑ 030 982 18 18; www.trattoriagos.it; Viale Repubblica 6; meals €25-35; ☉ 6pm-midnight daily, 11.30am-2pm Sat & Sun) Behind Gös' nondescript front sits a gleaming microbrewery where happy locals tuck into meat-rich, home-made pasta dishes – try the beef, butter and cheese *casoncelli* (stuffed pasta). It's all best washed down with a glass or two of Gös' own zesty unfiltered brew.

❶ Information

Iseo Tourist Office (☑ 030 374 87 33; www.iseolake.info; Lungolago Marconi 2; ☉ 10am-12.30pm & 3.30-6.30pm May-Sep, shorter hr winter) Facing the waterfront, this helpful office can give you the low-down on the region. Ask here about vineyards open for wine tasting in Franciacorta.

Sarnico

☑ 035 / POP 6630

Approaching Lake Iseo from the southwest brings you to Sarnico, prettily located on a corner of the lake and the Oglio river. It is characterised by several lovely *stile liberty* villas, many of them designed by Giuseppe Sommaruga. Among them, his lakeside

Villa Faccanoni (Via Veneto) is the most outstanding.

The heart of the old town, known as La Contrada, straggles back from its pretty riverside location on the mouth of the Oglio river and is perfect for a wander after a morning coffee along the riverside. Head up Via Lantieri, lined by shops and eateries, and along which you can make out vestiges of the past. Via Scaletta, which runs down to the lake, is where you'll find most evidence of Sarnico's medieval past, with the remnants of towers and stout surviving walls.

For information on attractions around the region, head for **Pro Loco Sarnico** (☑ 035 91 09 00; www.prolocosarnico.it; Via Tresanda 1, Sarnico; ⊙ 9am-12.30pm & 3-6.30pm Tue-Sat, 9.30am-12.30pm Sun). It's located near the bridge – go one block inland and turn left.

🍷 Drinking

★ **Enoteca Tresanda**   WINE BAR

(☑ 035 91 20 06; Via Tresanda 25; ⊙ 10am-midnight Tue-Sun; 🛜) A short stroll from the riverfront, this buzzing and jovial wine bar serves up phenomenal Italian vintages by the glass or bottle. Local varieties like bubbly Franciacorta and Valcalepio go nicely with cheese and meat boards, mushroom-topped bruschetta and a few baked dishes. Sit among the bottle-lined shelves inside or at one of the outdoor tables in front.

Lovere & Bossico

POP 5300 (LOVERE), 990 (BOSSICO)

Perched on the lake's northwestern tip, the port town of Lovere is a gem, with a working harbour and a wealth of walking trails nearby. Its cobbled old town, punctuated by the occasional medieval tower, curves around the harbour, shadowed by a leafy lake-front promenade. Those in need of an art shot should consider the waterfront **Accademia Tadini** (☑ 035 96 27 80; www. accademiatadini.it; Via Tadini 40, Lovere; adult/reduced €7/5; ⊙ 3-7pm Tue-Sat, 10am-noon & 3-7pm Sun May-Sep, weekends only Apr & Oct), home to a considerable art collection with works by Jacopo Bellini, Il Parmigiano, Giambattista Tiepolo, Francesco Hayez, Antonio Canova and more.

Those with vehicles might want to drive 12km out of town and up into the hills behind Lovere to the hamlet of Bossico (900m). Several panoramic viewpoints offer great vistas over Lake Iseo from the village

and nearby. Esmate, reached by Riva di Solto, 6km south of Lovere, offers further great lookout points over the lake.

Valle Camonica

Running northeast of Lake Iseo and marked by the course of the Oglio river, the Valle Camonica is best known locally for easy skiing at its northern extremity but internationally as the site of some quite extraordinary rock carvings – the whole lot of which encompass a Unesco World Heritage Site.

The rock carvings are concentrated in several sites around the small town of Capo di Ponte, which sits on the Oglio river.

The riverside town of Breno, 13km south of Capo di Ponte, is worth a stop for its extensive hilltop castle ruins. It is in fact a huddle of buildings built over centuries but consolidated as a defensive complex under Venetian rule from the 15th century on.

◎ Sights

Parco Nazionale delle
Incisioni Rupestri   PARK

(☑ 0364 43 34 65; www.arterupestre.it; Via Piana 29, Nadro di Ceto; adult/reduced €6/3; ⊙ 8.30am-7pm Tue-Sun Apr-Oct, to 4.30pm Nov-Mar; 🚻) About halfway between Darfo and Edolo, the Parco Nazionale delle Incisioni Rupestri is a 30-hectare open-air museum containing rock engravings that date back as far as the Bronze Age. Colour-coded paths loop through chestnut woods revealing an intriguing array of imagery, including antlered god figures, deer, weaponry, huntsmen on horseback, Latin inscriptions,

BERGAMO, BRESCIA & CREMONA LOVERE & BOSSICO

WORTH A TRIP

DUE COLOMBE

In the small village of Borgonato, **Due Colombe** (☑ 030 982 82 27; www. duecolombe.com; Via Foresti 13, Borgonato; tasting menu €70-90, 2-/3-course lunch €28/38; ⊙ 12.30-2pm & 7.30-10pm Tue-Sat, 12.30-2pm Sun) has earned a stellar reputation for its high-end cuisine thanks to the skills of head chef Stefano Cerveni. Delectable seasonal dishes coupled with an outstanding wine list (over 750 varieties) are a few reasons Due Colombe was awarded a Michelin star.

It's located about 4km southwest of Provaglio.

enigmatic shovel shapes, ploughing scenes, and duelling warriors all etched onto rock slabs.

Especially rich is Rock No 1 (aka Roccia Grande), upon which is carved a small labyrinth, among many other fascinating engravings.

Museo Nazionale della
Preistoria della Valle Camonica   MUSEUM
(MUPRE; Via San Martino 7; adult/reduced €6/3; ⊙2-6pm Wed-Sun) Capo di Ponte's newest attraction, which opened in 2014, delves into the fascinating prehistoric sites scattered around the Valle Camonica. The small museum on the ground floor has a collection of engraved stele and menhirs taken from nearby megalithic sites, and on the upper floor burial objects, household items and tools, which date back even earlier – to more than 10,000 BC.

The ticket price includes admission to Parco Nazionale delle Incisioni Rupestri (p165), and makes a great add-on to the archaeological park.

Parco Archeologico Comunale
di Seradina-Bedolina   ARCHAEOLOGICAL SITE
(�334 65756 28; www.parcoseradinabedolina.it; Strada della Greppa; ⊙9am-6pm Mar-Oct, 10am-5pm Nov-Feb) FREE Opened in 2005, this open-air site contains 150 engraved rocks, most dating from 2000 to 1000 BC. Carved hunters, plough scenes and single figures are spread along five colour-coded paths, with signage providing a helpful context.

The highlight is the so-called 'Bedolina map' found in the upper reaches of the park and believed to be a primitive topographic map of sorts depicting the surrounding territory.

ⓘ WINE TOURING

You could easily spend days exploring the vineyards of the Franciacorta region (www.stradadelfranciacorta.it). To that end, most tourist offices in the region should have a copy of the *Franciacorta Wine Route* brochure. It details numerous hiking and cycling itineraries through the region (some of which are possible by car), and includes a pull-out list with contact details for over 100 local wineries.

ⓘ Information

Pro Loco Capo di Ponte (☎0364 4 20 80; www.proloco.capo-di-ponte.bs.it; Via Briscioli 42, Capo di Ponte; ⊙9am-12.30pm Sun, Mon & holidays, to noon & 2.30-4.30pm Tue-Sat) Helpful office with tips on exploring the region. Located 500m south of the Capo di Ponte train station.

Franciacorta

South of Lake Iseo and stretching towards Brescia are the rolling fields, low hills and flourishing vineyards of the greatly applauded Franciacorta wine region. **Provaglio d'Iseo**, 3.5km south of Iseo, is dominated by a Romanesque monastery and the lush wetland of Riserva Naturale Torbiere del Sebino. The region also boasts an impressive medieval abbey in Rodengo Saiano and a 13th-century castle in Bornato.

◉ Sights

Castello di Bornato   CASTLE
(☎030 72 50 06; www.castellodibornato.com; Via Castello 24; ⊙10am-noon & 2.30-6pm Sun & holidays) Five kilometres south of Provaglio, in the hamlet of Bornato, stands a 13th-century castle, with imposing crenellated walls, and a Renaissance villa set inside the grounds. On Sunday the doors open to the public, allowing visitors to see some of the villa's grand fresco-covered rooms, its wine cellar and the lush gardens outside.

The villa's owners possess local vineyards in the area and sell their wine and offer tastings at the castle.

Riserva Naturale
Torbiere del Sebino   PARK
(☎030 982 31 41; www.torbiere.it; Via Europa 5, Provaglio d'Iseo; self-pay admission €1; ⊙7am-9pm) These 2-sq-km protected wetlands were formed from 18th-century peat beds. A reed-fringed 4km walking path – partly on muddy tracks, partly on wooden walkways – encircles the water, which in late spring is dotted with water lilies.

A handy access point is at the southeast corner of the reserve, a few steps from San Pietro in Lamosa. There's a metered parking area here.

Monastero San Pietro
in Lamosa   MONASTERY
(☎030 982 36 17; www.sanpietroinlamosa.org; Provaglio d'Iseo; ⊙10am-noon & 3-6pm Sat, Sun & holidays Apr-Oct, 10am-noon & 2-5pm Sat, Sun &

holidays Nov-Mar) An 11th-century monastery founded by the Cluniac monks who first started to cultivate the region. On weekends you can visit the church and have a look at 15th century frescoes in various states of decay.

BRESCIA

📞 030 / POP 196,800

Brescia's core takes the form of a fascinating old town, which more than compensates for the city's rather unappealing urban sprawl. The old town's narrow streets are home to some of the most important Roman ruins in Lombardy, and an extraordinary circular Romanesque church. While many visitors stop in only for a day, there's much to see here, from a sprawling collection of 2000-year old architecture to the fresco-filled corridors of a medieval monastery.

Start off with a panoramic overview of Brescia from the hilltop castle, then plunge down into the cobblestone centre for a memorable ramble that will take you back through the ages.

◉ Sights

In addition to the Roman sites and museums, don't forget to admire Il Broletto (Piazza Paolo VI), the medieval town hall with an 11th-century tower, and the nearby Torre dell'Orologio (Clocktower; Piazza della Loggia); the latter's exquisite astrological timepiece is modelled on the one in Venice's Piazza San Marco.

★ Santa Giulia   MUSEUM, MONASTERY
(Museo della Città; 📞 030 297 78 33; www.brescia musei.com; Via dei Musei 81; adult/reduced €10/5.50, combined ticket incl Tempio Capitolino €15/10; ⊙ 9.30am-5.30pm Tue-Sun Oct–mid-Jun, 10.30am-7pm Tue-Sun mid-Jun–Sep) The jumbled Monastero di Santa Giulia and Basilica di San Salvatore is Brescia's most intriguing sight. Inside this rambling church and convent complex, the Museo della Città houses collections that run the gamut from prehistory to the age of Venetian dominance. Highlights include Roman mosaics and medieval jewels.

The building of the monastery, which started as early as the 8th century, absorbed two *domus* (Roman houses), which were left standing in what would become the monk's garden (Ortaglia) near the north cloister. The remains have become known as the Domus dell'Ortaglia. Raised walkways allow

---

BRESCIA UNDERGROUND

For a different view of Lombardy, sign up for a tour with **Brescia Underground** (📞 349 0998697; www.bresciaunderground. com; tour per person from €10). True to name, this outfit takes you into the earth, on a ramble through the underground canals and waterways that still course beneath Brescia and its environs. Excursions range from 30-minute highlight tours to 2½-hour walks – some of which happen outside the city centre. Call or email for upcoming tours and meeting points.

you to wander round the Domus di Dioniso (so called because of a mosaic of Dionysius, god of wine) and the Domus delle Fontane (named after two marble fountains). The beautiful floor mosaics and colourful frescoes in these two *domus* rank among the highlights of the monastery-museum.

Other highlights of the monastery range from 1st-century-AD bronzes (including a beautifully rendered *Winged Victory*) to the Coro delle Monache (Nun's Choir), a marvellous two-storey chamber completed in the 16th century that is decorated with lavish frescoes.

Tempio Capitolino   RUINS
(www.bresciamusei.com; Via dei Musei; adult/ reduced €8/6, combined ticket incl Santa Giulia €15/10; ⊙ 9.30am-5.30pm Wed-Sun Oct–mid-Jun, 10.30am-7pm mid-Jun–Sep) Brescia's most impressive Roman relic is this temple built by Emperor Vespasian in AD 73. Today, six Corinthian columns stand before a series of cells. A ticket gets you admission to the temple chambers, where you can see original coloured marble floors, frescoed walls, altars in Botticino limestone and religious statues.

Panels in English and audiovisual displays (mostly in Italian) give an overview of the site in ancient times. Tickets also secure admission to Brescia's nearby Teatro Romano (p169).

Duomo Vecchio   CHURCH
(Old Cathedral; Piazza Paolo VI; ⊙ 9am-noon & 3-6pm Tue-Sat, 9-10.45am & 3-7pm Sun) The most compelling of all Brescia's religious monuments is the 11th-century Duomo Vecchio, a rare example of a circular-plan Romanesque basilica, built over a 6th-century church. The inside is surmounted

Brescia

by a dome borne by eight sturdy vaults resting on thick pillars.

Interesting features include fragmentary floor mosaics (perhaps from a thermal bath that might have stood here in the 1st century BC) and the elaborate 14th-century sarcophagus of Bishop Berado Maggi (which lies right at the entrance).

Palazzo Martinengo Cesaresco　　MUSEUM
(☑320 0130694; www.amicimartinengo.it; Via dei Musei 30; ⊘10am-6pm Tue-Sun) This 17th-century palace houses two separate museums, and it makes a worthwhile detour while exploring Brescia's historic sites. The Brixia Light Box (admission free) has an audiovisual projection that recreates in a rather dramatic fashion the ancient Roman forum during the Flavian dynasty. Displays of archaeological fragments round out the exhibition. Palazzo Martinengo's other galleries (admission €10) host excellent art exhibitions, showcasing works by well-known painters and sculptors from Italy and abroad.

Brixia Parco Archeologico　　RUINS
The most impressive of Brescia's Roman relics are the remains of the Tempio Capitolino (p167), a Roman temple built by the Emperor Vespasian in AD 73. Six Corinthian columns stand before a series of cells. About 50m to the east, cobbled Vicolo del Fontanon leads to the overgrown ruins of a Roman theatre (off Via dei Musei; adult/reduced €8/6; ⊘9:30am-5.30pm Wed-Sun Oct–mid-Jun, 10.30am-7pm mid-Jun–Sep). Limited remains of the Roman Forum (Piazza del Foro) FREE are nearby.

You can partially view these sights from the outside, but for a more in-depth look at Brescia's Roman legacy, it's worth visiting the Tempio Capitolino, which also gives you inside-the-gate access to the Roman theatre.

Museo Mille Miglia　　MUSEUM
(☑030 336 56 31; www.museomillemiglia.it; Viale della Rimembranza 3; adult/reduced €8/6; ⊘10am-6pm) The original Mille Miglia (Thousand Miles) ran between 1927 and 1957 and was one of Italy's most legendary endurance car races – it started in Brescia and took some 16 hours to complete. The race's colourful museum is loaded with some of the greatest cars to cross the finish line, as well as old-style petrol pumps and archived race footage.

The Mille Miglia proper was halted in 1957 after several high-profile fatalities.

But the event (www.1000miglia.it) was revived in the 1970s as a Brescia–Rome round trip, held in May, open only to pre-1957 cars. The Museo Mille Miglia is housed outside central Brescia in the sprawling 11th-century Monastero di Sant'Eufemia della Fonte.

Castello　　CASTLE
(Via del Castello; ⊘8am-8pm) FREE Brescia's historic centre is dominated by a hill, Colle Cidneo, crowned with the rambling castle that for centuries was at the core of the city's defences. Torre Mirabella, the main round tower, was built by the Viscontis in the 13th century. The main reason to come up is to amble around the grounds, but the castle hosts two mildly diverting museums.

Within the castle grounds, the Museo delle Armi Antiche (☑030 29 32 92; www.bresciamusei.it; adult/reduced €5/4 all admission to Museo Civico del Risorgimento; ⊘10am-4pm Thu-Sun Oct–mid-Jun, 11am-7pm Fri-Sun mid-Jun–Sep) has an extensive collection of vintage weaponry, while the Museo Civico del Risorgimento (☑030 29 32 92; ⊘9am-1pm, 2-5.30pm Tue-Sun) is dedicated to the history of Italian reunification (Risorgimento).

🍴 Eating & Drinking

La Vineria　　ITALIAN €€
(☑030 28 05 43; www.lavineriabrescia.it; Via X Giornate 4; meals €28-40; ⊘noon-3pm & 7-11pm Tue-Sat, noon-3pm Sun) Near the Piazza della Loggia, La Vineria serves up delectable regional cuisine at al fresco tables in the portico or in the classy downstairs dining room with vaulted ceilings. Try dishes like chestnut gnocchi with creamy Bagoss cheese, leeks and walnuts, or polenta prepared three different ways. True to name, 'the winery' has good wine selections.

The bread comes in a brown paper bag – a nice, if unusual, touch.

La Grotta　　ITALIAN €€
(☑030 4 40 68; www.osterialagrotta.it; Vicolo del Prezzemolo 10; meals €26-36; ⊘11am-3pm & 7pm-midnight Thu-Tue) Tucked down Parsley Lane off pleasant pedestrianised Corso Cavour, this is a hidden gem for good home cooking served at tables dressed in gingham. Frilly curtains and cheerful frescoes (food and wine-making scenes) watch over chattering diners. You can't go wrong with casoncelli al burro e salvia (typical local meat-filled pasta with butter and sage).

Osteria al Bianchi
OSTERIA €€

(☑030 29 23 28; www.osteriaalbianchi.it; Via Gasparo da Salò 32; meals €24-30; ⊙9am-2.30pm & 4.30pm-midnight Thu-Mon) Squeeze inside this classic bar, in business since 1880, or grab a pavement table and be tempted by the *pappardelle al taleggio e zucca* (broad ribbon pasta with Taleggio cheese and pumpkin), followed by anything from *brasato d'asino* (braised donkey) to *pestöm* (minced pork served with polenta).

La Sosta
ITALIAN €€€

(☑030 29 56 03; www.lasosta.it; Via San Martino della Battaglia 20; meals €40-55; ⊙noon-2pm & 8-10pm Tue-Sat, noon-2pm Sun, closed Aug) Set partly in the stables of a 1610 palace, flanked by columns, La Sosta excels at finely tuned gastronomic creations using the freshest regional produce. Start off with a creamy risotto before moving on to perfectly executed *orata al forno* (oven-baked bream) or rich *capretto alla bresciano con polenta* (Brescian-style kid with polenta).

La Bottega del Garzone
WINE BAR

(☑030 240 00 59; Via dei Musei 21; ⊙6pm-midnight Wed-Fri, noon-3pm & 6pm-1am Sat, 6-11pm Sun) A garrulous laid-back crowd crams into this buzzing bar to sip on luscious wines and sample platters of meats, cheeses and artichokes (€4 to €9).

❶ Information

Main Tourist Office (☑030 240 03 57; www.turismobrescia.it; Via Trieste 1; ⊙9am-7pm) Brescia's main tourist office, on the edge of Piazza Paolo VI, can advise on exploring the city's churches and Roman sites.

There's another, smaller tourist office at the train station (☑030 306 12 40; www.turismobrescia.it; Piazzale Stazione; ⊙9am-7pm).

IAT Brescia (☑030 374 99 16; www.provincia.brescia.it; Piazza del Foro 6; ⊙10am-6pm) Covers the wider Brescia region.

❶ Getting There & Away

BICYCLE

You can hire a bicycle (€1/4 per two hours/day) from the **Bike Station** (Il Parcheggio Biciclette; ☑030 306 11 00; Piazzale Stazione; ⊙7am-7.30pm Mon-Fri, 7.30am-1.40pm Sat) in front of the train station on Piazzale Stazione.

BUS

From Brescia's **main bus station** (☑030 288 99 11; Via Solferino) buses operated by **SIA** (☑030 288 99 11; www.arriva.it) serve destinations all over Brescia province. Some leave from another station off Viale della Stazione.

CAR

Brescia is on the A4 motorway between Milan and Verona. The A21 runs south to Cremona.

Driving in the old centre is restricted and monitored by camera. People staying in hotels in the centre need to give the hotel reception their number plate on arrival. You have 15 minutes to unload/load the vehicle before exiting again and parking elsewhere. There's free parking on the streets just south of the train station.

TRAIN

Brescia is on the Milan–Venice line, with regular services to Milan (€7.30 to €20, 45 minutes to 1¼ hours) and Verona (€6.75, 40 minutes). There are also secondary lines to Cremona (€5.50, one hour), Bergamo (€4.80, one hour) and Parma (€7.65, two hours).

A smart new metro (one ride €1.40) links the train station with Piazza della Vittoria (one stop) in the heart of the old town.

CREMONA

☑0372 / POP 72,000

A wealthy, independent city-state for centuries, Cremona boasts some fine medieval architecture. The Piazza del Comune, the heart of the city, is where Cremona's historic beauty is concentrated. It's a wonderful example of how the religious and secular affairs of cities were divided neatly in two. The city is best known around the world, however, for its violin-making traditions.

◉ Sights

★ Museo del Violino
MUSEUM

(☑0372 08 08 09; www.museodelviolino.org; Piazza Marconi 5; adult/reduced €10/7; ⊙10am-6pm Tue-Sun) The state-of-the-art Museo del Violino brings together the city's historic collection of violins and presents them alongside the tools of the trade. It also explores the development of the craft and why the instrument is so popular around the world. Highlights include a small workshop where you can see a luthier in action, a dramatically lit corridor full of gorgeous Cremona-made violins dating back to the 17th century, and a special room containing the drawings, moulds and tools Stradivari used in his workshop.

Cremona

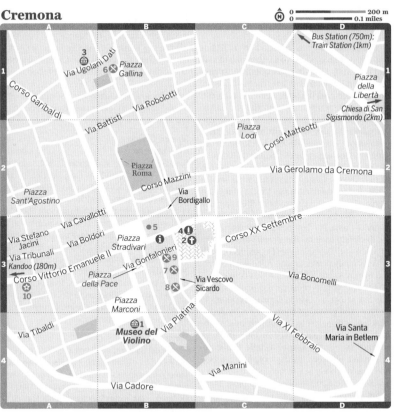

Cremona

Don't miss the enclosed wooden chamber where you can listen to the violin in action as videos of famous performances are projected on the ceiling (it's about as close as you can get to being inside the soundbox of a violin). The complex also features a specially engineered auditorium that hosts classical-music events. Pick up a free audio guide to explore the collection.

Cattedrale di Cremona CATHEDRAL
(Duomo; www.cattedraledicremona.it; Piazza del Comune; ☉ 10.30am-noon & 3.30-5pm Mon-Sat, noon-12.30pm & 3-5pm Sun) Cremona's cathedral started out as a Romanesque basilica, but the simplicity of that style later gave way to an extravagance of designs. The interior frescoes are utterly overwhelming, with the *Storie di Cristo* (Stories of Christ) by Pordenone

perhaps the highlights. One of the chapels contains what is said to be a thorn from Jesus' crown of thorns.

The cathedral was finished in 1107 but was badly damaged by an earthquake in 1117 and rebuilt by 1190. In subsequent centuries, various embellishments left traces of Gothic, Renaissance and baroque taste. As a result, Romanesque sculptures from the pre-earthquake church adorn the facade, whose upper part is largely the result of Renaissance renovation, meanwhile the brick north facade is a fine example of Lombard Gothic.

The central nave and apse have especially rich frescoes and paintings, with scenes dedicated to the lives of the Virgin Mary and Christ. The local, Ferrara-born Renaissance master Boccaccio Boccaccino carried out many of them. Pordenone's mesmerising *Storie di Cristo* include the *Crocifissione* (Crucifixion) and *Deposizione* (Deposition); both are especially powerful and filled with curvaceous movement and voluptuous colour.

The cathedral's most prized possession is the *Sacra Spina* (Holy Thorn), reputed to be from the crown of thorns worn by Jesus, which was donated to the church by Cremona-born Pope Gregory XIV in 1591. It's kept behind bars in the **Capella delle Reliquie**, in the left transept. In the **crypt**, the robed and masked body of Cremona's 12th-century patron saint, San Omobono Tucenghi, is on show in a glass casket.

Chiesa di San Sigismondo   CHURCH
(Largo Visconti; ⊘8am-noon & 3-6.30pm) A few kilometres southeast of the old city, the 15th-century Chiesa di San Sigismondo features a 16th-century fresco cycle that is a superb example of Mannerist painting. All the big names of the Cremona art scene contributed, including the Campi brothers and Camillo Boccaccino, son of Boccaccio. Camillo did the entire presbytery, with images including *Adultera* (Adultress) and *Risurrezione di Lazzaro* (Resurrection of Lazarus).

Museo Civico
Ala Ponzone   MUSEUM
(🗐0372 40 77 70; Via Ugolani Dati 4; adult/reduced €7/5; ⊘10am-5pm Tue-Sun) Set in the spacious halls of the Palazzo Affaitati, Cremona's finest art gallery houses an exquisite collection of paintings dating from the 15th to the 19th centuries. The museum's star is a stunning work by Caravaggio, which gets one moodily lit room largely to itself, *San Francesco in meditazione* (Saint Francis in Meditation). Other pieces from the treasure trove include paintings from Cremona masters such as Boccaccio Boccaccino, Bernardino Gatti and the Campi family (Antonio, Giulio, Vincenzo).

Torrazzo   TOWER
(Piazza del Comune; adult/reduced €5/4, incl Baptistry €6/5; ⊘10am-1pm & 2.30-6pm, closed Mon winter) Cremona's 111m-tall *torrazzo* (bell tower, although 'torrazzo' translates literally as 'great, fat tower') soars above the city's central square. A total of 502 steps wind up to the top. The effort is more than repaid with marvellous views across the city.

CREMONA'S VIOLINS

It was in Cremona that Antonio Stradivari lovingly put together his first Stradivarius violins, helping establish a tradition that continues today. Other great violin-making dynasties that started here include the Amati and Guarneri families.

Some 100 violin-making workshops occupy the streets around Piazza del Comune but very few accept casual visitors. To visit a workshop, you generally need to be looking to buy a violin, but the **Consorcio Liutai Antonio Stradivari**, which represents the workshops, can make appointments for visits. Count on €60 to €80 per group for a one-hour visit.

Various events dedicated to violin-making take place each year, while the **Triennale Internazionale degli Strumenti ad Arco** (International Stringed Instrument Expo; www.entetriennale.com) is held in Cremona every third year in September/October; if you're in town in 2018 or 2021, don't miss it.

If you really want to learn about the intricacies of Cremona's musical legacy, the best place to go is the **Museo del Violino** (p170). Here, you'll learn about the evolution of the violin, and how Cremona came to be known for its world-class luthiers (builders or repairers of stringed instruments).

🏃 Activities

Target Turismo
WALKING

(📞 0372 80 08 42; www.targetturismo.com) Offers historical walking tours around Cremona and can also arrange visits to the violin workshops. Book in advance (English-language guides aren't always available). Prices start at €10 per person.

Consorcio Liutai
Antonio Stradivari
MUSIC

(📞 0372 46 35 03; www.cremonaliuteria.it; Piazza Stradivari 1; ⊙11am-1pm & 4-6.30pm Tue-Fri) This organisation arranges visits to violin workshops around Cremona by advance appointments. Prices for a one-hour visit are steep, ranging from €60 to €80 per group. The Consorcio also has a small display of violins.

✨ Festivals & Events

Stradivari Festival
MUSIC

(www.stradivarifestival.it;   ⊙mid-Sep–mid-Oct) Focusing on music for string instruments. Held between mid-September and mid-October, it's organised by the Museo del Violino (p170).

Festival di Cremona Claudio
Monteverdi
MUSIC

(www.teatroponchielli.it; ⊙May) A month-long series of concerts centred on Monteverdi and other baroque-era composers, held in the Teatro Amilcare Ponchielli.

Festa del Torrone
FOOD & DRINK

(www.festadeltorronecremona.it; ⊙Nov) A weekend full of exhibitions, performances and tastings dedicated to that toffee-tough Cremona-made Christmas sweet: *torrone* (nougat).

🍴 Eating

Il Violino
ITALIAN €€

(📞 0372 46 10 10; www.ilviolino.it; Via Vescovo Sicardo 3; meals €40-50; ⊙12.30-2pm daily & 7.30-10pm Mon-Sat) Il Violino is Cremona's timeless class option. Smooth service is key to this elegant spot, where you might start with one of a number of risotto options or the *tortelli alle erbette al burro spumoso* (stuffed pasta in herbs and frothy hot butter), then move on to roast meat dishes and fresh fish of the day with polenta.

Hosteria '700
LOMBARD €€

(📞 0372 3 61 75; www.hosteria700.com; Piazza Gallina 1; meals €33-40; ⊙noon-2.45pm Wed-Mon, 7-11pm Wed-Sun) Behind the dilapidated facade lurks a sparkling gem. Some of the vaulted rooms come with ceiling frescoes, dark timber tables come with ancient wooden chairs, and the hearty Lombard cuisine comes at a refreshingly competitive cost.

Every second Thursday of the month, Hosteria '700 dedicates the entire savoury supper menu to risotto.

Kandoo
JAPANESE €€

(📞 0372 2 17 75; Piazza Luigi Cadorna 11; meals €30-45; ⊙11.30am-2.30pm & 6-11pm Tue-Sun) For a break from risottos and pastas, this elegant Japanese spot makes a fine destination. Amid vaulted brick ceilings and flickering candles, Kandoo serves beautifully prepared sashimi platters, mouth-watering sushi rolls, crispy tempura and satisfying bowls of miso soup. For a broad selection, opt for a *barca* (boat-shaped platter), with a mix of sushi, sashimi and nigiri (for one/two persons €20/40).

It's located about 700m west of the cathedral (just off Corso Vittoria Emmanuele II).

Ristorante Duomo
ITALIAN €€

(📞 0372 3 52 42; www.pizzeriaduomocremona.com; Via Gonfalonieri 13; meals €25-35; ⊙noon-3pm & 6.30-10pm) A few steps from the Piazza del Comune, this place is full every night with a happy mix of tourists and locals, with more of the latter – always a good sign. The pizzas are good, while the *risotto ai fruta di mare* is chock-full of shellfish. Large complimentary foccacia and a bruschetta round out an excellent overall package.

La Sosta
OSTERIA €€

(📞 0372 45 66 56; www.osterialasosta.it; Via Vescovo Sicardo 9; meals €35-45; ⊙12.15-2pm Tue-Sun, 7.15-10pm Tue-Sat) La Sosta is surrounded by violin-makers' workshops and is a suitably harmonious place to feast on regional delicacies such as stuffed quail with saffron rice or baked snails with wild herbs. The entrance is plastered with so many approving restaurant-guide stickers that you can't see through the glass.

⭐ Entertainment

Teatro Amilcare Ponchielli
THEATRE

(📞 0372 02 20 01; www.teatroponchielli.it; Corso Vittorio Emanuele II 52; ⊙box office 10.30am-1.30pm & 4.30-7.30pm Mon-Fri) To hear Cremona's violins in action, attend one of the

BERGAMO, BRESCIA & CREMONA CREMONA

OFF THE BEATEN TRACK

PIZZIGHETTONE

Just a 22km train ride west of Cremona, the walled town of Pizzighettone sits astride the Adda river. The bulk of the town, with its impressive defensive walls (☑ 0372 73 03 33; www.gvmpizzighettone.it; guided tours in Italian adult/child €5/free; ⊘ museum & prison 10am-noon Thu & Sat, to noon & 2-6pm Sun, tours 3pm & 4.30pm Sat, Sun & holidays, & 9pm Sat Jul & Aug), rests on the east bank. The main draw of the sleepy village is strolling the red-brick fortification and admiring the bucolic views over the riverside. Across the river from the main part of town is the pretty hamlet of La Gera.

Once you've finished wandering make a beeline for **Cascina Valentino** (☑ 0372 74 49 91; http://lnx.cascinavalentino.it; Cascina Valentino 37; meals €28-38; ⊘ 7-10pm Mon-Sat & 12.30-2.30pm Sun). Here on a working farm where cows are raised and asparagus is grown, the owners also offer up fine local cooking with only the freshest in-season ingredients – this is a real rural eating experience. The menu changes often, but creamy risottos (or perhaps a pumpkin tortellini) are the best way to start. Mains are mostly from the farm's own meat stocks. The dining area, with dark timber furniture, in the main farmhouse, is a treat in itself. It's 4km away from central Pizzighettone. Cross the bridge east to La Gera and turn right along the river, then follow the signs along a dirt track past a dairy farm until you reach this second dairy farm. Booking ahead is compulsory.

concerts held at the ornate 19th-century Teatro Amilcare Ponchielli. Its website has the latest listings.

❶ Information

Tourist Office (☑ 0372 40 70 81; www.turismocremona.it; Piazza del Comune 5; ⊘ 9.30am-1pm & 1.30-4.30pm Mon-Fri, 10am-1pm & 2-5pm Sat & Sun) Helpful staff in an office across from the cathedral.

❶ Getting There & Away

BUS

Buses to surrounding towns leave from the **bus station** (Cremona Autostazione; Via Dante) on Via Dante, near the train station.

CAR

From Milan, take the A1 motorway and then the A21 to Cremona. The A21 proceeds north to Brescia. The SP415 heads northwest to Crema and on to Milan.

Driving through the old town is a no-no – obey signs that talk of a 'zona limitato' or you'll be captured on camera and forced to pay a €120-plus fine. Street parking becomes easier as you move away from the centre, and there is huge car-park space near the bus station.

TRAIN

The **train station** (Via Dante) receives trains from Milan (from €7.30, one to two hours, several daily) and Brescia (€5.50, one hour, hourly).

AROUND CREMONA

Lodi

☑ 0371 / POP 44,900

Capital of an essentially agricultural province, Lodi was founded in the 12th century on the south bank of the Adda river after the original town (Lodi Vecchio, about 7km west) was destroyed by the Milanese army. The old town centre, with its stately architecture, cobblestone lanes and attractive cafe-dotted squares, is well worth a half-day visit.

◉ Sights

Catedrale Vegetale   SCULPTURE
(Tree Cathedral; http://en.cattedralevegetale.info; Via Pietro Ferrabini 1; ⊘ 24hr) On the north bank of the Adda river, a short stroll from the centre, this ambitious art installation blends the natural world with the religious in soaring wooden columns and branchlike finials that create something of an open-air cathedral. The work, completed in 2017, was designed by Lodi-born artist Giuliano Mauri and invites contemplation.

Oak saplings were planted within each lashed-together column, so that one day the framework can be removed and the trees will form their own living cathedral.

Tempio Civico dell'Incoronata
CHURCH

(Via Incoronata, btwn Nos 23 & 25; ⊙9-11.20am & 3.30-6pm Tue-Sun) The Tempio Civico dell' Incoronata was built in the late 15th century at the prompting of the local citizenry, apparently after a sighting of the Virgin Mary with crown (hence the church's name 'Civic Temple of the Crowned One') on the spot, close to an infamous brothel. The church is a splendid, octagonal Renaissance affair, whose inside is a riot of gold leaf, frescoes and paintings.

La Basilica Cattedrale della Vergine Assunta
CHURCH

(Duomo; Piazza della Vittoria 23) Lodi's iconic sight is its imposing cathedral. Work began in 1160 and its towering brick facade betrays Romanesque, Gothic and Renaissance elements (the rose window being the clearest sign of the latter).

✗ Eating

La Coldana
ITALIAN €€

(☑0371 43 17 42; www.lacoldana.it; Via del Costino; meals €32-42; ⊙noon-2.30pm & 8-10.30pm Sun-Fri, 8-10.30pm Sat) A sprawling yellow 18th-century farmhouse, La Coldana seats its guests in bustling dining rooms or out in a quiet garden. The kitchen is a cauldron of ideas, with delectable linguine with broccoli cream and fresh apples, saffron risotto with osso buco, and *tagliolini* with crab.

It's 2km southeast of the centre. Head southeast along Corso Mazzini from Porta Cremona in the southeast corner of the old centre. Turn left at Strada Vecchia Cremonese and left again into Via del Costino.

✪ Getting There & Away

Trains from Milan run every half hour to Lodi (€4, 30 minutes). Direct trains run every two hours or so between Lodi and Cremona (€5.50, 41 minutes). By car, Lodi is a short hop from Crema (19km) on the SP235 road.

BERGAMO, BRESCIA & CREMONA LODI

Lake Garda & Around

Why Go?

Covering 370 sq km, Lake Garda is the largest of the Italian lakes, straddling the border between three regions: the Lombard plains to the west, Alpine Trentino Alto-Adige to the north and the rolling hills of the Veneto to the east. Look around and you'll be surprised to see a Mediterranean landscape of vineyards, olive groves and citrus orchards that is thanks to the lake's uniquely mild microclimate.

Like the best Italian lunch, exploring this region can't be rushed. You'll want to linger in Sirmione's thermal pools, amble around Roman ruins and ferry-hop between villages. Then you might consider touring vineyards that feature in many sommeliers' top 10s: Valpolicella, Soave and Bardolino. Further south, in incurably romantic Verona, sit beneath the stars and enjoy world-class opera; and, in Mantua, feast on Renaissance frescoes. Uncork it, savour it, then come back for more.

Best Places to Eat

➡ Dal Pescatore (p208)

➡ La Rucola 2.0 (p180)

➡ Osteria Le Servite (p189)

➡ Agriturismo i Vegher (p182)

➡ Locanda San Vigilio (p33)

Best Tours

➡ Isola del Garda (p183)

➡ Allegrini (p201)

➡ Try Verona (p198)

➡ Azienda Agricola Zuliani (p182)

Road Distances (km)

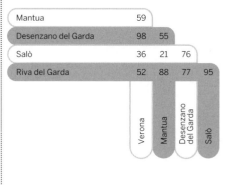

	Verona	Mantua	Desenzano del Garda	Salò
Mantua	59			
Desenzano del Garda	98	55		
Salò	36	21	76	
Riva del Garda	52	88	77	95

Poets and politicians, divas and dictators, they've all been drawn to captivating Lake Garda (Lago di Garda). In fact, 7% of all tourists to Italy head for the lake's shores, taking to its wind-ruffled waters in the north and village- and vineyard-hopping in the south. Surrounded by three distinct regions – Lombardy, Trentino Alto-Adige and the Veneto – the lake's cultural diversity attracts a cosmopolitan crowd. Mitteleuropeans colonise northern resorts such as Riva del Garda and Torbole, where restaurants serve air-dried ham and Austrian-style *carne salada* (salted beef), while in the south, French and Italian families bed down in Valtenesi farmhouses and family-friendly spa towns such as Sirmione and Bardolino.

❶ Getting There & Away

AIR

Verona-Villafranca airport (p200) is 20km from the lake. Regular buses link the airport with Mantua and Verona; Peschiera del Garda is 15 minutes by train from Verona.

BOAT

Navigazione Lago di Garda (☑ 030 914 95 11; www.navigazionelaghi.it) Lake Garda has a surprisingly extensive ferry network. One-day, unlimited-travel foot-passenger tickets include: lake-wide (adult/reduced €34.30/17.60); lower lake (€23.40/12.40); and upper lake (€20.50/11). Sample single passenger fares include Sirmione to Salò (adult/reduced €9.80/5.90) and Riva del Garda to Sirmione (adult/reduced €15.10/8.60). Car ferries link Toscolano-Maderno with Torri del Benaco and (seasonally) Limone with Malcesine.

There are no ferries in winter; services are reduced in spring and autumn.

BUS

ATV (☑ 045 805 79 22; www.atv.verona.it) Runs buses up the lake's west side, including regular connections between Desenzano del Garda train station and Riva del Garda, via Salò and Gardone. ATV also runs shuttles along the lake's east shore with regular services between Riva del Garda and Verona, via Garda.

SIA (☑ 840 620001; www.arriva.it) Operates regular buses from Brescia up the western side of the lake to Riva del Garda (€9, three hours, two-hourly). It also runs hourly buses linking Brescia with Desenzano, Sirmione, Peschiera and Verona along the southern shore.

Trentino Trasporti (☑ 0461 82 10 00; www.ttesercizio.it) Connects Riva del Garda with Trento (€4, one hour, every two hours).

CAR

Car is by far the best way of getting around. The lake sits just north of the A4 Milan–Venice autostrada, and just west of the A22 Modena–Trento route. A single-lane road circles the lake shore and is heavy with traffic in summer. Parking is difficult everywhere.

TRAIN

Desenzano del Garda and Peschiera del Garda are both on the Milan–Venice train line and have hourly trains in each direction. Excellent connections with Verona make the city an easy day trip.

LAKE GARDA SOUTH BANK

Sirmione

☑ 030 / POP 7650

Built on the end of an impossibly thin, appendix-like peninsula sticking out from the southern shore, pretty Sirmione has drawn the likes of Catullus and Maria Callas to its banks over the centuries, and today millions of visitors follow in their footsteps for a glimpse of Lake Garda's prettiest village and a dip in its only hot spring.

◉ Sights & Activities

★**Grotte di Catullo**　　ARCHAEOLOGICAL SITE
(☑ 030 91 61 57; www.grottedicatullo.beniculturali.it; Piazzale Orti Manara 4; adult/reduced €6/3, with Rocca Scaligera €10/5; ◷ 8.30am-7.30pm Tue-Sat & 9.30am-6.30pm Sun summer, 8.30am-5pm Tue-Sat & 8.30am-2pm Sun winter) Occupying 2 hectares at Sirmione's northern tip, this ruined 1st century AD Roman villa is a picturesque complex of teetering stone arches and tumbledown walls, some three storeys high. It's the largest domestic Roman villa in northern Italy and wandering its terraced hillsides offers fantastic views.

Despite the name, there's no evidence Catullus lived here, although the poet did have a home in the village. Significantly, the living quarters were on the top floor, offering 360-degree vistas of the surrounding waters; it seems the Romans too liked rooms with a view.

★**Aquaria**　　SPA
(☑ 030 91 60 44; www.termedisirmione.com; Piazza Piatti; pools per 90min/day €19/53, treatments from €30; ◷ pools 9am-10pm Sun-Wed, to midnight Thu-Sat Mar-Jun & Sep-Dec, 9am-midnight daily Jul & Aug, hours vary Jan & Feb) Sirmione is blessed with a series of offshore thermal springs that pump out water at a

LAKE GARDA & AROUND PLACES TO EAT

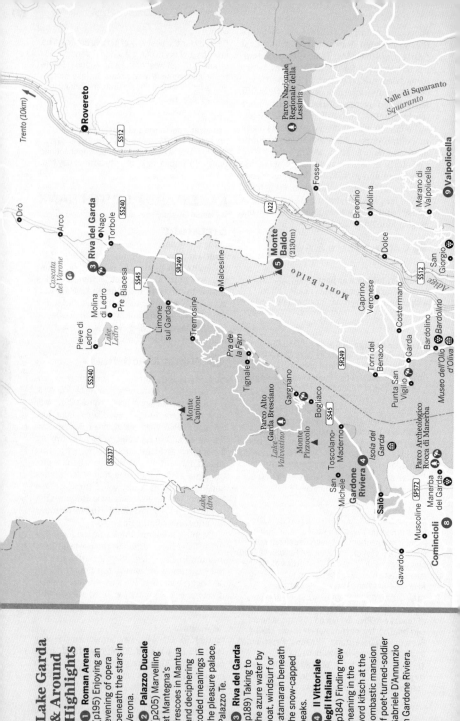

Lake Garda & Around Highlights

1 **Roman Arena** (p195) Enjoying an evening of opera beneath the stars in Verona.

2 **Palazzo Ducale** (p205) Marvelling at Mantegna's frescoes in Mantua and deciphering coded meanings in the pleasure palace, Palazzo Te.

3 **Riva del Garda** (p189) Taking to the azure water by boat, windsurf or catamaran beneath the snow-capped peaks.

4 **Il Vittoriale degli Italiani** (p184) Finding new meaning in the word kitsch at the bombastic mansion of poet-turned-soldier Gabriele D'Annunzio in Gardone Riviera.

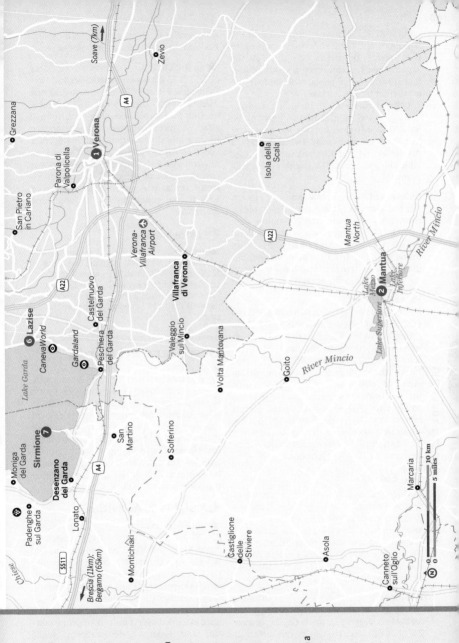

5 Monte Baldo
(p190) Hiking, biking and paragliding for a bird's-eye view of the lake.

6 Lazise (p194)
Doing a full circuit of the wonderfully well-preserved walls.

7 Aquaria (p177)
Watching the sunset over the lake through the rising steam of Sirmione's thermal spa.

8 Comincioli
(p182) Sampling Italy's finest olive oil cultivated with passion for over 500 years.

9 Valpolicella
(p200) Savouring world-class wines on a vineyard tour.

natural 37°C. They were discovered in the late 1800s and the town's been tapping into their healing properties ever since. At the Aquaria spa you can enjoy a soothing wallow in two thermal pools – the outdoor one is set right beside the lake.

Other treatments – including thermal massages and mud baths – have to be booked in advance, but for the pools you just turn up with your swimsuit; buy a day ticket and you'll be provided with cap, bathrobe and towel. The spa shop also sells swimwear.

Chiesa San Pietro in Mavino   CHURCH
(Via San Pietro in Mavino) Sirmione's oldest church and its crumbling bell tower date from the 14th century, though it was built on the site of a much older temple. The frescoes inside also date from the same period, but the attraction here is the peaceful setting on the top of a hill in the hotel zone.

Rocca Scaligera   CASTLE
(Castello Scaligero; ☑030 91 64 68; adult/reduced €5/2.50, with Grotte di Catullo €10/5; ☺8.30am-7.30pm Tue-Sat, to 1.30pm Sun) Expanding their influence northwards, the Scaligeri of Verona built this enormous square-cut castle right at the entrance to old Sirmione. Rising out of the still waters of the lake it guards the only bridge into town, looming over the scene with impressive crenellated turrets and towers. There's not a lot inside, but the climb up 146 steps to the top of the tower affords beautiful views over Sirmione's rooftops and the enclosed harbour.

✖ Eating

Al Boccondivino   LOMBARD €€
(Piazzetta Mosaici; meals €25-30; ☺11am-2am) Renaissance-style portraits dress the walls and a Roman olive-oil press is glassed in underfoot at this new Sirmione dining spot. The talking point here is the locally matured cheeses and hams as well as tasty pasta dishes available all day.

La Fiasca   TRATTORIA €€
(☑030 990 61 11; www.trattorialafiasca.it; Via Santa Maria Maggiore 11; meals €30-35; ☺noon-2.30pm & 7-10.30pm Thu-Tue) In this authentic trattoria, tucked away in a backstreet just off the main square, the atmosphere is warm and bustling, and the dishes are packed with traditional Lake Garda produce. Prepare for some gutsy flavours: *bigoli* (thick spaghetti)

with sardines, fillets of perch with asparagus, and duck with honey and orange.

★**La Rucola 2.0**   GASTRONOMIC, GARDESE €€€
(☑030 91 63 26; www.ristorantelarucola.it; Vicolo Strentelle 7; meals €75-120; ☺noon-2.30pm & 7-11pm Sat-Wed, 7-11pm Fri) Boasting a Michelin star, Sirmione's best eatery is a refined affair. A recent makeover lends modern freshness to the experience while the chefs add a touch of class to a menu strong on sea and lake fish. Expect sea bass, prawns and the catch of the day to feature in risottos, pastas and grilled guises, combined with flavour-enhancing confits, pâtés and marinades.

❶ Information

Tourist Office (☑030 91 61 14; iat.sirmione@provincia.brescia.it; Viale Marconi 8; ☺10am-12.30pm & 3-6.30pm daily summer, 10am-12.30pm & 3-6pm Mon-Fri, 9.30am-12.30pm Sat winter) Efficient if visitor-weary office on the main road into Sirmione, just before the castle.

Desenzano del Garda

☑030 / POP 27,800
An easygoing commuter town 9km southwest of Sirmione, Desenzano del Garda is not nearly as pretty as some of Garda's other lakeside settlements, but its ancient harbour, broad promenades and vibrant Piazza Matteotti and Piazza Malvezzi make for pleasant wanderings. Thanks to its mainline train station Desenzano is a popular jumping-off point for car hire and other transport around the Lake Garda area.

◎ Sights & Activities

★**Villa Romana**   HISTORIC SITE
(☑030 914 35 47; Via Crocifisso 2; adult/reduced €2/1; ☺8.30am-7pm mid-Mar–mid-Oct, to 4.30pm mid-Oct–mid-Mar, closed Mon) Before the Clooneys and Versaces, wealthy Roman senators and poets had holiday homes on Italy's northern lakes. One survivor is Desenzano's now-ruined Roman villa, which once extended over a hectare of prime lakeside land. Today, wooden walkways snake through the villa above a colourful collage of black, red, olive and orange mosaics, many depicting hunting, fishing and chariot riding, garlanded by fruits and flowers.

Built more than 2000 years ago, the villa was remodelled in the 2nd century, but continual renovations meant the interiors weren't completed until the 4th century. A short video explains the layout of the villa and is worth watching before exploring. The villa is a short walk from the Desenzano del Garda ferry landing stage.

Frantoio Montecroce FOOD
(📌 030 991 15 04; www.frantoiomontecroce.it; Viale Ettore Andreis 84; ⊙ by appointment) FREE Set in the hills above Desenzano, this olive mill offers tutored tastings of Lake Garda's olive oil. The same family has been harvesting the fruit from the surrounding trees for four generations, and family members conduct the tours and tastings.

✖ Eating & Drinking

★**La Goccia Trattoria** SEAFOOD €€
(📌 030 910 31 94; Via Montonale Basso 13; meals €40-50; ⊙ noon-2.30pm & 7.30-11pm, closed Wed) Positioned well back from the lake front, La Goccia is a fantastic find, especially for fish lovers. With a chef who hails from Puglia you can expect the freshest seafood carpaccio followed by fragrant home-made pasta tossed with razor clams and shrimp. The *fritto misto* (fried seafood platter) is also a delight. Pair with the local Lugana 'Muntunal' for the perfect meal.

La Cambusa BISTRO €€
(📌 342 1224813; www.allacambusabistrot.it; Via Canonica 12; meals €25-35; ⊙ 10.30am-midnight) Located in an old butcher's shop, La Cambusa is earning itself some heartfelt accolades with home-brewed beer, top-notch salami, *aperitivo* (aperitif) platters with hand-cut Parmesan and Parma ham as well as local wines. The always-around owners are on hand to explain the origin of everything they serve.

ℹ Information

Tourist Office (📌 030 914 15 10; www.comune. desenzano.brescia.it; Via Porto Vecchio 34; ⊙ 9.30am-noon & 3-6pm Mon-Sat)

ℹ Getting There & Away

Train station (Piazza Luigi Einaudi) The train station is 500m back from the lake shore and handles services to Verona (€4.45 to €15, 20 to 30 minutes, at least hourly) and Milan (€9.20 to €30, one to 1½ hours, twice hourly).

Ferry Departures Ferries depart for various locations around Lake Garda from opposite Piazza XXV Aprile.

LAKE GARDA WEST BANK

The western Lombard shore of Lake Garda is the most beautiful, lined with historic towns, stately villas, mountain-backed roads and frothing flower-filled gardens. North of Gardone, much of the shore is encompassed within the Parco Alto Garda Bresciano (www.parcoaltogarda.net), where it's easy to escape the summer crowds and find yourself amid some truly stunning scenery.

Valtenesi

The Valtenesi stretches languidly between Desenzano and Salò, its rolling hills etched with vine trellises and flecked with olive groves. The main lake road heads inland, allowing for gentle explorations of an array of wineries and small towns, including Padenghe sul Garda, Moniga del Garda, Manerba del Garda and San Felice del Benaco.

The area also constitutes the Garda Classico DOC wine region, its vineyards producing the light, rose-coloured Chiaretto, the rare, autochthonous Groppello and the full-bodied Rosso Superiore. Olives also thrive here and you can sample the light, spicy oils at many wineries and *agriturismi* (farmstay accommodation). The tourist office in Desenzano stocks the best information on the region.

◉ Sights

★**Parco Archeologico Rocca di Manerba** NATURE RESERVE
(📌 0365 55 25 33; www.parcoroccamanerba.net; Via Rocca 20, Manerba del Garda; ⊙ 10am-8pm Apr-Sep, to 6pm Thu-Sun Oct-Mar) FREE Protected by Unesco, the gorgeous 'rock of Minerva' juts out scenically into the lake just north of Moniga del Garda. The park contains the remaining low rubble walls of a medieval castle, a restful nature reserve of evergreen woods, orchid meadows and walking trails, and some of the best beaches on the lake.

Strolling from Pieve Vecchia to Porto del Torchio via Punta del Rio reveals glorious views and idyllic spots for a dip or a paddle. The park takes its name from a long-gone Roman temple dedicated to the goddess Minerva.

Santuario della Madonna del Carmine MONASTERY
(📌 0365 6 20 32; www.santuariodelcarmine-san felice.it; Via Fontanamonte 1, San Felice del Benaco;

⊙ 7am-noon & 3-6pm; P) The sanctuary of the Madonna del Carmine dates from 1452. Its simple Gothic-Romanesque exterior does little to prepare you for the technicolour frescoes inside, depicting images of Christ and the Virgin and scenes resonant with the Carmelite Order.

🏃 Activities

Frantoio San Felice del Benaco
FOOD

(🖉 0365 6 23 41; www.oliveoil-lakegarda.com; Via delle Gere 2, San Felice del Benaco; ⊙ shop 9am-noon & 3-6pm, happy hour 5.30-8pm) FREE With over 350 members, this DOP-accredited cooperative is a great place to sample Garda Breciano oils in a gorgeous rural setting. It's also possible to rock up for free tastings without reservations during the daily 'happy hour' (5pm to 7.30pm) and keep a eye out on Facebook for impromptu farmyard feasts when you can enjoy spit-roasts and live music.

Cicli Mata
CYCLING

(🖉 0365 55 43 01; www.matashop.it; Via Nazionale 63, Raffa di Puegnago; half/full day €20/27; ⊙ 9am-1pm & 2.30-7.30pm Tue-Sat, 2.30-7.30pm Sun & Mon) The Valtenesi is perfect cycling country, so pick up a bike from Cicli Mata in Raffa di Puegnago,

La Basia
HORSE RIDING

(🖉 0365 55 59 58; www.labasia.it; Via Predefitte 31, Puegnago del Garda; per hour €25) At this rambling vineyard and riding school you can have a formal riding lesson or head out for a trot among the vines, before sampling wines and wild honey on the terrace. Between March and September you can also bed down in one of the family-sized apartments (from €345 to €550 per week).

La Basia is just above the Viale Panoramico between Puegnano and Salò.

👉 Tours

Comincioli
FOOD

(🖉 0365 65 11 41; www.cominciolI.it; Via Roma 10, Puegnago del Garda; ⊙ 9.30am-noon & 2.30-7pm Mon-Sat by reservation) 🌿 FREE Cominciolì produces some of Italy's best olive oils – its Numero Uno is legendary. The family has been harvesting olives for nearly 500 years. Get an insight into that complex process and indulge in a tutored tasting at their farm-vineyard deep in the Valtenesi hills.

Azienda Agricola Zuliani
WINE

(🖉 030 990 70 26; www.vinizuliani.it; Via Tito Speri 28, Padenghe sul Garda; ⊙ 9am-1pm & 2.30-7pm Mon-Sat by reservation) FREE This family-run vineyard has been producing wine since 1589 and is an aristocratic Valtenesi brand. Of the farms' 22 hectares, 13 are devoted to vineyards while the other nine are covered in meadows, olive groves and pasture. Make a reservation for a tour and a tasting in the historic farmhouse kitchen.

🍴 Eating

★ Agriturismo i Vegher
AGRITURISMO €€

(🖉 0365 65 44 79; www.agriturismovegher.it; Via Mascontina 6, Puegnago del Garda; meals €25-35; ⊙ 7-10pm Wed-Sat & Mon, noon-2.30pm Sun; P 🚼) Well worth the journey along unsurfaced roads and the long booking lead times (book at least a month in advance for holiday weekends, otherwise about two weeks), I Vegher is a place you'll want to arrive at hungry. Awaiting you are numerous and delicious antipasti courses, home-made pasta and the unrivalled meat *secondi*.

La Dispensa
MODERN ITALIAN €€

(🖉 0365 55 70 23; Piazza Municipio 10, San Felice del Benaco; meals €30-45; ⊙ 7-11.30pm Wed-Sun) Situated on the main square in San Felice del Benaco, this fun and colourful wine bar and restaurant offers a mouth-watering modern Italian menu with a focus on sensational fish and handsome charcuterie platters. Ingredients are first rate, market fresh and locally sourced – and sometimes come accompanied by live jazz.

Ristorante Fior di Loto
STEAK €€

(🖉 0365 65 42 64; www.ristorantefiordiloto.it; Via Dei Laghi 8, Puegnago del Garda; meals €40-45; ⊙ 7.30-10pm Tue, 12.30-2pm & 7.30-10pm Wed-Sun; P) Describing Fior di Loto as a steakhouse is criminal given the Rolls Royce selection of meat cuts aged between 25 and 40 months. Ten different cuts of meat are displayed in the counter like finely veined pieces of marble. Take the chef's advice when selecting and then sit back on the patio overlooking Lake Sovenigo and wait for your succulent steak to appear.

Salò

📞 0365 / POP 10,600

Wedged between the lake and the foothills of Monte San Bartolomeo, Salò exudes an air of courtly grandeur, a legacy of its days as Garda's capital when the Venetian Republic held sway over the lake. Devoid of any singular sights, Salò's lovely historic centre is lined with fine *style liberty* buildings and small, ordinary shops and restaurants. In 1901 an earthquake levelled many of its older *palazzi*, although a few fine examples remain: the Torre dell'Orologio (the ancient city gate), the late Gothic *duomo* (cathedral) with its Renaissance facade and the grand porticoed Palazzo della Magnifica Patria.

◉ Sights

★ **Isola del Garda**   ISLAND
(📞 328 6126943; www.isoladelgarda.com; tour incl boat ride €27.50-33.50; ☉ Apr-Oct) It's not often you get to explore such a stunning private island, villa and grounds. Anchored just off Salò, this speck of land is crowned with impressive battlements, luxurious formal gardens and a sumptuous neo-Gothic Venetian villa. Boats depart from towns including Salò, San Felice del Benaco, Gardone Riviera and Sirmione, but in typical Italian fashion they only leave each location one or two times a week, so plan ahead. See the website for the precise timetable.

The island is owned by the Contessa Cavazza, and she and her seven children still live on the island with their families; you may well see some of them strolling around. The tour price includes a small *aperitivo*. Visits to the island are by guided tour only (in Italian, English, French and German) and last one and a half to two hours.

Republic of Salò   AREA
In 1943 Salò was named the capital of the Social Republic of Italy as part of Mussolini and Hitler's last efforts to organise Italian Fascism in the face of advancing American forces. This episode, known as the Republic of Salò, saw more than 16 public and private buildings in the town commandeered and turned into Mussolini's ministries and offices. Strolling between the sites is a surreal tour of the dictator's doomed mini-state. Look out for the multilingual plaques scattered around town.

The Palazzo della Magnifica Patria (now the town hall) was the Interpreters' Office

LAKE GARDA'S OLIVE OIL

Lake Garda's microclimate resembles the Mediterranean's, ensuring ideal olive-growing conditions. The lake's banks produce a tiny 1% of Italy's olive oil, but the product is renowned for being light, soft and sweet. Some 15 varieties of olives are grown here; the local black fruit produces subtler tasting oil, while the green olives are spicier – the oil makers' skill lies in achieving the perfect blend. Lake Garda's lighter oils work well with fish, the medium blends are delicious drizzled over mozzarella, and the stronger, spicier varieties are superb with grilled meats and soup. Locals advise not to use the best oils for salads, arguing if you're adding vinegar it ruins the taste.

Among the places where you can tour the olive groves, sample and purchase the oil are **Frantoio San Felice del Benaco** and **Comincioli** in the Valtenesi and the **Consorzio Olivicoltori di Malcesine** (p190) in Malcesine.

HQ, where foreign dispatches were translated. Bar Italia was the Casa del Fascio, home to Mussolini's guards, and the local primary school became the base for Agenzia Stefani, the news agency for Fascist propaganda.

✗ Eating

Ristorante Papillon   PIZZA €
(📞 0365 4 14 29; www.ristorantepapillon.it; Lungolago Zanardelli 69; pizza €8-15; ☉ 8am-10pm Tue-Sun summer, shorter hours winter) Surprisingly good thin-crust pizzas straight from the wood-fired oven. Enjoy them lakeside beside the weeping willow, but watch out for the pushy, pizza-loving ducks.

★ **Al Cantinone**   TRATTORIA €€
(📞 0365 2 02 34; Piazza Sant'Antonio 19; meals €25-30; ☉ noon-2.30pm & 7-10pm Fri-Wed) It's well worth heading just a few streets back from the waterfront to track down this friendly neighbourhood trattoria, home to gingham tablecloths, fabulous cooking smells and a clutch of regulars playing cards in the corner. The dishes draw on Salò's lake-meets-mountains setting.

Try the coregone fish simply grilled with lemon, or the mounds of intensely flavoured *tagliatelle* (ribbon pasta) with mushrooms and truffle oil.

Antica Trattoria alle Rose MODERN ITALIAN €€€
(☎0365 4 32 20; www.trattoriaallerose.it; Via Gasparo da Salò; meals €45-65; ☺noon-2pm & 7-11.30pm Thu-Tue) Go with the flow in this elegant trattoria where Rosanna Faè and Gianni Briarava have been turning out contemporary, local cuisine for 25 years. Say yes to the parade of mixed antipasti – the zucchini souffle in a puddle of melted mountain cheese is delicious – and the home-made pastas with seasonal finferli mushrooms. Then you'll have to agonise over the rabbit in cognac or the grilled lake sardines, before crashing out at dessert and petit fours.

Its sister restaurant, **Osteria dell'Orologio** (☎0365 29 01 58; www.osteriadellorologio.it; Via Butturini 26; meals €25-35; ☺noon-2.30pm & 6-11pm Thu-Tue), is equally good but more informal.

ℹ Information

Tourist Office (☎0365 2 14 23; www.gardalombardia.it; Piazza Sant'Antonio 4; ☺10am-12.30pm & 3-6pm Mon, Tue & Thu-Sat, 10am-12.30pm Wed)

Gardone Riviera

☎0365 / POP 2700

Once Lake Garda's most prestigious corner, Gardone is flush with belle-époque hotels, opulent villas and extravagant gardens. They tumble down the hillside from the historic centre, Gardone Sopra, complete with tiny chapel and piazza, to the cobbled *lungolago* (lake front) of Gardone Sotto, which is lined with cafes and other tourist paraphernalia. Although the haute glamour of Gardone's 19th-century heyday is long gone it is a pleasant enough place for a stroll and drink, although you'll probably want to base yourself elsewhere on the lake.

An hour of so uphill from Gardone is the pretty mountain village of San Michele from where you can pick up a number of panoramic walking trails. Ask at the tourist office in Gardone Sotto for details.

◉ Sights

★**Il Vittoriale degli Italiani** MUSEUM
(☎0365 29 65 11; www.vittoriale.it; Piazza Vittoriale; gardens & museums adult/reduced €16/13; ☺9am-8pm Apr-Oct, to 5pm Tue-Sun Nov-Mar; ℗) Poet, soldier, hypochondriac and proto-Fascist, Gabriele d'Annunzio (1863–1938) defies easy definition, and so does his estate. Bombastic, extravagant and unsettling, it's

home to every architectural and decorative excess imaginable and is full of quirks that help shed light on the man. Visit and you'll take in a dimly lit, highly idiosyncratic villa, a war museum and tiered gardens complete with full-sized battleship.

By 1914 d'Annunzio was an established poet, but his fame was cemented by a series of daring military adventures in WWI. His most dramatic exploit was an unsanctioned occupation of Fiume, now Rijeka, on the Adriatic. Outraged that it was to be handed over to Yugoslavia, not Italy, at the end of the war, he gathered a mini-army, invaded the port and proclaimed himself the ruler. Despite eventually surrendering he was hailed a national hero. In the 1920s d'Annunzio became a strong supporter of Fascism and Mussolini, while his affairs with wealthy women were legendary.

In his main house, the **Prioria**, stained-glass windows cast an eerie light on gloomy rooms with black-velvet drapes (he had an eye condition that made exposure to sunlight painful). The rooms are crammed with classical figurines, leather-bound books, leopard skins, gilded ornaments, lacquer boxes and chinoiserie. Highlights include the bronze tortoise that sits on the guests' dining table (in admonition of gluttony; it was cast from a pet that died of over-indulgence); the bright blue bathroom suite with more than 2000 pieces of bric-a-brac; his spare bedroom where he would retire to lie on a coffin-shaped bed and contemplate death; and his study with its low lintel – designed so visitors would have to bow as they entered. Guided visits, in Italian only, tour the house every 15 minutes and last half an hour.

If you aren't already overwhelmed by d'Annunzio's excesses, the estate's **Museo della Guerra** is housed nearby in the art-nouveau Casa Schifamondo ('Escape from the World'). It is full of mementoes, banners and medals of d'Annunzio's war-time exploits, while the **gardens** offer the chance to wander the deck of the full-sized battleship *Puglia*, which d'Annunzio used in his Fiume exploits.

★**Giardino Botanico Fondazione André Heller** GARDENS, SCULPTURE
(☎336 410877; www.hellergarden.com; Via Roma 2; adult/reduced €11/5; ☺9am-7pm Mar-Oct) Gardone's heyday was due in large part to its mild climate, something which benefits the thousands of exotic blooms that fill artist

André Heller's sculpture garden. Laid out in 1912 by Arturo Hruska, the garden is divided into pocket-sized climate zones, with tiny paths winding from central American plains to African savannah, via swathes of tulips and bamboo.

The playful touches hidden among the greenery include 30 pieces of contemporary sculpture – look out for the jagged red figure by Keith Haring near the entrance, Rudolf Hirt's Gaudi-esque *Ioanes, God of Water*, and Roy Lichtenstein's polka-dot take on the pyramids.

✖️ Eating

Antico Brolo   OSTERIA €€
(☑️0365 2 14 21; www.ristoranteanticobrolo.it; Via Carere 10; tasting menu €45, meals €35-45; ⊘noon-2pm & 7.30-10pm Tue-Sun) If you're a considering a date night, Antico Brolo is the place for you, with seating in an intimate walled courtyard or better still on a tiny balcony frothing with pink geraniums overlooking Gardone. The food is as elegant as the surroundings, serving tiny *amuse-bouche* and nouvelle plates of steamed fish and truffle pasta.

Locanda Agli Angeli   ITALIAN €€
(☑️0365 2 09 91; Piazza Garibaldi 2; meals €35; ⊘11am-11pm Wed-Mon) A shaded terrace, rattan chairs and burgundy tablecloths set the scene for some classic Lake Garda cooking. Tempting choices include veal ravioli, sardines with potatoes and herbs, and fettuccine with smoked eel. As Agli Angeli is tucked into the hillside on the way to Il Vittoriale, it makes an ideal post-sightseeing stop.

ℹ️ Information

Tourist Office (☑️0365 374 87 36; Corso della Repubblica 8; ⊘9am-12.30pm & 2.15-6pm Mon-Sat) The tourist office stocks information on activities.

Toscolano-Maderno

POP 8200

Straddling the Toscolano torrent are the twin villages of Toscolano and Maderno, joined at the hip and co-occupants of a stubby headland boasting some good beaches, arguably Lake Garda's finest. To the southwest, pretty, pastel-coloured Maderno marks the location of Benacum, the principal Roman town on the lake, while more industrial Toscolano, to the northeast, once supplied nails for Venetian galleys and thick, creamy paper for Martin Luther's Bible.

👁️ Sights & Activities

Museo della Carta   MUSEUM
(☑️0365 64 10 50; www.valledellecartiere.it; Via Valle delle Cartiere; adult/reduced €7/5; ⊘10am-6pm Apr-Sep, to 5pm Sat & Sun Oct) The Toscolano torrent upstream fed numerous paper mills in the Middle Ages and you can follow the riverside road up the wooded Valle delle Cartiere and explore their peaceful ruins. The largest of them is now the Paper Museum where you can see how Toscolano-Maderno's top-quality paper was made and learn about the history of this local industry.

Garda Yachting Charter   BOATING
(☑️0365 54 83 47; www.gyc.it; Lungolago Zanardelli; ⊘9am-7pm Mar-Nov) This professional outfit runs sailing courses on Lake Garda and rents out motorboats.

LOCAL KNOWLEDGE

LAKE GARDA'S LEMON INDUSTRY

It's thought monks from Genoa brought lemons to Gargnano when they arrived at the town's monastery of St Francis in the 13th century. Lake Garda's temperate climate provided good conditions for a fruit normally grown further south, and by the 18th century hundreds of *limonaie* (lemon houses) were being built. These kept the frosts off the trees by laying sheets of glass over a wooden latticework supported by ranks of tall, thin stone pillars. Hundreds of thousands of lemons were exported annually to Germany and Russia, providing a crucial local income. But by the second half of the 19th century the industry fell into terminal decline due to disease and the discovery of artificial citric acid.

Today, terraces of weathered stone pillars are evidence of this lost industry. You can visit restored lemon houses at **Limonaia del Castèl** (p187) in Limone sul Garda on the west bank of the lake and at Torri del Benaco's **Castello Scaligero** (p191) on the east bank.

✖ Eating

Osteria Gatto D'Oro   OSTERIA €€
(☎ 0339 621 94 93; www.osteriagattodoro.it; Via
Fratelli Bianchi 41; meals €25-35) This funky-
rustic place has shunned the sometimes
bland, traditional style of an Italian eatery
and added tons of colour to proceedings. But
it's no gimmick to hide second-rate food – the
pastas are to die for and the thin-crust pizza
is one of the best this side of Lake Garda.
Some guests moan about slow service here.

❶ Information

Tourist Office (☎ 0365 64 42 98; www.
prolocotoscolanomaderno.com; Via Garibaldi
24; ⊙ 9am-12.30pm & 3-6pm)

Gargnano

📞 0365 / POP 3000
Although they loom on the horizon for
much of the lake, it's around Gargnano that
the mountains really kick in. They rear so
steeply it's overwhelming – you don't just
look at views like these, you step into them.
Thanks to its awkward location (at the point
when the road north becomes a tortured set
of dynamite-blasted tunnels), Gargnano has
been spared the worst excesses of the tourism industry and it retains a pleasant, local
feel. It is linked with the hamlets of Bogliaco
and Villa, through which you pass before
you reach Gargnano proper. It's a perfect
spot to spend a couple of days relaxing and
exploring off-the-beaten-track nature trails.
For more information on walking itineraries around Gargnano visit www.gargnano
sulgarda.com.

LOCAL KNOWLEDGE

LAKE GARDA'S WINDS

Lake Garda has an unusual meteorological quirk – the winds that blow over
its surface are almost as regular as
clockwork. The Pelèr (also called Suer
or Vento) gusts gently from the north,
lasts 12 hours and is normally done by
10am, while the Ora blows from the
south between noon and sunset and is
felt mainly in the central and northern
parts of the lake. Their predictability has
ensured Riva, Torbole, Campione and
Malcesine are magnets for windsurfers
and sailors.

⊙ Sights & Activities

Parco la Fontanella   BEACH
(Via Rimembranze 18; ⊙ 9am-9pm mid-Mar–mid-
Sep, 10am-5.30pm mid-Sep–mid-Mar; 🚣) A
300m stroll north from the ferry landing
brings you to a beach where gleaming white
pebbles fringe shallow crystalline waters.
The shore, bar and restaurant are backed
by olive groves that look out directly at the
craggy heights of Monte Baldo opposite. If
you're here in late spring, the mountain often still has snow clinging to its tip.
   Popular with families, the beach is well
equipped with a shaded picnic area, ping-
pong tables, volleyball courts, and water-
sports hire outlets.

OKSurf   SURFING
(www.oksurf.it; Parco La Fontanella, Via Rimembranza) Offers windsurfing courses for adults and
children as well as mountain bike tours and
sailing on Lake Garda.

✸ Festivals & Events

Centomiglia   SPORTS
(www.centomiglia.it) In September, Gargnano hosts the lake's most prestigious sailing
regatta, the Centomiglia, which starts in
Bogliaco and circumnavigates the lake. It attracts international sailors and throughout
the week the village celebrates with markets
and open-air concerts.

✖ Eating

Ristorante Lido   CONTEMPORARY ITALIAN €€
(☎ 0365 79 10 42; Via Colletta 61, La Villa; meals
€30-45; ⊙ noon-3pm & 7.30-11pm Wed-Mon) The
sleek, modern Lido is a perfect lunch location, its terrace thrust out over the lake
shaded by a pergola and ancient olive tree.
Chef Gramatica's dishes are similarly simple
and pared back: fish carpaccio drizzled with
Limone lemons, home-made ravioli in sage
and butter and grilled lake fish. At night,
fairy lights add to the kitschsy romance.

La Tortuga   GASTRONOMIC €€€
(☎ 0365 7 12 51; www.ristorantelatortuga.it; Via
XXIV Maggio 5; tasting menu €90, meals €60-100;
⊙ noon-2.30pm & 7-10pm Wed-Mon) Despite its
homey appearance Michelin-starred La Tortuga serves a sophisticated menu without
undue pomp and ceremony. Appreciative
diners at its handful of tables enjoy Garda
classics such as pasta with lake perch in a
fragrant slow-cooked broth, and veal fillet
with truffles or morelles. Wines from the

encyclopaedic wine list are generously priced, with classics like Allegrini's La Grola a mere €35.

Limone sul Garda

📞 0365 / POP 1040

Limone sul Garda is the most worthwhile stopping-off point on the west bank between Gargnano and Riva del Garda. Here, stone houses tumble down steep slopes and cobbled lanes meander towards a waterfront lined with pastel-painted houses. Inevitably in the summer it's besieged by tourists (nearly 10,000 a day) and the trinket sellers and snack bars are there in force. The town gets its name from the lemons that once grew here in large glasshouses and lemon-inspired souvenirs are still all the rage.

◉ Sights

Limonaia del Castèl   HISTORIC BUILDING

(📞 0365 95 40 08; Via IV Novembre; €2; ⏰ 10am-6pm Apr, May & mid-Sep–Oct, Jun–mid-Sep to 10pm; 🅿) Limone's top attraction is this renovated Lemon orchard where you can learn a bit about the region's lemon-growing traditions, sample lemon-infused products and admire the views across Lake Garda. There's lots of info in English and parking opposite.

🍴 Eating

Al Veccio Fontec   LOMBARD €€

(📞 0365 95 41 85; Via Corda 21; meals €25-35) This titchy restaurant occupies an ancient building in the centre of Limone and serves a menu of Italian standards as well as locally inspired dishes involving mountain cheeses, seasonal forest-harvested ingredients and fish. Book ahead as table space is limited.

LAKE GARDA NORTH BANK

Riva del Garda & Around

POP 16,850 / ELEV 73M

Officially in the Alpine region of Trentino-Alto Adige, stunning and very popular Riva is encircled by towering rock faces and a looping landscaped lake front. Its appealing historic core is arranged around handsome Piazza III Novembre.

For centuries Riva's position at the northern tip of the lake, a key access for northern armies into Italy, lent it a vital strategic role. In the Middle Ages the town was a port for the Prince-Bishops of Trento, and throughout its history Riva was much fought over, ruled at various times by the Republic of Venice, Milan's Visconti and Verona's Della Scala families. In 1815 it became part of the Austrian Empire (Trentino itself is still considered the Südtirol) and soon became a holiday resort for the Archduke and the northern European intelligentsia. Stendhal, Thomas Mann and Kafka all summered here, drawn by Goethe's evocative descriptions in his 1817 bestseller, *Italian Journey.*

◉ Sights

★ **Cascata del Varone**   WATERFALL

(📞 0464 52 14 21; www.cascata-varone.com; Via Cascata 12; adult/reduced €5.50/2.50; ⏰ 9am-7pm May-Aug, to 6pm Apr & Sep, to 5pm Mar & Oct, 10am-5pm Jan & Feb) Prepare to get a soaking as this 100m waterfall thunders down sheer limestone cliffs through an immense, dripping gorge. Spray-soaked walkways snake 50m into the mountain beside the booming torrent, and ambling along them is like walking in a perpetual downpour. It's well signposted 3km northwest of Riva's centre.

Parco Arciducale   PARK

(Via Lomego; ⏰ 8am-7pm Apr-Sep, to 4pm Oct-Mar) **FREE** No doubt avoiding the summer tourists, Archduke Albrecht preferred to build his winter palace 5km north of Riva in pretty Arco in 1872. Around it he created a magnificent arboretum, now the Parco Arciducale, planted with huge holm-oaks, sequoias and dagger-sharp cypresses.

Punta Lido   BEACH

This area of pebble beaches, parkland, picnic spots, paddling toddlers and strolling Italian holidaymakers is also the launchpad for many a waterborne adventure with some of the sports agencies based here. It's particularly popular on sunny Sunday mornings when all Riva seems to take a well-dressed amble here.

Bastione   LANDMARK

FREE From the centre of Riva, the Bastione is the chalk-white castle clinging to sheer cliffs high above the west edge of town. The 3.5km hike to this picturesque ruin is as steep as it looks and leads up hairpin bends past oleanders, cypresses and wayside shrines. The castle was built by the Venetians in a desperate bid to hold onto power.

Pick up the signed path where Via Bastione joins Via Monte Oro.

Riva del Garda

N
0   200 m
0   0.1 miles

Via Bastione
Molina di Ledro (12km)
Arco (5km); Drò (12km)
Hotel Garni Villa Maria (830m); Cascata del Varone (3km); Trattoria Piè di Castello (5.5km)
Viale Dante
Piazza Cavour
Giardini Verdi
Viale Carducci
Viale San Francesco
Via Filzi
Osteria Il Gallo
Via Maffei
Largo Medaglie d'Oro
Garda Bike Shop
Via Monte Oro
Piazza III Novembre
Museo Alto Garda
Lido Palace
Piazza Cesare Battisti
Bastione
Cristallo Caffè
La Rocca
Blue Garden (320m); Restel de Fer (730m); Osteria Le Servite (2.5km); Surfsegnana (2.5km); Residence Filanda (2.8km)
Torbole (3.5km)
SS45bis
Punta Lido
Lake Garda
Limone sul Garda (10km); Gargnano (28km); Gardone Riviera (40km)

Museo Alto Garda   MUSEUM

(La Rocca; ☑ 0464 57 38 69; www.museoaltogarda. it; Piazza Cesare Battisti 3; adult/reduced €5/2.50; ☺ 10am-6pm Tue-Sun mid-Mar–May & Oct, daily Jun-Sep) Housed in Riva's compact medieval castle, the civic museum features local archaeology, frescoes from Roman Riva, documents and paintings. In light of Riva's much fought-over past, perhaps the most revealing exhibits are the antique maps dating from 1579 and 1667, and a 1774 *Atlas Tyrolensis,* which evocatively convey the area's shifting boundaries.

🏃 Activities

Along the gorgeous landscaped lake front gentle pursuits are possible such as swimming, sunbathing and cycling the 3km lakeside path to Torbole. The water here is safe for small children, and there are numerous play areas set back from the water.

Live Outdoor Life   OUTDOORS

(☑ 328 5486497; www.lol-garda.it) Professional Riva-based outdoor activities agency that can organise anything from canyoning and *via ferrata* (trails with cave and ladders) to ice climbing and skiing.

Garda Bike Shop   CYCLING

(☑ 0464 56 70 11; www.gardabikeshop.com; Viale Rovereto 3a; rental per day from €16, tours from €20; ☺ 9am-7.30pm) This big, professional outfit can take care of all your cycling needs, be it a popped inner tube or a week's mountainbike hire. They also run tours and a bike-shuttle service.

★★ Festivals & Events

Rockmaster Festival   SPORTS

(☑ 0464 47 25 67; www.rockmasterfestival.com; ☺ late-Aug) Arco is one of Europe's most popular climbing destinations and is the location of the Rockmaster festival and climbing competition in late summer.

🍴 Eating

Cristallo Caffè   GELATO €

(☑ 0464 55 38 44; www.cristallogelateria.com; Piazza Catena 17; cones €2.50; ☺ 7am-1am, closed Nov-Mar) More than 60 flavours of artisanal gelato are served up in this seasonal lakeside cafe, all of it crafted by the Pancieras, a Belluno gelato-producing family since 1892. It's also a top spot to sip a *spritz* (cocktail made with Prosecco) while enjoying lake views.

★ **Osteria Le Servite** OSTERIA €€
(☑ 0464 55 74 11; www.leservite.com; Via Passirone 68, Arco; meals €30-45; ⊙ 7-10.30pm Tue-Sun Apr-Sep, 7-10.30pm Wed-Sat Oct-Mar; P 🖶) Tucked away in Arco's wine-growing region, this elegant little *osteria* (tavern) serves dishes that are so seasonal the menu changes weekly. You might be eating mimosa gnocchi, tender *salmerino* (Arctic char) or organic ravioli with *stracchino* cheese.

Each dish comes with a suggested wine. In summer you can sit on the patio and sip small-production DOC Trentino vintages.

★ **Restel de Fer** ITALIAN €€
(☑ 0464 55 34 81; www.resteldefer.com; Via Restel de Fer 10; meals €40-60; ⊙ noon-2.30pm & 7-11pm daily Jul & Aug, Thu-Tue Sep, Oct & Dec-Jun; P 🛜) Going to the restaurant at this family-run *locanda* (inn) feels like dropping by a friend's rustic-chic house: expect worn leather armchairs, copper cooking pots and glinting blue glass. The menu focuses on seasonal, local delicacies such as rabbit wrapped in smoked mountain ham, char with crayfish, and veal with Monte Baldo truffles.

Upstairs, swish farmhouse-style accommodation (single €70, double €90 to €120) is chock-full of old oak dressers and hand-woven rugs. It's 1km east of the centre of Riva.

Osteria Il Gallo TRATTORIA €€
(☑ 0464 55 62 00; www.osteriailgallo.com; Piazza San Rocco; meals €25-35; ⊙ 11.45am-2.30pm & 7-10pm) Trentino specialities punctuate the menu of this cosy trattoria, which sits snug underneath the arches of one of Riva's lakeside squares. Try the *canederli* – breadcrumb and bacon dumplings bathed in butter – or the *persico*, perch plucked straight out of the lake.

🔒 Shopping

Blue Garden MALL
(www.blue-garden.it; Viale Rovereto; ⊙ 10am-8pm; 🛜) This 40-shop mall on busy Viale Rovereto boasts a free toilet, free wi-fi, a supermarket, free parking, a bookshop selling local maps, an outdoor-equipment store and an Indian restaurant when you tire of Alpine gourmet fare as well as enough lingerie and coffee to keep the Italians happy.

ACTIVITIES AROUND RIVA DEL GARDA

Riva makes a natural starting point for a host of activities, including hiking and biking trails around Monte Rocchetta (1575m), climbing in Arco and canyoning in the Val di Ledro. One of the town's top highlights is the easy 7km hike along **La Strada del Ponale** (www.ponale.eu).

Water Sports

Like its neighbour Torbole, Riva is well known for windsurfing and has several schools that hire out equipment on Porfina Beach. Fleets of operators provide equipment hire and tuition along the lake fronts in Riva and Torbole. One of the largest is **Surfsegnana** (☑ 0464 50 59 63; www.surfsegnana.it; Foci del Sarca, Torbole), which operates from Lido di Torbole and Porfina Beach in Riva.

Climbing

Surrounded by perfect waves of limestone, Arco is one of Europe's most popular climbing destinations. There are hundreds of routes of all grades to choose from divided between short, bolted, single-pitch sports routes and long, Dolomite-style climbs, some extending as much as 1400m. The 300m **Zanzara** is a classic route, a 7a+ climb directly above the Rockmaster competition wall. For information on climbing courses and routes contact **Arco Mountain Guide** (☑ 330 567285; www.arcomountainguide.com).

Canyoning

Thanks to glacial meltwaters, which have worn smooth the limestone mountains surrounding Riva and the Val di Ledro, canyoning here is a fantastic experience offering lots of slides, jumps and abseiling. Both **Canyon Adventures** (☑ 334 8698666; www.canyonadv.com; ⊙ May-Oct) and **Arco Mountain Guide** arrange trips to the Palvico and Rio Nero gorges in the Val di Ledro and the Vione canyon in Tignale.

ℹ Information

Tourist Office (📞 0464 55 44 44; www.garda trentino.it; Largo Medaglie d'Oro; ⊙ 9am-7pm daily May-Sep, to 6pm Mon-Fri Oct-Apr) Can advise on everything from climbing and paragliding to wine tasting and markets.

LAKE GARDA EAST BANK

Sitting in the Veneto region, the eastern shore of Lake Garda has a different character to its western counterpart. Its nickname, the Riviera degli Olivi comes from the silvery olive groves that line the shoreline and the lower reaches of Monte Baldo (2130m), a massive, muscular limestone ridge that stretches 40km between Lake Garda and the Adige valley.

Malcesine

📞 045 / POP 3647

With the lake lapping right up to the tables of its harbourside restaurants and the vast, snow-capped ridge of Monte Baldo looming behind, Malcesine is quintessential Lake Garda. Alas, its picturesque setting attracts thousands of holidaymakers and day trippers, who flood the town's tiny streets. However, Malcesine hasn't completely sold its soul to tourism and locals still inhabit the tangle of alleyways, hanging their washing between houses in typical Italian fashion and filling the place at mealtimes with mouth-watering aromas.

◉ Sights & Activities

Castello Scaligero   CASTLE
(Via Castello; adult/reduced €6/3; ⊙ 9.30am-6.30pm Tue-Sun; 🚐) From Via Capitanato winding lanes lead to the chalky-white Castello Scaligero. This late-6th-century fortress was built by the Franks and consolidated by the Della Scala family, who ruled Malcesine between 1277 and 1387. The poet Goethe thought the castle so beautiful he sketched it, was mistaken for a spy and temporarily thrown into its cells. The view of the castle from the lake is vastly superior to the views of the lake from the castle.

**Funivia Malcesine–
Monte Baldo**   CABLE CAR
(📞 045 740 02 06; www.funiviedelbaldo.it; Via Navene Vecchia 12; adult/reduced return €22/15; ⊙ 8am-7pm Apr-Sep, to 5pm Oct-Mar) Jump

aboard this cable car and glide 1760m above sea level for spectacular views – circular rotating cabins reveal the entire lake and surrounding mountains. For the first 400m the slopes are covered in oleanders, and olive and citrus trees – after that, oak and chestnut take over. Mountain-bike trails wind down from the summit.

Getting off the cable car at the intermediate station of San Michele (from Malcesine one way/return €6/10) opens up some excellent hikes; pick up a map from the tourist office before you set out. The hour-long walk back to Malcesine reveals a rural world of hillside houses and working farms.

Xtreme Malcesine   CYCLING
(📞 045 740 01 05; www.xtrememalcesine.com; Via Navene Vecchia 10; road/mountain bike per day €15/25; ⊙ 8am-7pm) Rents bikes from its shop, situated at the base of the Monte Baldo cable car. There's also a bike cafe and the owners run mountain-bike tours into them hills.

**Consorzio Olivicoltori
di Malcesine**   FOOD
(📞 045 740 12 86; www.oliomalcesine.it; Via Navene 21; ⊙ 9am-12.30pm & 3.30-6.30pm Mon-Sat, 9am-1pm Sun, shorter hours winter) FREE Olives harvested around Malcesine are milled into first-rate extra-virgin olive oil by this local consortium. You can sample the product here. Known as 'El nos Oio' (Our Oil), it's a gold-green liquid that's low in acidity and has a light, fruity, slightly sweet taste. Prices of the cold-pressed extra virgin DOP oil start at €8.50 for 0.25L.

🍴 Eating

Speck Stube   BARBECUE €
(📞 045 740 11 77; www.speckstube.com; Via Navene Vecchia 139; meals €15-25; ⊙ noon-11pm Mar-Oct; 🅿🚐) Catering for northern European tourists, the specialities at this family-friendly place 2.5km north of Malcesine are wood-roast chickens, sausages and pork on the bone. Help yourself to hearty portions and mugs of beer at trestle tables beneath the olive trees, while the kids let off steam in the play park.

⭐ **Vecchia Malcesine**   GASTRONOMIC €€€
(📞 045 740 04 69; www.vecchiamalcesine.com; Via Pisort 6; meals €55-110; ⊙ noon-2pm & 7-10pm Thu-Tue) The lake views from the terrace at hillside Vecchia Malcesine do their best to upstage the food. But the Michelin-

Malcesine

N 0 — 200 m
0 — 0.1 miles

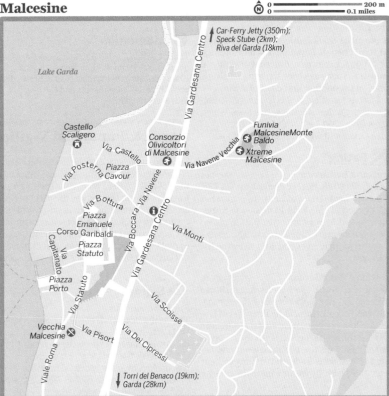

Car-Ferry Jetty (350m);
Speck Stube (2km);
Riva del Garda (18km)

Lake Garda

Via Gardesana Centro

Castello
Scaligero

Via Castello

Via Posterna

Piazza
Cavour

Consorzio
Olivicoltori
di Malcesine

Via Navene Vecchia

Funivia
MalcesineMonte
Baldo

Xtreme
Malcesine

Via Bottura

Piazza
Emanuele
Corso Garibaldi

Via Boccara

Via Navene

Via Gardesana Centro

Via Monti

Via Capitanato

Piazza
Statuto

Via Statuto

Piazza
Porto

Via Scoisse

Vecchia
Malcesine

Via Pisort

Via Dei Cipressi

Viale Roma

Torri del Benaco (19km);
Garda (28km)

LAKE GARDA & AROUND DEL BENACO

starred menu wins; its exquisitely present-ed, creative dishes might include trout with horseradish, smoked caviar and white chocolate, or risotto with lake fish, apple and raspberry.

Five-course menus (€75–80) focus on earth or sea ingredients, or you can put yourself in the chef's hands for a six-course surprise (€110). Inevitably, the dessert offer-ings are sublime.

The restaurant is well signposted, but hard to find. Don't try to drive to the gates as you'll get stuck in the narrow lanes.

🛈 Information

Tourist Office (☑ 045 740 00 44; www.tour-ismverona.it; Via Gardesana 238; ⊙ 9.30am-12.30pm & 3-6pm Mon-Sat, 9.30am-12.30pm Sun) Malcesine's tourist office is set back from the lake beside the bus station, on Via Garde-sana, the main road through town.

Torri del Benaco

☑ 045 / POP 3000

Picturesque Torri del Benaco is one of the most appealing stops on the eastern bank, its lanes, courtyards and tunnels a joy to ex-plore. Another 14th-century Scaligero castle, remodelled from the town's 10th-century walls, overlooks a pint-sized harbour, filled with swaying yacht masts. Arranged around a single cobbled street, Corso Dante, are ivy-draped 16th-century *palazzi*, relics of a past prosperity when Torri del Benaco was a kind of mini Garda capital with the right to levy customs duties on lake traffic.

◉ Sights

Castello Scaligero   MUSEUM
(☑ 045 629 61 11; Viale Frateli Lavanda 2; adult/reduced €5/3; ⊙ 9.30am-12.30pm & 2.30-6pm Apr–mid-Jun & mid-Sep–Oct, 9.30am-1pm & 4.30-7.30pm mid-Jun–mid-Sep) This atmospheric

museum packs a wealth of history into the rough stone walls of a 14th-century castle. The fortification was built in 1338 as part of the Della Scala family's attempts to fend off the Venetian Republic. Each of the castle's rooms explores a different traditional industry such as boat-building, fishing, olive-oil production and citrus growing.

Most interesting is the *limonaie* (lemon glasshouse), the oldest on the lake, which dates from 1760 – it's crowded with fragrant citrus trees and windfalls litter the floor.

Eating

Trattoria Bell'Arrivo VENETO €€
(☑045 629 90 28; Piazza Calderini 10; meals €35; ☺9.30am-2am) The excellent, if somewhat pricey food at this local harbourside trattoria is served by very attentive staff in a simple, undistracting dining room. The pastas here are particularly good, and the wine list is local.

Restaurant Gardesana RISTORANTE €€
(☑045 722 54 11; www.gardesana.eu; Piazza Calderini 20; pizzas €5-7, meals €35; ☺noon-2.30pm & 7-10pm) The artfully lit arches of Hotel Gardesana's restaurant make a romantic spot for dinner as the sun sinks over a pink-tinged lake and the distant mountains beyond. The food is understated but excellent – try the perch in white wine with brioche

---

OFF THE BEATEN TRACK

HORSE TREKKING ON MONTE BALDO

For a totally unique experience, saddle up one of **Ranch Barlot's** (☑348 7234082; www.ranchbarlot.com; Località Porcini, Caprino Veronese; treks per person per day €110-150) sweet Appaloosa or Argentinian ponies and ride Western-style up Monte Baldo or through the lushly forested Adige valley. Treks from two- to eight-days are possible and prices include everything from your mount and guide to accommodation in mountain refuges. Back at the ranch you can take expert lessons in Western-style riding in the school watched by the farm's friendly deer herd.

You'll find the ranch 14.5km northeast of Garda, up a steep, narrow country road just beyond the village of Caprino Veronese.

croutons – although you may be distracted by the views.

ℹ Information

Tourist Office (☑045 629 64 82; Via Gardesana; ☺9.30am-4.30pm Mon & Thu-Sat, 10am-3pm Sun) On the main road opposite the post office. Sells bus tickets and can help out with accommodation.

Garda & Punta San Vigilio

POP 4000

Situated in the shade of the Rocca del Garda is the 10th-century fishing village that gave the lake its name. Sadly, the picturesque town is now cut through by the main perimeter road around the lake making summer traffic overwhelming. Out of season, Garda's perfectly curved bay and fine shingle beaches make it a great lunch spot. Just 3km west of Garda is popular beauty spot, Punta San Vigilio.

◉ Sights

Punta San Vigilio BEACH
The leafy headland of Punta San Vigilio curls out into the lake 3km north of Garda. An avenue of cypress trees leads from the car park towards a gorgeous crescent of bay backed by olive groves. There the **Parco Baia delle Sirene** (☑045 725 58 84; www.parcobaiadellesirene.it; adult/reduced Punta San Vigilio €12/6, cheaper after 4.30pm; ☺10am-7pm Apr & May, 9.30am-8pm Jun-Aug; ℗) offers sun loungers beneath the trees; there's also a children's play area.

Entry is free at sunset. Alternatively, from the car park walk north a short distance and head off down the paths to a couple of smaller, quieter public coves.

Market MARKET
(Piazza Catullo; ☺8am-1pm Fri) It's worth timing a visit to Garda to coincide with its exuberant Friday market, one of the biggest on the lake's eastern bank. Look out for Lake Garda lemons and jars of golden local honey.

Eating & Drinking

★ **Taverna San Vigilio** CAFE €
(☑045 725 51 90; Punta San Vigilio; meals €20-30; ☺10am-5.30pm; ℗) With an olive-tree-shaded garden and tables strung out along a tiny crab-claw harbour, the Taverna San Vigilio is one of the most atmospheric bars on the

lake. Nibbles include lobster, veal and *prosciutto crudo* (cured ham).

Art Cafe Alla Torre   CAFE
(Piazza Calderini 1; ⊙7am-11pm) This hip, multitasking cafe-bar next to a medieval tower can be a laid-back cafe in the morning, an exhibition space after lunch, a cocktail halt as the sun goes down and a jazz venue after dark. Live music and tango nights complete the programme.

Bardolino

⚏ 045 / POP 6700

Gathered around a tiny harbour, prosperous Bardolino is a town in love with the grape. More than 70 vineyards and wine cellars grace the gentle hills that roll east from Bardolino's shores, many within DOC and the even stricter DOCG quality boundaries. They produce an impressive array of pink Chiaretto, ruby classico, dry superiore and young novello.

Bardolino is at its most Bacchic during the Festa dell'Uva e del Vino in early October, when the town's waterfront fills with food and wine stands, as well as musicians and dancers. The tourist office stocks a map of local producers on the Bardolino Strada del Vino (www.stradadelbardolino.com). Otherwise, plan your visit on a Thursday in order to catch the weekly market.

Bardolino is also also a spa town and the springboard for the ancient walled village of Lazise.

◉ Sights

Pieve di San Zeno   CHURCH
(Corte San Zeno) Flee the gelato and Aperol brigade for a pilgrimage to this ancient miniature church, concealed in a picturesquely shabby courtyard north of the main road. Dating from the 9th century, it's one of the finest pieces of Carolingian architecture to have survived in northern Italy, and its almost windowless form and moody interior give visitors a good impression of how early Christian worship must have felt. The original painted decoration is still visible in places.

Museo dell'Olio d'Oliva   MUSEUM
(⚏045 622 90 47; www.museum.it; Via Peschiera 54, Cisano; ⊙9am-12.30pm & 2.30-7pm year-round, 9am-12.30pm Sun Mar-Dec; ℗) FREE Some 2km south of Bardolino in Cisano, the most impressive exhibits at this well-

laid-out museum are the monster grape presses, some of which used mule power to drive them. Other displays chart the history of olive oil production around Lake Garda and explain how the crop is harvested today. There's also an olive-oil library and an exhibition of glassware used to serve and store oil. The shop upstairs sells everything from olive-wood chopping boards to olive-based cosmetics.

Museo del Vino   MUSEUM
(⚏045 622 83 31; www.museodelvino.it; Via Costabella 9; ⊙9am-12.30pm & 2.30-7pm mid-Mar–Sep, hours vary Oct–mid-Mar) FREE Just off the main lake road, the Museo del Vino is set within the Zeni winery (⚏045 721 00 22; www.zeni.it; ⊙2.30-7pm daily, 9am-12.30pm Sat & Sun) and rarely has a museum smelt this good. Rich scents waft around displays of wicker grape baskets, cooper's tools, drying racks and gigantic timber grape presses. Tastings of Zeni's red, white and rosé wines are free, or pay to sample pricier vintages, including barrel-aged Amarone.

🏃 Activities

Aqualux Hotel Spa   SPA
(⚏045 622 99 99; www.aqualuxhotel.com; Via Europa Unita 24; adult Mon-Fri/Sat & Sun €30/35, child free; ⊙9am-7pm Mar-Dec; ⊕) Treat yourself to a day at Bardolino's four-star Aqualux spa where over 1000 sq metres, eight pools and a fitness room are dedicated to your wellbeing. A circulating whirlpool, hydromassage jets and warm waterfalls get the circulation going and double as fairground rides for older kids, while designated children's pools and play areas keep little ones amused.

Guerrieri Rizzardi   WINE
(⚏045 721 00 28; www.guerrieri-rizzardi.com; Via Verdi 4; tastings €15; ⊙by appointment 5pm Wed May-Oct) One of the most enjoyable ways to savour Bardolino's bitter cherry flavours is a tutored tasting at Guerrieri Rizzardi. After a tour of wine cellars full of cobweb-laced bottles, relaxed tastings take place in the ancient walled kitchen garden. Booking required.

🍴 Eating & Drinking

Cristallo   GELATO €
(Piazza Matteotti 1; gelato from €1.50; ⊙7am-2am daily) The best ice cream in Bardolino has been scooped at this family-run parlour since 1969. Choose your flavour before joining

LAKE GARDA'S AMUSEMENT PARKS

For adrenalin-sparking rides and stunt shows, it's hard to beat northern Italy's Lake Garda. The lake's eastern shore is home to larger-than-life dinosaurs, pirate ships, roller coasters and an aquarium at the kid-oriented Gardaland (☑045 644 97 77; www.garda-land.it; Via Dema 4, Castelnuovo del Garda; adult/reduced €40.50/34; family €102-170; ☉10am-11pm mid-Jun–mid-Sep, 10am-6pm Apr–mid-Jun).

To its north CanevaWorld (☑045 696 99 00; www.canevaworld.it; Località Fossalta 58) features an aqua park (www.canevapark.it; adult/child €28/22; ☉10am-7pm Jul & Aug, 10am-6pm mid-May–Jun & Sep) and medieval shows (adult/reduced dinner & show €30/20; ☉2 shows daily May–mid-Sep) complete with medieval banquet. Within the same sprawling park is CanevaWorld's Movieland Studios (www.movieland.it; adult/reduced €28/22), featuring stunt-packed action shows. Opening times vary slightly throughout the year, so check the website for details. Cheaper deals and family tickets are also available online.

Both parks are just off the main lake road. Gardaland is 2km from Peschiera del Garda. CanevaWorld is a similar distance from Lazise. Free buses shuttle visitors to both parks from Peschiera del Garda train station.

the fast-moving queue as the *solo italiano* servers don't wait around.

★ Il Giardino delle Esperidi   OSTERIA €€
(☑045 621 04 77; Via Goffredo Mameli 1; meals €35-50; ☉7-10pm Mon & Wed-Fri, noon-2.30pm & 7-10pm Sat & Sun) Holidaying gourmets should head for this intimate little *osteria*, where sourcing local delicacies is a labour of love for its sommelier-owner. The intensely flavoured baked truffles with *parmigiano reggiano* (Parmesan) are legendary, and the highly seasonal menu may feature rarities such as red grouse or bull meat marinaded in Garda olive oil.

La Bottega del Vino   WINE BAR
(☑348 6041800; Piazza Matteotti 46; ☉10.30am-2pm & 5-10pm Sun-Thu, to midnight Fri & Sat) To experience some authentic Bardolino atmosphere head to this no-nonsense bar in the centre of town. Inside, a stream of lively banter passes between locals and staff beside walls lined with bottles four deep.

❶ Information

Tourist Office (☑045 721 00 78; www.tourism.verona.it; Piazzale Aldo Moro 5; ☉9am-noon & 3-6pm Mon-Sat, 10am-2pm Sun) Operates a hotel booking service and can advise on the surrounding wine region.

Lazise

☑045 / POP 6900

Some 5km south of Bardolino, Lazise is picturesque even by Lake Garda's high standards. The old centre is still guarded by its water-to-water town walls that ape the town's chessboard square. This opens onto one of Garda's most delightful tiny harbours, slender fishing boats occupying one side, bars and restaurants the other. As the lake's most lovely spot, the summer crowds are enormous.

◉ Sights

Paved in waves of marble and brick, Lazise's promenade is the best on this side of Lake Garda. Grab an ice cream, feed the swans and lap up those views.

Chiesa di San Nicolò   CHURCH
(Via San Marco) The Romanesque Church of Saint Nick, the patron of fishermen, sits squat by the lapping harbour as it has done since the 11th century. Inside lurk the remnants of 14th-century frescoes.

Rocca Scaligera   CASTLE
(Via Castello) The five towers of the privately owned Rocca Scaligera rise to the south of the harbour – look out for the huge hole in the north wall of its main tower, made by a canon during the 15th-century wars between Venice and Milan. The town's south gate, known as the Porta del Lion due to the bas-relief of the Venetian lion carved on it, is alongside.

✕ Eating

Alla Grotta   SEAFOOD €€
(☑045 758 00 35; www.allagrotta.it; Via Francesco Fontana 5; meals €30-35; ☉noon-2pm & 7-10pm Wed-Mon) The resemblance of this harbourside restaurant to an aquarium is

perfectly apt as the menu here offers almost exclusively seafood. Don't even think of asking for a lake-dweller to be grilled for you lunch – they simply don't do freshwater fish, the gourmet dishes are made from fresh ingredients shipped in from other bodies of water on a daily basis.

🛈 Information

Tourist Office (☑ 045 758 01 14; www.visit garda.com; Via Francesco Fontana 14; ⊗ 9am-1pm & 2.30-6pm Mon-Fri, 9am-1pm Sat) In the library next to the harbour. There's a free toilet right behind.

VERONA

☑ 045 / POP 260,000

Best known for its Shakespeare associations, Verona attracts a multinational gaggle of tourists to its pretty piazzas and knot of lanes, most in search of Romeo, Juliet and all that. But beyond the heart-shaped kitsch and Renaissance romance, Verona is a bustling centre, its heart dominated by a mammoth, remarkably well-preserved 1st-century amphitheatre, the venue for the city's annual summer opera festival. Add to that countless churches, a couple of architecturally fascinating bridges over the Adige, regional wine and food from the Veneto hinterland and some impressive art, and Verona shapes up as one of northern Italy's most attractive cities. And all this just a short hop from the shores of stunning Lake Garda.

◉ Sights

⭐**Roman Arena**   RUINS
(☑ 045 800 32 04; Piazza Brà; adult/reduced €10/7.50; ⊗ 8.30am-7.30pm Tue-Sun, from 1.30pm Mon) Built of pink-tinged marble in the 1st century AD, Verona's Roman amphitheatre survived a 12th-century earthquake to become the city's legendary open-air opera house, with seating for 30,000 people. You can visit the arena year-round, though it's at its best during the summer opera festival. In winter months, concerts are held at the Teatro Filarmonico (☑ 045 800 28 80; www. arena.it; Via dei Mutilati 4; opera €23-60, concerts €25-50). From January to May and October to December, admission is €1 on the first Sunday of the month.

The eighth biggest amphitheatre in the Roman Empire and predating the Colosse-um in Rome, nothing of the incredible inside is visible from outside. Pass through the dingy ancient corridors, wide enough to drive a gladiator's chariot down, to re-emerge into the massive, sunlit stone arena, at least 50 levels of seating rising from the mammoth, oval showground. Note the amphitheatre is completely open so this is not a great place to visit in the rain.

⭐**Museo di Castelvecchio**   MUSEUM
(☑ 045 806 26 11; https://museodicastelvecchio. comune.verona.it; Corso Castelvecchio 2; adult/ reduced €6/4.50; ⊗ 1.30-7.30pm Mon, 8.30am-7.30pm Tue-Sun) Bristling with fishtail battlements along the River Adige, Castelvecchio was built in the 1350s by Cangrande II. Severely damaged by Napoleon and WWII bombings, the fortress was reinvented by architect Carlo Scarpa, who constructed bridges over exposed foundations, filled gaping holes with glass panels, and balanced a statue of Cangrande I above the courtyard on a concrete gangplank. The complex is now home to a diverse collection of statuary, frescoes, jewellery, medieval artefacts and paintings.

ROMEO & JULIET IN VERONA

Shakespeare had no idea what he'd start when he set his (heavily derivative) tale of star-crossed lovers in Verona, but the city has seized the commercial possibilities with both hands – everything from *osterie* and hotels to embroidered kitchen aprons get the R&J branding. While the play's depiction of feuding families has genuine provenance, the lead characters themselves are fictional.

Undaunted, in the 1930s the authorities settled on a house in Via Cappello (think Capulet) as Juliet's and added a 14th-century-style balcony and a bronze statue of our heroine. You can squeeze onto the balcony itself at the altogether underwhelming **Casa di Giulietta** (Juliet's House; ☑ 045 803 43 03; Via Cappello 23; adult/reduced €6/4.50, free with VeronaCard; ⊗ 1.30-7.30pm Mon, 8.30am-7.30pm Tue-Sun), or – more sensibly – see the circus from the square below, a spot framed by a slew of lovesick sticky notes.

Verona

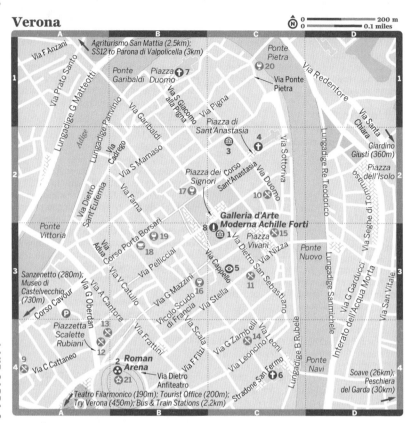

Verona

Top Sights

Sights

Eating

Drinking & Nightlife

Entertainment

Scarpa's modern remodelling of the interior comes as a surprise after the austere medieval exterior and provides a contrasting backdrop for the exhibits. Highlights include some wonderful 14th-century glass, the Pisanello room with its well-preserved frescoes, the collection of Flemish art and works by Renaissance Veronese and

Venetian painters. Look out for the Cangrande coat of arms throughout – Cangrande means 'Top Dog' and the family's comedy shield features two dogs climbing a ladder! After viewing the exhibition, clamber out onto the ramparts for views of the river and old city defences.

★ **Giardino Giusti**   GARDENS
(☑ 045 803 40 29; Via Giardino Giusti 2; adult/reduced €8.50/5; ⊘ 9am-8pm Apr-Sep, to 7pm Oct-Mar) Across the river from the historic centre, these sculpted gardens are considered a masterpiece of Renaissance landscaping, and named after the noble family that has tended them since opening them to the public in 1591. The vegetation is an Italianate mix of the manicured and natural, graced by soaring cypresses, one of which the German poet Goethe immortalised in his travel writings.

According to local legend, lovers who manage to find each other in the gardens' petite labyrinth are destined to stay together. If you do, whisper sweet nothings while gazing out at the city from the *belvedere* (lookout), accessed from the back of the gardens. Forget the Casa di Giulietta, this is where the real romance is in Verona.

Torre dei Lamberti   TOWER
(☑ 045 927 30 27; Via della Costa 1; adult/reduced incl Galleria d'Arte Moderna Achille Forti €8/5, with VeronaCard €1; ⊘ 10am-7pm) One of Verona's most popular attractions, this 84m-high watchtower provides panoramic views of Verona and nearby mountains. Begun in the 12th century and finished in 1463 – too late to notice invading Venetians – it sports an octagonal bell tower whose two bells retain their ancient names: Rengo once called meetings of the city council, while Marangona warned citizens of fire. A lift whisks you up two-thirds of the way but you have to walk the last few storeys.

★ **Galleria d'Arte**
Moderna Achille Forti   MUSEUM
(Palazzo della Ragione; ☑ 045 800 19 03; www.palazzodellaragioneverona.it; Cortile Mercato Vecchio; adult/reduced €4/2.50, incl Torre dei Lamberti €8/5; ⊘ 10am-6pm Tue-Fri, 11am-7pm Sat & Sun) In the shadow of the Torre dei Lamberti, the Romanesque Palazzo della Ragione is home to Verona's jewel-box Gallery of Modern Art. Reached via the Gothic Scala della Ragione (Stairs of Reason), the collection of paintings and sculpture spans 1840 to 1940

and includes influential Italian artists such as Giorgio Morandi and Umberto Boccioni. Among the numerous highlights are Francesco Hayez' arresting portrait *Meditazione* (Meditation), Angelo Dall'Oca's haunting *Foglie cadenti* (Falling Leaves) and Ettore Berladini's darkly humourous *I vecchi* (Old Men).

The gallery's architectural pièce de résistance is the vaulted Cappella dei Notai (Chapel of Notaries), bursting with late 17th- and early 18th-century biblical scenes executed by Alessandro Marchesini, Giambattista Bellotti, Santo Prunati and Louis Dorigny.

Basilica di San Zeno Maggiore   BASILICA
(www.basilicasanzeno.it; Piazza San Zeno; €2.50; ⊘ 8.30am-6pm Mon-Sat, 12.30-6pm Sun Mar-Oct, 10am-1pm & 1.30-5pm Mon-Sat, 12.30-5pm Sun Nov-Feb) A masterpiece of Romanesque architecture, the striped brick and stone basilica was built in honour of the city's patron saint. Enter through the flower-filled cloister into the nave – a vast space lined with 12th- to 15th-century frescoes. Painstaking restoration has revived Mantegna's 1457–59 *Majesty of the Virgin* altarpiece, painted with such astonishing perspective that you actually believe there are garlands of fresh fruit hanging behind the Madonna's throne.

Under the rose window depicting the Wheel of Fortune you'll find meticulously detailed 12th-century bronze doors, which include a scene of an exorcism with a demon being yanked from a woman's mouth. Beneath the main altar lies a brooding crypt, with faces carved into medieval capitals and St Zeno's corpse glowing in a transparent sarcophagus.

Basilica di Sant'Anastasia   BASILICA
(www.chieseverona.it; Piazza di Sant'Anastasia; €2.50; ⊘ 9am-6pm Mon-Sat, 1-6pm Sun Mar-Oct, 10am-1pm & 1.30-5pm Mon-Sat, 1-5pm Sun Nov-Feb) Dating from the 13th to 15th centuries and featuring an elegantly decorated vaulted ceiling, the Gothic Basilica di Sant'Anastasia is Verona's largest church and a showcase for local art. The multitude of frescoes is overwhelming, but don't overlook Pisanello's story-book-quality fresco *St George and the Princess* above the entrance to the Pellegrini Chapel, or the 1495 holy water font featuring a hunchback carved by Paolo Veronese's father, Gabriele Caliari.

LAKE GARDA & AROUND VERONA

Arena Museo Opera - AMO MUSEUM
(✆045 80 30 461; www.arenamuseopera.com; Palazzo Forti, Via Massalongo 7; adult/reduced €10/8; ⊙2.30-7.30pm Mon, 9.30am-7.30pm Thu-Sun) Opera fans shouldn't miss this under-visited multimedia museum dedicated entirely to the great Italian opera culture. Exhibits include scores, letters and notes by big names such as Bellini, Rossini, Donizetti, Verdi and Puccini as well as costumes, sets and photographs of great operatic events of grander times gone by.

Chiesa di San Fermo CHURCH
(Stradone San Fermo; admission €2.50, combined Verona church ticket €6 or with VeronaCard; ⊙10am-6pm Mon-Sat, 1-6pm Sun Mar-Oct, 10am-1pm & 1.30-5pm Mon-Sat, 1-5pm Sun) At the river end of Via Leoni, Chiesa di San Fermo is actually two churches in one: Franciscan monks raised the 13th-century Gothic church right over an original 11th-century Romanesque structure. Inside the main Gothic church, you'll notice a magnificent timber *carena di nave,* a ceiling reminiscent of an upturned boat's hull. In the right transept are 14th-century frescoes, including some fragments depicting episodes in the life of St Francis. Stairs from the cloister lead underground to the spare but atmospheric Romanesque church below.

Duomo CATHEDRAL
(✆045 59 28 13; Piazza Duomo; €2.50, combined Verona church ticket €6 or with VeronaCard; ⊙10am-5.30pm Mon-Sat, 1.30-5.30pm Sun Mar-Oct, 10am-1pm & 1.30-5pm Mon-Fri, to 4pm Sat, 1.30-5pm Sun Nov-Feb) Verona's 12th-century cathedral is a striking Romanesque creation, with bug-eyed statues of Charlemagne's paladins Roland and Oliver, crafted by medieval master Nicolò, on the west porch. Nothing about this sober facade hints at the extravagant 16th- to 17th-century frescoed interior with angels aloft amid *trompe l'œil* architecture. At the left end of

the nave is **Cartolari-Nichesola Chapel**, designed by Renaissance master Jacopo Sansovino and featuring a vibrant Titian *Assumption.*

👉 Tours

Try Verona TOURS
(www.tryverona.com; Via Pallone 16) This superb outfit run myriad tours focusing on anything from local cuisine, shopping to Romeo & Juliet. It also runs tours to neighbouring towns and out to Lake Garda, many of them themed.

Simonetta Bike Tours CYCLING
(✆045 834 6104; www.simonettabiketours.it) This cycle tour company operates a variety of pedal-powered jaunts around the city, one involving cycling and rafting on the Adige. It also arranges longer bike tours of the Veneto, Lake Garda and the Dolomites.

🍴 Eating

Hostaria La Vecchia Fontanina TRATTORIA €
(✆045 59 11 59; www.ristorantevecchiafontanina .com; Piazzetta Chiavica 5; meals €20-25; ⊙10.30am-3.30pm & 6.30-midnight Mon-Sat) With tables on a pint-sized piazza, cosy indoor rooms and excellent food, this historic, knick-knack-filled eatery stands out from the crowd. The menu features typical Veronese dishes alongside a number of more unusual creations such as *bigoli con ortica e ricotta affumicata* (thick spaghetti with nettles and smoked ricotta) and several heavenly desserts. Queuing to get in is normal.

Enocibus VENETO €
(✆045 594 010; www.enocibus.com; Vicolo Pomodoro 3; meals €20-25; ⊙11am-3pm & 7-11pm) Owners Claudio and Titti keep things low key, cheap and local at this central but well-concealed eatery. Some of the best-priced food in Verona is served with real care and attention and you can fill up here on pasta and salad for under €15. Only when you add wine does the bill go up.

La Tradision VENETIAN €
(✆045 594 226; Via Oberdan 6; meals €15-25; ⊙8am-10pm Mon-Thu, to midnight Fri & Sat) Join locals and visitors at this relaxed gastro-bar to sample local cheeses, salamis and wines for prices that won't require emergency money wired from home. The cold meat and cheese board is the signature dish,

---

ⓘ VERONA CARD

••

The **VeronaCard** (€18/22 per 24/72 hours; www.tourism.verona.it), available at tourist sights, tobacconists and numerous hotels, offers access to most major monuments and churches, unlimited use of town buses, and discounted tickets to selected concerts and opera and theatre productions.

VERONA'S OPERA FESTIVAL

On balmy summer nights, when 14,000 music lovers fill the Roman Arena during the opera festival and light their candles at sunset, expect goosebumps even before the performance starts. The festival (☑ 045 800 51 51; www.arena.it; Via Dietro Anfiteatro 6; ☺ late Jun–late Aug) was started in 1913 and is now the biggest open-air lyrical music event in the world. It draws international stars and the staging is legendary – highlights have included Franco Zeffirelli's lavish productions of *Carmen* and *Aida*.

Prices rise at weekends, ranging from €22 on unreserved stone steps and costing over €200 on the central gold seats. Performances usually start at 8.45pm or 9pm with locals booking their dinner table for after the show. Tucking into a preshow picnic on the unreserved stone steps is fine, so decant that wine into a plastic bottle (glass and knives aren't allowed), arrive early, rent a cushion and prepare for an utterly unforgettable evening.

perfect for two to share with a glass of Valpolicella or two. A great place to start the evening.

Osteria da Ugo   VENETIAN €€
(www.osteriadaugo.com; Vicolo Dietro Sant'Andrea 1b; meals €25-30; ☺ noon-2.30pm & 7.30-10.30pm, closed Sun dinner) Lost in a backstreet away from the tourism, this *osteria* is a popular treat typically frequented at mealtimes by whole families. Surrounded by stained glass, elegantly laid tables and hundreds of wine bottles, enjoy a menu of Italian favourites as well as Vicenza-style codfish and tortellini with Lessinia truffles. Be prepared to queue to get a table during busy periods.

La Taverna di Via Stella   VENETO €€
(☑ 045 800 80 08; www.tavernadiviastella.com; Via Stella 5c; meals €30-35; ☺ 12.15-2.30pm & 7.15-11pm, closed Wed & Mon evening) Brush past the haunches of prosciutto dangling over the deli bar and make your way into the dining room, decorated Tiepolo-style with rustic murals of chivalric knights and maidens. This is the place you'll want to sample traditional Veronese dishes such as *pastissada* (horse stew), tripe and DOP Lessinia cheeses from Monte Veronese.

★ **Locanda 4 Cuochi**   MODERN ITALIAN €€
(☑ 045 803 03 11; www.locanda4cuochi.it; Via Alberto Mario 12; meals €40, 3-course set menu €25; ☺ 12.30-2.30pm & 7.30-10.30pm, closed lunch Mon-Wed; ☎) With its open kitchen, urbane vibe and hotshot chefs, you're right to expect great things from Locanda. Culinary acrobatics play second fiddle to prime produce cooked with skill and subtle twists. Whether it's perfectly crisp suckling pig lacquered with liquorice, or an epilogue of

gianduja ganache with sesame crumble and banana, expect to to be gastronomically impressed.

★ **Pescheria I Masenini**   SEAFOOD €€€
(☑ 045 929 80 15; www.imasenini.com; Piazzetta Pescheria 9; meals €40-50; ☺ 12.40-2pm & 7.40-10pm, closed Sun evening & Mon) Located on the piazza where Verona's Roman fish market once held sway, softly lit Masenini quietly serves up Verona's most imaginative, modern fish dishes. Inspired flavour combinations might see fresh sea bass carpaccio paired with zesty green apple and pink pepper, black-ink gnocchi schmoozing with lobster *ragù*, or sliced amberjack delightfully matched with crumbed almonds, honey, spinach and raspberries.

🍷 Drinking & Nightlife

Antica Bottega del Vino   WINE BAR
(☑ 045 800 45 35; www.bottegavini.it; Vicolo Scudo di Francia 3; ☺ 11am-1am) While *vino* is the primary consideration at this historic, baronial-style wine bar (the cellar holds around 18,000 bottles), the linen-lined tables promise a satisfying feed. Ask the sommelier to recommend a worthy vintage for your braised donkey, Vicenza-style codfish or Venetian liver – some of the best wines here are bottled specifically for the *bottega*.

Archivio   COCKTAIL BAR
(☑ 345 8169663; Via Rosa 3; ☺ 8am-midnight Mon-Fri, from 9am Sat, from 11am Sun) Fragrant with aromatic cocktail ingredients, this sidestreet micro-bar is one of the best places for a night-launching drink. Imaginative mixology combines with craft beers to give a lot of choice to drinkers, and the friendly owner knows his tipples.

Cafe Borsari   COFFEE

(☑ 045 803 13 13; Corso Porta Borsari 15d; ☺ 7.30am-8.15pm) It might look like a ceramics shop from the outside, but open the door and you'll discover this magically minuscule coffee house that's been roasting its own coffee and supplying hot chocolate to tables since 1969. It also sells quirky Christmas gifts year-round.

Osteria del Bugiardo   WINE BAR

(☑ 045 59 18 69; Corso Porta Borsari 17a; ☺ 11am-midnight, to 1am Fri & Sat) Crowds converge at friendly Bugiardo for glasses of upstanding Valpolicella bottled specifically for the *osteria*. Feeling peckish? Order the yellow polenta with creamy gorgonzola and salami. On weekdays from November to January, pair a delicious Amarone with the very local *lesso e pearà* (boiled meat stew with a peppery beef, hen, bone-marrow and breadcrumb sauce).

Terrazza Bar al Ponte   BAR

(☑ 045 927 50 32; www.terrazzabaralponte.eu; Via Ponte di Pietra 26; ☺ 9am-2am) Mingle with hip, young locals for *spritz* (*prosecco* cocktails) beneath the giant chandelier in this retro-cool bar. Come early enough and you might even nab a table on the tiny terrace overlooking the river and the Ponte Pietra.

ⓘ Information

Tourist Office (☑ 045 806 86 80; www.tourism.verona.it; Via degli Alpini 9; ☺ 10am-7pm Mon-Sat, to 3pm Sun) Just off Piazza Brà. Knowledgeable and helpful.

ⓘ Getting There & Away

AIR

Verona-Villafranca Airport (☑ 045 809 56 66; www.aeroportoverona.it) is 12km outside town and accessible by **ATV** (Azienda Trasporti Verona; www.atv.verona.it) Aerobus to/from the train station (€6, 15 minutes, every 20 minutes 6.30am to 11.30pm). A taxi costs between €25 and €30, depending on the time of day. Flights arrive from all over Italy and some European cities, including Amsterdam, Barcelona, Berlin, Brussels, Dusseldorf, London and Paris.

BUS

The main intercity bus station is in front of the train station in the Porta Nuova area. Buses run to Padua, Vicenza and Venice.

ATV city buses 11, 12 and 13 (bus 92 or 93 on Sundays and holidays) connect the train

station with Piazza Brà. Buy tickets from newsagents, tobacconists, ticket machines or the ATV office within the train station before you board the bus (tickets valid for 90 minutes, €1.30).

CAR

Verona is at the intersection of the A4 autostrada between Milan and Venice (exit at Verona East) and the A22 between Modena and Trento (exit at Verona North). Southern Lake Garda is 30km away.

The centre of Verona is restricted to traffic. Useful car parks fringe the city, some as cheap as €5 a day. The nearest car park to the city centre is at Piazza Cittadella.

Tourists staying within the limited traffic zone (ZIL) need to obtain a permit from their hotel or B&B in order to park within the historic centre.

TRAIN

Verona Porta Nuova station is a major stop on the Italian rail network with direct services to numerous northern Italian towns and cities, including Venice (€8.85 to €27, 70 minutes to 2¼ hours, one to four hourly) and Milan (€12.75 to €25, 1¼ to two hours, one to three hourly). Local services also connect with Mantua (€3.95, 40 minutes) and Desenzano del Garda (€4.45, 25 minutes).

VERONA'S WINE COUNTRY

The Veneto produces more DOC (*denominazione di origine controllata*) quality-controlled wines than any other region in Italy, with the most productive vineyards – Soave and Valpolicella – within easy reach of Verona. Northwest, Valpolicella is celebrated for Amarone, an intense red made from partially dried grapes, while Soave, to the east, delivers its crisp, namesake whites amid story-book medieval walls.

Valpolicella

The 'valley of many cellars', from which Valpolicella gets its name, has been in the business of wine production since the ancient Greeks introduced their *passito* technique (the use of partially dried grapes) to create the blockbuster flavours we still enjoy in the region's Amarone and Recioto wines.

Seven *comuni* compose the DOC quality-controlled area: Pescantina, San Pietro in Cariano, Negrar, Marano di Valpolicella, Fumane, Sant'Ambrogio di Valpolicella and

Sant'Anna d'Alfaedo. Situated in the foothills of Monte Lessini, the valleys benefit from a happy microclimate created by the enormous body of Lake Garda to the west and cooling breezes from the Alps to the north. No wonder Veronese nobility got busy building weekend retreats here. Many of them, like the extraordinary Villa della Torre, still house noble wineries, while others have been transformed into idyllic places to stay and eat.

◎ Sights

Villa della Torre HISTORIC BUILDING
(☑ 045 683 20 70; www.villadellatorre.it; Via della Torre 25, Fumane; villa guided tours €10, with wine tasting & snack €30-40; ⊙ villa tours 11am & 4pm Mon-Sat by appointment; P) The jewel in the Allegrini crown, this historic villa dates to the mid-16th century and was built by intellectual and humanist Giulio della Torre. Numerous starchitects contributed to its construction: the classically inspired peristyle and fish pond are attributed to Giulio Romana (of Palazzo Te fame), the chapel to Michele Sanmicheli, and the monstrous, gaping-mouthed fireplaces to Bartolomeo Ridolfi and Giovanni Battista Scultori.

Villa Mosconi Bertani WINERY
(☑ 045 602 07 44; www.mosconibertani.it; Via Novare, Arbizzano; tours €10, tastings from €20; ⊙ wine tastings & tours 2pm & 4pm Sun-Fri, 10am Tue-Sun) This grand winery housed in a small chateau offers both wine tastings and tours of the building. There is a choice of four tasting sessions, most of them involving superior Valpolicello wines such as Lepia Soave DOC, Amarone Classico DOCG and Torre Pieve Chardonnay. Afterwards, take a turn around the sumptuously romantic chateau gardens.

Pieve di San Floriano CHURCH
(Via della Pieve, Località San Floriano; ⊙ 7.30am-noon & 3.30-6pm) Considered one of the most attractive Romanesque churches in the region, this austere place of worship dates back to between the 10th and 13th centuries. Particularly impressive are the cloisters, a peaceful oasis with an ancient feel.

✖ Eating

★ **Osteria Numero Uno** OSTERIA €€
(☑ 045 770 13 75; www.osterianumero1.com; Via Flaminio Pellegrini 2, Fumane; meals €15-30; ⊙ noon-2.30pm & 7-10.30pm Thu-Mon, noon-2.30pm Tue) The archetypal *osteria* with a wooden bar packed with overall-clad vintners

LAKE GARDA & AROUND VALPOLICELLA

OFF THE BEATEN TRACK

TOP WINERIES

Allegrini (☑ 045 683 20 11; www.allegrini.it; Via Giare 9/11, Fumane; wine tasting & cellar tour €20, tour of villa €10, tour of villa with wine tasting & snack €30-40; ⊙ cellar tour & wine tasting 10.30am & 3.30pm Mon-Fri by appointment, villa tours 11am & 4pm Mon-Sat by appointment; P) Valpolicella aristocracy, the Allegrini family has been producing grand crus from Corvinia and Rondinella grapes since the 16th century.

Giuseppe Quintarelli (☑ 045 750 00 16; giuseppe.quintarelli@tin.it; Via Cerè 1; wine tastings €20; ⊙ by appointment) The late Giuseppe Quintarelli put the Valpolicella region on the world wine map, and his limited-production Amarone – made using Corvina, Corvinone, Rondinella, cabernet, Nebbiolo, Croatina and Sangiovese grapes – is a Holy Grail for oenophiles.

Massimago (☑ 045 888 01 43; Via Giare 21, Mezzane di Sotto; wine tastings from €10, 2-person apt €120-150, 4-person apt €220-250; ⊙ 9am-6pm Mon-Fri, by appointment Sat & Sun; P) Breaking the traditional mould, Camilla Chauvet concentrates on a limited range of lighter, more modern Valpolicellas at her winery-come-relais, including a rosé and an unusual sparkling variety.

Valentina Cubi (☑ 045 770 18 06; www.valentinacubi.it; Località Casterna 60, Fumane; wine tastings €20; ⊙ 10am-noon & 3-6pm Mon-Sat by appointment; P) 🌿 Blazing a trail with her state-of-the-art, certified organic winery, Cubi uses biodynamic methods to produce one of the few 'natural', sulphate-free Valpolicellas.

Zýmē (☑ 045 770 11 08; www.zyme.it; Via Cà del Pipa 1; wine tastings €15; ⊙ shop 9am-5pm Mon-Sat, tastings by appointment 9am-noon & 2-6pm Mon-Sat) An award-winning winery with striking contemporary architecture by Moreno Zurlo, an ancient quarry turned cellar, and a reputation for bold, big-blend wines.

ROAD TRIP: VALPOLICELLA WINE TOUR

Wine has been made in these hills since the Romans ruled the roost, and today the Valpolicella area produces some of Italy's most renowned reds, including the blockbuster Amarone. Situated within easy striking distance of Lake Garda's western shore and a 20-minute drive north of Verona, its historic and avant-garde wineries make for a pleasant one-day road trip.

1 Arbizzano

From Verona, pick up the SS12 highway northwest out of town. At the turning for Parona di Valpolicella, a warren of narrow country lanes straggle north. Turn on to the SP4 and drive into the hills. Before you reach Negrar take a quick 1.5km detour down Via Novare to **Villa Mosconi Bertani** (p201) in **Arbizzano**. Arguably one of the

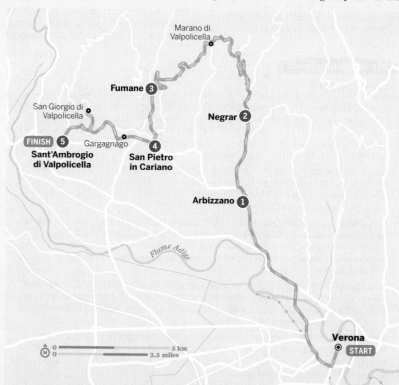

A day 43km/27 miles

Great for.... Food & Drink, History & Culture

Best Time to Go Autumn, when the grapes are harvested

most beautifully sited villas in Valpolicella, this winery is one of the oldest continuously operating wine businesses in Italy. What's more, the lovely neoclassical residence, completed in 1769, with a phalanx of Greek gods perched on the the facade and a grand frescoed Chamber of the Muses, is a listed historic landmark. Tours and tastings run between April and October, but require pre-booking.

❷ Negrar

Return to the SP4 and turn right towards Negrar. Tiny Negrar, so-called 'city of wine', is the largest of Valpolicella's five DOC communities. It sits amid a patchwork of pergola vineyards, criss-crossed by lines of *marogne* (dry stone walls) typical of the region. Amarone acolytes flock here to the iconic winery of **Giuseppe Quintarelli** (p201) which, despite its modest appearance, produces one of the biggest, deepest, richest red wines this side of Porto. Younger vintners such as **Fratelli Vogadori** (☑ 328 941 72 28; www.vogadorivini.it; Via Vigolo 16; ⊙ 8am-noon & 1-6pm Mon-Sat, 9am-noon Sun) 🖉 are also worth a visit to sample unusual native varieties such as Oseleta and Negrara.

❸ Fumane

Follow the SP12 north out of Negrar and after 3km turn left onto Via Ca'Righetto, climbing into the terraced hills before dropping down to Marano di Valpolicella, with its Romanesque church. From here, take the SP33b to Fumane and **Allegrini** (p201), where wine tastings are held in the 16th-century **Villa della Torre** (p201). On its surface the villa and its garden appear to present a regular Renaissance scene, but look closer and you'll find grotesque masks spitting water at promenaders, fireplaces that look like roaring monsters and a grotto that resembles a snarling hell's mouth. It subversively suggests that the veneer of civilisation

is fragile and despite men's best efforts the forces of nature are always lurking just beneath the surface.

If you're feeling peckish, join the locals who flock to **Osteria Numero Uno** (p201) for superb *cucina casalinga* (home cooking).

❹ San Pietro in Cariano

Drive south on the SP33 for 6km to the ancient hamlet of San Pietro in Cariano. Traces of the towns Roman heritage are visible in the 12th-century **Pieve di San Floriano** (p201) and the town is surrounded by elegant Palladian villas, such as San Giona, dating to the period of Venetian domination. But despite its impressive heritage San Pietro hasn't stayed stuck in the past as witnessed by the strikingly modern, award-winning winery **Zýmē** (p201). Headed up by Moreno Zurlo, the winery has a reputation for big-blend wines, the most famous being Harlequin, a thrilling IGP wine made using 15 local grape varieties.

❺ Sant'Ambrogio di Valpolicella

A short 10km drive west on the SP4 gets you from San Pietro to Sant'Ambrogio di Valpolicella via San Giorgio. Part of the wealth of Valpolicella comes from the marble quarries at Sant'Ambrogio, which have been worked for their Rosso Broccato and Bronzetto marble since Roman times. Much of it went to build Verona's Arena, and even today the Marble School is the only one of its kind in Italy. Perched 375m up on a hill, in the fraction of San Giorgio di Valpolicella, the Romanesque **Pieve di San Giorgio** (☑ 347 248 67 87; www.sangiorgiodivalpolicella.it; Piazza della Pieve; ⊙ 7am-6pm) **FREE**, is the area's oldest Christian church, dating back to 712. Behind the church you can pick up the Sentiero della Salute, a 2.5km (one hour) walk through the woods.

and delicious aromas wafting out of the kitchen. Glasses of Valpolicella (around 120 types) range from just €2 to €5 for a good Amarone. Pair them with salty speck and belly-filling duck with wild garlic and gnocchi.

★**Enoteca**
della Valpolicella   VENETIAN €€
(☑ 045 683 91 46; www.enotecadellavalpolicella.it; Via Osan 47, Fumane; meals €25; ☺ noon-2.30pm Sun, noon-2.30pm & 7.30-10pm Tue-Sat) Gastronomes flock to the town of Fumane, just a few kilometres north of San Pietro in Cariano, where an ancient farmhouse has found renewed vigour as a rustically elegant restaurant. Put your trust in gracious owners Ada and Carlotta, who will eagerly guide you through the day's menu, a showcase for fresh, local produce.

Trattoria Caprini   TRATTORIA €€
(☑ 045 750 05 11; www.trattoriacaprini.it; Via Zanotti 9, Torbe; meals €30; ☺ noon-2.30pm & 7-10pm Thu-Tue) A little north of Negrar in the hamlet of Torbe, family-run Caprini serves heart-warming fare you wish your mamma could make. Many menu items are home made, including the delicious *lasagnetta* with hand-rolled pasta, and a *ragù* of beef, tomato, porcini and finferlo mushrooms. Downstairs, beside the fire of the old *pistoria* (bakery), you can sample some 200 Valpolicella labels.

Trattoria Dalla
Rosa Alda   TRATTORIA €€
(☑ 045 770 10 18; www.dallarosalda.it; Via Sengia 15, San Giorgio di Valpolicella; meals €30-35; ☺ noon-2pm & 7-10pm Tue-Sat, noon-2pm Sun Mar–mid-Nov; ℗) In San Giorgio, Trattoria Dalla Rosa Alda has been serving honest local fare since 1853, including house-made gnocchi and beef braised in Amarone. The wine cellar carved out of the rock features an excellent Veronese selection. There are also 10 rooms for overnighters (singles €65, doubles €90 to €120).

Soave

Southeast of Verona and an easy day trip, Soave serves its namesake DOC white wine in a story-book setting. The town is entirely encircled by medieval fortifications, including 24 bristling watchtowers guarding a medieval castle. Wine is the main reason to come here, with tastings available throughout the year.

◉ Sights

Castello di Soave   HISTORIC BUILDING
(☑ 045 768 00 36; www.castellodisoave.it; adult/reduced €7/4; ☺ 9am-noon & 3-6.30pm Tue-Sun Apr-Oct, 9am-noon & 2-4pm daily Nov-Mar) Built on a medieval base by Verona's fratricidal Scaligeri family, the Castello complex encompasses an early Renaissance villa, grassy courtyards, the remnants of a Romanesque church and the Mastio (the defensive tower apparently used as a dungeon): during restoration, a mound of human bones was unearthed here. The highlight for most, however, will be the panoramas of the surrounding countryside from the many rampart viewing points.

★**Suavia**   WINERY
(☑ 045 767 50 89; www.suavia.it; Via Centro 14, Fittà; ☺ 9am-1pm & 2.30-6.30pm Mon-Fri, 9am-1pm Sat & by appointment; ℗) Soave is not known as a complex white, but this trailblazing winery, located 8km outside Soave via the SP39, has been changing the viticultural landscape in recent years. Don't miss DOC Monte Carbonare Soave Classico, with its mineral, ocean-breeze finish.

Azienda Agricola Coffele   WINERY
(☑ 045 768 00 07; www.coffele.it; Via Roma 5; wine tasting €9-12; ☺ 9.30am-7.30pm Mon-Sat, 10am-1pm & 2-7pm Sun) Across from the old-town church, this family-run winery offers tastings of lemon-zesty DOC Soave Classico and an elegant, creamy DOC Coffele Ca' Visco Classico. The family also rents out rooms among vineyards a few kilometres from town. Book wine tastings in advance; at least a day ahead in winter and about a week ahead in summer.

✖ Eating

★**Locanda Lo Scudo**   MODERN ITALIAN €€
(☑ 045 768 07 66; www.loscudo.vr.it; Via Covergnino 9; meals €35; ☺ noon-2.30pm & 7.30-10.30pm Tue-Sat, noon-2.30pm Sun; 🖘) Just outside the medieval walls of Soave, Lo Scudo is half country inn and half high-powered gastronomy. Cult classics include a risotto of scallops and porcini mushrooms, though – if it's on the menu – only a fool would resist the extraordinary dish of tortelloni stuffed with local pumpkin, Grana Padano, cinnamon, mustard and Amaretto, and topped with crispy fried sage.

Above the restaurant, the owners rent out four bright, lovely rooms (single/double €85/95) that continue the theme of countrified sophistication.

ℹ Information

Soave's **tourist office** (☏ 045 619 07 73; www.soaveturismo.it; Piazza Foro Boario I; ◷10am-5pm Mon, 9am-6pm Tue-Fri, 9am-3pm Sat & Sun Apr-Oct, 9am-5pm Tue-Fri, to 2pm Sat & Sun Nov-Mar) is just outside the medieval wall, in front of the central bus stop.

ℹ Getting There & Away

To reach Soave from Verona, take ATV bus 130 (€3.40, around one hour) from Corso Porta Nuova (the main road that links Verona's city centre to its train station). Buy tickets from the machines on the platforms. If driving, exit the A4 autostrada at San Bonifacio and follow the Viale della Vittoria 2km north into town.

MANTUA

☏ 0376 / POP 46,670

As serene as the three lakes it sits beside, Mantua (Mantova) is home to sumptuous ducal palaces and a string of atmospheric cobbled squares. Settled by the Etruscans in the 10th century, it has long been prosperous. The Latin poet Virgil was born just outside the modern town in 70 BC, Shakespeare's Romeo heard of Juliet's death here and Verdi set his tragic, 19th-century opera, *Rigoletto,* in its melancholy fog-bound streets.

◉ Sights

The intimate, tight-knit centre of Mantua is like an al fresco architectural museum – the interlocking piazzas a series of medieval and Renaissance rooms, comprising from north to south: Piazza Sordello, Piazza Broletto, Piazza delle Erbe and Piazza Mantegna. All four are packed solid with market stalls at the weekends and come early evening, waves of promenading Mantuans ebb and flow between them.

★**Palazzo Ducale**   PALACE
(☏ 041 241 18 97; www.ducalemantova.org; Piazza Sordello 40; adult/reduced €12/7.50; ◷8.15am-7.15pm Tue-Sat, from 1.45pm Sun) For more than 300 years the enormous Palazzo Ducale was the seat of the Gonzaga – a family of wealthy horse breeders who rose to power in the 14th century to become one

of Italy's leading Renaissance families. Their 500-room, 35,000-sq-metre palace is vast; a visit today winds through 40 of the finest chambers. Along with works by Morone and Rubens, the highlight is the witty mid-15th-century fresco by Mantegna in the Camera degli Sposi (Bridal Chamber).

Executed between 1465 and 1474, the room, which is entirely painted, shows the marquis, Lodovico, going about his courtly business with family and courtiers in tow in impressive 3D. Painted naturalistically and with great attention to perspective, the arched walls appear like windows on the courtly world – looking up at the Duke's wife Barbara, you can even see the underside of her dress as if she's seated above you. Most playful of all though is the *trompe l'œil* oculus featuring bare-bottomed *putti* (cherubs) – the point of view is quite distastefully realistic in places – balancing precariously on a painted balcony, while smirking courtly pranksters appear ready to drop a large potted plant on gawping tourists below.

Other palace highlights are the Sala di Troia, Frederico II's council chamber entirely done out in Trojan War scenes and Rubens' *Adoration of the Holy Trinity* in the Sala degli Arcieri (Room of Archers), which Napoleonic troops brutally dismembered in 1797. In room 8, the Sala del Pisanello, fragments and preliminary sketches of Pisanello's frescoes of Arthurian knights remain, while room 24, the Sala dello Zodiaco sports a ceiling representing the heavens studded with starry constellations.

The palace's finest remaining features are its frescoed and gilt ceilings including, in room 2, a labyrinth, prophetically predicting the capricious nature of good fortune. Below it, as if in illustration, are two portraits of Eleanor Gonzaga (1630–86), who rose to marry a Habsburg emperor, and Vicenzo II (1594–1627), who lost the entire family fortune and one of Europe's most enviable art collections.

ℹ **MANTUA CARD**

The Mantova Card (adult/reduced €20/€8) covers entry to all the main attractions, plus discounted entry to other regional museums such as those in Sabbioneta. Ask at the tourist office.

Mantua

Rooms 34 to 36 house the **Stanze degli Arazzi**, some of the only original artworks commissioned by the family: nine 16th-century Flemish tapestries reproduced from Raphael's original designs for the Sistine Chapel. Woven in Brussels using the finest English wool, Indian silk and Cypriot gold and silver thread, they represent the cosmopolitan sophistication of the Gonzaga court at the height of its power.

0 200 m
0 0.1 miles
E
F
1
2
3
4
5
6
Lake Mezzo
Boats to San Benedetto Po, Venice & Mincio
Verona (38km)
8
Via San Giorgio
Via Legnago
Piazza Castello
1
Piazza Santa Barbara
Palazzo Ducale
Boats to San Benedetto Po, Venice & Mincio
Lungolago dei Gonzaga
Piazza Arche
11
Lake Inferiore
Via Fondamenta

Mantua

Top Sights
1 Palazzo Ducale E3

Sights
2 Basilica di Sant'Andrea C4
3 Palazzo della Ragione C4
4 Piazza delle Erbe C4
5 Rotonda di San Lorenzo C4
6 Teatro Bibiena D5

Activities, Courses & Tours
7 La Rigola D6
8 Motonavi Andes E3
9 Navi Andes Office D4
10 Visit Mantua D4

Eating
11 Fragoletta E5
12 Il Cigno A3
13 Osteria delle Quattro Tette C3
14 Salumeria C5

Drinking & Nightlife
15 Bar Caravatti C4

★ **Palazzo Te** PALACE

(☎0376 36 58 86; www.palazzote.it; Viale Te 13; adult/reduced €12/8; ⏲1-6.30pm Mon, 9am-6.30pm Tue-Sun) Palazzo Te was where Frederico II Gonzaga escaped for love trysts with his mistress Isabella Boschetti, and it's decorated in playboy style with stunning frescoes, playful motifs and encoded symbols. A Renaissance pleasure-dome, it is the finest work of star architect Giulio Romano, whose sumptuous Mannerist scheme fills the palace with fanciful flights of imagination.

Having escaped a Roman prison sentence for designing pornographic prints, Romano, Raphael's most gifted student, was the perfect choice for the Palazzo Te commission. Using the *trompe l'œil* technique, he eschewed the cool classicism of the past in favour of wildly distorted perspectives, a pastel colour palette and esoteric symbols.

The second room, the **Camera delle Imprese** (Room of the Devices), sets the scene with a number of key symbols: the salamander, the symbol of Federico; the four eagles of the Gonzaga standard; and Mt Olympus, the symbol of Charles V, Holy Roman Emperor, from whom the Gonzaga received their titles and in whose name they ruled Mantua. The purpose of Renaissance devices was to encode messages, mottos and virtues so that visitors to the palace could 'read' where loyalties lay and navigate political power structures. Federico's device, the salamander, is accompanied by the quote: *Quod hic deest, me torquet* (What you lack, torments me), alluding to his notoriously

WORTH A TRIP

DAL PESCATORE

Petals of egg pasta frame slices of guinea fowl caramelised in honey saffron; silky tortellini are stuffed to bursting with pumpkin, nutmeg, cinnamon and candied *mostarda* (fruit in a sweet-mustard sauce). You practically eat the Mantuan countryside in Nadia Santini's internationally acclaimed restaurant, **Dal Pescatore** (☎ 0376 72 30 01; www. dalpescatore.com; Località Runate, Canneto sull'Oglio; meals €160-260; ☺ noon-4pm & 7.30pm-late Thu-Sun, 7.30pm-late Wed; P ☀).

What's even more surprising is that the triple-Michelin-starred chef is entirely self-taught and has only ever cooked here, in what was originally the modest trattoria of her husband's family. Beneath the tutelage of her mother-in-law, who still cooks in the kitchen, Nadia learnt to create Mantuan cuisine deftly and creatively. Despite a background in food science, her food isn't remotely high-tech, but rather quietly brilliant, focusing on the essentials and balancing simplicity with the very finest natural produce.

The restaurant is located 40km west of Mantua in a green glade beside the Oglio river. Nearby, **9 Muse B&B** (☎ 335 8007601; www.9muse.it; Via Giordano Bruno 42a, Canneto sull'Oglio; s €45-55, d €73-90; P ☀ @) provides elegant and charming accommodation.

passionate nature when compared to the cold-blooded salamander.

The culmination of the symbolic narrative, however, comes together masterfully in the **Camera dei Giganti** (Chamber of the Giants), a domed room where frescoes cover every inch of wall with towering figures of the rebellious giants (disloyal subjects) clawing their way up Mt Olympus (symbol of Charles V) only to be laid low by Jupiter's (Charles') thunderbolt. The effect is spectacular. As the viewer you are both spectator and participant, standing in the centre of the scene, the worried faces of Olympian gods staring down at you.

Piazza delle Erbe   PIAZZA
Once the location of the town's vegetable market, Piazza delle Erbe is Mantua's most lively piazza. Its 13th-century **Palazzo della Ragione** (Town Hall; ☎ 0376 22 00 97; adult/reduced €3/1.50; ☺ exhibitions 10am-1pm & 3-6pm Tue-Fri, 10am-6pm Sat & Sun) sports a 15th-century clock tower at its south end that marks the phases of the moon and signs of the zodiac.

Mantua's oldest church, the 11th-century **Rotonda di San Lorenzo** (☺ 10am-1pm & 2.30-6.30pm Mon-Fri, 10am-7pm Sat & Sun) FREE, sits just below street level alongside Palazzo della Ragione.

Basilica di Sant'Andrea   BASILICA
(Piazza Mantegna; ☺ 8am-noon & 3-7pm) This towering basilica safeguards the golden vessels said to hold earth soaked by the blood of Christ. Longinus, the Roman soldier who speared Christ on the cross, is said to have scooped up the earth and buried it in Mantua after leaving Palestine. Today, these containers rest beneath a marble octagon in front of the altar and are paraded around Mantua in a grand procession on Good Friday.

Ludovico II Gonzaga commissioned Leon Battista Alberti to design the basilica in 1472. Its vast, arched interior is free from pillars and has just one sweeping central aisle, which is dotted with frescoes, gilded ceiling bosses and columns cleverly painted to look like carved stone.

The first chapel on the left contains the tomb of Andrea Mantegna, the man responsible for the splendours of Mantua's most famous paintings – those in the Camera degli Sposi in the Palazzo Ducale. The chapel is beautifully lit and also contains a painting of the Holy Family and John the Baptist, attributed to Mantegna and his school.

Teatro Bibiena   THEATRE
(Teatro Scientifico; ☎ 0376 28 82 08; Via dell'Accademia 47; adult/reduced €2/1.20; ☺ 10am-1pm & 3-6pm Tue-Fri, 10am-6pm Sat & Sun) If ever a theatre were set to upstage the actors, it's the 18th-century Teatro Bibiena. Dimly lit and festooned with plush velvet, its highly unusual, intimate bell-shaped design sees four storeys of ornate, stucco balconies arranged around curving walls. It was specifically intended to allow its patrons to be seen – balconies even fill the wall behind the stage. You

can wander round at will during the day or come to an evening performance to see the building come alive. Just a few weeks after it opened in 1769 the theatre hosted a concert by a 14-year-old prodigy – one Wolfgang Amadeus Mozart.

🏃 Activities

On a sunny day the people of Mantua head for the waterfront, where grassy banks throng with fishermen and picnicking families. Each of the three lakes has a distinct style. The shore of **Lake Mezzo**, complete with the child-friendly gadgets of the **Parco dell Scienza** (outdoor science park), is the most crowded; the quieter path beside **Lake Superiore** meanders amid reed beds and wading birds; while the shore of **Lake Inferiore** brings broad views.

La Rigola   CYCLING
(☑ 0335 605 49 58; Via Trieste 5; per day from €10; ⊙ 9.30am-12.30pm & 2.30-7.30pm) Rent bikes by the day to explore the surrounding lakes, the Po river and the Parco del Mincio (www.parcodelmincio.it). The shortest route (a couple of hours) takes cyclists around Lago Superiore to the Santuario di Santa Maria delle Grazie, while longer routes meander south to the abbey of San Benedetto Po and the Gonzaga town of Sabbioneta

👣 Tours

★Visit Mantua   WALKING
(☑ 347 4022020; www.visitmantua.it; tours per 2 people 90min/5hr €100/300) Get the insider view of Renaissance dukes and duchesses – what they ate for breakfast, how they conspired at court and the wardrobe crises of the day – with Lorenzo Bonoldi's fascinating conversational tours of Mantua's highlight palaces. Tours leave from Piazza Sordello 40.

Motonavi Andes   BOATING
(☑ 0376 32 28 75; www.motonaviandes.it; Via San Giorgio 2) Motonavi Andes run frequent boat tours of Mantua's lakes (starting from €9 for 1½ hours) as well as other occasional cruises along the Po and to the Parco del Mincio.

Navi Andes Office   BOATING
(☑ 0376 32 45 06; www.naviandes.com; Piazza Sordello 48) Runs a wide range of boat trips, including a two-hour cruise on Lago Superiore (€13) and trips to Parco del Mincio (adult/reduced from €10/8.)

🍴 Eating & Drinking

Osteria delle Quattro Tette   OSTERIA €
(☑ 0376 32 94 78; Vicolo Nazione 4; meals €10-15; ⊙ 12.30-2.30pm Mon-Sat) Queue then grab a pew at rough-hewn wooden tables beneath unadorned barrel-vaulted ceilings and order up pumpkin pancakes, pike in sweet salsa or *risotto alla pilota* (risotto with spiced sausage). It's spartan but extremely well priced, which is why half of Mantua is in here at lunchtime. Lingering after your meal is not the done thing. It's easy to miss – look out for the cobbled alley (Vicolo Nazione) leading off Via Cavour. Cash only.

Salumeria   DELI €
(Via Orefici 16; ⊙ 7.30am-1pm & 4-7.30pm Tue-Sun, 7.30am-1pm Mon) Step into this traditional deli and feel the clock turning right back. Hanging hams and salami, stacks of pungent local cheese and see-through vats of Mantua's speciality *mostarda* ensure prime picnic shopping. There are wines to wash it all down with, too.

Fragoletta   LOMBARD €€
(☑ 0376 32 33 00; www.fragoletta.it; Piazza Arche 5; meals €35; ⊙ noon-3pm & 8pm-midnight Tue-Sun) Wooden chairs scrape against the tiled floor as diners eagerly tuck into Slow Food–accredited *culatello di Zibello* (lard) at this friendly local trattoria. Other Mantuan specialities feature, such as *risotto alla pilota* (rice studded with sausage meat) and pumpkin ravioli with melted butter and sage. Dine in the back room and you'll be surrounded by bright home-made art amid stacks of wine crates.

★Il Cigno   MODERN ITALIAN €€€
(☑ 0376 32 71 01; Piazza d'Arco 1; meals €60; ⊙ 12.30-1.45pm & 7.30-9.45pm Wed-Sun) The building is as beautiful as the food: a lemon-yellow facade dotted with faded olive-green shutters. Inside, Mantua's gourmets graze on delicately steamed risotto with spring greens, poached cod with polenta or gamey guinea fowl with spicy Mantuan *mostarda*.

Bar Caravatti   BAR
(☑ 0376 32 78 26; Portici Broletto 16; ⊙ 7am-8.30pm Sun-Thu, to midnight Fri & Sat) All of Mantua passes through Caravatti at some point during the day for coffee, *spritz* or Signor Caravatti's 19th-century *aperitivo* of aromatic bitters and wine.

ⓘ Information

Tourist Office (☎ 0376 43 24 32; www.turismo.mantova.it; Piazza Mantegna 6; ☺ 9am-5pm Sun-Thu, to 6pm Fri & Sat)

ⓘ Getting There & Away

BOAT

Boats depart from the jetties on **Viale Mincio** and **Longolaga dei Gonzaga** to San Benedetto Po, Venice and Mincio. The **Motonavi Andes boats to Lake Superiore** depart from the jetty north of the train station.

BUS

APAM (☎ 0376 23 03 39; www.apam.it) operates buses to Sabbioneta, San Benedetto Po and Brescia. Most leave from the **bus station**, near the **train station** on Piazza Don Leoni, but some leave from Viale Risorgimento.

At the weekend, a special service leaves from outside Palazzo Ducale to the Gonzaga's smaller country fiefdom of Sabbioneta (€8 return,

one hour, 3pm Saturday, 9am and 1.15pm Sunday).

An express service also operates from Piazza Sordello and Piazza don Leoni for Verona airport (adult/child €5/free, 45 minutes, four daily).

CAR

Mantua is just west of the A22 Modena–Verona–Trento autostrada; the best exit is Mantua North. The city is 45km south of Verona and around 50km south of Lake Garda.

Much of old Mantua is a traffic-restricted zone. There is free parking along the city's northern lake road (Viale Mincio) and to the south of the city along Viale Isonzo, near Palazzo Te.

TRAIN

Direct trains link Mantua with Verona (€3.95, 50 minutes, hourly) and Milan (€11.50, two hours, every two hours). The trip to Lake Garda's Peschiera del Garda train station (€6.25, 70 minutes, hourly) involves a change in Verona.

Understand the Italian Lakes

The Italian Lakes Today

News flash: Italy was not cryogenically frozen six centuries ago. Lombardy is one of Europe's most creative corners, contributing 20% of Italian GDP, standing alongside Baden-Württemberg, Rhône-Alpes and Catalonia as one of the Four Motors for Europe. Just look around you, and you'll see breakthrough ideas literally popping up: urban art projects, sustainable architecture and cutting-edge design and fashion. As Leonardo da Vinci did in the past, Lombards are busy pioneering the future.

Best on Film

Miracolo a Milano (Miracle in Milan; 1951) Vittorio de Sica's fairy tale about a boy given the gift of miracles.

Rocco and His Brothers (1960) Luchino Visconti's take on southern immigration, boxing and brotherhood.

Romeo & Juliet (1968) Franco Zeffirelli's film is still the best adaptation of Shakespeare's love story.

Teorema (1968) Pier Paolo Pasolini sets Terence Stamp loose on a haute-bourgeois Milanese family.

Che Bella Giornata (What a Beautiful Day; 2011) Gennaro Nunziante's comedy about a security guard from Brianza is Italy's most commercially successful film.

Best in Print

I Promessi Sposi (The Betrothed; 1827) Alessandro Manzoni's tale of two lovers, and a country, longing to be united.

Design as Art (1966) Illuminating text by designer Bruno Munari.

Accidental Death of an Anarchist (1970) A sly comedy by Dario Fo.

Voices from the Plains (1985) Gianni Celati's arresting stories of chance encounters on the Po plains.

Italian Neighbours (1992) Tim Parks writing about his home town, Verona.

Northern Powerhouse

Stand at the base of Milan's cloud-piercing, LEED-certified UniCredit Tower and you'll understand why Lombards think their regional capital, Milan, is Italy's guiding light. This region – home to 17% of all Italians, 826,000 businesses and 30% of all multinationals in Italy – has in the last few years become an irresistible magnet for the brightest and best, who flock here to work in design, media, fashion, food, biotech, finance, engineering and technology. Milan and Lombardy play a vital role in European manufacturing and agriculture, bringing together industry and services, art and culture, university research and new technology giants.

Towns like Brescia, Bergamo, Monza, Brianza, Varese, Lecco and Como, let alone Milan, represent some of the most specialised manufacturing areas on the continent, placing the region 10th when compared with other European countries. Since the financial crash of 2008, vast sums of money have been invested in Milan's Porta Nuova and CityLife developments, the largest in the country since WWII. And, in the wake of the successful Expo 2015, Milan now has some of the best infrastructure in Europe: reachable by high-speed rail, three highways and an intercontinental airport. By 2024, the Expo area itself is earmarked to become a 'Human Technopole', housing the scientific faculties of the University of Milan and a new life sciences research centre.

A Cultural Renaissance

It's not just business, finance and science that this region excels at – the fashion, design, food and art worlds speak Lombard too. The 'Made in Italy' brand (much of it made in northern Italy) accounts for 30% of the €32 billion global design market. Fashion mecca Milan, bustles with over 12,000 fashion and design companies, 800 showrooms and 6000 sales outlets, and the Salone del Mobile is now a global reference point for design.

Public spaces have also been transformed with new contemporary architecture dedicated to cultural institutions such as the Fondazione Prada and the Fondazione Feltrinelli; La Scala and Piccolo Teatro are enjoying their best and most diverse seasons in a decade; Milan's and Verona's contemporary art fairs continue to garner increasing international attention; and Milan's fashion shows, criticised as 'grandmotherly' in 2014, are once again contending with Paris following Gucci's headline-grabbing AW17 show.

Important restoration work has also drawn attention to regional gems such as Monza's magnificent Villa Reale (reopened in 2014); Bergamo's world-class fine art museum, Accademia Carrara (reopened in 2015); San Pellegrino's lovely art nouveau casino (reopened in 2015); and Mantua's fabulous art and architecture, highlighted when the city was nominated a Capital of Culture in 2016. In the same year, Unioncamere and Fondazione Symbola released a report confirming that Lombardy's cultural assets generate €23 million per year (26% of the Italian total). Hardly surprising, then, that tourism is an increasingly important part of the region's economy: with 49 million registered arrivals in 2016, Milan now ranks as the world's 14th most visited city.

The Future is Sustainable

Expo 2015's focus on sustainable food production continues in Lombardy. In May 2017, Milan hosted Seeds & Chips, a global conference on technology and food innovation, where former US president Barack Obama appeared as the keynote speaker – a major coup for the conference and the city.

Aside from Milan's Urban Food Policy Pact, which commits the city to the development of a sustainable urban food system (including the largest composting initiative in the world), this emphasis on sustainability has resulted in positive spin-offs for regional development. Lombard universities have an ambitious agenda to build a global brand around Lombard food expertise; the newly formed Cluster CAT.AL aims to drive innovation in the agrifood sector; biogas plants are sprouting up in Cremona, Brescia and Pavia; and silk company Canepa is pioneering a new water-friendly eco-material. Furthermore, an increasing number of LEED Gold Certified buildings, such as the new Gucci headquarters in Milan, demonstrate northern Italy's commitment to building a future that is not only beautiful, but healthy as well.

POPULATION: **10.03 MILLION**

AREA: **23,844 SQ KM**

GDP: **€330 BILLION**

GDP PER CAPITA: **€33,100**

UNEMPLOYMENT: **7.9%**

if the Italian lakes were 100 people

91 would be Italian
3 would be Romanian
2 would be Moroccan
2 would be Albanian
2 would be Other

employment rate
(% of population)

74 Men
56 Women

population per sq km

MILAN | LOMBARDY | ITALY

† ≈ 205 people

History

Northern Italy, with its head full of jagged Alpine teeth and its feet paddling in the deltas of the Po river, has been both blessed and cursed by its geography. Despite their awesome appearance, Alpine passes have been in use since the Bronze Age. Carthaginian general Hannibal brought his army and elephants across the Alps, and Alaric and Attila marauded from the east. Yet those pearly white peaks and broad delta have also been the making of the northern Italian powerhouse.

Cisalpine Gaul

The Romans didn't consider wild Cisalpine Gaul (meaning Gaul on the near side of the Alps) part of Italy at all and stayed well away until the Gauls swept south through Etruria and sacked Rome in 387 BC. Then they sided with the Carthaginians in the Punic Wars (264–146 BC) so Rome marched north, subduing Mediolanum (Milan) in 221 BC and establishing Roman garrisons at Piacenza, Como and Cremona. The Romanisation of the region was accomplished through a combination of military and political inducement: adversaries were disarmed by the grant of citizenship (which brought with it social, legal and economic privileges), while Roman culture wowed the masses with its impressive civic buildings, literature and philosophy.

Julius Caesar was made consul of northern Italy in 59 BC and found it a fruitful recruitment ground. He took his legions into neighbouring Gaul (modern France) on a campaign of conquests that would last until 51 BC. They provided him with a strong-enough power base to cross the Rubicon and embark on the Italian civil war (49–46 BC) that would lead him to absolute power in 45 BC. None of this would have been possible without the loyalty of Cisalpine Gaul.

Mediolanum was by then a prosperous city astride key routes. The city supplied arms for the empire's insatiable war machine, traded wool, hides and metal, and boasted a theatre, university, forum, mint and many fine temples and palaces, remnants of which survive in the Basilica di San Lorenzo and the palace ruins in Via Brisa. The lakes became

Lombardy's first designers set to zealously decorating their surrounds; the rocky Val Camonica to Milan's northeast is covered in 150,000 engraved petroglyphs dating back to 8000 BC that gleefully depict figures hunting, farming, making magic and indulging in wild sexual antics. It was recognised a World Heritage Site in 1979.

TIMELINE	11,000 BC	c 600–400 BC	218 BC
	Accounts of Roman historian Titus Livius point to the invasion of the Lombard plains and Po valley by Gallic tribes from southern France as early as the 10th century BC.	According to legend, the Insubri Gauls chose the site of Milan when their greedy king glimpsed a bristle-backed boar across the plains. They call it Mediolanum (Middle of the Plains).	Carthaginian general Hannibal crosses the Alps into the Lombard plains and 50,000 Gauls join his forces. After several defeats, Rome emerges master of the Mediterranean.

a favoured holiday destination for the Roman elite; it was to a villa in Sirmione that the poet Catullus retreated when 1st-century-BC 'it girl' Clodia Metelli broke his heart. As the empire crumbled in the 4th century, Mediolanum, with its strategic position by the Rhine frontier, became home to the imperial court.

The Long Beards & Franks

Despite an unprecedented three centuries of relative tranquillity, Lombardy got its name not from the Romans, but the *langobardi* (long beards). A Germanic people from across the Danube, they marched into northern Italy almost unopposed in 568. Led by King Alboino (c 530s–572), they rapidly captured all the cities of the Po valley, first taking Verona and then, over the next four years, besieging Bergamo, Brescia and Milan. In 572 they captured Pavia and made it their capital.

Between this Lombard kingdom in the north and the reduced Roman seat of power in Ravenna, an uneasy peace survived for nearly 200 years, long enough for the heartlands of both to become known as Lombardy and Romagna. Much of this tenuous peace was based on a shared and growing Christian faith, championed by Milan's Archbishop Ambrose (c 340–97), Pope Gregory (540–604) and the devout Queen Theodolinda (c 570–628). Married to two Lombard kings, and Queen Regent for her young son from 616, Theodolinda was instrumental in restoring mainstream (Nicene) Christianity to the northern provinces and routing its rival, Arianism. She patronised many new churches – the oratory at Modena, the cathedral at Monza and the first baptistry in Florence – and in 628 she donated the Lombard Corrona Ferrae (Iron Crown) to the Italian Church in Monza.

Despite history dismissing this period as Italy's Dark Age, the cathedral museum at Monza houses a spectacular collection of early medieval artworks, much of it collected by Theodolinda. It includes a rich stash of Barbarian and Carolingian art, Lombard gold jewellery and 16 6th-century Palestinian ampullae (flasks) sporting the earliest depictions of the Crucifixion and the Nativity in medieval art.

With the fall of the Roman frontier at Ravenna to the Lombards in 727, when the city rebelled against a new edict banning icons, Pope Stephen II (715–57) became increasingly alarmed at expanding Lombard ambitions and turned to the Frankish ruler Pepin for military support. In return for Pepin's help and the assumption of conquered Lombard territories, Stephen named Pepin protector of the Church. It was Pepin's son, Charles, more famously known as Charlemagne (742–814), who eventually swept away the Lombard kingdom and was crowned King of Italy in 774 and Holy Roman Emperor in 800.

Roman Italia was a land of city-states that largely ran themselves. Yet the empire engendered loyalty and prosperity through free trade and a common currency, the provision of justice, and a broadminded attitude about race and class that modern Europe is having trouble emulating today.

HISTORY THE LONG BEARDS & FRANKS

49 BC	AD 313	568	773–74
The Cisalpine cities of northern Italy are granted the right to declare 'civis romanus sum' (I am a Roman citizen) in the year Caesar marched on Rome.	Roman Emperor Constantine issues the Edict of Milan, declaring Christianity the official state religion. St Ambrose becomes Bishop of Milan 61 years later.	Germanic tribes known as Lombards (or Langobards) occupy northern Italy, making Pavia their capital and giving the Po valley its present name.	Charlemagne leads Frankish troops into Italy, defeats the Lombards and has himself crowned with the legendary Iron Crown. The Lombards pay homage to him at Pavia.

Frederick Barbarossa

By the 11th century, the overextended Holy Roman Empire was ill equipped to administer its thriving Italian colonies. The growth and prosperity of the cities gave their citizens the desire to run their own affairs. Unwilling to accept an absentee foreigner with doubtful rights of sovereignty, they were soon electing their own leaders, running their own courts and raising their own militias.

Frederick I (1122–90), Duke of Swabia, who became emperor in 1155, was determined to reverse this drift and restore the empire to the powerful force it had been under Charlemagne. A feted warrior, with grandiose notions of his rights, he became renown as a symbol of Teutonic unity, a hero to German romantics and an inspiration for Adolf Hitler.

The defiance of anti-imperial Milan, the largest Italian city, and its subjugation of pro-imperial neighbours Pavia, Lodi and Como, inspired Frederick to invade Italy. He captured Milan in 1162 and destroyed it utterly, earning his nickname Barbarossa (red beard) both for the colour of his beard and the ferocity with which he fought. He also obliterated the towns of Cremona and Crema, which likewise resisted him.

But these triumphs and the humiliations of the conquered, who were made to parade before Frederick barefoot with swords and ropes around their necks, were to be short lived as his actions prompted the formation of the Lombard League (1167). Uniting 16 Lombard cities, the League promised to aid anyone threatened by Frederick's armies, and although a few member states dropped out in subsequent years, the League held long enough to rout Frederick's armies at Legnano in 1176. This historic defeat forced Barbarossa to the negotiating table, and at the Treaty of Constance in 1183 he conceded the rights of the *comune* (city-state) to elect their own leaders, make their own laws and administer their own territories.

Feminist Icons

Queen Theodolinda
Church builder and art collector

Beatrice d'Este
Fashion icon and art patron

Isabella d'Este
Political maven and intellectual

Sofonisba Anguissola
Renaissance painter

Empress Maria Theresa
Civil rights champion

A New Law & Order

Medieval Italians described their *comuni* as if it were an earthly paradise, where life was regulated by sublime statutes framed by learned lawyers. They were proud of their appearances, too. Since things were constructed in their name they could take proprietorial interest in the paving of streets, the layout of squares and the building of bridges.

Bonvesin de la Riva was a typical medieval citizen. A well-to-do Milanese, he belonged to an order of monks called the Umilati. Thanks to his magnus opus, *De Magnalibus Mediolani* (The Marvels of Medieval Milan), which he penned in the spring of 1288, we have quite an image of medieval Milan, the largest city of the peninsula in the 13th century. Milan, he tells us, is exalted among cities 'like the eagle above birds'. He

800	1098	1176	1329
Having conquered and Christianised Friuli, Saxony, Swabia, Bavaria, Hungary, Gascony and northern Spain, Pope Leo III crowns Charles Holy Roman Emperor on Christmas Day.	Milan becomes a *commune*, an increasingly independent city-state. Bergamo, Brescia, Como, Cremona, Mantua and Verona follow suit in the ensuing 30 years.	Defeated by the Lombard League, Frederick Barbarossa sues for peace. Peace between Frederick and Pope Alexander III is achieved in 1177 with the Treaty of Venice.	Azzone Visconti becomes the first strongman of Milan. In his 10 years as Lord of Milan he annexes Bergamo, Como, Crema, Cremona, Lecco, Lodi and Vercelli among other territories.

THE IRON CROWN
....

Despite its small size, the heavily jewelled Corrona Ferrae (Iron Crown) is one of the most significant symbols of royalty in Western Europe. It is called the Iron Crown because of the 'iron' band (revealed to be silver in later tests) that encircles the inside of the diadem, which according to legend was beaten out of a nail used at the Crucifixion. This makes the crown both a religious relic worthy of veneration, as well as a potent symbol of monarchy.

As with most medieval relics, the nail is said to have been discovered by St Helena, mother to Constantine, the first Christian Roman Emperor, who allegedly dispatched it to Theodolinda, regent of the Lombards, for her good work in converting her people to Christianity. Although no pre-12th-century records survive, the crown was purportedly used in the coronation of Charlemagne and in 34 subsequent coronations, including those of Frederick Barbarossa, Charles V, Napoleon and Ferdinand I of Austria, who was the last Italian king to be crowned with it in 1838.

Before surrendering Lombardy to the newly unified Italian state, the Austrians removed the crown to Vienna, but in 1866 when they were finally defeated, the peace terms stipulated the return of the crown to Monza where it is now on display in the cathedral museum. While the new Italian monarchs eschewed coronations, the Iron Crown was carried behind the funeral cortege of King Vittorio Emanuele II (1820–78), the first king of independent Italy.

HISTORY A NEW LAW & ORDER

goes on to enumerate its admirable features: aside from its 'wondrous rotundity', it had 6km of city wall, six monasteries and 94 chapels, 80 farriers, 440 butchers and over a thousand tavern owners. The city Bonvesin loved had a population nearing 150,000. Florence and Venice were not far behind.

But left to themselves, the *comuni* had a tendency to expand – to strengthen their borders, thwart their rivals and acquire land from weaker neighbours. By the 14th century, Milan and Venice controlled most of northern Italy and wars between the two rumbled on for decades. This endless internecine conflict, coupled with the devastating effects of the Black Death between 1348 and 1350, which killed more than 30,000 people in Milan, left people yearning for strong leadership even if losing some of their liberties was the price.

Comuni thus began inviting in strong men who could lead their cities out of crisis. The most successful of these 'temporary' leaders often refused to retire and instead became *signori,* founding long-lasting dynasties. Among the strongest were the Visconti in Milan, the Della Scala (or Scaliger) in Verona and the Gonzaga in Mantua. Under Azzone Visconti (who ruled from 1330–37), Milan took control of Bergamo, Brescia,

1386	1428	1450	1495–98
Work begins on Milan's Duomo. The Candoglia marble quarries on Lake Maggiore are requisitioned in perpetuity and new canals are built to transport materials to the city.	After defeat at the hands of Venice in the Battle of Maclodio, Milan permanently cedes control of Bergamo, Brescia and Ferrara to La Serenissima.	Soldier of fortune Francesco Sforza, married to Filippo Maria Visconti's daughter, grabs power in Milan. He aims to maintain a balance of power within Italy and keep the French out.	At the behest of Ludovico Sforza, Leonardo da Vinci starts work on *The Last Supper*. He opts for an experimental new medium, oil paint, and robes Christ in a dazzling ultramarine cloak.

Ludovico Sforza's downfall in 1499 deprived Leonardo da Vinci of his best patron. Ironically, he and Ludovico died barely 32km apart in the Loire valley in France: the duke imprisoned in the dungeon of Loches castle in 1508, and Leonardo in the manor house of Cloux at Amboise in 1519.

Como, Cremona, Lodi, Novara, Piacenza and Sondrio, extending its influence from the Ticino and the Alps in the north to the Po river in the south. In 1395 Milan annexed Verona and Vicenza, as well as Bologna, Siena and Perugia.

Southeast along the Po valley were two small but vigorous principalities, the duchy of Ferrara and the marquessate of Mantua, which by the 1400s even challenged the cultural primacy of Florence. The success of Mantua's Gonzaga dynasty owed much to their skill in choosing the winning side in regional wars. It owed even more to the political talents of Isabella d'Este, a daughter of the Duke of Ferrara who became regent of Mantua in 1519 and so enhanced the prestige of her domain that her first son became a duke and her second a cardinal.

Ludovico & Leonardo

Ludovico Sforza (1452–1508) was as handsome, vigorous and cunning as a Renaissance prince could hope to be. Known to all as Il Moro (the Moor) thanks to his dark complexion, he became de facto ruler of Milan in 1481 after usurping his feckless nephew Giangaleazzo. Under his cultured and crafty rule, Ludovico turned the duchy into the 'most flourishing realm in Italy', according to the envious Holy Roman Emperor Maximilian I.

He married the brilliant Beatrice d'Este (1475–97), who is widely credited with luring high-calibre Renaissance painters, musicians and architects to the court. Law and medicine flourished at the universities of Milan and Pavia. New buildings were commissioned from Bramante, and Ludovico laid the first stone of the beautiful church of Santa

THE GOOD, THE GREAT & THEIR LEGACIES

The della ScalaClan Verona's paranoid ruling *signori* who built the Castelvecchio and Arche Scaligeri.

The Gonzaga Dynasty Renaissance patrons of frescoes by Andrea Mantegna and Giulio Romano, and a grand cathedral by Leon Battista Alberti.

Giangaleazzo Visconti The figure behind Milan's Duomo and the Certosa di Pavia.

Ludovico Sforza Patron to Leonarda da Vinci and commissioner of *The Last Supper*.

Bartolomeo Colleoni Venice's mercenary commander whose mausoleum is the Cappella Colleoni in Bergamo.

Empress Maria Theresa The empress who ordered the building of La Scala in Milan.

Benito Mussolini Author of Milan's Fascist icon the Stazione Centrale and Brescia's Piazza della Vittoria.

1499	1510	1515	c 1550
A confederation of Swiss-German cantons wins independence from Austrian Habsburg control. Four years afterwards, they take Bellinzona from the Sforzas.	Pliny, Ovid and Virgil all wrote about mulberry trees. In 1510 entrepreneur Pietro Boldoni realises their profit-making potential and establishes the first silk spinning mills on Lake Como.	Milanese and Swiss forces are defeated by François I at Marignano (modern-day Melegnano); the present-day border between Lombardy and Ticino is established.	Following Columbus' return from the New World in the late 1400s with maize, Lombard farmers take up corn production. Corn, in the form of polenta, becomes a staple.

Maria dei Miracoli with his own hands. But Ludovico could not rest easy. Giangaleazzo's father-in-law was Alfonso II, the king of Naples, whose daughter Isabella deplored Ludovico's scheming and did not fail to report her sufferings to her father. Ludovico was told to beware of assassins.

Among the brilliant courtiers in Ludovico's court was Leonardo da Vinci, who was the same age as the duke. By the accounts of early biographers he, too, was strikingly handsome. He had long hair, long eyelashes and a very long beard. One itemised list of clothing notes a rose-coloured Catalan gown, dusty-rose hose, a purple cape with a velvet hood and another of crimson satin. He had brawn and vigour too. During his absences from court, he climbed the barren peaks north of Lake Como, seeking fossils and developing a taste for Valtellina wines. An epitome of masculinity, he bore the title *pictor et ingeniarius ducalis:* the duke's painter and engineer.

Leonardo had come to Milan, aged 30, in the hopes of inventing and constructing fearsome war machines such as chariots, cannons and catapults. His hopes were no doubt bolstered by the fact that Milan was at war with Venice, with Ludovico spending almost 75% of his revenues on warfare. But although visions of war filled his head, he was set to work on more modest tasks such as designing costumes for weddings and banquets, decorating the halls of the castle, fashioning elaborate stage sets for pageants, and painting portraits of Il Moro's mistresses, Cecilia Gallerani and Lucrezia Crivelli.

But if Il Moro underused Leonardo, he at least offered the temperamental artist creative latitude and financial security. For the better part of two decades, Leonardo was allowed to pursue his intellectual explorations through aeronautics, anatomy, architecture, mathematics and mechanics (the wonders of which are on display in Milan's Biblioteca e Pinacoteca Ambrosiana and the Museo Nazionale della Scienza e della Tecnologia) and finally furnished the world with *The Last Supper* (Il Cenacolo), an artwork of such unquestionable superiority it swept away the efforts of even the greatest masters before him. In 1489, commissioners for the decorations in Orvieto cathedral in Umbria declared Pietro Perugino the most famous painter in all of Italy. But when Perugino unveiled his altarpiece in 1505, he was ridiculed for his lack of ability and want of originality. By 1505, Leonardo had changed the way people saw the world.

Historical Reads

Twilight in Italy (1911),
DH Lawrence

Mussolini (2002),
RJ Bosworth

Dark Heart of Italy (2003),
Tobias Jones

Silvio Berlusconi: Television, Power and Patrimony (2004),
Paul Ginsborg

Winning at All Costs (2007),
John Foot

The Pursuit of Italy (2012),
David Gilmour

Foreign Rule

As a relation of the Angevins, Charles VIII had a weak claim to the throne of Naples, which he was encouraged to revive by Ludovico Sforza, who wanted to rid himself of the Neapolitan threat, Alfonso II. And so, in 1494, the French king marched down the peninsula unopposed and occupied Naples in February 1495.

1630–31	1713	1760s	1799
Neglected by Spanish governors, Lombardy sinks into provincial decay and a devastating plague sweeps across the region, killing almost half the population of Milan.	The Treaty of Utrecht ends the War of the Spanish Succession and thwarts French ambitions. Spanish territories, including Lombardy, are given to Austria to restore the balance of continental power.	Milan, along with Venice, Turin, Florence and the lakes, becomes an essential stop for British aristocrats on the Grand Tour, a trend that continues until the 1840s.	Como's most famous son, Alessandro Volta (1745–1827), invents the electric battery. Professor at the University of Pavia, he is made a count by Napoleon in 1810.

In 1512 the Swiss helped Ludovico's son Massimiliano return to the ducal throne of Milan, but a Franco-Venetian alliance soon reversed that situation. Beaten by the forces of François I at the Battle of Marignano in 1515, the Swiss retreated over the border and never embarked on foreign war again.

After an enthusiastic welcome, Charles made himself popular by slashing taxes and throwing banquets, but he was far too venal for his popularity to last. As the French army sickened from syphilis he found himself opposed by a Holy League that included Venice, Mantua, Florence, the Pope as well as Ludovico who, perturbed by the garrisoning of Charles' cousin and would-be claimant to the Milanese duchy, Louis of Orléans, at Asti, had switched sides.

Making a run for the north, troops of the Holy League, led by Francesco II Gonzaga, caught up with Charles at Fornovo. Outnumbered three to one and with their artillery rendered useless by the pouring rain, the French were brutally exposed. But instead of inflicting a crushing defeat, the Italian troops broke rank and made straight for the booty-laden French wagons. Since the French continued retreating after the battle, Francesco claimed a dubious victory and even had Mantegna paint the *Madonna della Vittoria* (The Madonna of Victory) in commemoration.

Charles' uncontested march on Naples showed how easy a conquest Italy was. It encouraged Charles' cousin, and the next king of France, Louis of Orléans, to emulate him in 1499 – leading an invasion which led to the overthrow and capture of Ludovico Sforza.

As the struggle for supremacy in western Europe escalated between the French and Spanish in the 16th century, the French invasions of Italy brought Spain into the northern half of the country. Lying directly between Naples, which Emperor Charles V inherited from his Spanish mother, and Germany, which he claimed through his Habsburg grandfather, Lombardy was the inevitable battleground. Following the death of the last Sforza duke in 1535, Charles took control of the duchy of Milan and gave it to his son Philip II (1527–98), the future Spanish king. Thus the political and cultural independence of Milan was extinguished forever.

The Five-Day Revolt

Napoleon's greatest legacy as the king of Italy (1805–14) was a new-found sense of nationalism. When his adversaries gathered in Vienna in 1814 to restore Europe's pre-Napoleonic borders and Lombardy's previous Austrian rulers, many Milanese in the Italian contingent complained. One of them told Lord Castlereagh, the British foreign secretary, that Italians were no longer satisfied to languish beneath paternalistic Austrian rule. But the great powers of Europe – Britain, Russia, Prussia and Austria – weren't inclined to listen. If the Austrians were going to have to give up the Netherlands, then they wanted their northern Italian territories back.

Filled with prosperous industrialists and intellectuals, Milan now chaffed under Austrian rule, not because it was bad, but because they were occupiers. Poet-prophet Vittorio Alfieri (1749–1803) and statesman Massimo d'Azeglio (1798–1866) were ashamed by Italy's subjugation and

1805	1805–14	1814–15	1848
Milan's Duomo is finished for the coronation of Napoleon Bonaparte, who crowns himself King of Italy with the Iron Crown and the words, 'God gives it to me, beware whoever touches it'.	Italy becomes a battle-ground between Napoleon, the Habsburgs and their Russian allies, thousands of Italians are conscripted and much of the region's cultural patrimony is stolen.	The Congress of Vienna re-establishes the pre-Napoleonic European borders with Lombardy and the Veneto joined as a single 'kingdom' beneath Austrian rule.	Revolts across Europe spark rebellion in Italy. King Carlo Alberto of Piedmont joins the Lombards against Austria, but within a year the latter recovers Lombardy and the Veneto.

were convinced that the country's dignity could only be restored through martial ardour. Other artists and intellectuals joined Azeglio in searching history for material they could weave into their patriotic propaganda promoting unity and independence, but they had a hard time finding suitable examples (after all the Battle of Legnano was over 600 years ago). The only work of the era that has truly lasted is Alessandro Manzoni's *I Promessi Sposi* (The Betrothed; 1827), a book that acquired the status of national monument soon after its publication, written as it was in the new 'Italian' language.

Other idealogues like Milanese philosopher Carlo Cattaneo (1801–69) advocated for a federal system, arguing that Italy's 'ancient love of liberty' was more important that 'the cult of unity'. Cattaneo pointed out how medieval Italy had prospered from civic competition and he presciently argued that a political system that failed to take into account the communal ethos would not succeed.

In 1848, Italy began the year with revolution. First an uprising broke out in Sicily in January, where insurgents forced Ferdinand II to grant his kingdom a constitution. By March, constitutions had also been proclaimed in Tuscany, Piedmont and Rome and further insurrections were breaking out in Venice, Milan, Parma and Modena. When the Cinque Giornate di Milano (Five Days of Milan) broke out on 18 March, Cattaneo threw himself into the street fighting, joining rebels bent on forcing Austrian commander, Marshal Radetzky, out of the city. Together with democrats Enrico Cernuschi, Giulio Terzaghi and Giorgio Clerici, Cattaneo formed a council of war in Via Bigli from where he helped direct operations, refusing all offers of an armistice and insisting on the complete evacuation of Radetzky's forces from Lombardy.

The revolts in Milan and, more importantly, in Venice (where the rebels held out until well into 1849) may have failed but they provided essential fuel for those clamouring for Italian unification. The diplomatic offensive to this end came from the Duchy of Savoy, whose capital was in Turin. Ably led by prime minister Count Camillo Benso Cavour, the House of Savoy struck a deal with France's Napoleon III. In 1859, Savoyard and Napoleonic troops defeated the Austrians at Magenta (4 June) and Solferino (24 June) and within a year all of Lombardy had joined the nascent Italian kingdom. Venice did so in 1866 and unification was completed in 1870 with the taking of Rome.

Bombs & Blackshirts

Milan hadn't yet recovered from its WWI losses when influenza struck in 1918, and the economy faltered. Benito Mussolini's political career began in Milan, swiftly moving from words to direct action at the hands of his paramilitary Blackshirts. His promises of strength and national unity

---

History on Show

....

Valle Camonica
Bronze Age rock art

Santa Giulia
Brescia museum housing two Roman villas

....

Duomo, Monza
Home of the Iron Crown

....

Castello Sforzesco
Milan's mighty medieval castle

....

Science Museum, Milan
Leonardo da Vinci's models

....

Mantua
Renaissance art and architecture

1861	1870–1915	1915	1921–22
Two decades of insurrections culminate in a new Italian government, with a parliament. Vittorio Emanuele II is proclaimed king of a newly united Italy.	Milan booms, becoming the country's main railway hub and leading industrial centre. Milanese banks dominate financial markets and in 1883 one of Europe's first electric power stations is opened.	Italy enters WWI on the side of the Allies to win Italian territories still in Austrian hands. Austria had offered to cede some of these territories but Italy insists the offer is insufficient.	Mussolini forms the Fascist Party and marches on Rome. King Vittorio Emanuele III, fearful of the movement's popular power, asks Mussolini to form a government in 1922.

The Cimitero Monumentale contains a memorial to the Milanese who died in Nazi concentration camps. Designed by Studio BBPR, the pure form of a cube is traced in steel and slab marble. At its centre is earth from the camp where Gianluigi Banfi, one of BBPR's four partners, died.

had broad appeal and by 1922 he was prime minister (many turned a blind eye to his rapid assumption of absolute power until 1938, when at Hilter's behest, he introduced anti-Semitic 'race laws'). The city's Fascist monuments include San Siro, Stazione Centrale, the Triennale, Palazzo dell'Arengario and the massive Armani shop on Via Manzotti.

During WWII, the Allied forces destroyed over a quarter of the city, leaving La Scala and the Palazzo Reale in ruins. The Italian Resistance and anti-Fascist trade unions paralysed Milan with strikes and demonstrations in 1943. Italy surrendered to Allied forces on 8 September, but two weeks later Mussolini declared a new Fascist republic in Salò on Lake Garda, forcing a long, bloody fight against the Allies and a civil guerrilla war. The partisans prevailed in 1945 and Brescia earned a Gold Medal for its brave resistance against the Fascists.

Mussolini was captured near Como as he tried to escape to the border. He was executed along with his mistress, Clara Petacci, their bodies brought to Milan and displayed at a petrol station.

Comebacks & Kickbacks

A postwar manufacturing boom produced a vital growth spurt in northern Italy and change was in the air. In 1963 Umberto Eco, chafing against the conformity and insularity of Italian intellectual life, cofounded the avant-garde literary group Gruppo 63. The year 1968 brought dissent, free love and psychedelic fashions to Milan's students. The Quadrilatero d'Oro became synonymous with the fashion industry. At the same time, growing income gaps and mass migration from southern Italy inflamed underlying tensions and old political rivalries. Brigade Rosse terrorism and repressive anti-terror laws created further turmoil, giving rise to extremist groups like the right-wing Lega Nord (Northern League).

Claudia Cardinale starred in the 1984 film *Claretta* about the racy life and tragic end of Clara Petacci, Mussolini's lover. Given the chance to flee when they were captured, she instead tried in vain to shield Il Duce from the partisan execution squad's bullets.

Increasing prosperity and the glamour of the '80s and '90s brought more stability, or so it seemed. But corruption and organised crime mushroomed behind closed doors until the Tangentopoli (or 'kickback city') scandals broke in 1992. Milanese judges opened investigations and trials implicating thousands of northern politicians and high-flyers in a panoply of white-collar crimes. Led by judge Antonio di Pietro, the trials came to be known as Mani Pulite (Clean Hands) and rocked the political and business establishment.

Many spoke of the coming of a new republic, as traditional parties such as the centre-right conservative Catholic Democrazia Cristiana and centre-left Partito Socialista Italiano (PSI) crumbled. PSI chief and former prime minister Bettino Craxi chose exile in Tunisia rather than face the courts. An old pal of his, the Milan business magnate Silvio Berlusconi, saw his political opportunity and launched his Forza Italia (Go Italy!)

1940–43	1945	1946	1961
The Fascist Italian Empire joins Germany in declaring war. Italy surrenders in 1943; Mussolini refuses to comply and establishes the so-called Republic of Salò.	Partisans capture and execute Mussolini and his companion Clara Petacci on the shores of Lake Como. Their bodies are later strung up in Milan's Piazzale Loreto.	Italians vote to abolish the monarchy and King Umberto II leaves Italy, refusing to recognise the result. Sixty-three percent of Lombards vote for a republic.	With low salaries and a booming export business, Milan and its surrounding area attract vast waves of immigrants from the south – more than 80,000 settle in Milan.

campaign. He was elected prime minister in 1994 with the support of an equally colourful character from near Varese – Umberto Bossi.

Bossi's Lega Nord, founded in the 1980s on a narrow anti-immigration, anti-Rome and pro-secession (now watered down to devolution) platform, quickly pulled the rug from under Berlusconi's feet by withdrawing from the coalition, but stood with him again in his election victories of 2001 and 2008. These days Lega Nord and Liga Veneta candidates dominate the regional councils of Lombardy and Veneto. That said, although the Lega Nord polls well in regional elections its support nationally is just 12% to 13% and virtually all of Lombardy's powerful cities, with the exception of Varese, voted for centre-left candidate Umberto Ambrosoli in 2013. In June 2016, Milan voted decisively for left-leaning, independent candidate Giuseppe Sala who now leads a progressive alliance composed of the Democratic Party and Italian Left.

Reinventing the Future

When the financial crisis hit, it was estimated that throughout Lombardy the contraction in business cost companies some €12 billion in the first three months of 2009, while gross domestic product fell by 6.3%. But, in the face of global recession, Lombard entrepreneurs do what they do best, and reinvented their future with a €2.6 billion World Exposition in 2015. While critics carped that it was a costly farce, Expo's resounding success – 21 million visitors and estimated tourism profits of €6 billion – put northern Italy back on the *New York Times* 'Best List', imbued depressed citizens with a sense of optimism and kick-started the regeneration of numerous northern cities.

Milan is the seat of the Italian Stock Exchange and one of the most important European financial centres. The reliability of Lombardy's economic system is endorsed by the Moody's agency report, which conferred an Aa1 rating on the region in December 2016.

HISTORY REINVENTING THE FUTURE

1984	1994–2006	2015	2017
Umberto Bossi founds the right-wing, separatist Lega Lombarda movement, which in 1991 becomes Lega Nord and later an ally of prime minister Silvio Berlusconi.	Milanese Berlusconi's right-wing Casa delle Libertà (Liberties House) coalition wins in national polls. His decade in power is marked by economic stagnation, corruption and scandal.	Milan hosts the World Exposition on the theme 'Feeding the Planet, Energy for Life'. It occupies a 100-hectare site in Rho-Pero and is attended by 145 countries and 50 international organisations.	Work begins on the 'Human Technopole', Milan's new life sciences research centre. With seven high-tech laboratories planned, it aims to become Italy's Silicon Valley and the premier genomics institute in the world.

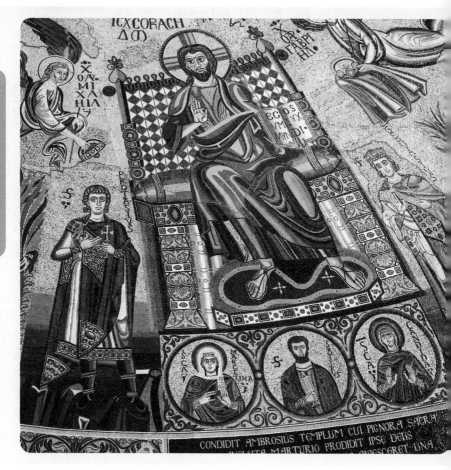

The Arts

A young Michelangelo Merisi, now better known by the name of his Lombard home town Caravaggio, got noticed in Milan with his singular style of extreme realism in 1584, while art maverick and true Renaissance man Leonardo da Vinci hung around long enough to paint *The Last Supper* and install a system of locks and levees for the city's canals. Art and architecture in Milan have always been about innovation.

Lingua Franca

Above Mosaic, Basilica di Sant'Ambrogio (p60), Milan

Virgil (70–19 BC), son of Mantua, was poet laureate of Roman Italia, penning the national epic *The Aeneid* in which he promoted the idea of Italianism by fusing Greeks, Trojans and Italic peoples into a shared Roman ancestry. His poetry had an enduring and widespread influence, providing inspiration for medieval humanists like Petrarch, Boccaccio and Dante, who made Virgil his guide in his underworld peregrinations in the *Divina Commedia* (Divine Comedy; 1555).

Other northern luminaries included poet Catullus (84–54 BC), naturalist and philosopher Pliny the Elder (23–79), writer Pliny the Younger (61–112) and historian Tacitus (56–117). Through them Romanisation continued apace, carried to all corners of the empire through its legionnaires, who spoke in Latin and retired to villas in the Po valley and around the lakes. To make them comfortable, extensive building projects were commissioned: a castrum at Como and Castelseprio, a grand arena in Verona, a forum, theatre and multitude of basilicas and temples in Mediolanum (Milan) and Brixia (Brescia), and commodious country villas at Sirmione, Desenzano del Garda and Bellagio. Many of these, such as the well-preserved Domus dell'Ortaglia in Brescia's Museo della Città, were decorated with fine mosaics, elegant peristyles (internal courtyards) and frescoes.

This rash of building gave the peninsula a common (vernacular) architectural language. The red-brick basilica with its colonnaded interior, plain facade and semicircular apses is still discernable in many of Milan's oldest churches (Sant'Eustorgio, Sant'Ambrogio, Santa Maria delle Grazie, San Lorenzo); while in Cremona, Lodi and Monza, and around the lakes, especially Lake Como, dozens of towns and villages boast Lombard Romanesque churches, distinguished by their plain facades, symmetrical layout, vaulted interiors and rounded, ornamental arcades. The Maestri Comacini (Como Masterbuilders) spread across Lombardy and Europe, some travelling as far as Catalonia (Spain) and St Petersburg (Russia).

Likewise, *volgare latino* (vernacular Latin) cut across diverse regional dialects, providing Italy with its first lingua franca. From this, modern Italian was to finally emerge nearly 1800 years later, promoted over the centuries through the works of Virgil, Petrarch, Dante and Milan's most famous novelist, Alessandro Manzoni, whose immense novel *I Promessi Sposi* (1827) is considered the first modern 'Italian' novel. On his death in 1873, Manzoni's funeral at the Cimitero Monumentale was attended by royal princes and all the heads of state, and Verdi penned his *Requiem* in honour of his memory.

A Humanist View

Almost 200 years before da Vinci's *The Last Supper* came Giotto's Renaissance breakthrough: the moving, modern 1303–05 frescoes in Padua's Capella degli Scrovegni. Medieval churchgoers were accustomed to blank stares from flat, far-off saints perched on high golden Gothic thrones, but Giotto introduced biblical figures as characters in recognisable settings, caught up in extraordinary circumstances. Onlookers gossip as middle-aged Anne tenderly kisses Joachim, and then late in life gives birth to miracle-baby Mary, and Jesus stares down Judas as the traitor puckers up with a fateful kiss.

Dante, da Vinci and Boccaccio all honour Giotto (1267-1337) as the artist who officially ended the Dark Ages. His humane approach changed how people saw themselves; not as lowly vassals but as vessels for the divine. This radical idea was the product of a new generation of Italian scholars who were rediscovering classical ideals. Poet Francesco Petrarch (1304–74) was just such a man. Like Giotto, Petrarch was patronised by Azzone Visconti, for whom he worked as an ambassador in Milan between 1353 and 1361, and where he spent his time writing to Boccaccio extolling the glories of Pavia's well-endowed library.

A seat of humanist scholarship and debate, Pavia's library contained many richly illuminated manuscripts in the *ouvraige de lombardie* tradition, a highly decorative style that emanated from Po valley workshops. At the time, manuscript illumination led the visual arts agenda in Italy

Medieval English poet Geoffrey Chaucer was linked with Milan's Visconti dukes through his patron, Lionel, Duke of Clarence, who married Violante Visconti in 1368. Chaucer mentions Bernabò Visconti ('God of delit and scourge of Lumbardye') in the exempla of tyrants in the *Monk's Tale,* while Pavia provides the setting for *The Merchant's Tale.*

and Europe and many proponents of the style like Giovannino de'Grassi (c 1340–98) – a pupil of Giotto whose Sketch Book is the prized possession of Bergamo's Angelo Mai library – and the Zavattari brothers, who executed the frescoes in Theodolinda's chapel in Monza in 1444, were extraordinary artisans.

These artist-artisans specialised in manuscript illumination, fresco, stained glass and sculpture. In fact, Grassi was also a master builder on Milan's Duomo and a consultant on the building of Pavia's cathedral. In their work they emulated Giotto's richness of colour, anecdotal representation of character and well-defined perspective. You can see the close connections between the frescoes in the Mocchirolo Oratory (reconstructed wholesale in the Pinacoteca di Brera) and the exquisite detail in Grassi's illuminated Tarocchi Brambilla (Brambilla tarot cards), also sometimes displayed in Brera, where the Lombard decorative sensibility and attention to fashion are wonderfully rendered in the costumes of Milanese nobles and St Catherine's ermine-tasselled gown.

Architecture of the Imagination

The Duomo may be the enduring symbol of Milan, but it is also one of the most famous and complex constructions of Italian Gothic architecture. Begun by Giangaleazzo Visconti in 1387, its ambitious design was considered impossible to build. Canals were constructed to transport marble to the centre of town and new technologies were invented to adapt to the never-before-attempted scale. And its slow construction – over 500 years – made its name a byword for an impossible task (*fabrica del Dom* in the Milanese dialect).

During his stint as King of Italy, Napoleon, never one to miss a chance to be associated with something monumental, offered to fund its completion in 1805. The appointed architect piled on the neo-Gothic details, displaying a prescient use of fashion logic, ie everything old is new again. The organic ferment of petrified pinnacles, cusps, buttresses, rampant arches, cyma and acroteria are almost all products of the 19th century but pay faithful homage to the original design.

The choice of the Duomo's Gothic style was inspired by 14th-century European trends, reflecting the Visconti's close links with France, Germany and Bohemia, through marriage and alliance. Although the designer is unknown, we do know that Giovannino de'Grassi was listed among the engineers in 1389. In 1395 he was painting the sacristy sculpture, and from 1396 he was involved in illuminating the transcript of Beroldo's *Treatise on the Usage of Milan Cathedral*, which he decorated with swirling plants and pinnacles. In it the close relationship between organic forms and the cathedral's architectural detail are clear. The macrocosm of the Duomo and the microcosm of manuscript decoration were part and parcel of the same stylistic universe.

The Visconti-Sforza tarot deck (1463) is one of the oldest card decks in the world. When they were commissioned, the cards were still known as Trionfi ('triumphs', ie trump) cards, and used for everyday playing. They had a significant impact on the visual composition, card numbering and interpretation of modern decks.

French, Flemish, Venetian, German and Alpine influences are evident throughout the enormous structure. Initially designed so Milan's then-population of around 40,000 could fit within, the cathedral's elegant, hysterical and sublimely spiritual architecture can even transport 21st-century types back to a medieval mindset. Inside, once your eyes adjust to the subdued light, how not to stare up, and up, to the largest stained-glass windows in all of Christendom? In the north (left) transept the Trivulzio Candelabra is one of the cathedral's original decorations. Attributed to Anglo-Norman master Nicolas de Verdun, its roiling, writhing composition of biblical figures, flora and fauna reflects the same naturalistic detail and simplicity of form that marks out Grassi's manuscripts and Baldassare degli Embriachi's extraordinary triptych (c 1390–1400) in hippopotamus ivory in the Duomo's only contemporary, the Certosa di Pavia.

Although nothing else of scale remains from the Gothic period, the era's highly decorative tradition, love of naturalism and representation of an anecdotal character captured the northern imagination and resonate across the centuries. Men like Grassi were forerunners to the burgeoning Renaissance talent of Stefano da Verona (c 1379–1438), Gentile da Fabriano (c 1370–1427) and the great Pisanello (1395–1455), who worked at the courts of Verona, Ferrara, Mantua, Milan, Rome and Naples. Pisanello foreshadowed the coming brilliance of the Renaissance with his naturalistic style so wonderfully captured in his fresco *St George and the Princess of Trebizond* in Verona's church of Sant'Anastasia, and the graphic cartoons in Mantua's Palazzo Ducale.

Classicism

In 1452 the most important Renaissance treatise on architecture, *De Re Aedificatoria* (On the Art of Building; 1485), was written by Genovese polymath Leon Battista Alberti (1404–72). Like Petrarch before him, Alberti loved the classics and grasped how the lessons of ancient Rome were pertinent to the city-states of 15th-century Italy. Regarding mathematics as the common ground between art and the sciences, Alberti made an effort to explain his thinking in his earlier publication, *De Pictura* (On Painting; 1435), which formed the first scientific study of perspective. He dedicated the treatise to Gian Francesco Gonzaga, his generous Mantuan patron.

As the Pope's architectural adviser, Alberti had plenty of time to study ancient ruins and the writings of Roman architect and engineer Vitruvius (c 80–c 15 BC). His detailed observations appeared in the 10-volume *De Re Aedificatoria,* which was to become the major reference for Renaissance architects. Eager to put his theories into practice, Alberti then set about building things. His most notable projects are the church of Santa Maria Novella in Florence and the soaring cathedral of Sant'Andrea in Mantua.

In Mantua, Alberti was given free rein to create a monumental edifice to house the Gonzaga's most precious relic, two ampoules of Christ's blood. Alberti recreated an Etruscan temple with a huge barrel-vaulted nave fronted with a triumphal arch for a facade. Fittingly, in the first chapel on the left, rests that other great classical artist Andrea Mantegna (1431–1506), whose outstanding depiction of the *Dead Christ* (1480) is thought to have been created for this chapel.

Like Alberti, Mantegna was fascinated with the classical world and experimented widely with perspective. His painted room, the *Camera degli Sposi,* in the Gonzaga's Palazzo Ducale, is the apotheosis of this study. Apprenticed in Padua, he would have come into contact with the work

Directly across from the Duomo sits Milan's other precocious feat of engineering, the Galleria Vittoria Emanuele. This soaring iron-and-glass neoclassical arcade heralded the new industrial Italy of the Risorgimento. Highly innovative for its time, the building has spawned countless imitators, right down to the glazed-roofed megamalls of today.

THE COURT PAINTER: ANDREA MANTEGNA

The first Renaissance court painter was Andrea Mantegna, who was employed by the Gonzaga marquesses of Mantua from 1460 until his death in 1506. He was a good choice for a dynasty with political pretensions. With his understanding of perspective and knowledge of the classical world, Mantegna glorified his subjects, making his nobles seem like ancient heroes as well as contemporary men. Viewers of his powerful series *The Triumph of Julius Caesar* (1484–92; now at Hampton Court in London) can sense the implied connection between his patrons and the conquering Caesar. For his pains Mantegna, a poor woodworker's son, received an extravagant income (75 lire a month), and the Gonzaga got their propaganda and the reputation they still enjoy today – that of being great patrons of the arts. Bramante, Leonardo da Vinci, Raphael and Michelangelo all followed in his footsteps and worked as court painters for powerful patrons.

Better known as an architect, Bramante embarked on numerous architectural projects in the city, most notably the church of Santa Maria presso San Satiro. With a tiny plot to work on, Bramante used all of his skills as a painter to create the illusion of a grander space with his theatrical trompe l'œil apse.

of Tuscans Paolo Uccello, Filippo Lippi and Donatello, and in 1453 he married Nicolosia Bellini, bringing him into the orbit of the celebrated Venetian Bellini brothers, Giovanni and Gentile. Synergies between their work are evident in Mantegna's gorgeous, garlanded Madonna in San Zeno Maggiore, in Verona, and the softer, more luminous *Madonna of the Cherubim* (c 1485), which sits next to Bellini's Mantegna-esque *Pietà* (1460) in the Brera gallery.

Donato Bramante (1444–1514) took his lead from Mantegna, producing the intensely poignant, but restrained, *Christ at the Column* (c 1490). Commissioned by Cardinal Ascanio Sforza for the Chiaravalle Abbey on the outskirts of Milan, the image demonstrates Bramante's research into perspective and the volumetric construction of a human body. Christ's profoundly tragic gaze, however, shows a clear dialogue with the work of Leonardo da Vinci who was working in Milan at the same time.

In the same way as Bramante, Brescian artist Vicenzo Foppa, who frescoed the Portinari chapel in Sant'Eustorgio, combined the perspective-based classicism of Mantegna with the intense compassion and realism of Leonardo.

Leonardo da Vinci

During the 15th century, wealthy Lombards like the Della Scala family in Verona and the Gonzaga in Mantua played a key role in patronising and promoting the great artists of the day, and even wealthy merchants, abbots and bankers spent their hard-earned coin on frescoing their townhouses, fashioning extraordinary mausoleums and commissioning frescoes and portraits. Medici banker Pigello Portinari commissioned Vicenzo Foppa to paint his private chapel in Milan; Venetian commander Bartolomeo Colleoni engaged Pavian architect and sculptor Giovanni Amadeo to fashion his polychrome marble mausoleum, the Cappella Colleoni, in Bergamo; and Cardinal Castiglioni hired Florentine Masolino to paint the charming frescoes in Castiglione Olona in Varese province.

From the fruitful partnership between Ludovico Sforza and Leonardo da Vinci, Milan's (and possibly the world's) most famous painting was to emerge. Leonardo's depiction of *The Last Supper* (Il Cenacolo; 1495–98), painted on a wall of the refectory adjoining the Chiesa di Santa Maria delle Grazie, shows Christ and his disciples at dinner during the

AN ENLIGHTENED VISION

The great museum tradition for which Milan is famous can be traced back to the educational aims of Counter-Reformation cardinal Federico Borromeo (1564–1631). During his 36 years as Milan's cardinal, he distinguished himself through his incorruptible episcopal virtue, academic zeal and civic patronage, applying everywhere the reformed principles laid down by the Council of Trent (1545–63).

In 1609 he founded the Biblioteca Ambrosiana, which along with Oxford's Bodleian, was one of the first public libraries in Europe. In 1618 he also donated his art collection to the Ambrosian academy and laid the foundation of a public institution that could work with the school training artists and supplying them with models and examples to copy. Not only did he make his collection available, but he compiled a catalogue called the *Musaeum,* in which he gave an explanation of his tastes and ideas about art.

In contrast to the tradition of the time, Borromeo's collection included many anti-academic works like Caravaggio's *Basket of Fruit* (1599) along with genre paintings, still lifes by Breugel and Paul Bril, and miniatures, portraits and landscapes that reflected his scientific approach and interest in visual realism. Despite being struck by the plague while feeding the poor in 1630, which led to the closure of the academy for many years, the public tradition and universal intention introduced by him were to leave an indelible mark on Milan.

dramatic moment when Christ reveals he is aware one of his followers will betray him. It is a masterful psychological study.

Painting for Leonardo was all about capturing the details, which he tirelessly recorded in his famous sketchbook. In his treatise on painting, he stated the artist had two goals: the first to represent man, and the second to capture the intentions of his mind. While the first had already been ably demonstrated by Pisanello, Mantegna, Bramante and Foppa, the second was much harder. Leonardo concluded the only way to do this was by capturing men's expressive 'gestures and movements'. It was this that he so masterfully translated into *The Last Supper,* where the drama of the scene is embodied in the disciples' reactions, both physical (upsetting glasses, recoiling backwards, lifting knives and leaning in) and in their varied facial expressions (mouths agape, brows furrowed, expressions incredulous).

So outstandingly good was Leonardo's composition that almost before the paint dried demand grew for copies. Princes, cardinals, churches and monasteries all wanted a replica, much in the way that everyone wanted a relic of the True Cross. *The Last Supper* was engraved as early as 1498; Giampietrino executed the most faithful copy on canvas in 1520 and many other copies followed in fresco, panel, canvas, marble and tapestry. Copies were produced in Venice, Antwerp and Paris. The Certosa di Pavia even had two versions. But while the results were spectacular, Leonardo's choice of oil paint was flawed; unlike traditional egg tempera, the oil paint did not bond successfully with the plaster and within a few decades began to flake. After 22 years of diligent restoration (completed in 1999), conservators estimate that 80% of the original colour has been lost.

But the legacy remains. *The Last Supper* ushered in the High Renaissance with a flourish, influencing generations of Lombard artists (Giovanni Boltraffio, Marco d'Oggiono, Bernardino Luini, Salaino, Giampietrino, Cesare da Sesto, Andrea Solari and Cristoforo Solari, whose works are scattered through the collections of the Pinacoteca di Brera, Accademia Carrara, Museo di Poldi Pezzoli and Certosa di Pavia) and laying the groundwork for Michelangelo and Raphael.

Cremonese Sofonisba Anguissola (c 1561–1625) was one of the few professional female artists of the 16th century. She set a precedent for women to be accepted as students of art and she pursued an international career at the royal court in Madrid. Despite two marriages she worked as a professional artist her whole life, until she died aged 93 in 1625.

Academies & Collectors

When Pope Clement XIV (1769–74) suppressed the Jesuit order, their grand palace and well-stocked library on Via Brera was appropriated by the ruling Austrian state. At the time Maria Theresa and her son Joseph II were engaged in a wide-ranging program of reforms in Milan, which extended to the city's educational establishments. Giuseppe Piermarini, who had designed La Scala, was chosen to adapt the palace for use as a new art academy and in 1801 Giuseppe Bossi was appointed secretary. An ardent republican, artist, connoisseur and friend of Canova and Angelica Kauffmann, Bossi assembled the nucleus of Brera's art collection.

The *pinacoteca* (gallery) was to come later in 1809, under the direction of Viceroy Eugène de Beaubarnais, in fulfilment of Napoleonic policy intent on creating cultural repositories for public edification much in the same vein as the Louvre. Prestigious works of art, considered symbols of national identity, were confiscated from churches and monasteries in the Veneto, Mantua, Ferrara, Bologna, Ravenna, Urbino and the Papal States and brought to Brera. The focus, naturally, was on the Italians (Bellini, Bramante, Luini, Mantegna, Raphael and Titian), reflecting the museum's social context and role as a great workshop of art.

At the same time men like Count Giacomo Carrara (1714–96), descended from that long line of wealthy Lombard art patrons, sought to establish a similar institution in Bergamo. Well educated and well travelled, Carrara was an art connoisseur who believed passionately in the values

Detail from *Stories of Saint Barbara* by Lorenzo Lotto, Oratorio di Suardi (p163)

Top Frescoes

The Last Supper (Milan)

Chiesa di San Maurizio (Milan)

Basilica di San Giulio (Lake Orta)

Palazzo Te (Mantua)

Chiesa di Santa Maria Foris Portas (Castelseprio)

Basilica di Sant'Abbondio (Como)

Basilica di San Zeno Maggiore (Verona)

of the Renaissance in northern Italy. By his death he had amassed 1300 works of art, all of which he bequeathed to his new Accademia Carrara in the hope of reviving the local Bergamo school, which boasted great talents such as portraitist Giovanni Moroni and Lorenzo Lotto. Although Venetian by birth, Lotto spent his most productive years in Bergamo and Brescia, leaving the glorious *Pala Martinengo* in the church of San Stefano, frescoes in the Suardi chapel in Trescore and some 20 canvases commissioned by wealthy merchants and aristocrats, many of which now live in the Carrara collection.

Although the Carrara is the grandest expression of civic-minded private patronage in Lombardy, many other enlightened individuals formed smaller, but equally impressive, collections. Count Guglielmo Lochis (1789–1859), the pro-Austrian podestà of Bergamo, donated many works from his collection to Carrara, as did art critic Giovanni Morelli (1816–91). In Milan, Gian Giacomo Poldi Pezzoli (1822–79) amassed one of the finest private collections in Europe and modelled his apartments on the house-museum that he had seen in London (which was later to become the Victoria & Albert Museum). His contemporaries, Fausto (1843–1914) and Joseph Bagatti Valsecchi (1845–1934), transformed their Milanese townhouse into a faithful copy of a Lombard-Renaissance palazzo and filled it with paintings, sculptures, glass, ceramics, textiles, books and crafts belonging to the Lombard Renaissance tradition. Other noble families, like the Melzi d'Eril, branched out into landscapes, such as those by Bernardo Bellotti, a student of Canaletto, who painted their villa at Gazzada on Lake Varese, while Napoleonic politician Count Giovanni Sommariva collected Canova statues and romantic Hayez paintings at Villa Carlotta in Tremezzo.

Stile Liberty

From the latter end of the 19th century, there was a boom in villa construction on the lakes, a symbol of self-worth among moneyed families at a time of confidence following Italian unification. The villas became the focus of a high-class *dolce vita*, as well as their gardens, which were seen as a kind of open-air salon where a coterie of socialites and artists were entertained.

It was the belle époque, and for some decades a fresh new wave in art and architecture had been spreading across Europe, taking its cue from applied arts and strong Japanese influences. Known as art nouveau in France, it came to be called *stile liberty* (Liberty style) in Italy. Key points for identifying such buildings are the proud and visible use of materials previously considered 'ignoble', such as wrought iron, ceramics, stained glass, brick and, in some cases, cement. In addition, Liberty and art nouveau designers and architects favoured curves and natural motifs (flowers, vines etc) over straight lines, particularly in decorative elements (from door handles to windows, sculptural reliefs to door frames). The style reached its apotheosis in the spa of San Pellegrino Terme and in the residential area around Corso Venezia in Milan, where there are many examples, like the exotic natural history museum and the civic aquarium, and Casa Galimberti, with its ceramic facade, on Via Malpighi.

It is hardly surprising that many buildings in this style should have popped up on the lakes. They did so mainly in more popular resorts. Since the opening of the Sempione (Simplon) Pass from Switzerland and the arrival of rail connections, Stresa on Lake Maggiore had become a key holiday destination, as had sunny Gardone Riviera on Lake Garda. Both are dotted with Liberty villas like the Grand Hotel Borromees and Villa Barberis on Lake Maggiore and Villa Simonini (now Hotel Laurin) and Villa Feltrinelli (also a hotel) on Lake Garda. One of the great Italian Liberty architects was Giuseppe Sommaruga, who left several villas in Sarnico (the most noteworthy is Villa Faccanoni) on Lake Iseo. On Lake Como, only the Villa Bernasconi is a clear Liberty example, although it's one of the best.

Fascism & Futurism

With the advent of war the effete, decorative style of *stile liberty* was no longer fit for purpose in a world where Mussolini blustered about the Roman ideals of strength, masculinity and rationalism. San Siro Stadium was built in 1926, embodying Fascism's disconcerting mix of rationalist modernity with Mussolini's fetish for the camper side of imperial Rome. As Italy's biggest rail terminus, Mussolini commissioned a fitting palace for rail transport on Piazza Duca d'Aosta in Milan. Begun in 1912, but finally realised between 1925 and 1931, the extraordinary design is flush with national fervour. Most of the overtly Fascist symbolism was removed or obscured but the deco-tinged neo-Babylonian architecture can hardly hide its intent. Milan's other former Fascist monuments include the Triennale, Palazzo dell'Arengario and the massive Armani shop on Via Manzotti.

Best Art Books

Painters of Reality
(Andrea Bayer et al)
Sumptuous, illustrated exploration of the Lombard Renaissance.

Maurizio Cattelan
(Francesco Bonami, Massimiliano Gioni et al)
A monograph of Milan's bad boy artist.

Design City Milan
(Cecilia Bolognesi)
Photographic tour of cutting-edge architecture.

Giò Ponti
(Ugo La Pietra)
Monograph from local publisher Rizzoli.

Villas on the Lakes
(Elizabeth Minchilli)
Mouth-watering villa interiors.

Leonardo & The Last Supper
(Ross King)
The story of the world's most famous painting.

THE MORELLIAN TECHNIQUE

The brilliant art critic and intellectual Giovanni Morelli (1816–91) devised the 'Morellian' technique of identifying authorship of a painting by studying the characteristic 'hands' of painters, by which the minor details of a portrait or scene, such as the painting of a subject's ears or hands, reveals the artist's subconscious shorthand. The Morellian technique of finding hidden clues in the details was to have a much wider cultural influence, when the method was mentioned in Arthur Conan Doyle's best-selling series, *Sherlock Holmes*, and in the work of Sigmund Freud.

Contemporaneous with Fascism was FT Marinetti's violent, history-hating futurist credo, intent on dispatching the deadening weight of the past in order to speed Italy into the modern age. Futurist painter Gino Severini described the artistic atmosphere of early 20th-century Milan as 'messier and more destructive than you could imagine'. Launched by a gang of drawing-room revolutionaries, Marinetti's 1910 manifesto railed against museums, the past and even pasta, and looked presciently to a new century forged by violence, war, machines and speed. The movement was a broad church, ranging from Marinetti's card-carrying Fascism to those more interested in aesthetic liberation and the search for a poetic of the industrial age. These included Giacomo Balla, Umberto Boccioni and a young Bruno Munaris whose work is displayed in Milan's Museo del Novecento.

Post WWII, the Informels captured the frustrated but heady energy of the early boom years in paintings marked by 'formlessness'. Initially an Informel, Lucio Fontana went on to poke holes and slash canvases, and with Piero Manzoni, famous for exhibiting cans of 'Artist's Shit', was Italy's seminal conceptual artist. Crowded salon-style into the Piero Portaluppi–designed 1930s apartment of Pirelli engineer, Antonio Boschi and his wife, Marieda di Stefano, now the Casa Museo Boschi-di Stefano, are some 300 examples of futurist and Informel works, where Fontana's slashed canvases hang side-by-side with Manzoni's surface-busting *Anchromes*.

The Contemporary Scene

In addition to the private gallery scene, a number of dynamic private foundations champion some of the region's most avant-garde art. Prada (www.fondazioneprada.org), Trussardi (www.fondazionenicolatrussardi.com) and Hangar Bicocca (www.hangarbicocca.org) all stage programs of important, ground-breaking work.

Until recently, the Milanese were fond of carping that despite claims they were Italy's most modern city, they hadn't produced a significant building since Giò Ponti erected the Torre Pirelli. Then the World Exposition (Expo) came to town in 2015 and Milan transformed itself into Italy's city of the future. Glittering skyscrapers sprouted almost overnight at Porta Nuova – the country's largest development since WWII – while the 186-hectare CityLife project has delivered a trio of extraordinary towers and a series of sinuous residences designed by world-class architects Arata Isozaki, Daniel Libeskind and the late Zaha Hadid. Elsewhere in the city Mario Cucinelli, Herzog & de Meuron and Norman Foster are busy at work on striking contemporary structures such as the super-sustainable Vertical Nest, Fondazione Feltrinelli's magnificent slanted 'greenhouse', and Apple's first Lombard store on Piazza Liberty, which promises to be one of the most technologically advanced stores in the world.

Other major players in the city's fashion industry, such as Gucci, Prada and Armani, are also making waves in developing Milan's cultural scene. In 2015, Prada opened its OMA-designed Fondazione Prada focused on contemporary art, while Armani Silos now houses 40 years of the designer's work. Fashion, design, advertising, publishing – Milan is now the go-to city for all these sectors, and along with Turin and Venice (which hosts the Biennale, the world's most important art show) is the beating heart of Italy's contemporary art scene. As a result, the majority of Italy's living artists choose to call Milan home, at least between sojourns in New York or Berlin, and there's a network of dozens of commercial galleries, including big names such as Lia Rumma and Galleria Cardi, many of which exhibit at the annual MiArt Fair.

Beyond these big-city bright lights, Bergamo's GAMeC gallery houses a collection of over 300 works by contemporary Italian artists. MART, in Rovereto, a half-hour drive east of Riva del Garda, is one of the most important modern and contemporary art museums in the country. Even medieval Verona is upping its game with a burgeoning annual art fair, Art Verona, which aims to support emerging artists and cater to the 65% of all Italian collectors who live between Milan, Verona, Turin and Bologna.

Villas & Gardens

First they fixed the drawing room and then they started on the garden: Italy's penchant for the 'outdoor room' has been going strong since wealthy Romans realised the benefits of regular rest and relaxation, and situated their holiday villas beside the tranquil northern lakes. Medieval humanists revived their interest in botany and pharmacology, and Renaissance princes used never-before-seen engineering techniques to mould Italian landscapes into dramatic and dynamic statements of wealth and power.

Classical Ideals

As early as the 1st century AD, the rough date of the Grotte di Catullo, sited on the headland of Sirmione on Lake Garda, the garden landscape played a significant role in classical culture. Writers such as Ovid, Cicero, Pliny the Elder and Younger set their stories in fantastical gardens full of grottos and groves and wrote treatises on agriculture, outdoor dining, summerhouses and the pleasure of aviaries.

Above Villa Carlotta (p136), Tremezzo

Classical poet Ovid records the myth that explains the association of the cypress with the handsome boy Cyparissus, a favourite of Apollo, accidentally killed a beloved tame stag. He was so distraught that he asked to weep forever in punishment and so he was transformed into *cupressus sempervirens*, whose sap eternally weeps his tears.

For the Romans, a garden was not only a practical place to cultivate vegetables, but also a place of relaxation and physical well-being. Pliny the Younger is known to have used his garden at Bellagio as a place of meditation, while Plato used a garden to host his philosophy lessons. Other ruins at Desenzano del Garda reveal an indoor-outdoor colonnaded peristyle and lavish mosaics, while the Domus dell'Ortaglia, in Brescia, overlooks a grassy viridarium, a contemplative space lined with fruit trees, laurel hedges and fragrant roses.

In the more cash-strapped Middle Ages, medieval gardeners seemed to lose the pleasure principle of the Roman *horti* (garden) and focused solely on a protected area or walled garden *(hortus conclusus)* for the production of food, fruit and medicinal herbs. Cloisters in medieval abbeys and churches were often cultivated in this way, supplying essential pharmacological treatments to surrounding communities. At the Certosa di Pavia, monks still cultivate medicinal plants and make natural remedies and products, such as soap. While, in Milan, at the Basilica di Sant'Ambrogio, the monks allowed humanist scholar Francesco Petrarch (1304–74) to experiment growing spinach, beets, fennel and laurels. Petrarch wrote extensively about these experiments and through his work, among that of others, the classical ideals of the garden as an aesthetic place began to be revived.

Renaissance Revival

In 1452 one of the Renaissance's most gifted men, polymath Leon Battista Alberti (1404–72), wrote a radical new treatise on architecture and the architecture of gardens. *De Re Aedificatoria* (On the Art of Building), published in 1485, suggested that the Renaissance retreat should not look inwards, but instead sit at an elevated position so its inhabitants could both 'see' and 'be seen'. To create a beautiful garden in a magnificent landscape was to tame nature and introduce culture, something to be widely applauded. This new showiness appealed greatly to fashionable cardinals, princes and popes, who commissioned daring new pleasure gardens such as Bramante's Cortile del Belvedere (1484) and Raphael's Villa Madama (1518), both in Rome.

These ground-breaking commissions introduced new rules of proportion, perspective and symmetry to the garden. Off Alberti's central

SECRET GARDENS

Secret gardens abounded during the Renaissance, providing the celebrities of the day with one of their only truly private spaces. Aside from privacy, the secret garden was also a place for prized plants and exotic specimens, acting as an extension of the indoor cabinet of curiosities.

Isabella d'Este's apartments in the Corte Vecchia at the Palazzo Ducale in Mantua house the perfect example of this private space. Designed in 1522 by Mantuan architect Gian Battista Covo, the garden is completely surrounded by walls and can only be seen from Isabella's private rooms.

Classical features abound: Ionic columns line the walls and were originally interspersed with classical statuary lodged in the niches in the walls, while around the top runs an inscription singing Isabella's praises and reminding visitors that she is a daughter of the King of Naples and the powerful Este house, as well as a wife and mother of the Gonzaga dynasty. The garden adjoins Isabella's *studiolo* (study), where the walls are lined with inlaid cabinets stamped with her monogram. These cabinets housed her most precious jewels and treasures in countless tiny drawers. Likewise, the design of the flower beds mirrors the compartmentalisation of the *studiolo*, divided into small sections sometimes called *cassette* or boxes.

Villa Balbianello (p133), Lenno

axis, the Renaissance landscaper divided up the garden with hedges and rows of trees, while open terraces created powerful architectural planes and loggias linked indoor and outdoor rooms. Hedges and topiary added sculptural possibilities and organised space, contrasting openness with enclosures. The neatly clipped labyrinth, serried ranks of cypresses and geometric axes of the Giardino Giusti (1580) in Verona and the two-storeyed loggia, Roman statuary and 'garden rooms' of Villa Guarienti (1538) at Punta San Vigilio, provide classic examples.

Water, too, was a key component of the Renaissance garden. Still a luxury in the 16th century, it was vital in enlivening the garden, attracting both birds and animals in summer months. Ingenious new hydraulic engineering meant it was possible to pipe water further and in greater quantities, allowing for elaborate fountains and humorous *giochi d'acqua* (water tricks), which were liable to drench silk-clad guests at any moment to the great amusement of their hosts.

Such a garden was the Gonzaga's garden at their suburban villa, Palazzo Te, where Giulio Romano, Raphael's most gifted student, came to work after a dispute at Villa Madama. Although the planting schemes are now long gone, the garden's structure remains: a square house, built around a cloistered courtyard where a formal garden divided by a central access would have been laid out. At the far end, a *giardino segreto* (secret garden) was added where Duke Federico could court his mistress in private. And beneath it is a shell-encrusted grotto complete with *giochi d'acqua,* which splashed visiting courtiers standing on the covered balcony.

Baroque Splendour

By the end of the 16th century the idea of the garden as a quiet, contemplative space had completely given way to an outdoor room expressing wealth and culture. The garden was now a place where new and

A *parterre* is a formal garden constructed on a level surface, consisting of planting beds arranged to form a pleasing, usually symmetrical pattern, with gravel paths laid between. The beds are edged in stone or tightly clipped hedging and need not contain any flowers.

MASTER1305 / SHUTTERSTOCK ©

Isola Bella (p93)

Giardino Giusti
Renaissance rules

Garden Greats

Giardino Giusti
Renaissance rules

Villa Balbianello
Perfect lakeside promenade

Isola Bella *Baroque theatrics*

Isola Madre *English informality*

Villa Carlotta
English and Italian harmony

San Pancrazio
Tropical botanical blooms

ingenious hydraulic devices transported many litres of water to costly, elaborate fountains; where rare and expensive plants demonstrated a patron's knowledge and culture; and where artfully arranged sculptures imbued with layers of meaning carried symbolic messages and displayed refined artistic sensibilities. All these ingredients ultimately combined to form the bold gardens of the baroque era.

Around this time, the first great lakeside villas were being built or bought, designed as holiday pleasure homes for the wealthy. The Marquis Stanga acquired Villa Serbelloni, in Bellagio, and set about creating its gardens. Until then, here and in a handful of other older villas, the grounds had served as orchards and herb gardens, grown amid chestnut forests and freely running streams. All this was gradually cleared to make way for symmetrically laid out lawns and topiary, pergolas and terraces. In 1565 work on what is now Villa d'Este began, and in around 1600 the Sfondrati family came into possession of what would be transformed into Villa Monastero.

Of these, the Borromean garden of Isola Bella is Italy's finest example of the baroque garden. It was built between 1632 and 1671 on the instruction of Count Carlo Borromeo III, who wanted to transform a barren island in Lake Maggiore into his own version of the Garden of the Hesperides, that blissful orchard of classical mythology where immortality-giving golden apples grew.

His vision was for a pyramid of terraces that would mimic the shape of a baroque galleon at anchor in the lake. The island's handful of inhabitants, who were asked to relocate from their homes, understandably didn't share the Count's enthusiasms so plans had to be modified and the galleon lost its pointed prow and the central axis linking the garden to the palace.

Nevertheless, the garden wrought by the otherwise unremarkable architect from Milan, Angelo Crivelli, was nothing short of spectacular. Fountains, terraces, grottos and a water theatre combine to form a theatrical and energetic space. Vast quantities of soil were ferried from the mainland, clothing the jagged rock with 10 sloping terraces. Marble from Baveno followed and stone from Viggiù. Later, boats packed with Spanish lemon trees, lilies and lotus flowers brought the flora for its rising galleries and, finally, statues of Agriculture and Arts, waving putti and the triumphant Borromeo unicorn were set atop Carlo Fontana's spectacular shell-encrusted water theatre. It is the perfect expression of the confidence and power of the Borromean family who had furnished Milan with two cardinals, one of whom was canonised by Pope Paul V in 1610.

French Influences

Arguably the most famous garden in the world isn't Italian, but French. Yet 'garden' is hardly a word to apply to the vastness of Versailles. Designed by André Le Nôtre, gardener to Louis XIV, in the latter half of the 17th century, it came to epitomise a modern expression of wealth and power. Unlike Italian gardens it did away completely with any sense of enclosure, intimacy or humour, instead making a statement of illimitable power.

With the fashion for all things French taking Italy by storm in the 17th century, it wasn't long before Le Nôtre was making his way south with plans for the Palazzo Reale in Turin. Needless to say, he thought little of Italian garden design. But try as they might to imitate Le Nôtre, the monumental scale of his gardens was not possible in the intensely cultivated landscape of northern Italy. Although imitated with some success at the Venaria Reale, the Savoy hunting lodge in Piedmont, the closest Lombardy came to the *jardin à la francaise* were the park at Monza and the exposed formal garden at Villa Olmo, which runs into a tree-filled park.

Giovanni Battista Ferrari's *Flora, overo cultura dei fiori* (1638) was the most influential florilegium of the 17th century. It was the first book ever written about plants cultivated for purely ornamental purposes and it tackles every detail, from the choice of garden guard dog to the modification of flower colour, scent and form.

VILLAS & GARDENS FRENCH INFLUENCES

A BOTANICAL BENT

Renaissance and baroque gardens flourished against a backdrop of scientific discovery. With human dissection new on the syllabus at Padua University, students of medicine were rapidly gaining a greater understanding of anatomy and phramacology and coming to terms with the shortcomings of existing medical texts, many of them dating back to the 1st century AD. What's more, merchant ships docking in Venice were starting to offload strange and exotic plants along with medicinal herbs, which were fetching prices just shy of gold and spices in the Rialto market.

This new interest in botany, and the fabulous specimens (such as maize) arriving from voyages of discovery, such as those by Christopher Columbus in 1492 and 1493, captured the popular imagination of villa owners who coveted rare plants for display in their newly designed gardens. Aristocratic families like the Medicis, Estes and Borromee funded many early botanic gardens, and through their patronage plant collecting developed into a full-blown mania in the 17th and 18th centuries.

At Villa Monastero on Lake Como, African and American palms tower above groupings of agave and dragon trees. Aubergines were introduced from Asia and tulips from Persia and some 80,000 bulbs, representing 65 varieties, are planted at Villa Taranto on Lake Maggiore. Although there was a fashionable element to plant collecting, the trend was part of a wider intellectual landscape of discovery. Count Vitaliano IX Borromeo, who introduced species from China, New Zealand, India, the Himalayas and South America to Isola Madre, was a serious and passionate botanist, as was Baroness Antoinette Saint Leger, who transformed San Pancrazio, the larger of the Isole di Brissago on Lake Maggiore, with thousands of exotic specimens into an enormous island garden.

The English Garden

Other international influences were also gaining ground in the south at the Bourbon court in Naples, where English prime minister Sir John Acton was a favourite of Queen Maria Carolina (the daughter of Maria Theresa, Habsburg Empress and Duchess of Milan). Under the English influence, a section of the fabulous new gardens at the Bourbon palace at Caserta, just outside Naples, were to be laid out in English style, that is under a seemingly 'natural' design of irregular paths and profuse plantings, rather than the more formal, geometric French or Italian style.

This romantic English tradition suited the awkward Italian landscape and appealed to Italian tastes with its element of surprise and delight in the changing perspectives. It was also easier to incorporate into traditional Italian schemes, and many gardens around the lakes are now a hybrid of Italian and English styles; a more formal Italianate layout fronting the villa or palace gradually gives way to softer more varied planting schemes incorporating thickets and clearings set around curvaceous ponds and paths.

Villa Carlotta, built in the 17th century on Lake Como, follows just such a design. Around the villa itself the ordered layout suggests the Italianate approach though, as you explore, this changes radically. At one part of the northern end of the garden is the cool and magical Valle delle Felci (Fern Valley), a dense forest full of ferns and trees, including towering sequoias. This 'wilderness' is perhaps the best example of the English ideal on the lakes. Villa Melzi d'Eril, in Bellagio, is another good example. Likewise, Villa Balbianello, the most visually striking of Lake Como's gardens, follows the same pattern. Perched on a promontory, the villa buildings have a neoclassical flavour with some lightly baroque elements while the surrounding terraced gardens are a mix of Italian and English plantings. But of all the gardens around the lakes, the most English is the romantic garden of Isola Madre.

In 1801 Ercole Silva published *Dell'arte dei giardini inglesi*, the first treatise on the English garden, advising the 'artist-gardener' to abandon the architectural approach, which hampered true creativity and genius.

Public Gardens

Plantsmen rather than architects were the heroes of 19th-century gardens thanks to gardeners such as the Rovelli brothers, who worked for the Borromean family. Experts in cultivation and hybridisation, the brothers ran a nursery on the sidelines at Verbania Pallanza, where they sold some of the count's 500 varieties of camellia.

It also became the fashion for aristocratic families to send their gardeners and landscapers on educational voyages around Europe. One of the earliest examples of this is the trip Archduke Ferdinand (1754–1806) took between 1783 and 1786 with Ercole Silva (1756–1840). Ercole was primarily a writer, but oversaw a number of garden designs in Milan, including the Palazzo Reale overlooking the Giardini Pubblici, Villa Litta in the suburb of Affori, and Villa Reale at Monza.

This growing exchange of information popularised gardening as a pastime. The Rovelli brothers even published a catalogue on camellias while others, such as the Roda brothers working for the House of Savoy in Piedmont, wrote gardening manuals and features for monthly magazines. New horticultural societies were established in Piedmont and Lombardy, nurseries proliferated around Milan and Padua, and space was cleared for public parks in Milan, Turin and Venice. Finally, with the Unification of Italy in 1861, a new middle class began to emerge keen on tending their own small patch of paradise. This passion persists today, as evidenced by the enthusiastic crowds at Lake Maggiore's camellia and tulip festivals and Milan's annual Orticola festival.

Italian Villas and Their Gardens is Pulitzer Prize–winner Edith Wharton's pioneering collection of essays on Italian gardens. Written during a four-month tour of the country in 1903, it is one of the first books to explore Italian garden architecture and it influenced a generation of landscape architects.

The Lakes Kitchen

Is there a particular lake cuisine? No, not if you're looking for a homogenous gastronomic tradition. Northern Italy's cultural history and varied terrain preclude a single culinary style. But Lombardy divides naturally into distinct zones: the Po plain with its rice paddies, rivers and game birds; the lakes teeming with freshwater fish; the Alpine foothills where cows and goats graze, providing milk and meat; and the mountains with their chestnut forests, mushrooms and wild herbs. Eat your way around here and you'll learn much about Italy's history and changing tastes.

A Rich & Industrious Kitchen

Northern Italy was never a naturally rich or fertile region. Centuries of human labour and know-how have adapted the shifting Po Delta and shorn up the mountain sides, while a cosmopolitan outlook has incorporated and refined the endlessly varied flavours we delight in when we sit down to enjoy a meal.

Above Vegetables for sale at an open-air market

PROTECTED DESIGNATION OF ORIGIN
• •

Like much bureaucratic legislation, DOP (Protected Designation of Origin) and IGP (Protected Geographical Indication) accreditation is boring but important: quite simply, there is a huge amount of money at stake. At last count, Italy had 266 DOP and IGP products, 20% of which are Lombard specialities, including a wide range of cheese, salami and rice, but also Mantovan pears, peaches from Verona, asparagus, nuts, olive oil from Lake Garda, *bresaola* (air-cured beef) from the Valtellina and *cotecchino* (pork sausage). In total, the country boasts 4698 accredited regional specialities, a number unrivalled by any other European country. Together these Italian products generate annual sales of around €33 billion. In a 'post-horsemeat-masquerading-as-beef' world where consumers are ever more sensitive to the quality of produce, and the price of anonymous ingredients, the little blue and yellow badge that signals a DOP pedigree is priceless.

But what is remarkable about Lombard cuisine is that despite industrialisation and the radical dietary changes in northern Italy's fast-paced modern cities (Italy's first supermarket opened in Milan in 1957 and its first fast-food outlet arrived in 1982), the food on the table remains largely local, seasonal and artisanal. Italians buy just a quarter of the frozen products that the British do, and 50% of their spending is still on fresh, unpackaged goods. Just check out the food markets in Milan, Mantua and Verona to witness the health of the local food economy.

But northern Italy is not some timeless land of peasant cooks, nonnas and mammas. There are over 70,000 registered agribusinesses in Lombardy, producing 15% of Italy's food and, together with Piedmont, 30% of Europe's rice crop. But many of these industrial-scale products are actually some of the country's most genuine: ham, cheese, salami and rice were designed for preservation, transport and trade. Northern Italy's agribusinesses may cater to the masses but they include 25% of Italy's DOP and IGP quality-assured meat and cheese products, and 60% of the nation's quality-assured wines.

The Urban Kitchen

'A good cook in a great city is more or less like a general in a vast theatre of war... It is not just that big cities are ever more bountifully provisioned with all sorts of fine ingredients. They have people whose job it is to supply you with the tiny things that may have little intrinsic importance, but which help to make your handiwork varied, elegant and precise.' *Science in the Kitchen and the Art of Eating Well*, 1891, Pellegrino Artusi

Northern Italian food is city food originating from one of the richest urban cultures on the planet. Peasants may have toiled in the fields, but they rarely had the means to eat anything more exciting than wild garlic, greens, frogs and polenta. The latter, a coarsely ground barley/farro/spelt/chestnut-meal (maize was not cultivated in Europe until the 16th century), has been a staple since Roman times and such was the consumption that regular outbreaks of pellagra (a devastating disease caused by niacin deficiency) were common. Baked, fried or grilled, modern variations include *polenta taragna* (with buckwheat flour), *polenta uncia* (made with cheese) and *missultin e polenta* (cooked with dried fish from Lake Como).

The people with the knowledge to transform the country's growing abundance of ingredients were the inhabitants of wealthy and cosmopolitan cities like Milan, Pavia, Verona, Cremona, Brescia and Mantua. With the rise of Venice's mercantile empire in the 10th century, northern Italy was at the vanguard of Europe's transformation from an agricultural society to a medieval powerhouse of trade and commerce. As Venetian and Genoese seamen offloaded their cargoes of spices, sugar cane, saffron, figs, lemons, almonds and more from around the Mediterranean, tradesmen distributed them via the region's navigable network of rivers that connected Milan to Lake Maggiore and Como, Venice to Vicenza and Mantua to Ferrara, Parma and Piacenza. By the 13th century cartloads of wine were trundling over the Brenner pass into Austria.

Powerful clans such as the Della Scala family in Verona, the Gonzaga in Mantua and the Sforza in Milan competed for a slice of the profits, dividing up and taxing the countryside and establishing themselves as political dynasties. It was in this competitive, commercial environment that Italy's great cuisine was born.

The Marvels of Medieval Milan

De Magnalibus Mediolani (The Marvels of Medieval Milan) was written in 1288 by Milanese monk Bonvesin de la Riva. In his proud depiction of his home town's finest features, Bonvesin gives us a rare insight into one of Europe's largest medieval cities and its surprisingly rich diet.

Butchers, fishmongers and bakers were important men, members of powerful organised guilds, and it's no wonder when you consider the animals, wild birds, poultry, fruits and fish they supplied. Dishes such as *nervetti* (veal cartilage), *busecca* (tripe stew), *bollito* (boiled meats) and *carpione* (fried, floured fish) were becoming standard and Bonvesin also lists damascene plums, early figs, hyssop and white horehound, exotic ingredients even by today's standards. And already land-locked Milan was one of the best places in Italy to eat fish, thanks to its access to the northern lakes. There was even an abundant supply of prawns from the city's moat.

To accompany this medieval city guide, Bonvesin wrote *Fifty Courtesies at Table*. With this in hand, city sophisticates could avoid such faux pas as sneezing into the communal plate, and were reminded to wipe their mouths before drinking from the communal goblet. Good manners were no longer the preserve of aristocrats, but a badge of success for the upwardly mobile middle class.

Cooking in the Renaissance

As with art, music and architecture, the Renaissance was a period of culinary creativity. Italy's urban food system became more sophisticated, and political power and wealth were increasingly displayed at table. Sugar and spices became a European addiction, and saffron, nutmeg, cloves, cardamom and pepper entered the cooking repertoire, giving us sweet and sour dishes such as *agnoli* (ravioli stuffed with capon, cinnamon and cloves), *sbrisolona* (a hard biscuit with almonds) and *mostarda* (candied fruit and mustard relish).

Opulent banquets combined food with theatre, music and dance for the first time. Leonardo da Vinci was even drafted in to design sets for

Born in Dumenza on Lake Maggiore, Bartolomeo Scappi was one of the greatest cooks of the Italian Renaissance. In his six-volume *Opera di Bartolomeo Scappi* (1570) he left a meticulously illustrated monument to the aspirations of Italian Renaissance cuisine.

THE LAKES KITCHEN THE MARVELS OF MEDIEVAL MILAN

BEYOND PASTA

Food historians generally agree that rice came to Europe by way of India. During Roman times it was an expensive commodity, used in small quantities for medicinal purposes. The earliest documentation of rice growing in Italy dates to 1475, when its cultivation on the Lombard plain was promoted by Galeazzo Maria Sforza, Duke of Milan. These days some 50 varieties of rice are grown in the Po valley, making Italy Europe's largest producer with an output of 1.33 million tonnes. Sure, pasta (an import from the south in the 17th century) abounds, but rice is the number one staple in Lombardy. Among the best known is *carnaroli,* a medium-grain rice mostly grown in Piedmont. Others, such as *arborio* (a short grain) and *vialone nano* (a thicker grain), are grown around Pavia – the rice capital of Italy.

How should we count the ways of preparing risotto? The Milan standard is with saffron and a meat broth. In Pavia a speciality is *risotto con le rane* (with crispy fried frogs). *Risotto al porcini* (with porcini mushrooms) is a universal favourite, while risottos done with wines as a base, such as Barolo or Amarone, are typical in wine regions. In Mantua, *risotto alla pilota* (with minced pork) is a signature dish and seafood variations from the Veneto include *risotto al nero* (with black octopus or squid ink).

Sbrisolona (a hard biscuit with almonds)

the wedding banquet of Milan's Giangaleazzo Sforza and Isabella of Aragón in 1489. Cristoforo da Messisbugo's 1548 *Banquets* gives us some idea of their scale and extravagance. A record of the wedding feast of the Duke of Ferrara's son Ercole to Renée, the daughter of Louis XII of France, offers us an endless list of courses, gifts and entertainments – shocking in light of the plague that was decimating the countryside around Ferrara at the time.

At a rough calculation each of the guests had to plough through 18 large portions of fish, three whole birds, three portions of meat, sausage, salami and ham, 15 pastries and pies, as well as sweetmeats and an early morning collation of fruit in sugar and syrup. They were seated carefully, according to rank, their places affording access (or not) to the choicest dishes. The Duke's sister, Isabella d'Este, the Marchioness of Mantua, and one of the most esteemed dinner guests of the Renaissance, sat at his right hand, and the Venetian ambassador was prominently placed so he could report back on the costly spectacle.

Below stairs, a similar charade of political manoeuvring was going on in the kitchen as the Este's cook brokered new relationships with possible patrons and suppliers. Unlike courtiers, cooks came from rural backgrounds. As the seasons and their employers' fancies changed, they networked constantly to find suppliers and discover new recipes. It was through cooks that an understanding of good food circulated between rich and poor, the country and the town.

In 1661 the first known law for the protection of a local Italian speciality was issued, protecting the heritage recipe for *mortadella* (pork cold cut).

The French & Austrian Influences

Between the 1600s and 1800s foreign influences brought new flavours to bear and spices went out of fashion. The French introduced butter and cream (*crema di asparagi*, a creamed asparagus soup, is typical) while the Austrians introduced a penchant for sausages and schnitzel (*scaloppina* and *cotoletto alla Milanese* are variations on the Austrian breaded cutlet, Wiener Schnitzel) and a tradition of *viennoisserie* that is still evident in Milan's glut of elegant *pasticcerie* (pastry shops).

A new centralised bureaucracy and a reformed tax system increased agricultural output, while new farming methods and crops (potatoes, tomatoes and maize from the New World) revolutionised the diet of the masses. From across the Alps came Grand Tourists, French recipe books and the fashion of eating *a la russe* (Russian style), in separate courses comprising individual plates. Piedmontese chefs trained in France were most in demand.

With new political ideas came new places to meet and eat. Cafes, serving a new drink, coffee, and Austrian doughnuts (*ciambella* and *castagnole*) and strudels, were hothouses of political debate and the rise of the restaurant democratised access to good food. New advances in medicine raised the profile of vegetables and fruit. Sweet peppers from the New World found their way into Voghera's version of risotto, the potato craze began (*gnocchi di patate* is now a Verona speciality) and herbs, lemon juice and olive oil became acceptable, even desirable, flavourings for delicate fish dishes.

According to futurist Filippo Marinetti food wasn't simply fuel for the body, but an aesthetic experience that affected the way people thought, dreamt and acted. In a modern era of molecular gastronomy, recipes from *The Futurist Cookbook* (1932) no longer look quite so kooky.

Home Cooking

Up until the early 20th century, the only Italian cookery books in circulation were written by men: chefs, stewards and courtiers working in the wealthiest city households with the finest ingredients. *Cucina casalinga* (home cooking) had no place at this elite table. That is, until the deprivation of two world wars pushed middle-class housewives out of the kitchen and into print.

The first Italian cookery book written by a woman was *Come Posso Mangiar Bene?* (How Can I Eat Well?) by home cook Giulia Tamburini and published in Milan, by Hoepli, in 1900. She was to be the first in a long line of northern Italian housewives – including, most recently, Anna del Conte, whose biography, *Risotto With Nettles,* recalls her wartime Milanese childhood and its influence on her cooking – who valued good food but, by necessity, had to work within a limited budget.

Thanks to them, a simple, filling *primo* (first course) of *minestra* (soup), gnocchi or risotto now sits at the heart of the northern Italian meal. 'Make-do' classics such as *mondeghili* (Milanese meatballs made with leftover chopped, boiled meat), *minestrone* (a rich vegetable soup

---

LIVING WELL IN DIFFICULT TIMES: JEWISH SPECIALITIES

One surprising cookery writer working in Fascist Milan was Fernanda Momigliano, a middle-aged, Jewish intellectual who lived with her ailing mother.

Her first book, *Vivere bene in tempi difficili: come le donne affrontano le crisi economiche* (Living Well in Difficult Times: How Women Face Up to the Economic Crisis), attempted to address the issues faced by housewives in the wake of the 1929 Wall Street crash. Advocating 'economy, not deprivation or waste', Momigliano's manual showed Italian women how they might eat well on their diminishing budget. As Italy lurched from deprivation to hunger in the wake UN sanctions in 1935, these reassuring tips on making ends meet, using cheaper cuts of meat and making home preserves put home cooking firmly on the modern Lombard table.

But it was her follow-up book, *Eating Italian,* published in 1936, which is even more interesting not least because it includes 16 Jewish recipes, many of them typical of northern Italy. They range from carp with porcini mushrooms cooked in white wine, to a saffron risotto prepared on the eve of the Sabbath, and goose ham and salami, a specialist product from Mortara that now holds the prestigious Slow Food badge of approval.

Top Potato gnocchi with burnt sage

Bottom Minestrone soup

including rice and pancetta) and *pasta rasa* (egg pasta cooked in a soup with tomatoes, beans, potatoes, onions and garlic) were elevated. Whether it came in the form of soup, rice or pasta, *minestra* allowed middle-class families to live with a modicum of comfort. The more expensive second course was a secondary concern: liver, or butter-fried eggs during the week, roast chicken or veal cutlets on Sunday.

The Perfect Cheeseboard

Counters in northern Italian *alimentari* (food stores) overflow with cheeses. They come in every possible size, form, colour and texture, which isn't surprising considering Lombardy produces nearly 40% of Italy's cheese.

One of the most widespread and best-known Lombard cheeses is *stracchino*. The name is derived from *stracca,* meaning tiredness. It is said that the milk of tired cows (during the seasonal move to and from Alpine pastures) is richer in fats and acids, giving this cheese its tang. It is usually eaten as a dessert cheese. Bitto, from the Valtellina, is similarly dry and sharp as it ages. Once known as green *stracchino,* gorgonzola is made of autumn cow's milk (collected after the return from the Alps) and is one of several cheeses made laced with blue mould.

Another popular autumn cheese is Taleggio, a soft cheese originally made in the like-named valley north of Bergamo. It is a mild cheese matured in six to 10 weeks and regularly washed to prevent mould or a thick rind forming. Other mountain cheeses from the Val Brembana, north of Bergamo, are generically called *formai de mut* (cheese of the mountains).

Originating from the Lodi area is the soft cream cheese known as mascarpone, a versatile product obtained from milk cream and used to make desserts (most famously tiramisu). Lodi also produces Pannerone (a soft, fatty cheese made without salt) and Grana Lodigiano. The latter is similar to Parmesan and Grana Padano, but 'weeps' a drop of whey when flakes of it are cut away.

From the province of Brescia comes Bagoss, a well-matured, straw-coloured cheese traditionally made in cow herds' huts in the summer mountain pastures. Robiola is a soft pasteurised cow's milk cheese made in Lombardy and Ticino. It comes in small discs. A cool, fresh alternative in Ticino is *robiolino* (tubes of pasteurised cow's milk cheese often seasoned with herbs or pepper). Various types of *formaggella* (a semi-hard cheese with a greyish crust) are produced throughout the region.

Several goat cheeses, such as *cadolet di capra* (from the Valle Camonica north of Lake Iseo) and *fatuli,* are made in spring and summer and lightly smoked. Caprino Lombardo, a generic name, covers a range of such cheeses. True goat-milk cheese ranges from the fresh, soft white variety to those matured over several months in oil and laurel leaves. Cingherlin, from Varese and Como, is drizzled with olive oil and vinegar and served with beans.

At Italian unification in 1861, the average consumption of meat was 12kg per person per year, equivalent to 33 grams per day or half the weight of an egg. By 2009 Italians were more fond of meat than the British, consuming 91kg per person.

Tipicita, or 'typicality', describes the magical aura that food acquires when local identity is invested in it. In Italian, *tipico* has become synonymous with *buono* – good, wholesome, delicious.

On the Wine Trail

The region around the northern Italian lakes has been producing wine since Roman times and today produces an enormous variety, from fizzy red lambruscos to bombastic Sforzato and chilly, mineral-rich whites. The tradition of selling many of these modestly priced wines in local *osterie* (taverns), *cantine* (cellars) and *enoteche* (wine bars) has led to the impression that they are of lesser quality than wines from other areas, but the region claims five DOCG, 19 DOC and 15 IGT wines.

Franciacorta

Above Oltrepò Pavese vineyards (p83)

DOCG spumante (sparkling) whites and rosés lead the way in Franciacorta (www.franciacorta.net), an area stretching between Brescia and Lake Iseo. Look out also for Satèn, a *blanc de blanc* almost exclusively made of chardonnay grapes. The Curtefranca DOC covers a series of whites and reds, the latter dominated by cabernet franc and the local carmenere grape varieties.

Oltrepò Pavese

Riots broke out in the Middle Ages when Milan was cut off from Oltrepò, Lombardy's most renowned wine region (www.vinoltrepo.org). No fewer than 20 wines are classified as DOC in this area, and the Oltrepò Pavese spumante is a DOCG. Keep an eye out for reds like the Oltrepò Pavese Barbera and the Bonarda, among the stars of the area's DOC wines made from the local croatina grape. A curious sweet dessert red is the Sangue di Giuda (Judas' Blood).

Riviera del Garda & Bardolino

Along the western shore of Lake Garda, vineyards blanket the Valtenesi area all the way up to Lake Idro. Look for Garda DOC or Garda Classico DOC (www.stradadeivini.it). The reds predominantly use the local gropello grape.

On the southeastern shore, one of the Veneto's best-known reds is cultivated around the town of Bardolino. Of its namesake reds, the Bardolino Superiore DOCG is a delicate, dry drop that pairs well with meat and game. If you're looking for a fine white, try Lugana DOC (www.consorziolugana.it).

Soave

West of Verona, the town of Soave (www.ilsoave.com) rests next to a castle-topped hill whose slopes are dense with vineyards. Some of Italy's finest white wines come from here. The local garganega grape dominates the area's two white DOCGs, Recioto di Soave and Soave Superiore.

Valcalepio

The Valcalepio (www.valcalepio.org) wine region between Bergamo and Lake Iseo is just beginning to make a name for itself. Established as a DOC in 1976, small local holdings have since been continually refining their two main DOC products: a red that blends merlot and cabernet sauvignon (and which also comes in an aged *riserva* version) and whites that combine pinot bianco and pinot grigio varieties. You will also come across a sweet dessert *passito* using moscato grapes, which is perfect as an accompaniment for pastries and dessert.

Valpolicella

Led by the outstanding Amarone della Valpolicella DOC (using dried corvina, rondinella and molinara grapes), this region, which stretches north–northwest up the valleys parallel to Lake Garda from Verona, is one of the best-known names in northern Italian wine. While many Valpolicella (www.consorziovalpolicella.it) reds are light, pleasant table wines, the flagship Amarone (literally 'big sour one') is big, bold and dry. It is accompanied by another signature red, also made with dried grapes, the somewhat sweeter Recioto.

Valtellina

Like a well-behaved Milanese dinner companion, the Valtellina (www.vinidivaltellina.it) red is distinctive and rich without being too forward – Leonardo da Vinci loved the stuff. The area boasts two DOCG classifications, a general one (Valtellina Superiore DOCG) and one applied to a particular style of wine, the Sforzato (or Sfursat) di Valtellina DOCG. The nebbiolo grape (locally known as chiavennasca) is the most important.

ON THE WINE TRAIL OLTREPÒ PAVESE

Compared with the 30,000-hectare French wine region of Champagne, Italy's finest sparkling wine region, Franciacorta covers just 2200 hectares. That said, it is quickly becoming one of the fastest-growing wine regions in Europe. In the early 1990s, there were just 15 producers. Now there are over 100.

Alongside France, Italy is the largest wine producer in the world, processing 45 to 50 million hectolitres per year, around 20% of the world's combined total. Of this, 1.3 million hectolitres come from Lombardy.

Fashion & Design

Lombardy's creative reputation is inextricably linked to the fashion and design industries, which power the local economy and drive an endless round of influential and fabulous designer fairs. Today Milan is home to all the major showrooms and continues to be a centre of fashion and design education and publishing. Design isn't merely functional here; it is also suffused with emotion: expressive, inventive and humorous.

Above Fashion store display, Milan

Fashion

Italians have strong opinions about aesthetics and aren't afraid to share them. A common refrain in Milan is *che brutta!* (how hideous!), which may strike visitors as tactless. But consider it from an Italian point of view – everyone in this fashion town is rooting for you to look good, and allowing you to step out in an unflattering get-up would be considered a serious failure of taste on their part. After all, Italy's centuries-old reputation for style is at stake.

Medieval Trendsetters

Northern Italian artisans and designers have been shoeing, dressing and adorning Europe's affluent classes since the early Middle Ages, when Venetian merchants imported dyes from the East and Leonardo da Vinci helped design Milan's canal system, connecting the wool merchants and silk weavers of Lake Maggiore and Lake Como to the city's marketplaces. Further south, Florence's wool guild grew so rich and powerful it was able to fund a Renaissance.

As this cultural reimagining transformed philosophy, art, music and literature, fashion flourished as a new expression of taste and status. Dresses and men's doublets grew shorter and fuller; impractical, pointy Gothic headdresses were tossed aside; and hair reappeared trimmed with golden ribbons and covered in fine Venetian lace. Patterned velvet and brocade were in vogue, and robes, sleeves and skirts were slashed to reveal shockingly bright silks and dainty jewelled shoes.

Promoted by the celebrities of the day – the Sforza of Milan, the Este of Ferrara, Mantua's Gonzaga dukes and the extravagant Florentine Medici – they immortalised their style choices in newly commissioned portraits and public works. Da Vinci painted three of Ludovico Sforza's mistresses and Mantegna's frescoes in the Camera degli Sposi depict the latest men's trend, pastel hose. On her wedding to Henry, Duke of Orléans (later King of France), in 1533, Tuscany's Catherine de'Medici (1519–89) single handedly transformed French fashions, wearing the first pair of four-inch, high-heeled shoes. Some courtesans and trophy wives were so widely imitated that sumptuary laws were passed restricting necklines, stacked heels and trailing cauls.

In Venice and Milan, the advent of illustrated pamphlets, forerunners to Italian *Vogue,* sent these fashions global. What's more, as feudalism waned and northern city-states revelled in periods of relative peace and prosperity, new forms of mass culture emerged. In 1637 the first public opera house opened in Venice and La Scala's precursor, the Teatro Regio Ducale, opened in Milan in 1717. Regular public appearances required the careful cultivation of image and a gradually expanding wardrobe.

Como Silk

Smuggled out of China inside a bamboo pole, the first silkworms reached northern Italy in the 13th century. At the time, the majority of peasants around Lake Como were employed in woollen mills, but given the abundance of mulberry trees in the Po valley a few canny entrepreneurs, such as Pietro Boldone, spotted the potential for sericulture and established Como's first silk spinning mill in the early 1500s.

Although nurturing the worms and harvesting the silk was brutally hard work, silk cultivation gradually became an annual sideline for lower- and middle-class families, many of whom risked their annual savings trying to capitalise on the rich harvest. Entire sections of farmhouses were turned over to the worms, which women and children tirelessly fed mulberry leaves by hand until they spun their silken cocoons. To make just one tie, a hundred cocoons were needed.

Incorporating both the production and processing of silk, Como manufacturers, especially those around Lecco, produced some of the world's finest, most durable silks. The weavers had a knack for knowing a quality thread, which was both fine and elastic and wouldn't snap on the weaving rack. By the 18th and 19th centuries, Como was the third-largest silk-producing sector in the world (not far behind China and Japan) and silk constituted Italy's most important national export. So valuable was the trade that silk represented a third of the value of all Italian exports.

The beret originated in Italy during the Renaissance. It was made of a circular piece of cloth gathered onto a band decorated with jewels or embroidery. Inside the band was a string, which could be tightened to fit any head.

FASHION & DESIGN FASHION

In 2016, the price of raw silk reached its highest level (over $50 per kilo). The reason? Chinese farmers are turning away from the arduous work to other more lucrative crops, and rapid industrialisation is consuming farmland in the silk-producing region of Shanghai.

Even after the devastating prebina epidemic of 1855, which all but wiped out the Italian moth species, necessitating the import of raw silk from the Far East, the Como weaving industry retained a significant world presence. It was only in the early 20th century, following the economic crash of 1929 and the advent of new synthetic fabrics, that the European silk industry fell into terminal decline. Still, through high-quality craftsmanship, Como maintained its world-class reputation into the 1990s when it was the most important centre for silk production in the world, supplying all the major fashion houses.

Since then, cheaper Chinese silk has made the production of silk in Como unviable and these days the city focuses on finishing, dying and printing raw silk imported from China or Brazil. That said, 18,000 people (nearly a quarter of the population) still work in the silk industry, which generates approximately 80% of Europe's entire output. Out of literally hundreds of silk houses only three big firms remain: Seteria Ratti, Mantero and Canepa, while Como's Istituto Tecnico Industriale di Setificio, founded in 1869, continues to turn out world-class designers, printers and chemical-dying experts.

Global Powerhouses

Although Italy ceded ground as global tastemaker to France, Austria and even England between the 17th and 20th centuries, when foreign domination of the Italian peninsula sent power and vertigo-inducing pomaded wigs elsewhere, the streamlined look of Italian futurism and the industrial revolution of the 19th century brought fashion back to Florence. Where once Italian cobblers, seamstresses and leatherworkers crafted only made-to-measure designs for aristocrats and royalty, in 1950s Florence the idea of a seasonal fashion show was born. Held in the Palazzo Pitti, these shows were an extraordinary success, launching some of world's most famous fashion empires.

But Milan literally stole the show in 1958 when it hosted Italy's first Fashion Week. Away from the constraints of the Florentine fashion establishment, where designers had to be invited to show and shows were heavily formatted, the Milan Fashion Week gave designers creative power. Thanks to this, the first ready-to-wear collections aimed at mass

LUISA CASATI

Before Lady Gaga's meat dress or Italian style-star Anna dello Russo's Star Wars–style feathered headgear, there was the Marquesa Casati (1881–1957). The first female style icon to realise the power of fashion in creating legend, the Marquesa proudly proclaimed, 'I want to be a living work of art'.

Born in Milan, the daughter of a wealthy cotton merchant, Luisa was one of Italy's wealthiest heiresses by the age of 15. She married well and all seemed to be going according to plan, until she met notorious Italian writer and war hero Gabriele d'Annunzio, with whom she started a shockingly open love affair.

Unfettered by d'Annunzio's unorthodox nature, Luisa began to transform her appearance, dying her hair flame red, highlighting her huge green eyes with droplets of poisonous belladonna, and dressing in lustrous Bakst velvets.

Luisa Casati is one of the most widely represented women in history. She has been painted, sculpted, drawn and photographed by some of the 20th century's most avant-garde artists (Boldoni, Singer Seargeant, Dali, Epstein, Man Ray and Cecil Beaton, to name but a few). She played muse to many movements, including the Italian futurists, and launched the careers of countless artists through her generous patronage. But her greatest impact was in the world of fashion, where she is considered the original female dandy. Buried in Brompton Cemetery with her false eyelashes, her tombstone reads: 'Age cannot wither her, nor custom stale her infinite variety'.

markets were launched and fashion finally found a way to make money from the business of dressing people.

Recognising the huge potential of mass markets, designers like Armani, Missoni and Versace began creating and following trends, selling their 'image' through advertising and promotion. In the 1980s, Armani's power suits gave rise to new unisex fashions, Dolce & Gabbana became a byword for Italian sex appeal, and Miuccia Prada transformed her father's ailing luxury luggage business with democratic, durable totes and backpacks made out of radical new fabrics like waterproof Pocone, silk faille and parachute nylon.

Even more ubiquitous was the sportswear and casual chic look of fashion houses like Diesel and Benetton – the provocative advertising campaigns of the latter broadcasting an image of an irreverent brand with a social conscience. Fashion, it seemed, had something to say and now had the power to say it on a global scale. This trend of influential cultural commentary continues today in the internationally acclaimed AW17 collection from Gucci director Alessandro Michele, which posed the question 'What are we going to do with all this future?', and Fondazione Prada's provocative contemporary art exhibits exploring where the world is headed in the 21st century.

Fashion Mecca Milan

Milan's rise to global fashion prominence was far from random. No other Italian city, not even Rome, was so well suited to take on this mantle. First, thanks to its geographic position, the city had historically strong links with European markets. It was also Italy's capital of finance, advertising, television and publishing, with both *Vogue* and *Amica* magazines based here. What's more, Milan had always had a fashion and clothing industry based around the historic textile and silk production of upper Lombardy. And, with the city's postwar focus on trade fairs and special events, it provided a natural marketplace for the exchange of goods and ideas.

As a result, Milan rapidly emerged as Italy's top fashion exporter. Many of the world's top fashion houses are Italian, and most of them are based in Milan. The Quadrilatero d'Oro, or 'Golden Quad', is now dominated by over 500 fashion outlets in an area of barely 6000 sq metres. Such is the level of display, tourists now travel to Milan to 'see' the fashion.

If you feel so inclined, you can also drop by during one of the four Fashion Weeks (the 'week' is now nine days long) for male and female summer and winter collections. They are held, respectively, in January and February, and June and September.

Design

Better living by design: what could be more Milanese? From the cup that holds your morning espresso to the bedside light you switch off before you go to sleep, there's a designer responsible, and almost everyone in Milan will know their name. Design here is a way of life.

Modern Italian Design

Italy's design roots are in 1930s Milan, with the opening of the Triennale, the founding of *Domus* and *Casabella* magazines, Rinascente's visionary commissions (Giorgio Armani started as a window dresser here) and the development of the Fiera. Where elaborate French rococo and ornate Austrian art nouveau had captured the imagination of a genteel pre–world war Europe, the dynamic deco style of Italian futurism was a perfect partner for the industrial revolution and thrusting Fascist philosophies.

For a full time-table of Fashion Week shows, check the Camera Nazionale della Moda Italiana (National Chamber of Italian Fashion; www.cameramoda.it) website.

FASHION & DESIGN DESIGN

Fashion Classics

....

Borsalino
Montecristi Panama

....

Prada
Cashmere sweater

....

Aspesi
Trench coat

....

Gallo
Silk socks

....

Car Shoe
Loafers

....

Ermenegildo Zegna
Midnight-blue suit

Alessi's famous bird-whistle kettle by American Michael Graves was designed not only to boil water, but to bring users joy when it sang its morning song. Launched in 1985 it captured the public imagination and has been a bestseller for over 30 years.

Like cogs in a political wheel, Fascist propaganda co-opted the radical, neoclassical streamlining that futurism inspired and put it to work in posters, architecture, furniture and design. Modern factories were needed to aid the war effort and Fascist tendencies to hierarchical organisation and centralised control boosted Italian manufacturing. Through an inherent eye for purity of line, modern Italian design found beauty in balance and symmetry. This refreshing lack of detail appealed greatly to a fiercely democratising wartorn Europe where minimalism and utility came to represent the very essence of modernity.

After WWII, the military industrial complexes in Turin and Milan became the centrepieces of a new, global consumer-centric economy. Turin's strength was industrial design, from Lavazza espresso machines to the Fiat 500 car; Milan focused on fashion and home decor. Italian films and pioneering magazines such as *Domus* showcased these newly mass-produced design objects, making them seem both desirable and, more importantly, attainable.

From the Spoon to the City

Milan's philosopher-architects and designers – Giò Ponti, Vico Magistretti, Gae Aulenti, Achille Castiglioni, Ettore Sottsass and Piero Fornasetti – were imbued with a modernist sense of optimism. They saw their postwar mission not only to rebuild the bomb-damaged city but to redesign the whole urban environment. A defining statement of the era was the assertion by Milanese architect Ernesto Rogers that he wished to design 'everything, from the spoon to the city', while philosopher Enzo Paci believed designers sat somewhere between 'art and society'.

Far from being mere intellectual theorists, this cadre of architect-designers benefited from a unique proximity to a mosaic of artisanal businesses that spread across the Lombard hinterland north of Milan. This industrial district, known as Brianza, had grown up organically from rural society, thus retaining many specialist peasant craft skills and hundreds of years of manufacturing experience. While these production houses remained true to the craft aspect of their work, they were able to move towards modern sales and production techniques via the central marketplace of the Triennale, which opened in 1947.

This direct connection between producer and marketplace meant that Milanese designers remained attuned to the demands of the market. As producers of goods, they were unashamedly involved in the business of making profits. It was this happy symbiosis between creativity and commercialism that ultimately fine-tuned Italian design to achieve the modernist ideal of creating beautiful, *useful* objects. If you fancy a glimpse into the homes, offices and urban spaces of the future, visit Milan's mega Salone Internazionale del Mobile (p68); it's still the largest most prestigious furniture in the world.

Iconic Designs
....
Alessi
Kitchen utensils designed by architects
....
Vespa Piaggio
1946 mini-motor
....
Cassina
Furniture by Frank Lloyd Wright
....
Alfa Romeo
Milan's sexy racing roadster
....
Mezzadro
Castiglioni's cantilevered stool

Survival
Guide

Directory A–Z

Climate

Milan

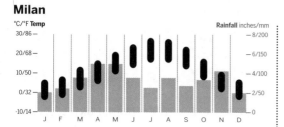

Electricity

Type C
230V/50Hz

Customs Regulations

Duty-free sales within the EU no longer exist (but goods are sold tax-free in European airports). On leaving the EU, non-EU citizens can reclaim any Value Added Tax (VAT) on expensive purchases. Note that this applies to Swiss citizens and residents too.

Discount Cards

City & Regional Discount Cards

Musei Lombardia Milano (www.abbonamentomusei.it; adult/reduced €45/35) Offers discounted access to 100 regional museums, villas and royal residences (including the Violin Museum in Cremona, Bergamo's Accademia Carrara and the Villa Reale in Monza) and is valid for one year.

Civic Museum Card (www.turismo.milano.it; €12) This three-day cumulative ticket

allows admission to Milan's nine civic museums. Purchase tickets online or at any of the museums.

VeronaCard (24/48hr €18/22; www.turismoverona.eu) Verona's cumulative discount card offers access to most major monuments and churches, unlimited use of town buses, plus discounted tickets to selected concerts, opera and theatre productions.

Senior & Youth Cards

International Student Identity Card (www.isic.org) Handy for minor transport, theatre and cinema discounts, as well as occasional discounts in some hotels and restaurants. For nonstudent travellers under 25, the European Youth Card (www.eyca.org) offers similar benefits.

Carta d'Argento (€30/free for 60-75 years/over 75) For seniors who are travelling extensively by rail. Provides discounts of 10% to 15% on national travel and 25% on international trains. The card is valid for a year.

Type F
230V/50Hz

Gay & Lesbian Travellers

Homosexuality is legal in Italy and well tolerated in Milan, but a little less so in other towns. Overt displays of affection by homosexual couples could attract a negative response in smaller towns. There are gay clubs in Milan but otherwise pickings are slim. For more information:

Arcigay (www.arcigay.it) National organisation for the LGBTI community.

Gay.it (www.gay.it) Website featuring LGBT news, feature articles and gossip.

GayFriendlyItaly.com (www.gayfriendlyitaly.com) English-language site produced by Gay.it, featuring information on everything from hotels and events, to LGBT politics and rights.

Health

Before You Go

No special health insurance is required in northern Italy. If you're an EU citizen (or from Switzerland, Norway or Iceland), a European Health Insurance Card (EHIC) covers you for most medical care in public hospitals free of charge, but not for emergency repatriation home or nonemergencies. The card is available from health centres and (in the UK) post offices. Likewise, Australian citizens are entitled to free public health care thanks to a reciprocal arrangement with Italy – carry your Medicare card.

Citizens of other countries, including USA, Canada and New Zealand, have to pay for anything other than emergency treatment. Most travel-insurance policies include medical coverage.

In the Italian Lakes

Lombardy's health care system is well known for its high standards and efficiency. There are over 200 private and public accredited hospitals in the region, the majority of which are run by the Lombardy Health Service. Most hospital physicians speak English, while a number of nurses and nurse assistants speak other languages, particularly Spanish and Russian. The official working language within hospitals is Italian.

If you need to attend a clinic, and are already on medication, bring them along in their original, labelled containers. If carrying syringes or needles, be sure to have a physician's letter documenting their medical necessity. No jabs are required to travel to Italy.

For emergency treatment, head straight to the *pronto soccorso* (casualty) section of a public hospital, where you can also get emergency dental treatment (carry your ID/passport and any relevant insurance card).

TAP WATER

Tap water is drinkable in northern Italy and Switzerland.

MEDICAL SERVICES

American International Medical Centre (AIMC; ☑02 5831 9808; www.aimclinic.it; Via Mercalli 11; ⊙9am-5.30pm Mon-Fri; Ⓜ Crocetta) Private, international health clinic in Milan with English-speaking staff.

ASST Papa Giovanni XXIII (☑035 26 71 11; Piazza OMS 1; ⊙24hr) Located 4km west of Bergamo, this modern, state-of-the-art hospital has excellent facilities.

Ospedale Borgo Trento (☑045 812 11 11; Piazza A Stefani; ⊙24hr) Verona's health centre is of national importance and offers top-quality diagnostics, surgery and outpatient care.

Ospedale Maggiore Policlinico (☑24hr 02 5 50 31; www.policlinico.mi.it; Via Francesco Sforza 35; Ⓜ Crocetta) Milan's main hospital; offers an outpatient service.

Insurance

A travel-insurance policy to cover theft, loss and medical problems is a good idea. It may also cover you for cancellation or delays to your travel arrangements. Paying for your ticket with a credit card can often provide limited travel accident insurance and you may be able to reclaim the payment if the operator doesn't deliver. Ask your credit-card company what it will cover.

Worldwide travel insurance is available at www.lonelyplanet.com/travel-insurance. You can buy, extend and claim online anytime – even if you're already on the road.

Internet Access

Wireless internet access is widespread in most hotels and some cafes and restaurants – access is usually (but not always) free. Otherwise, there are just a handful of internet cafes around, charging €2 to €6 per hour.

Legal Matters

The average tourist will have a brush with the law only if they are a victim of petty theft. If you're stopped by the police in both Italy and Switzerland, you will be required to show your passport.

Possession of any controlled substances, including cannabis or marijuana, is illegal. Those caught in possession of 5g of cannabis can be considered traffickers and prosecuted as such. The same applies to tiny amounts of other drugs. Those caught with amounts below this threshold can be subject to minor penalties. You should be equally circumspect in Switzerland.

If driving, the legal limit in both countries for blood-alcohol level is 0.05% and random breath tests do occur.

Maps

Driving Maps

If driving, the Automobile Association's (AA) *Road Atlas Italy,* available in the UK, is scaled at 1:250,000 and includes town maps. Just as good is Michelin's *Tourist and Motoring Atlas Italy,* scaled at 1:300,000.

In Italy, De Agostini publishes a comprehensive *Atlante Turistico Stradale d'Italia* (1:250,000), which includes 140 city maps (the AA *Road Atlas* is based on this). Perhaps handier for the lakes is TCI's *Atlante Stradale d'Italia* (1:200,000), which is divided into three parts – grab the Nord volume (www.touringclub.com).

Michelin's fold-out Map 353 *(Lombardia),* scaled at 1:200,000, is good and covers the entire area of this guide, except for Lake Orta and a sliver of territory in the west (for which you'd need neighbouring Map 351, *Piemonte & Valle d'Aosta*). The 1:400,000 *Italy: North-West* (Map 561) covers the whole area.

Many of these are available online.

Walking Maps

Maps of walking trails around the lakes, the Lombard Alps and Ticino are available at all major bookshops in Italy and Switzerland. In Italy, the best are the TCI bookshops. Kompass (www.kompass-\italia. it) publishes several 1:50,000 scale maps to the lakes region, including the following titles: *Lago di Como-Lago di Lugano, Lago di Garda-Monte Baldo, Le Tre Valli Bresciane, Lecco-Valle Brembana, Lago Maggiore-Lago di Varese* and *Bernina-Sondrio.*

Most of western Ticino is covered by the 1:50,000 map Val Verzasca, produced by the government body Swisstopo.

Money

The euro is Italy's currency and euro notes come in denominations of €500, €200, €100, €50, €20, €10 and €5. The euro coins are in denominations of €2 and €1, and 50, 20, 10, five, two and one cents.

Switzerland's currency is the Swiss franc. The six notes come in denominations of Sfr1000 (which you'll hardly ever see), Sfr200, Sfr100, Sfr50, Sfr20 and Sfr10. Coins are in denominations of Sfr5, Sfr2, Sfr1, Sfr½ (ie 50 Swiss cents), and 20, 10 and five cents. As a rule, it's pretty easy to use euros in Ticino, although generally you'll get change in francs and the rate will not necessarily be all that favourable.

ATMs

There are *bancomats* (ATMs) that accept international credit and debit cards in all northern Italian cities and towns. Visa and MasterCard are the most widely recognised cards, but others like Cirrus and Maestro are also well covered. Bank fees apply to withdrawals and there's a daily limit of €250.

Money Changers

You can change cash and travellers cheques at a bank, post office or *cambio* (exchange office). Post offices and most banks are reliable and tend to offer the best rates.

Travellers Cheques

Although travellers cheques are now fairly uncommon, Visa, Travelex and Amex are still accepted brands. Get most of your cheques in fairly large denominations to save on per cheque commission charges.

Opening Hours

Opening hours in Italy tend to be longer in summer. In August, in Milan, many shops and restaurants close for several weeks' holiday, or have reduced hours, and clubs move their activities out of town. Conversely, in winter, around the lakes, many places are shut.

Banks 8.30am–1.30pm and 3.30–4.30pm Monday–Friday

Cafes & bars 7.30am–8pm; most serve alcoholic drinks in the evening

Nightclubs 10pm–4am; may open earlier if they have restaurants

Restaurants noon–2.30pm and 7.30–11pm (kitchens close at 10pm); most close at least once a week

Shops 9am–1pm and 3.30–7.30pm (or 4–8pm) Monday–Saturday; some shops only open for half the day on Monday

Post

Le Poste (www.poste.it), Italy's postal system, is reasonably reliable. The most efficient mail service is *posta prioritaria* (priority mail).

In Switzerland, the main categories for international post are Economy and Priority. For details on the Swiss postal system, see www. post.ch.

Francobolli (stamps) are available at post offices and, in Italy, at authorised *tabacchi* (tobacconists; look for the official sign – a big 'T', usually white on black).

Public Holidays

Many Italians and Ticinesi take their annual holiday in August. This means that, depending on where you are, many businesses and shops close for at least a part of that month. Milan and cities like Bergamo, Brescia and Cremona can be eerily quiet in August, while lakeside towns such as Como, Locarno and Lugano bustle with holiday activity. Settimana Santa (Easter Week) is another busy holiday period.

Individual towns have public holidays to celebrate the feasts of their patron saints.

Italy

New Year's Day (Capodanno or Anno Nuovo) 1 January

Epiphany (Epifania or Befana) 6 January

Good Friday (Venerdì Santo) March/April

Easter Monday (Pasquetta or Lunedì dell'Angelo) March/April

Liberation Day (Giorno della Liberazione) 25 April marks the Allied Victory in Italy, and the end of the German presence and Mussolini, in 1945

Labour Day (Festa del Lavoro) 1 May

Republic Day (Festa della Repubblica) 2 June

Feast of the Assumption (Assunzione or Ferragosto) 15 August

All Saints' Day (Ognissanti) 1 November

Feast of the Immaculate Conception (Immaculata Concezione) 8 December

Christmas Day (Natale) 25 December

Boxing Day (Festa di Santo Stefano) 26 December

Switzerland

New Year's Day 1 January

Easter March/April

Ascension Day 40th day after Easter

Whit Sunday & Monday 7th week after Easter

National Day 1 August

Christmas Day 25 December

St Stephen's Day 26 December

Safe Travel

Pollution

Air pollution, caused mainly by heavy traffic, can be a problem in Milan, particularly in summer. On especially bad days, traffic curbing restrictions are put in place.

Theft

Pickpockets operate in Milan and around major train stations, especially in Brescia and Verona.

In case of theft or loss, always report the incident to police within 24 hours and ask for a statement; otherwise, your travel-insurance company won't pay out.

Traffic

Driving into and around Milan can be nerve-wracking. Traffic is dense and the sign-posting is not always immediately clear. In other cities around the region, things are calmer. Pedestrians should be watchful wherever they are, as drivers will not always automatically halt at crossings.

Traffic can be heavy on minor lakeside roads in summer. Some mountain roads are very narrow, particularly around Lakes Como and Garda, and you'll be sharing the road with everything from buses to bicycles. Be prepared for some poorly lit tunnels at the northern end of Lake Garda.

Telephone

Mobile Phones

➡ Italy and Switzerland use GSM 900/1800, which is compatible with the rest of Europe and Australia but not with North America GSM 1900 or the Japanese system.

➡ To buy a SIM card you'll need to show your passport and the address of your accommodation.

➡ Prepaid SIM cards are readily available at telephone and electronics stores. Purchase recharge cards at tobacconists and newsstands.

➡ Since June 2017 roaming charges have been abolished within the EU.

Phone Codes

ITALY

The dialling code for Italy is 39. The city code is an integral part of the number and must always be dialled. Toll-free (free-phone) numbers, known as *numeri verdi*, start with 800.

International directory enquiries ⏺176

Local directory enquiries ⏺12

SWITZERLAND

The dialling code for Switzerland is 41. When calling Switzerland from abroad, the leading 0 in area codes must not be dialled.

Area codes begin with 0, which must always be dialled when calling locally. Telephone numbers with the code 079 are mobile phones, those with the code 0800 are toll-free and those beginning with 156 or 157 are premium rate.

National telecom provider Swisscom (www.swisscom.ch) provides public phone booths that accept coins and major credit cards.

Time

Italy and Switzerland are one hour ahead of GMT. Daylight-saving time, when clocks are moved forward one hour, starts on the last Sunday in March. Clocks are put back an hour on the last Sunday in October. Italy operates on a 24-hour clock.

Toilets

Here and there you'll find public toilets in city centres, but more often than not you'll probably want to duck into a cafe or bar. The polite thing to do is order something at the bar, although more often than not no one will say anything if you don't, especially if things are busy. Most service stations have toilets.

Tourist Information

The lakes area takes in four Italian regions – Piedmont, Lombardy, Trentino-Alto Adige and the Veneto – and the Swiss canton of Ticino. Tourist offices can be found in most cities and towns throughout the region.

Italy

The main regional websites covering northern Italy are those for Lombardy (www.in-lombardia.it), Piedmont (www.piemonteitalia.eu) and Veneto (www.veneto.eu).

Websites dedicated to the lakes include:

Lake Maggiore (www.illagomaggiore.com) Covers the southern (Italian) half of Lake Maggiore, Lake Orta, Varese and the Ossola valleys.

Lake Como (www.lakecomo.org) Covers the whole Como area.

Lake Garda (www.visitgarda.com) Covers all the towns and cities surrounding Italy's largest lake, including a list of all tourist offices.

The most useful tourist offices in the region are:

Bergamo (Città Alta) Tourist Office (Map p154; ⏺035 24 22 26; www.visitbergamo.net; Via Gombito 13; ⏺9am-5.30pm) Helpful, multilingual office in the upper town.

Como Tourist Office (Map p122; ⏺031 26 97 12; www.visitcomo.eu; Piazza Cavour 17; ⏺9am-1pm & 2.30-6pm Mon-Sat year-round, 9.30am-1pm Sun Jun-Sep) The main tourist office on Lake Como with helpful English-speaking staff.

Laveno Tourist Office (⏺0332 66 72 23; www.stradasaporivallivaresine.it; Piazzale Europa 1; ⏺10.30am-4pm Tue-Fri, to 5.30pm Sat & Sun) Particularly good for hiking and walking information, and insider tips about Lake Maggiore.

Mantua Tourist Office (Map p206; ⏺0376 43 24 32; www.turismo.mantova.it; Piazza Mantegna 6; ⏺9am-5pm Sun-Thu, to 6pm Fri & Sat) Useful office in the centre of Mantua with excellent information on the city and surrounding area.

Milan Tourist Office (Map p66; ⏺02 8845 5555; www.turismo.milano.it; Galleria Vittorio Emanuele II 11-12; ⏺9am-7pm Mon-Fri, to 6pm Sat, 10am-6pm Sun; Ⓜ Duomo) Centrally located with helpful English-speaking staff and tonnes of maps and brochures.

Sirmione Tourist Office (⏺030 91 61 14; iat.sirmione@provincia.brescia.it; Viale Marconi 8; ⏺10am-12.30pm & 3-6.30pm daily summer, 10am-12.30pm & 3-6pm Mon-Fri, 9.30am-12.30pm Sat winter) Efficient office on the main road into Sirmione, just before the castle.

Stresa Tourist Office (Map p90; ⏺0323 3 13 08; www.stresaturismo.it; Piazza Marconi 16; ⏺10am-12.30pm & 3-6.30pm summer, closed Sat afternoon & Sun winter) Located at the ferry dock. Has brochures and tips on Lake Maggiore activities.

Varenna Tourist Office (⏺0341 83 03 67; www.varennaitaly.com; Via 4 Novembre 3; ⏺10am-3pm Mon, 10am-1pm & 2-6pm Tue-Sun Jul, shorter hours rest of year) Provides information on Lake Como's entire eastern shore.

Verona Tourist Office (⏺045 806 86 80; www.tourism.verona.it; Via degli Alpini 9; ⏺10am-7pm Mon-Sat, to 3pm Sun) Excellent, multilingual service. Also offers discount cards and advises on tours and booking services.

Switzerland

Ticino (www.ticino.ch) is the Italian-speaking Swiss canton that borders the northern end of Lake Maggiore. Bellinzona is the capital but Locarno is its most touristed city. The most useful tourist offices are:

Ascona-Locarno Tourism (Map p112; ⏺0848 091 091; www.ascona-locarno.com; Piazza Stazione; ⏺9am-6pm Mon-Fri, 10am-6pm Sat, 10am-1.30pm & 2.30-5pm Sun) Conveniently located at Locarno's train station, this tourist office has stacks of information about Locarno and the surrounding region. Ask about the Ticino Discovery Card and its discounts.

Bellinzona Tourist Office (Map p148; ⏺091 825 21 31; www.bellinzonaturismo.ch; Piazza Nosetto; ⏺9am-6.30pm Mon-Fri, 9am-2pm Sat, 10am-2pm Sun

Apr-Oct, shorter hours rest of year) Helpful information office located in the restored Renaissance Palazzo del Comune (town hall).

Travellers with Disabilities

Much like the rest of Italy, the northern part of the country is not easy to get around for travellers with disabilities. Even a short journey in a city or town can become a major expedition if cobblestone streets have to be negotiated. Although many buildings have lifts, they are not always wide enough for wheelchairs. Not an awful lot has been done to make life for the deaf and/or blind any easier either.

The Italian National Tourist Office in your country may be able to provide advice and may also carry a small book titled *Services for Disabled Passengers*, published by Trenitalia (Italian railways), which details facilities at stations and on trains. **Trenitalia** (☑199 30 30 60; www.trenitalia.it) also has a national helpline for people with disabilities. For more information, see the 'Information & Support' section of the Trenitalia website and click on the English version.

Resources

In Milan and Verona, general guides on accessibility are published.

Accessible Italy (www.accessibleitaly.com) is a San Marino–based company that specialises in holiday services for people with disabilities, ranging from tours to the hiring of adapted transport. It can even arrange romantic Italian weddings. This is the best first port of call.

Milano per Tutti (www.milanopertutti.it) offers information on Milan.

For tips on accessibility in Locarno, see www.ascona-locarno.com/it/turismo-accessibile.html.

In addition, you can download Lonely Planet's free Accessible Travel guide at http://lptravel.to/Accessible Travel.

Visas

Citizens of EU countries, Iceland, Norway and Switzerland do not need a visa to visit Italy. Nationals of some other countries, including Australia, Brazil, Canada, Israel, Japan, New Zealand and the US, do not require visas for tourist visits of up to 90 days. For more information and a list of countries whose citizens require a visa, check the website of the Italian foreign ministry (www.esteri.it).

The standard tourist visa issued by Italian consulates is the Schengen visa, valid for up to 90 days. This visa is valid for travel in Italy and in several other European countries with which Italy has a reciprocal visa agreement (see www.eurovisa.info for the full list). These visas are not renewable inside Italy.

Women Travellers

The lakes area of northern Italy and Switzerland is very safe for female travellers. While some city savvy should be exercised in Milan, women travellers generally encounter no real problems. Be aware that eye-to-eye contact is the norm in Italy's daily flirtatious interplay.

Transport

GETTING THERE & AWAY

Italy is exceptionally well connected to the rest of the world by air, and to neighbouring countries by road and rail. Switzerland is similarly well connected, although with fewer air connections. Flights, tours and rail tickets can be booked online at www.lonelyplanet.com/bookings.

Entering the Country

Entering both Italy and Switzerland is usually trouble-free and rarely involves anything more than cursory customs and immigration checks.

Air

Alitalia is Italy's national carrier. Its main hub is Leonardo da Vinci-Fiumicino Airport,

Rome, and a secondary hub is Linate Airport, Milan.

Airports

Malpensa (MXP; ☑02 23 23 23; www.milanomalpensa-airport.com; 🚆Malpensa Express) Located 50km northwest of Milan, Malpensa is northern Italy's main international airport. It consists of two terminals, which are linked by a free shuttle bus and the Malpensa Express.

Linate (LIN; ☑02 23 23 23; www.milanolinate-airport.com) Linate is 7km east of Milan and handles the majority of domestic and a handful of European flights. It's also the secondary hub of Alitalia, the national carrier.

Orio al Serio (☑035 32 63 23; www.sacbo.it) Located 4km southeast of Bergamo and 45km northeast of Milan. It's served by a coterie of budget airlines, including Ryanair, with daily flights to/from the UK and other popular European destinations.

Verona Villafranca (☑045 809 56 66; www.aeroportoverona.it) Located 12km southwest of

Verona and 22km southeast of Lake Garda. It's served by an array of domestic and European flights from cities including Amsterdam, Barcelona, Berlin, Brussels, London and Paris.

Land

Border Crossings

AUSTRIA & EASTERN EUROPE

The Brenner Pass connects with the A22 and parallel rail line south to Verona.

Other autostradas and train lines converge from Eastern Europe through Venice, en route to Verona and Lombardy along the six-lane A4, one of Italy's busiest motorways.

FRANCE

The main points of entry by road include:

Coast Road From Nice on what becomes the A10 motorway along the Ligurian coast (then take the A7 from Genoa north to Milan).

CLIMATE CHANGE & TRAVEL

Every form of transport that relies on carbon-based fuel generates CO_2, the main cause of human-induced climate change. Modern travel is dependent on aeroplanes, which might use less fuel per kilometre per person than most cars but travel much greater distances. The altitude at which aircraft emit gases (including CO_2) and particles also contributes to their climate change impact. Many websites offer 'carbon calculators' that allow people to estimate the carbon emissions generated by their journey and, for those who wish to do so, to offset the impact of the greenhouse gases emitted with contributions to portfolios of climate-friendly initiatives throughout the world. Lonely Planet offsets the carbon footprint of all staff and author travel.

TRANSPORT LAND

Mont Blanc Tunnel Begins near Chamonix and connects with the A5 for Turin and Milan.

SWITZERLAND

Grand St Bernard Tunnel Connects with the A5 and the Simplon tunnel connects with the SS33 road that leads to Lake Maggiore.

St Gotthard Tunnel The A2 runs from Basel, through the tunnel and into Ticino via Bellinzona to Lake Lugano.

Bus

Buses converge on Milan from major cities across Europe. Most national and international buses start and terminate at Milan's **Lampugnano Bus Terminal** (Via Giulia Natta; ⓂLampugnano), which is located by the Lampugnano metro station on Via Giulia Natta, 5km west of the city centre.

Eurolines (⌨0861 199 1900; www.eurolines.it) A consortium of European coach companies that operates across Europe with offices in all major European cities.

Autostradale (Map p66;⌨02 3008 9300; www.autostradale. it) Runs the bulk of Italian national services and has a ticket office at the main tourist office. It also sells international tickets for Eurolines services.

Car & Motorcycle

If driving into northern Italy, you'll need:

➡ proof of ownership of a private vehicle or proof of car rental

➡ a valid national licence plate

➡ a sticker identifying the car's country of registration (unless it has the standard EU number plates with the blue strip and country ID)

➡ car registration certificate or card.

DRIVING LICENCE & DOCUMENTATION

➡ All EU member state driving licences are fully recognised throughout Europe.

➡ Drivers from non-EU member states should obtain an International Driving Permit (IDP) to accompany their national licence. Issued by your national automobile association, it's valid for 12 months and must be kept with your proper licence.

INSURANCE

You must have evidence of third-party insurance. If driving a vehicle registered and insured in an EU country (and Switzerland), your home-country insurance is sufficient.

Ask your insurer for a European Accident Statement (EAS) form, which can simplify matters in the event of an accident. A European breakdown assistance policy is a good investment. If for whatever reason you don't have such a policy, assistance can be obtained through:

Automobile Club d'Italia (ACI;⌨80 31 16, from a mobile phone 800 11 68 00; www.aci. it) Foreigners do not have to join, but instead pay a per-incident fee. The numbers operate 24 hours a day.

Automobil Club der Schweiz (⌨41 31 328 31 11; www.acs.ch) The Swiss equivalent of Automobile Club d'Italia.

Train

Milan is a major European rail hub. High-speed services arrive from across Italy, from France via Turin in the west and from major Swiss cities like Zürich and Geneva to the north. An overnight sleeper train also runs from Barcelona (Spain).

For train timetables and fares, visit www.trenitalia. com (Italy), www.sbb.ch (Switzerland) or www.bahn. de (Germany). Another useful site for planning intercontinental train travel is www. seat61.com.

FRANCE, SWITZERLAND & UK

Geneva–Milan Cisalpino high-speed services converge on Milan from Geneva (via Lausanne, Brig and Domodossola) and Zürich (via Ticino). The trip takes four to six hours (Sfr95 one way).

London–Milan Eurostar passenger trains travel between London and Paris from where there are TGV connections to Milan. For the latest information on journeys to Italy, check out www. raileurope.co.uk.

Paris–Milan Fast direct trains (TGV) run from Gare de Lyon to Stazione Centrale (from €90, seven to eight hours) in Milan.

ITALIAN RAIL NETWORK

The partially privatised state train system **Trenitalia** (⌨199 30 30 60; www.tren italia.it) runs most services. Travelling by train in Italy is relatively cheap compared with other European countries. The most useful types of train include the following:

Alta Velocità (High Speed) – Frecciarossa Variously known as AV and/or ESA, they operate on the Turin–Milan–Bologna–Florence–Rome–Naples–Salerno route. Nonstop trains between Milan and Rome take three hours. Prices vary according to the time of travel and how far in advance you book.

Alta Velocità (High Speed) – Frecciabianca Connects Milan with Venice in 2½ hours.

Regionale or Interregionale Local trains that usually stop at all stations.

Intercity (IC) Medium-speed services that operate between major cities.

GETTING AROUND

Trains will get you to the main Lombard towns and to some strategic launch pads on and around the lakes. Elsewhere, you'll be relying on a fairly dense network of buses, although infrequency of some services and the need to change buses at times can make the process a little slow.

Ferries ply the lakes, offering not only commuter services but also a range of day-ticket options. Some handy car ferries cross at several points on Lakes Maggiore, Como and Garda. Clearly, having your own transport provides much greater liberty.

Milan has an excellent public transport network with both buses and the metro covering just about anywhere you'd need to go. Buses and trains connect Milan's airports to the city centre.

Bicycle

Cyclists are a common sight on Italian roads, but that doesn't necessarily mean that drivers will take cyclists into account. There are, nonetheless, some fabulous cycling routes around the region and roads are well maintained.

Although cycling in Milan can be nerve-wracking for those unaccustomed to Italian traffic, it can be an enjoyable experience if you

avoid the major thoroughfares. Both Milan and Verona have public bicycle schemes, while some city centres have been closed to motorised transport, making cycling a pleasant way to get around – Cremona is an excellent example of this.

Bikes can be taken on any train displaying the bicycle logo. Folding bikes and bikes packed in bags (110x80x-40cm) are admitted free of charge. Otherwise, you need to buy a separate bicycle ticket (€3.50, or €6 to €15 on Intercity, Eurostar and Euronight trains), available even at the self-service kiosks. You can use this ticket for 24 hours. On high-speed Frecciarossa and Frecciargento services your bike must be packed in a bag.

Boat

Ferries criss-cross all of the lakes, though timetables are cut back quite drastically in the off-season (November to Easter).

Gestione Navigazione Laghi (☑800 55 18 01; www.navigazione laghi.it) Covers ferry services on the three main lakes (Lakes Maggiore, Como and Garda). The website includes timetables and pricing. Lakeside ticketing booths and tourist offices also have timetables. A popular option are one-day tickets allowing unlimited travel.

Navigazione Lago d'Orta (☑345 5170005; www.navigazione lagodorta.it) For Lake Orta. From its landing stage on Piazza Motta in Orta San Giulio, services run to numerous spots on that lake, including Isola San Giulio.

Navigazione sul Lago d'Iseo (☑035 97 14 83; www.navigazione lagoiseo.it) For Lake Iseo. Operates up to eight ferries daily on routes from (south to north) Sarnico, Iseo, Monte Isola, Lovere and Pisogne (and other smaller stops).

Bus

Getting around the Po valley towns and to some of the main settlements at the southern end of the main lakes is easier by train than by bus. To get any further and explore the lake shores and beyond, however, taking the bus is often the only option for those without their own transport.

Italy

Services are mainly organised around provincial capitals, which act as hubs for the towns nearby. You will rarely be able to scoot from one lake directly to another by bus.

Most bus services from Milan leave from **Lampugna-no bus terminal** (Via Giulia Natta; Ⓜ Lampugnano) or **Stazione Centrale** (www.milanocentrale.it; Piazza Duca d'Aosta; ⊘4am-1am; Ⓜ Centrale). Elsewhere, in bigger towns the bus station is often handily located near the train station. Sometimes you buy tickets at the station ticket counters (where timetables are posted), but often they can be bought on board. Most of the bus company websites have timetables.

Bus companies operating across the area include the following:

APAM (☑0376 23 03 39; www.apam.it) Buses around Mantua.

ASF Autolinee (☑031 24 72 47; www.sptlinea.it) Regular buses around Lake Como.

ATV (☑045 805 79 22; www.atv.verona.it) Buses run from/to Lake Garda, and connect towns along both shores of the lake.

SAB (Map p154; ☑035 28 90 11; www.arriva.it) Bergamo-based company operating services around Bergamo province, and to Lake Como, Lake Iseo and the mountains.

SAF (☑0323 55 21 72; www.safduemila.com) Buses from Milan to and around Lake Maggiore.

SIA (Map p168; ☎030 288 99 11; www.arriva.it) Also serves Brescia province and connects the city with the western shore of Lake Garda.

Trentino Trasporti (☎0461 82 10 00; www.ttesercizio.it) Buses between Trento and Rovereto and the north end of Lake Garda (including Riva del Garda and Arco).

Switzerland

In Ticino, on the Swiss side of the lakes, train is the easiest way to get between the three main cities (Lugano, Locarno and Bellinzona). Local buses and private trains cover some of the lakeside spots. Otherwise, the country's network of postal buses serves the valleys north of Locarno and Bellinzona.

Car & Motorcycle

Road Networks

ITALY

Northern Italy has an extensive privatised network of autostradas (motorways), represented on road signs by a white A followed by a number on a green background. You can pay tolls on Italian motorways with cash or credit card as you leave the autostrada.

Beyond the motorways, you'll be doing most of your travelling on the spiderweb network of state and regional roads, which are generally maintained in good condition.

The following are the key motorways in northern Italy:

A4 Runs east–west, linking Milan with Bergamo, Brescia, Lake Garda and Verona.

A8 Leads northwest out of Milan and, in a slightly confusing tangle, becomes the A8-A26 as it approaches the southern end of Lake Maggiore. A branch of the A8 reaches Varese.

A9 Once you're about 11km out of Milan along the A8, the A9 branches north to Como and on across the Swiss border, where it continues as the A2.

A26 Follows the western shore via Arona and Stresa before it peters out in a smaller route to Domodossola and the Swiss frontier. If you're coming from Milan and heading to Lake Maggiore, follow the signs to Gravellona Toce.

SWITZERLAND

In Switzerland, an autostrada (A2, represented with the number on a red background) also traverses Ticino roughly north–south. If you intend to use the A2 and other motorways in Switzerland, you must buy a one-off vignette (Sfr40) on entering the country. This windscreen sticker is valid on all Swiss motorways for a calendar year.

The A2 connects with Italy's A9 and passes through Lugano, Bellinzona and north through Ticino into the heart of Switzerland.

Fuel

Fuel prices are among the highest in Europe and vary from one service station (benzinaio, stazione di servizio) to another. Lead free (senza piombo; 95 octane) costs up to €1.55/L. A 98-octane variant costs as much as €1.65/L. Diesel (gasolio) comes in at €1.40/L. Prices tend to be slightly cheaper in Switzerland.

Hire

To rent a car in Italy you have to be aged 25 or over and have a credit card. Most firms will accept your standard licence or IDP for identification purposes. Consider hiring a small car, which you'll be grateful for when negotiating narrow city or village lanes.

Multinational car-rental agencies can be found at regional airports and in local towns, as well as local agencies including **Autos Abroad** (☎0844 826 65 36; www.autos abroad.com), **Italy by Car** (☎091 507 92 89; www.italyby car.it) and **Maggiore** (☎199 151120; www.maggiore.it).

Parking

Parking in most cities in the region can be complicated. The historic centre of most cities is generally off limits to traffic, although partial exceptions are sometimes made for tourists (in such cases you may be able to enter the city centre long enough to unload at your hotel).

Street-side parking around the lakes costs between €2 and €3 per hour and is easy to find. As a guide, blue lines indicate metered/paid parking, white lines indicate free parking, and yellow lines mean parking is reserved for special pass holders.

If you require parking at your hotel, you'll need to book in advance and some places levy a fee of around €10 to €20 per night.

Milan has instituted a congestion charge, which obliges drivers to pay to enter the centre of town between 7.30am and 7.30pm Monday to Wednesday (to 6pm on Thursday). To enter, you need to buy a daily pass costing €5. You can purchase it online at www.muoversi. milano.it.

Car parks in Milan charge between €25 and €40 for 24 hours.

Road Rules

➡ Drive on the right, overtake on the left.

➡ Give way to cars entering an intersection from a road on your right.

➡ Seatbelts are compulsory for all passengers.

➡ A warning triangle (to be used in the event of a breakdown) must be carried, and if your car breaks down and you get out of the vehicle, you must wear an approved yellow or orange safety vest (available at bicycle shops and outdoor stores).

➡ Random breath tests take place in Italy and Switzerland. The blood-alcohol limit is 0.05%.

Train Routes

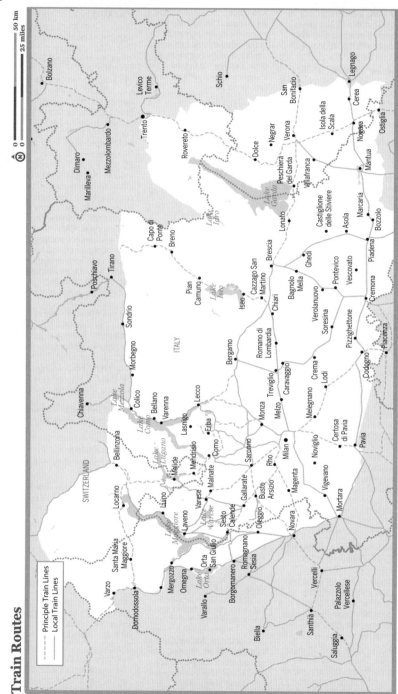

Key
Principle Train Lines
Local Train Lines

Bolzano

Levico Terme

Schio

San Bonifacio

Legnago

Cerea

Mezzolombardo

Trento

Rovereto

Dolce

Negrar

Verona

Isola della Scala

Nogara

Ostiglia

Dimaro

Marilleva

Peschiera del Garda

Villafranca

Mantua

Marcaria

Poschiavo

Tirano

Capo di Ponte

Breno

Lake Garda

Lake Idro

Lonato

Castiglione delle Stiviere

Asola

Bozzolo

Piadena

Pian Camuno

Brescia

Ghedi

Pontevico

Vescovato

Cremona

Sondrio

Lake Iseo

Cazzago San Martino

Bagnolo Mella

Verolanuovo

Soresina

Piacenza

Morbegno

Iseo

Chiari

Romano di Lombardia

Pizzighettone

Codogno

Chiavenna

Colico

Bellano

Varenna

Bergamo

Crema

Lodi

Certosa di Pavia

Pavia

ITALY

Lake Mezzola

Lecco

Trevíglio

Caravaggio

Melzo

Melegnano

Bellinzona

Lasnigo

Erba

Monza

Locarno

Lake Como

Lake Lugano

Melide

Mendrisio

Como

Saronno

Rho

Milan

Novíglio

Vigevano

Luino

Malnate

Gallarate

Busto Arsizio

Magenta

Mortara

Santa Maria Maggiore

Laveno

Varese

Sesto Calende

Oleggio

Novara

Varzo

Mergozzo

Omegna

Orta

San Giulio

Romagnano Sesia

Lake Maggiore

Lake Orta

Borgomanero

Vercelli

Palazzolo Vercellese

Domodossola

Varallo

Biella

Santhià

Saluggia

SWITZERLAND

Lake Maggiore

➡ All vehicles must use headlights by day on the autostradas. It is advisable for motorcycles on all roads at all times.

➡ Speed cameras operate in Italy and Switzerland and fines are increasingly being sent to the home countries of offenders, so beware!

Local Transport

Bus, Metro & Tram

ATM (Azienda Trasporti Milano; 📞02 4860 7607; www.atm.it) runs Milan's public transport network, including the metro, trams and buses.

The metro consists of four major lines: M1 (red) connects Duomo with Porta Venezia, the castle, Corsa Magenta and the Fiera; M2 (green) connects Porta Garibaldi with Brera and Navigli; M3 (yellow) connects the Quad with Porta Romana; and M5 (lilac) connects San Siro with Porta Garibaldi and Isola. Work on the M4 (blue) line, which will eventually connect the city with Linate Airport, is currently halted due to the discovery of archaeological artefacts beneath Via Molina delle Armi.

Metro services operate between 5.40am and 12.20am (from 6.15am on Sunday). A night service runs on buses and trams between 12.20am and 5.40am, when the metro is closed.

A ticket costs €1.50 and is valid for one metro ride or 90 minutes on trams and buses. It must be validated when boarding.

Tickets are sold at electronic ticket machines in the station, or at tobacconists and news stands.

Download the free ATM app for network maps and timetables.

Taxi

Taxis cannot be hailed, but must be picked up at designated ranks, usually outside train stations, large hotels and in major piazzas. Outside major cities, taxis mainly congregate at the train station and in the historic centre. Be aware that when you call for a cab, the meter runs from receipt of call, not pick up. The average short city ride costs €5 to €10.

Train

Trenitalia (📞892021; www.trenitalia.com) operates most trains in the Italian network. From Milan, all the main cities are easily reached by train. Brescia, the south-shore towns on Lake Garda and Verona are on the main line connecting Milan with Venice.

With the exception of fast trains operating on the Milan–Brescia–Verona line, and fast(ish) Cisalpino trains running to/from Milan to Switzerland via Stresa and Lugano, most trains are *regionali* calling in at most, if not all, stops.

You can buy tickets at the station counter or machines. Only on some services (such as Eurostar City and Cisalpino) will you need a seat reservation, but this can be made when you buy the ticket.

Most major train stations have some kind of left-luggage service or lockers.

USEFUL ROUTES

Lake Como West Bank & Lake Lugano Regular trains, Swiss or Italian, connect Milan's Stazione Centrale with Lugano via Mendrisio and Como (San Giovanni station). Ferrovie Nord Milano (FNM; www.ferrovienord.it), a private company, operates trains stopping at all stations from Milan's Stazione Nord, terminating at Como's lakeside Como Nord Lago stop. From Como there are numerous trains along the West Bank.

Lake Como East Bank Trains run from Milan's Stazione Centrale to Lecco, up the eastern shore of Lake Como and turn east along the Valtellina valley to Sondrio and wind up in Tirano, a town that sits on a sliver of Lombard territory between the Swiss border and the region of Trentino-Alto Adige. The Lecco–Tirano part of this 2½-hour trip is delightful.

Lake Maggiore Hourly trains connect Milan's Stazione Centrale with Stresa via Arona, on the western shore of Lake Maggiore, on their way to Domodossola and Switzerland. Connecting services run up the eastern shore.

Lake Iseo An assortment of trains run from Brescia along the eastern shore of Lake Iseo as far as Edolo.

Ticino, Switzerland The Milan–Lugano train line continues north to Bellinzona and up the Valle Leventina, to cross the St Gotthard pass into central Switzerland. A branch line connects Bellinzona with Locarno.

Language

Standard Italian is taught and spoken throughout Italy. Dialects are an important part of regional identity, but you'll have no trouble being understood anywhere if you stick to standard Italian, which we've also used in this chapter.

The sounds used in spoken Italian can all be found in English. If you read our coloured pronunciation guides as if they were English, you'll be understood. The stressed syllables are indicated with italics. Note that ai is pronounced as in 'aisle', ay as in 'say', ow as in 'how', dz as the 'ds' in 'lids', and r is a strong and rolled sound. Keep in mind that Italian consonants can have a stronger, emphatic pronunciation – if the consonant is written as a double letter, it should be pronounced a little stronger, eg *sonno son*·no (sleep) versus *sono so*·no (I am).

BASICS

Hello.	*Buongiorno.*	bwon·*jor*·no
Goodbye.	*Arrivederci.*	a·ree·ve·*der*·chee
Yes./No.	*Sì./No.*	see/no
Excuse me.	*Mi scusi.* (pol)	mee *skoo*·zee
	Scusami. (inf)	*skoo*·za·mee
Sorry.	*Mi dispiace.*	mee dees·*pya*·che
Please.	*Per favore.*	per fa·vo·re
Thank you.	*Grazie.*	*gra*·tsye
You're welcome.	*Prego.*	*pre*·go

How are you?
Come sta/stai? (pol/inf)   ko·me sta/stai

Fine. And you?
Bene. E Lei/tu? (pol/inf)   be·ne e lay/too

What's your name?
Come si chiama? pol   ko·me see *kya*·ma
Come ti chiami? inf   ko·me tee *kya*·mee

My name is ...
Mi chiamo ...   mee *kya*·mo ...

Do you speak English?
Parla/Parli   par·la/par·lee
inglese? (pol/inf)   een·*gle*·ze

I don't understand.
Non capisco.   non ka·*pee*·sko

ACCOMMODATION

Do you have a ... room?	*Avete una camera ...?*	a·*ve*·te oo·na *ka*·me·ra ...
double	*doppia con letto matri- moniale*	*do*·pya kon *le*·to ma·tree· mo·*nya*·le
single	*singola*	*seen*·go·la

How much is it per ...?	*Quanto costa per ...?*	*kwan*·to *kos*·ta per ...
night	*una notte*	*oo*·na *no*·te
person	*persona*	per·*so*·na

Is breakfast included?
La colazione è   la ko·la·*tsyo*·ne e
compresa?   kom·*pre*·sa

air-con	*aria condizionata*	*a*·rya kon·dee·tsyo·*na*·ta
bathroom	*bagno*	*ba*·nyo
campsite	*campeggio*	kam·*pe*·jo
guesthouse	*pensione*	pen·*syo*·ne
hotel	*albergo*	al·*ber*·go
youth hostel	*ostello della gioventù*	os·*te*·lo de·la jo·ven·*too*
window	*finestra*	fee·*nes*·tra

DIRECTIONS

Where's ...?
Dov'è ...?   do·ve ...

What's the address?
Qual'è l'indirizzo?   kwa·le leen·dee·*ree*·tso

Could you please write it down?
Può scriverlo,   pwo skree·ver·lo
per favore?   per fa·vo·re

Can you show me (on the map)?
Può mostrarmi   pwo mos·trar·mee
(sulla pianta)?   (soo·la pyan·ta)

at the corner	*all'angolo*	a·lan·go·lo
at the traffic lights	*al semaforo*	al se·ma·fo·ro
left	*a sinistra*	a see·nee·stra
right	*a destra*	a de·stra
straight ahead	*sempre diritto*	sem·pre dee·ree·to

EATING & DRINKING

What would you recommend?
Cosa mi consiglia?   ko·za mee kon·see·lya

What's in that dish?
Quali ingredienti   kwa·li een·gre·dyen·tee
ci sono in   chee so·no een
questo piatto?   kwe·sto pya·to

What's the local speciality?
Qual'è la specialità   kwa·le la spe·cha·lee·ta
di questa regione?   dee kwe·sta re·jo·ne

That was delicious!
Era squisito!   e·ra skwee·zee·to

Cheers!
Salute!   sa·loo·te

Please bring the bill.
Mi porta il conto,   mee por·ta eel kon·to
per favore?   per fa·vo·re

I'd like to reserve a table for ...	*Vorrei prenotare un tavolo per ...*	vo·ray pre·no·ta·re oon ta·vo·lo per ...
(eight) o'clock	*le (otto)*	le (o·to)
(two) people	*(due) persone*	(doo·e) per·so·ne
I don't eat ...	*Non mangio ...*	non man·jo ...
eggs	*uova*	wo·va
fish	*pesce*	pe·she
nuts	*noci*	no·chee
(red) meat	*carne (rossa)*	kar·ne (ro·sa)

Key Words

bar	*locale*	lo·ka·le
beer	*birra*	bee·ra
bottle	*bottiglia*	bo·tee·lya
breakfast	*prima colazione*	pree·ma ko·la·tsyo·ne

KEY PATTERNS

To get by in Italian, mix and match these simple patterns with words of your choice:

When's (the next flight)?
A che ora è   a ke o·ra e
(il prossimo volo)?   (eel pro·see·mo vo·lo)

Where's (the station)?
Dov'è (la stazione)?   do·ve (la sta·tsyo·ne)

I'm looking for (a hotel).
Sto cercando   sto cher·kan·do
(un albergo).   (oon al·ber·go)

Do you have (a map)?
Ha (una pianta)?   a (oo·na pyan·ta)

Is there (a toilet)?
C'è (un gabinetto)?   che (oon ga·bee·ne·to)

I'd like (a coffee).
Vorrei (un caffè).   vo·ray (oon ka·fe)

I'd like to (hire a car).
Vorrei (noleggiare   vo·ray (no·le·ja·re
una macchina).   oo·na ma·kee·na)

Can I (enter)?
Posso (entrare)?   po·so (en·tra·re)

Could you please (help me)?
Può (aiutarmi),   pwo (a·yoo·tar·mee)
per favore?   per fa·vo·re

Do I have to (book a seat)?
Devo (prenotare   de·vo (pre·no·ta·re
un posto)?   oon po·sto)

cafe	*bar*	bar
coffee	*caffè*	ka·fe
cold	*freddo*	fre·do
dinner	*cena*	che·na
drink list	*lista delle bevande*	lee·sta de·le be·van·de
fish	*pesce*	pe·she
fork	*forchetta*	for·ke·ta
fruit	*frutta*	froo·ta
glass	*bicchiere*	bee·kye·re
grocery store	*alimentari*	a·lee·men·ta·ree
hot	*caldo*	kal·do
(orange) juice	*succo (d'arancia)*	soo·ko (da·ran·cha)
knife	*coltello*	kol·te·lo
lunch	*pranzo*	pran·dzo
market	*mercato*	mer·ka·to
meat	*carne*	kar·ne
menu	*menù*	me·noo
milk	*latte*	la·te
plate	*piatto*	pya·to

red wine	*vino rosso*	vee·no ro·so
restaurant	*ristorante*	ree·sto·ran·te
seafood	*frutti di mare*	froo·tee dee ma·re
soft drink	*bibita*	bee·bee·ta
soup	*minestra*	mee·nes·tra
spicy	*piccante*	pee·kan·te
spoon	*cucchiaio*	koo·kya·yo
tea	*tè*	te
vegetables	*verdura*	ver·doo·ra
vegetarian (food)	*vegetariano*	ve·je·ta·rya·no
(mineral) water	*acqua (minerale)*	a·kwa (mee·ne·ra·le)
white wine	*vino bianco*	vee·no byan·ko
with	*con*	kon
without	*senza*	sen·tsa

EMERGENCIES

Help!
Aiuto!   a·yoo·to

Leave me alone!
Lasciami in pace!   la·sha·mee een pa·che

I'm lost.
Mi sono perso/a. (m/f)   mee so·no per·so/a

There's been an accident.
C'è stato un incidente.   che sta·to oon een·chee·den·te

Call the police!
Chiami la polizia!   kya·mee la po·lee·tsee·a

Call a doctor!
Chiami un medico!   kya·mee oon me·dee·ko

Where are the toilets?
Dove sono i gabinetti?   do·ve so·no ee ga·bee·ne·tee

I'm sick.
Mi sento male.   mee sen·to ma·le

It hurts here.
Mi fa male qui.   mee fa ma·le kwee

I'm allergic to ...
Sono allergico/a a ... (m/f)   so·no a·ler·jee·ko/a a ...

SHOPPING & SERVICES

I'd like to buy ...
Vorrei comprare ...   vo·ray kom·pra·re ...

I'm just looking.
Sto solo guardando.   sto so·lo gwar·dan·do

Can I look at it?
Posso dare un'occhiata?   po·so da·re oo·no·kya·ta

How much is this?
Quanto costa questo?   kwan·to kos·ta kwe·sto

It's too expensive.
È troppo caro/a. (m/f)   e tro·po ka·ro/a

Can you lower the price?
Può farmi lo sconto?   pwo far·mee lo skon·to

There's a mistake in the bill.
C'è un errore nel conto.   che oo·ne·ro·re nel kon·to

ATM	*bancomat*	ban·ko·mat
post office	*ufficio postale*	oo·fee·cho pos·ta·le
tourist office	*ufficio del turismo*	oo·fee·cho del too·reez·mo

TIME & DATES

What time is it?
Che ora è?   ke o·ra e

It's one o'clock.
È l'una.   e loo·na

It's (two) o'clock.
Sono le (due).   so·no le (doo·e)

Half past (one).
(L'una) e mezza.   (loo·na) e me·dza

in the morning	*di mattina*	dee ma·tee·na
in the afternoon	*di pomeriggio*	dee po·me·ree·jo
in the evening	*di sera*	dee se·ra

yesterday	*ieri*	ye·ree
today	*oggi*	o·jee
tomorrow	*domani*	do·ma·nee

Monday	*lunedì*	loo·ne·dee
Tuesday	*martedì*	mar·te·dee
Wednesday	*mercoledì*	mer·ko·le·dee
Thursday	*giovedì*	jo·ve·dee
Friday	*venerdì*	ve·ner·dee
Saturday	*sabato*	sa·ba·to
Sunday	*domenica*	do·me·nee·ka

Signs

Entrata/Ingresso	Entrance
Uscita	Exit
Aperto	Open
Chiuso	Closed
Informazioni	Information
Proibito/Vietato	Prohibited
Gabinetti/Servizi	Toilets
Uomini	Men
Donne	Women

January	gennaio	je·na·yo
February	febbraio	fe·bra·yo
March	marzo	mar·tso
April	aprile	a·pree·le
May	maggio	ma·jo
June	giugno	joo·nyo
July	luglio	loo·lyo
August	agosto	a·gos·to
September	settembre	se·tem·bre
October	ottobre	o·to·bre
November	novembre	no·vem·bre
December	dicembre	dee·chem·bre

TRANSPORT

Public Transport

At what time does the ... leave/arrive?	A che ora parte/ arriva ...?	a ke o·ra par·te/ a·ree·va ...
boat	la nave	la na·ve
bus	l'autobus	low·to·boos
ferry	il traghetto	eel tra·ge·to
metro	la metropolitana	la me·tro·po·lee·ta·na
plane	l'aereo	la·e·re·o
train	il treno	eel tre·no

Numbers		
1	uno	oo·no
2	due	doo·e
3	tre	tre
4	quattro	kwa·tro
5	cinque	cheen·kwe
6	sei	say
7	sette	se·te
8	otto	o·to
9	nove	no·ve
10	dieci	dye·chee
20	venti	ven·tee
30	trenta	tren·ta
40	quaranta	kwa·ran·ta
50	cinquanta	cheen·kwan·ta
60	sessanta	se·san·ta
70	settanta	se·tan·ta
80	ottanta	o·tan·ta
90	novanta	no·van·ta
100	cento	chen·to
1000	mille	mee·lel

... ticket	un biglietto ...	oon bee·lye·to
one-way	di sola andata	dee so·la an·da·ta
return	di andata e ritorno	dee an·da·ta e ree·tor·no
bus stop	fermata dell'autobus	fer·ma·ta del ow·to·boos
platform	binario	bee·na·ryo
ticket office	biglietteria	bee·lye·te·ree·a
timetable	orario	o·ra·ryo
train station	stazione ferroviaria	sta·tsyo·ne fe·ro·vyar·ya

Does it stop at ...?
Si ferma a ...? — see fer·ma a ...

Please tell me when we get to ...
Mi dica per favore quando arriviamo a ... — mee dee·ka per fa·vo·re kwan·do a·ree·vya·mo a ...

I want to get off here.
Voglio scendere qui. — vo·lyo shen·de·re kwee

Driving & Cycling

I'd like to hire a/an ...	Vorrei noleggiare un/una ... (m/f)	vo·ray no·le·ja·re oon/oo·na ...
4WD	fuoristrada (m)	fwo·ree·stra·da
bicycle	bicicletta (f)	bee·chee·kle·ta
car	macchina (f)	ma·kee·na
motorbike	moto (f)	mo·to

bicycle pump	pompa della bicicletta	pom·pa de·la bee·chee·kle·ta
child seat	seggiolino	se·jo·lee·no
helmet	casco	kas·ko
mechanic	meccanico	me·ka·nee·ko
petrol/gas	benzina	ben·dzee·na
service station	stazione di servizio	sta·tsyo·ne dee ser·vee·tsyo

Is this the road to ...?
Questa strada porta a ...? — kwe·sta stra·da por·ta a ...

Can I park here?
Posso parcheggiare qui? — po·so par·ke·ja·re kwee

The car/motorbike has broken down (at ...).
La macchina/moto si è guastata (a ...). — la ma·kee·na/mo·to see e gwas·ta·ta (a ...)

I have a flat tyre.
Ho una gomma bucata. — o oo·na go·ma boo·ka·ta

I've run out of petrol.
Ho esaurito la benzina. — o e·zow·ree·to la ben·dzee·na

GLOSSARY

abbazia – abbey

agriturismo – tourist accommodation on farms; farmstays

albergo – hotel

alimentari – grocery shops; delicatessens

alto – high

APT – Azienda di Promozione Turistica; local town or city tourist office

autonoleggio – car hire

autostrada – motorway; highway

AV – Alta Velocità, high-speed trains that began servicing Turin–Milan–Bologna–Florence–Rome–Naples–Salerno in late 2009

bambino – child

bancomat – ATM

benzina – petrol

bianco – white

biblioteca – library

borgo – archaic name for small town, village or town sector (often dating to Middle Ages)

calcio – football

cambio – money-exchange office

camera – room

campo – field; also a square in Venice

cappella – chapel

carabinieri – police with military and civil duties

casa – house

castello – castle

cattedrale – cathedral

centro – city centre

centro storico – historic centre

certosa – monastery belonging to or founded by Carthusian monks

chiesa – church

cima – summit

città alta – upper town

città bassa – lower town

città vecchia – old town

colle – hill

colonna – column

comune – equivalent to a municipality or county; a town or city council; historically, a self-governing town or city

contrada – district or street (in some towns)

coperto – cover charge in restaurants

corso – boulevard

duomo – cathedral

ENIT – Ente Nazionale Italiano per il Turismo; Italian National Tourist Board

ES – Eurostar Italia; fast train

espresso – express mail; express train; short black coffee

est – east

estate – summer

ferrovia – railway

festa – feast day; holiday

fiume – river

fontana – fountain

foro – forum

funicolare – funicular railway

funivia – cable car

gelateria – ice-cream shop

giardino – garden

golfo – gulf

grotta – cave

IAT – Informazione e Assistenza ai Turisti; local tourist office

IC – Intercity; limited stops train

inverno – winter

isola – island

IVA – Imposta di Valore Aggiunto; value-added tax

lago – lake

largo – small square

Lega Nord – Northern League; political party

lido – beach

locanda – inn; small hotel

loggia – covered area on the side of a building; porch; lodge

mar, mare – sea

mercato – market

MM – Metropolitana Milano (aka il metrò); Milan's underground transport system

monte – mountain

municipio – town hall

nord – north

palazzo – mansion; palace; large building of any type, including an apartment block

palio – contest

parco – park

passeggiata – traditional evening stroll

pensione – guesthouse

piazza – square

piazzale – large open square

pietà – literally 'pity' or 'compassion'; sculpture, drawing or painting of the dead Christ supported by the Madonna

pinacoteca – art gallery

ponte – bridge

porta – gate; door

portico – covered walkway, usually attached to the outside of a building

porto – port

posta – post office; also *ufficio postale*

reale – royal

rifugio – mountain hut; accommodation in the Alps

rocca – fortress

sala – room; hall

santuario – sanctuary

scalinata – staircase

stazione – station

stile liberty – 'liberty style', Italian version of art nouveau

strada – street; road

sud – south

teatro – theatre

tempio – temple

terme – thermal baths

torre – tower

torrente – stream

Trenitalia – Italian State Railways; also known as Ferrovie dello Stato (FS)

via – street; road

viale – avenue

villa – townhouse; country house; also the park surrounding the house

FOOD GLOSSARY

The Basics

alla griglia – grilled (broiled)
arrosto/a (m/f) – roasted
bollito/a (m/f) – boiled
cena – dinner
coltello – knife
cotto/a (m/f) – cooked
crudo/a (m/f) – raw
cucchiaio – spoon
enoteca – wine bar
forchetta – fork
fritto/a (m/f) – fried
osteria – simple, trattoria-style restaurant, usually with a bar
(pizza) al taglio – (pizza) by the slice
pranzo – lunch
prima collazione – breakfast
riso – rice
ristorante – restaurant
spuntino – snack
trattoria – informal, family-style restaurant

Staples

aceto – vinegar
aglio – garlic
burro – butter
formaggio – cheese
olio – oil
oliva – olive
pane – bread
panna – cream
pepe – pepper
polenta – maize-based meal
sale – salt
uovo/uova – egg/eggs
zucchero – sugar

Frutta e Verdura (Fruit & Vegetables)

arancia – orange
asparago/i – asparagus
fungo/hi – mushroom/s
limone – lemon
mela – apple
melanzane – aubergines
patata – potato

peperoncino – chilli
peperone – capsicum; pepper
pomodoro – tomato
tartufo – truffle
zucca – pumpkin

Carne (Meat)

agnello – lamb
bistecca – steak
coniglio – rabbit
manzo – beef
pollo – chicken
prosciutto crudo – cured ham
salsiccia – sausage

Pesce & Frutti di Mare (Fish & Seafood)

acciuga – anchovy
aragosta – lobster
branzino – sea bass
coregone – whitefish
cozza – mussel
gambero – prawn
merluzzo – cod
persico – perch
pesce spada – swordfish
polpo – octopus
tonno – tuna
trota – trout
vongola – clam

Colazione (Breakfast)

brioche – Italian croissant
ciambella – kind of doughnut
cornetto – croissant
crostata – breakfast tart with buttery crust and jam
zeppola – chewy doughnut with ricotta or pumpkin

Antipasti (Appetisers) & Primi Patti (First Courses)

câsonséi (aka casoncelli) – large egg-based ravioli stuffed with meat, cheese or spinach

crespelle – cross between pasta and crepes
insalata – salad
minestra – soup
minestrone – broth of vegetables and other ingredients
orecchiette – ear-shaped pasta
pappardelle – broad ribbon pasta
pizzoccheri – buckwheat *tagliatelle*
risotto – typical rice course
strozzapreti – strips of pasta
zuppa – soup

Secondi (Second Courses)

brasato d'asino – braised donkey
cazzoeula – stew of pork rib chops, skin and sausage
cotechino – boiled pork sausage
filetto ai ferri – grilled beef fillet
fritto misto – mixed fried fish
lumache alla bresciana – snails cooked with Parmesan and fresh spinach
maialino da latte – suckling pig
ossobuco con piselli – sliced shin of veal with peas
pestöm – minced pork meat with polenta
San Pietro al vapore con salsa di limone e capperi – John Dory in a lemon sauce with capers
stinco di maiale – pork shank
tagliata di scottona lombarda – a cut of rare Lombard beef
vitello tonnato – veal in tuna sauce

Desserts & Sweets

miele – honey
mostarda (di frutta) – fruit in a sweet mustard sauce
pandoro – sweet yeast bread
panettone – the Milanese version of *pandoro*
panna cotta – wobbly set dessert usually in a fruit sauce
polenta e osei – cakes filled with jam and cream, topped with sugared polenta icing
torta sbrisolana – crumble with yellow flower, almonds and lard

Behind the Scenes

SEND US YOUR FEEDBACK

We love to hear from travellers – your comments keep us on our toes and help make our books better. Our well-travelled team reads every word on what you loved or loathed about this book. Although we cannot reply individually to your submissions, we always guarantee that your feedback goes straight to the appropriate authors, in time for the next edition. Each person who sends us information is thanked in the next edition – the most useful submissions are rewarded with a selection of digital PDF chapters.

Visit **lonelyplanet.com/contact** to submit your updates and suggestions or to ask for help. Our award-winning website also features inspirational travel stories, news and discussions.

Note: We may edit, reproduce and incorporate your comments in Lonely Planet products such as guidebooks, websites and digital products, so let us know if you don't want your comments reproduced or your name acknowledged. For a copy of our privacy policy visit lonelyplanet.com/privacy.

WRITER THANKS

Paula Hardy

Grazie mille to all the fun and fashionable Venetians and Milanese who spilled the beans on their remarkable cities: Paola dalla Valentina, Costanza Cecchini, Sara Porro, Lucia Cattaneo, Monica Cesarato, Francesca Giubilei, Luca Berta, Marco Secchi and Nan McElroy. Thanks, too, to co-authors Regis and Marc for their contributions, and to Anna Tyler for all the support. Finally, much love to Rob for sharing the beauty of the *bel paese.*

Marc Di Duca

A big *grazie mille* goes to the many tourist offices around the Veneto, especially those in Verona, Vicenza, Padua and Mantua, as well as to Antonio in Belluno. Also huge thanks to Ukrainian grandma and grandpa for looking after my two sons while I was in Italy, and to my wife for suffering my lengthy absences.

Regis St Louis

I'm grateful to countless tourist office staff, innkeepers, chefs, baristas, market vendors, store clerks, students and many other locals who provided helpful tips and advice along the way. Warm thanks to Cassandra and daughters Magdalena and Genevieve, who make this enterprise all the more worthwhile.

ACKNOWLEDGEMENTS

Climate map data adapted from Peel MC, Finlayson BL & McMahon TA (2007) 'Updated World Map of the Köppen-Geiger Climate Classification', Hydrology and Earth System Sciences, 11, 1633–44.

Cover photograph: Bellagio, Lake Como, Francesco Iacobelli/AWL ©

THIS BOOK

This 3rd edition of Lonely Planet's *Italian Lakes* guidebook was researched and written by Paula Hardy, Marc Di Duca and Regis St Louis. The previous edition was written by Paula Hardy and Anthony Ham.

This guidebook was produced by the following:

Destination Editor Anna Tyler
Product Editors Alison Ridgway, Jenna Myers
Senior Cartographer Anthony Phelan
Book Designer Wibowo Rusli
Assisting Editors Imogen Bannister, Heather Champion, Carly Hall, Gabrielle Innes, Kate James, Jodie Martire, Anne Mulvaney, Monique Perrin, Ross Taylor, Simon Williamson
Assisting Cartographer Rachel Imeson
Cover Researcher Naomi Parker
Thanks to Sasha Baskett, Nigel Chin, Francesca Leadlay, Catherine Naghten, Claire Naylor, Mazzy Prinsep, Rachel Rawling, Kirsten Rawlings, Victoria Smith, Victoria Warrick-Ormerod, Tony Wheeler

Index

Map Legend

Sights

- Beach
- Bird Sanctuary
- Buddhist
- Castle/Palace
- Christian
- Confucian
- Hindu
- Islamic
- Jain
- Jewish
- Monument
- Museum/Gallery/Historic Building
- Ruin
- Shinto
- Sikh
- Taoist
- Winery/Vineyard
- Zoo/Wildlife Sanctuary
- Other Sight

Activities, Courses & Tours

- Bodysurfing
- Diving
- Canoeing/Kayaking
- Course/Tour
- Sento Hot Baths/Onsen
- Skiing
- Snorkelling
- Surfing
- Swimming/Pool
- Walking
- Windsurfing
- Other Activity

Sleeping

- Sleeping
- Camping
- Hut/Shelter

Eating

- Eating

Drinking & Nightlife

- Drinking & Nightlife
- Cafe

Entertainment

- Entertainment

Shopping

- Shopping

Information

- Bank
- Embassy/Consulate
- Hospital/Medical
- Internet
- Police
- Post Office
- Telephone
- Toilet
- Tourist Information
- Other Information

Geographic

- Beach
- Gate
- Hut/Shelter
- Lighthouse
- Lookout
- Mountain/Volcano
- Oasis
- Park
- Pass
- Picnic Area
- Waterfall

Population

- Capital (National)
- Capital (State/Province)
- City/Large Town
- Town/Village

Transport

- Airport
- Border crossing
- Bus
- Cable car/Funicular
- Cycling
- Ferry
- Metro station
- Monorail
- Parking
- Petrol station
- S-Bahn/Subway station
- Taxi
- T-bane/Tunnelbana station
- Train station/Railway
- Tram
- Tube station
- U-Bahn/Underground station
- Other Transport

Routes

- Tollway
- Freeway
- Primary
- Secondary
- Tertiary
- Lane
- Unsealed road
- Road under construction
- Plaza/Mall
- Steps
- Tunnel
- Pedestrian overpass
- Walking Tour
- Walking Tour detour
- Path/Walking Trail

Boundaries

- International
- State/Province
- Disputed
- Regional/Suburb
- Marine Park
- Cliff
- Wall

Hydrography

- River, Creek
- Intermittent River
- Canal
- Water
- Dry/Salt/Intermittent Lake
- Reef

Areas

- Airport/Runway
- Beach/Desert
- Cemetery (Christian)
- Cemetery (Other)
- Glacier
- Mudflat
- Park/Forest
- Sight (Building)
- Sportsground
- Swamp/Mangrove

Note: Not all symbols displayed above appear on the maps in this book

OUR STORY

A beat-up old car, a few dollars in the pocket and a sense of adventure. In 1972 that's all Tony and Maureen Wheeler needed for the trip of a lifetime – across Europe and Asia overland to Australia. It took several months, and at the end – broke but inspired – they sat at their kitchen table writing and stapling together their first travel guide, *Across Asia on the Cheap*. Within a week they'd sold 1500 copies. Lonely Planet was born.

Today, Lonely Planet has offices in Franklin, London, Melbourne, Oakland, Dublin, Beijing and Delhi, with more than 600 staff and writers. We share Tony's belief that 'a great guidebook should do three things: inform, educate and amuse'.

OUR WRITERS

Paula Hardy

Paula Hardy is an independent travel writer and editorial consultant, whose work for Lonely Planet and other flagship publications has taken her from nomadic camps in the Danakil Depression to Seychellois beach huts and the jewel-like bar at the Gritti Palace on the Grand Canal. Over two decades, she has authored more than 30 Lonely Planet guidebooks and spent five years as commissioning editor of Lonely Planet's bestselling Italian list. These days you'll find her hunting down new hotels, hip bars and up-and-coming artisans primarily in Milan, Venice and Marrakech. Get in touch at www.paulahardy.com.

Marc Di Duca

A travel author for the last decade, Marc has worked for Lonely Planet in Siberia, Slovakia, Bavaria, England, Ukraine, Austria, Poland, Croatia, Portugal, Madeira and on the Trans-Siberian Railway, as well as writing and updating tens of other guides for other publishers. When not on the road, Marc lives between Sandwich, Kent and Mariánské Lázně in the Czech Republic with his wife and two sons.

Regis St Louis

Regis grew up in a small town in the American Midwest – the kind of place that fuels big dreams of travel—and he developed an early fascination with foreign dialects and world cultures. He spent his formative years learning Russian and a handful of Romance languages, which served him well on journeys across much of the globe. Regis has contributed to more than 50 Lonely Planet titles, covering destinations across six continents. His travels have taken him from the mountains of Kamchatka to remote island villages in Melanesia, and to many grand urban landscapes. When not on the road, he lives in New Orleans. Follow him on www.instagram.com/regisstlouis.

31901062556404

Published by Lonely Planet Global Limited
CRN 554153
3rd edition – Jan 2018
ISBN 978 1 78657 251 6
© Lonely Planet 2018   Photographs © as indicated 2018
10 9 8 7 6 5 4 3 2 1
Printed in China

Although the authors and Lonely Planet have taken all reasonable care in preparing this book, we make no warranty about the accuracy or completeness of its content and, to the maximum extent permitted, disclaim all liability arising from its use.